DATE DUE			
NOV 1 8 1980			
MAR 21 1994			
MAR 17 1998			

THERAPEIA

PLATO'S
CONCEPTION OF
PHILOSOPHY

Therapeia

PLATO'S CONCEPTION OF PHILOSOPHY

By ROBERT E. CUSHMAN

GREENWOOD PRESS, PUBLISHERS
WESTPORT, CONNECTICUT

Library of Congress Cataloging in Publication Data

Cushman, Robert Earl.
    Therapeia : Plato's conception of philosophy.

    Reprint of the ed. published by University of
North Carolina Press, Chapel Hill.
    Includes bibliographical references and index.
    1. Plato. I. Title.
B395.C8 1976   184   76-6518
ISBN 0-8371-8879-2

Originally published in 1958 by the University of North
Carolina Press, Chapel Hill

Reprinted with the permission of University of North
Carolina Press, Inc.

Reprinted in 1976 by Greenwood Press, Inc.,
51 Riverside Avenue, Westport, Conn. 06880

Library of Congress catalog card number 76-6518

ISBN 0-8371-8879-2

Printed in the United States of America

10 9 8 7 6 5 4 3 2

To

My Mother and Father

Contents

PREFACE   xi

PROLOGUE   xv

I. THE SOCRATIC PERSPECTIVE   3
    1. Socrates, the Integral Man   3
    2. A Revolution of Perspective   11
    3. The Prophetic Soul and Teleology   16
    Notes   26

II. THE HUMAN PLIGHT AND PLATO'S TASK   30
    1. The Rationale of the Ideal   30
    2. Three Inadequate Sources of Virtue   34
    3. Man the Measure   38
    4. Upside-down Existence   44
    Notes   48

III. VIRTUE AND KNOWLEDGE   52
    1. The Augustinian Deduction   52
    2. *Katharsis:* Knowledge through Amendment of Life   55
    3. Ignorance an Affection of the Soul   59
    4. Ignorance Is Folly   62
    5. Truth and Character   68
    Notes   73

IV. KNOWLEDGE AS RE-COGNITION   77
    1. Knowledge Is Not Transmissible   77
    2. From Cognition to Re-cognition through Dialectic   82

3. *Doxa Alêthês:* The *A Priori* in Knowing   88
Notes   97

V. TRUE OPINION EXAMINED   101
  1. *Doxa Alêthês*   101
  2. *Doxa* and *Doxa Alêthês*   105
  3. *Doxa Alêthês* in the Later Dialogues   113
  Notes   129

VI. KNOWLEDGE THROUGH CONVERSION   135
  1. The Structure of Knowledge   135
  2. Of Human Bondage   139
  3. The Nature of Conversion   147
  4. The Habit of the Good   150
  Notes   155

VII. THE MEANS OF CONVERSION   161
  1. The Propaedeutic Studies   161
  2. The Power of Dialectic   166
  3. Ascent to the First Principle   177
  Notes   181

VIII. THE ROLE OF LOVE IN KNOWLEDGE   185
  1. Contrariety and the Primal Affection of the Soul   185
  2. Misconception of Eros   188
  3. The *Symposium:* Love as Mediatorial   193
  4. The Higher Madness   197
  Notes   205

IX. THE TRUE RHETORICAL AND PERSUASIVE ART   211
  1. Pedagogy and Indemonstrable Knowledge   211
  2. Two Modes of Certainty   217
  3. Critique of Rhetoric as a Persuasive Art   219
  4. The True Rhetorical and Persuasive Art   224
  5. Insight and the Irenic Art   233
  Notes   236

X. THE SOVEREIGNTY OF THE GOOD   242

    1. Issues of Metaphysical Knowledge   242

    2. The Nature of Judgment   246

    3. Knowledge as Personal Decision   251

    4. Decision and First Principles   254

    5. Preference for Certainty: Aristotle and Bacon   261

    6. The Final Preference of the Human Mind   269

    Notes   276

XI. WISDOM: THE FRUIT OF *THERAPEIA*   282

    1. Greek Wisdom in Its Succession   282

    2. Plato's Conception of Wisdom   287

    3. Wisdom as Concord in the Soul   291

    4. Plato's *Therapeia*: An Evaluation   295

    Notes   301

APPENDIX   304

    Plato's Depreciation of the Written Word   304

    Notes   309

INDEX   311

Preface

PLATO'S *philosophia*, as a method of education, represents the supreme and most influential attainment of classical Greek thought respecting the way of human salvation. For Plato, salvation presupposes a profound and well-nigh universal distortion of the human soul, entailing a whole range of disastrous consequences for man's social and political existence. Plato's diagnosis of the plight of man as well as his *therapeia*, his provision for its remedy, form the central preoccupation of this study. And while it is an inclusive purpose here to see Plato's philosophy steadily and to see it whole, it will be our special task to reappraise the basis of Plato's pervasive and unyielding conviction that "metaphysical" relations actually obtain for man's finite existence, whether recognized or not, and that upon these rest his present and his ultimate hope. It will also be necessary to indicate under what conditions Plato believed these same ontological relations are discoverable and, conversely, under what circumstances they are hidden from the sight of the mind. If in our time, or, for that matter, since that of Francis Bacon, metaphysics is to be regarded as the relic of outworn thought, then it will be our business to show that Plato long ago anticipated the kind of mentality for which this judgment is inevitable and even proposed means for its radical transformation.

There is still some reason for the interpreter of Plato to declare, even if he cannot prove, his understanding of the chronological order of the dialogues. It suffices to say that I judge the *Symposium*, the *Phaedrus*, the *Cratylus* as well as the *Theaetetus* and the *Parmenides*, and probably in this order, to follow the writing of the *Republic*. I accept the usual ordering of the late dialogues, and believe what is regularly conceded, that the *Sophist* must be regarded as preceding the *Philebus* and the *Timaeus*. The *Cratylus*, along with the *Theaetetus* and the *Parmenides*, shows Plato at a stage of reconsideration preparatory to the articulation of a more capacious ontology—a task the main purpose of which was to embrace the order of Becoming within an expanded conception of the frame of Being. This was first definitively accomplished in the *Sophist*, although it was already implied and prepared for in *Republic* V, xx-xxii. It is important, however, to stress the point that this development of Plato's ontology on the empirical side involves, so far as I can see, no significant alteration of his conception of *philosophia* as unfolded through the writing of the *Phaedrus*. It does indicate, however, a real development of what today would be called, more strictly, his scientific interest or, to be exact, his cosmology.

All references are to the Greek text of Plato as supplied by the Loeb Library edition; furthermore, all block translations are from the Loeb. I am greatly indebted to the Harvard University Press, publishers of the Loeb Classical Library, for permission to use quoted matter.

Wherever a Greek word or phrase has been used in the text, either in Greek characters or transliterated, the English equivalent has regularly been supplied immediately following. The weight of the argument may be checked by recourse to the text of the dialogues, to which, it is believed, ample reference is made. The use of Greek characters has been restricted as far as possible to the first occurrence of concepts. Thereafter they have usually been transliterated.

The richness of man's life is proportionate to the measure of his indebtedness to others. It is quite impossible to mention by name all who have, in varying ways, contributed to the outcome of this study; but a preface invites to conscious and grateful recollection. During the prolonged period of composition I have owed very much to the friendship of Professor Albert C. Outler of Southern Methodist University for continuous support, pointed criticism, and timely suggestion. Professor Robert L. Calhoun of Yale graciously advised with me concerning the structure of the work in its early stages; and to him, as also to Professor Cornelius Kruse of Wesleyan University, I owe the groundwork of my later researches in Plato. Now after many years' delay, and with uncommon personal satisfaction, I am able to make public acknowledgment to both of my constant appreciation.

It would be an inexcusable neglect of the privileges as well as of the obligations of friendship, should I fail to register my warm thanks to Mrs. Ray C. Petry, friend of the family and neighbor, for her rigorous but gracious insistencies in matters of style in the early stages of manuscript preparation. In the later and final revisions of the work, I have prized the judicious criticism of several staunch colleagues, and each has contributed valuably to the clarity, coherence, and cogency of the work. I make mention, with respect and thanks, of Professors McMurry S. Richey, John H. Hallowell, Thomas A. Schafer, and Stuart C. Henry. Professor W. D. Davies of Princeton and Dr. John Chamberlain of Goucher College, both esteemed former colleagues at Duke, have each kindly checked the Greek materials. Accepting full responsibility for any remaining errors, I thank them, as I do the others, with ever-renewing awareness that the work of scholarship and reflection is an adventure in community. And although she has already been "mentioned in numerous prefaces," my typist, Mrs. Donn Michael Farris, amply deserves to be remembered here also, not alone for her indubitable competence, but for her faithful assistance and unflagging commitment and attention to a task that has extended itself well beyond expectations. In this work I have bent every effort to the end of allowing Plato to speak again, though doubtless in a different idiom, his word which is, I believe, forever timely. I am therefore especially grateful to the Duke University Council on Research for generous assistance in aid of publication of the volume. I would also like to acknowledge my indebtedness to the Ford Foundation for a grant under its program for assisting American university presses in the publication of works in the humanities and the social sciences.

It is my parents, Ralph S. and Maud E. Cushman—to whom this book is dedicated—who take first place in my consciousness of final indebtedness; and words that are suitable to an academic preface are ill-fitted to bespeak the affection and gratitude that is mine for such an inheritance as they have been and have given. For my wife, she is, *Deo volente,* ever with me, and my right hand.

ROBERT E. CUSHMAN

Duke University
March, 1957

The Prologue

I

IT is hardly extravagant to claim that Plato's conception of *philo-sophia* has relevance to man's present-day search for an interpretation of existence. For Plato, philosophy is not disinterested ratiocination, though there is plenty of room in it for acute logical analysis and for probing reflection. Rather, it is, essentially, a way of life, a way out of chaos in human existence. Its root impulse is man in trouble with unresolved contradiction in his spirit, a contradiction which manifests itself in calamitous social derangements. As called forth by a destructive distortion in human life and experience, philosophy offers itself as a therapy. But it begins with diagnosis, and only thereafter supplies its distinctive method of release and transformation.

Nineteenth-century interpretation of Plato puts us forever in its debt, but it was too largely under the controlling influence either of Hegel or of Kant. The Hegelian tradition tended to see only the Platonic metaphysics and therefore unduly stressed the theory of Ideas. Plato was forced into the Procrustean bed of idealism and falsely ascribed to him was a doctrine of the unreality of Becoming, a fundamental indifference to the whole sphere of process. The centrality of the Good in Plato was profoundly appreciated by the Kantians; but, being unable to retain metaphysics, they undertook to "subjectivize" the Ideas, making them constitutive of the "understanding."

Neither approach is acceptable. Against the Kantian, it must be affirmed that the Ideas stand for an antecedently real Ideal Structure with which, as a condition of knowledge, the human mind is essentially akin and must become explicitly conformed. On the other hand, it must be said against the Hegelians, that, while Plato is indeed a metaphysician, his philosophy is wrongly approached if we propose to understand him exclusively in terms of the dictum: the Real is the Rational. On the contrary, the approach to the ultimately Real, in Plato's thought, is properly made by way of his interpretation of man, man whose rational existence is in jeopardy because he is divorced from his ground of Being despite the telltale signs of his essential kinship with it.

This study of Plato is so far indebted to the Kantian tradition as to deplore a long-prevailing disposition in Western thought to ignore the function of the "practical reason" in ontological knowledge and, reversing the position of Kant, to assert the primacy of the "theoretical" over the "practical reason." In our culture this has resulted, as Paul Tillich has lately argued, in the dominance of "technical" over "ontological reason," the flowering of technological civilization at the fearful price of loss of depth. Against this trend Plato long ago strove to vindicate the rightful superiority of *philosophia* to *technê*. But in our time the ascendancy of *technê* over *philosophia* has entailed the disastrous subordination of wisdom to science. And, with the eclipse of ultimate ends of life, not only has human culture become devoid of unconditional loyalties, but, for many, the very meaningfulness of life has been threatened.

If we allow Plato to speak, he will suggest that the question before us is whether we shall shrivel on the positivist vine or, with him, plumb again the resources of the human soul and so recover, it may be, faith in the dignity of man. So we come to our point: It was the Socratic-Platonic probing of the human *psuchê* which led to the Platonic metaphysics and, thus, to the subordination of science to wisdom (*philosophia*). For Plato, the judgment about the dignity of man rests with the answer made to the question regarding man's maximum environment and, hence, his ultimately significant relationship. Plato believed that when man is cut loose from any metempirical rootage and, so, dispossessed of all trans-phenomenal responsibility, he is shorn of moral dignity and shrinks to the status which is allowed to him by those who exercise supreme power in the state. Long ago Thomas Hobbes enforced the view that, if there is no absolute in heaven, there must needs be, for man's good (!), one upon earth. Political philosophies of our time imbibed the lesson well and have accordingly contrived the earthly counterpart—the varying forms of the great Leviathan. Plato's absolute is not exclusively in heaven; neither can it be comfortably domesticated upon earth. But Plato found no solution to the human plight apart from winning for the Ideal Structure of Being the common acknowledgment of men. We are concerned to understand the basis of his conviction that the ultimate Reality may be discovered as a guide to life.

II

All who undertake an interpretation of Plato's thought have been fully warned of the hazards by Plato himself. Interpreters are obliged to deal with a written text; yet Plato has stated that he who believes "that anything in writing will be clear and certain, would be an utterly simple person" (*Phaedr.* 275c). The written word is barely a pale image of "the living and breathing word" of free and fair discussion (276a). Of written words Plato says: "You might think they spoke as if they had intelligence, but if you question them, wishing to know about their sayings, they always say only one and the same thing. And every word, when once it is written, is bandied about, alike among those who understand and those who have no interest in it, . . . When ill-treated or unjustly reviled it always needs its father to help it; for it has no power to protect or help itself" (*Phaedr.* 275d-e). For this and for other reasons, Plato did not believe that truth could be encapsuled in treatises and conveyed to others. Nevertheless Plato did write dialogues and evidently with the intent of communication.

In spite of Plato's warning, it is altogether likely that every generation, in its serious moments, will undertake commentary upon Plato's dialogues. The explanation is not obscure. In good part, it is because Plato is less intent on propounding neat answers to the riddle of human existence than on locating the genuinely fruitful questions by the exploration of which others may be assisted to find answers for themselves. This is by intention, for, where things ultimate are at issue, Plato has no faith in borrowed findings, no faith in so-called truths which a man does not achieve for himself as a personal possession. And here indeed is a fundamental difference from Aristotle, who was subtly lured by definitive answers of supposedly enforceable demonstrations and who, consequently, was impatient with dialogue and preferred the declarative treatise.

Plato wrote only dialogues, and his results commonly annoy readers easily exasperated by tentative and provisional conclusions or, seemingly, no conclusions at all. Often Plato appears to be wholly absorbed in the quest and indifferent to the outcome; yet he is fully convinced that the dialogue alone preserves, in some measure, the form of "living speech" in search of truth and is alone, therefore, suited to be the vehicle of dialectic. Dialectic, especially in the form of *elenchos* or cross-examination, is the art of inquiry rather than of demonstration. It is a method calculated not so much to enforce a thesis as to discover one. It does not derive consequences from postulates; its business is to authenticate postulates. Through its power of crystallization, a man formulates the real issues and asks the fertile questions which may lead of themselves to self-confirming answers. For we cannot comprehend what Plato means to accomplish with *elenchos* unless we understand that, in the proper sphere of its operation, Plato discounts all answers except those a man gives to himself, inwardly consenting to the import of the converging lines of evidence. So he provides a method by which a man may be both inquisitor and witness. *Elenchos* is primarily, if not exclusively, the instrument of metaphysics. In this sphere issues may be isolated which lead, or may lead, to "agreements" which are neither forced nor enforceable. Hence, in metaphysics, a judgment is worth nothing if it is not one's own. If it is, it is a conviction and a commitment. It is, even more profoundly, an agreement of the mind with itself and with ideal Being.

Philosophy, whose best helper is dialectic, is not in Plato's view—and contrary to Aristotle's occasional indication—simply knowledge of the truth. On the contrary, for Plato philosophy is a way and a life, a way to a moment of existence in which there is direct confrontation with reality. Correspondingly, Plato's conception of Wisdom is governed by his conviction that truth relating to ultimate reality resists propositional status and cannot be corralled and contained. Truth *about* reality is subordinated to truth *as* reality. Where man's relation to ultimate Being is involved, truth and reality are inseparable, for reality is embraced in immediate apprehension. Manifestly, then, truth *as* reality is not something admissible of transference by some men to others. Accordingly, the function of philosophy is that of rightly disposing men toward truth.

Plato was doubtless the first to understand and declare that demonstrative truths, the truths of the "abstract" sciences, are certain and enforceable just because they are also hypothetical. In proportion as propositions are rigorous, in the same measure, they are hypothetical, and *vice versa*. Apodictic knowledge is rigorous because it is cogently derived from "arbitrary" or unexamined postulates which are simply taken for granted. But Plato perceived that apodictic knowledge is not the most significant kind. It possesses, among other defects, a purely hypothetical nature.

It is an intention of this study to show how Plato identified the main occupation of philosophy with a totally different sort of truth, which we may call decisional truth. Its subject matter is such reality as represents man's ultimate and ultimately significant environment, namely, truth as reality. When attained, this truth is axiomatic without any condition whatsoever; but, curiously, not for any and all. It is self-authenticating only for those who are possessed, both by nature and discipline, of a character and disposition to acknowledgment. It is one and the same thing, for Plato, that highest knowledge, in the final analysis, is self-confirmatory, and that it is a matter of acknowledgment through the assistance of dialectic.

Decisional in nature, metaphysical knowledge depends upon a volitional disposition favorable to the acknowledgment of reality or First Principle which, in its turn, answers to the native structure of human intelligence. Knowledge is *event* and exists in the moment of conformity of the mind with Being. It is in this sense that Plato understands the First Principle to be "hypothesis without any supposition." It is, thereafter, known to be the presupposition, *ne plus ultra*, of the knowledge of all else. As ultimate presupposition, it waits upon volitional disposition in conformity with it. The manifest sign of conformity is virtue or an affectional balance in the soul inclining it toward the Good. Thus virtue is a precondition of knowledge, and Plato readily concedes that the Ideal Structure of Being is inaccessible to corrupted minds.

The express interdependence of knowledge and virtue is the ground motif of this study. Apprehension of the ultimate structure of Being is conditioned upon *êthos* or the right state of balance of affection (*pathêma*) within the soul. In like manner, a certain perverse indisposition conduces to ignorance of Being. It is Plato's regular teaching that character is not irrelevant, but determinative, either for veridical knowledge or for ignorance. Hence Plato must be taken strictly at his word when, in the *Seventh Epistle* (344a), he asserts that knowledge of "abiding reality" cannot begin to germinate in "alien states of mind" or in the mind of him who is of a perverse "habit" of soul.

Among important corollaries of this general view of knowledge is Plato's total unfamiliarity with a pure, theoretical, or disinterested exercise of reason. On the contrary, every sort of knowledge is premised and conditioned upon some foundational interest. This, in turn, gives us a clue to the distinction which Plato customarily entertains between knowledge and Wisdom. The highest knowledge possible to man comprises the sphere of Wisdom. But Wisdom includes love of that reality of which justice, courage, temperance, and their kin are derivative refractions. More especially, Wisdom is the indissoluble union of highest knowledge with virtue in a single life.

The philosopher is a mathematician and a dialectician; but he is more. He is one in whom the distinctively humane, aboriginal, and insuppressible love of true Being has somehow become emancipated and received nurture. He is a man with vocation and is bent upon a quest. Unlike other men, however, he is ingenuous in his pursuit of truth. Possessed of "goodwill," he follows the path of dialectical discussion wherever it leads—as glad to be refuted as to refute if error can be purged and truth disclosed. But no man can take up this course unless he is possessed of a love of truth weightier than his commitment to present opinions and presently ruling passions. The philosopher therefore begins with honest self-inquiry. He must begin there, because the prime data of dialectical analysis are accessible only to that man who is disposed to probe unflinchingly his own inwardness. He must sometime have the candor to admit that, beyond the imperious claims of private desire, he is sensible of being laid under an undismissible obligation to honor every species of the Good that so far accosts him.

III

In Plato, the prime data of metaphysical knowledge are taken from the realm of man's distinctive experience, namely, the axiological. These data are given; but, as Socrates perceived, they are not given by way of the exteriorized standpoint occupied by the earlier "nature philosophy." Philosophic knowledge has its inception by way of man's honest encounter with himself. This Socratic alteration of standpoint is, above all else, responsible for the Socratic-Platonic conception of philosophy. The Socratic revolution is implied by Socrates' whimsical remark to Phaedrus in explanation for his indifference to rural jaunts: "the country places and the trees won't teach me anything and the people in the city do" (*Phaedrus* 230d). Socrates, and Plato after him, adopted the distinctively humane as the privileged analogy for the interpretation of reality; and in this standpoint we may with assurance locate the motive principle of Platonic humanism.

Plato's metaphysical effort, then, rests upon a distinctive reading of the human spirit. While the uniquely humane is the reliable clue to the nature of ultimate reality, nevertheless the ruling affection or prevailing *êthos* of man or culture decisively controls what will be adjudged the structure of Being, for knowledge is powerfully regulated by interest. The man or culture in whom sensuous appetition (*epithumia*) is presently ruling ordinarily will be content with some variety of phenomenalism. In Plato's estimate, this standpoint was in fact occupied by the mass of Athenian citizenry and was adroitly rationalized by the Sophists. Because of an obsessive sensate concern, men conspired to invert the true order of reality, turning it "upside-down," so that Being was identified with what is not Being but only Becoming.

The problem of education, therefore, was severely complicated. The cure for human ignorance encountered stubborn resistance since it rooted in something which, with etymological correctness, may be described as a pathological condition of the whole soul. Since the ontological perspective was tendentialized by an inferior eros, Plato perceived that education required the revolutionizing of the entire mind. Plato's *paideusis*, or educational discipline, is literally a *therapeia*. It is so described as early as the *Charmides*, where the Socratic *elenchos* is offered as the fitting initial therapy of the soul (*Charm.* 156a-157c); and it is still alluded to as *therapeia* as late as the *Timaeus* (90c). Nothing less than "conversion," as Plato recurrently insists in the *Republic*, is able to cope with an ignorance which Plato is not loath to term "corruption of mind" due to the tyranny of insubordinate eros. Plato's conception of *philosophia* is, consequently, correlated with his diagnosis of the human plight. His realism cannot be overstressed. The suitable approach to his conception of philosophy must always be through Plato's twofold conviction: the present misery and the possible glory of man. His philosophy is a way out of the misery of man's present self-contradictory existence.

Every ontology derives its principles of starting from an ultimate and usually unexamined but ruling preference of the mind. But Plato believed that some specifiable preferences are finally authentic and, therefore, of larger interpretative power than others. We shall be concerned to make plain what, in his view, was the true ruling preference of the human mind—and why. Plato sought his answer in the region of antithesis specified by the misery and glory of man. Behind the façade of the actual, he espied, as he believed, the essential man. Because Plato discerned a real difference between the two, he could also descry the outlines of an ontology which supplied an adequate context and sufficient reason for essential man. But Plato would be the first to concede that those who cannot make out a real difference between actual and essential man—his present misery and possible glory—will have no need of metaphysics. In Plato's sober opinion, their alternative must needs be a phenomenalistic world-view in which, almost certainly, the man described and acquitted by Thrasymachus will be forever having his day and yielding to his better. In that event, Power will be king, and the world must remain unintelligible to axiologically determined intelligence. These were the alternatives Plato tried to clarify for his contemporaries, to the end of forcing a decision for the Good and, thus, for a transcendent relation for man's present existence in time.

THERAPEIA

PLATO'S
CONCEPTION OF
PHILOSOPHY

For there is a dim glimmering of light unput-out in men:
let them walk, let them walk, that the darkness overtake
them not.

Why now doth truth bring forth hatred, . . . ?
Therefore do they hate the truth, for the sake of the
thing which they love instead of truth.

For because they would not willingly be deceived, . . .
do they love it when it discovers itself, but they hate it,
when it discovers them.

St. Augustine's Confessions, X, 23.

CHAPTER I

The Socratic Perspective

Such was the end, Echecrates, of our friend, who was, as we may say, of all those of his time whom we have known, the best and wisest and most righteous man.—*Phaedo* 118

1. Socrates, the Integral Man

THE martyrdom of Socrates in all likelihood cut Plato loose from any lingering intention of pursuing a political career. It crystallized his already maturing conviction of a warfare between good and evil in human life and political arrangements, the outcome of which was in serious doubt. The condemnation of Socrates exposed not merely the degeneracy of existing politics but the veneer of rectitude which barely concealed the potentialities for private and public wrong lurking beneath the surface of existing culture and rooting deep in human nature. In the death of Socrates Plato saw the ugly exhibition of a prevalent feature of human life in association: Righteousness, as manifested in the life of an individual, was beset, and seemingly overcome, by the multitude's torpor and moral obliquity.

For Plato it was a question whether the popular repudiation of goodness and integrity in the person of Socrates was an inevitable accompaniment of social existence or whether better things might be hoped for under other conditions. It was this issue which forced Plato to pursue, with even greater urgency than Socrates before him, the question: Can virtue be taught?[1] If virtue could not be taught, then the victory of ignorance over truth and righteousness, dramatized in the death of Socrates, was the likely and dreadful expectation of man's political destiny. If, on the other hand, virtue could be taught, there yet might be a way out of despair regarding man's political future. From first to last, even to the final pages of the *Laws*, Plato labored to secure for man a political salvation, a way out of social chaos.[2]

One originating source, then, of Plato's philosophical reflection was, undoubtedly, a resolute effort to cast off a dark and encompassing pessimism respecting the moral obtuseness of mankind and the iniquities incident to human political life. Although ill-founded popular tradition goes on attributing to Plato utopian optimism, certainly no Greek thinker looked with more sober and open eyes into the miserable realities of the human situation. None peered with more unflinching gaze into the awesome and dark recesses of human nature. Although Plato taught something like the deiformity of man, a kinship with the Divine in his inmost nature, Plato was aware that it was potential only and that its actualization was obstructed by turbulent and bestial elements in man's total make-up.

Plato was no optimist concerning man or society. He was not even what William James calls a meliorist. He was a tentative pessimist who labored with all his vast powers in order not to be bereaved finally of hope for the betterment of human-kind. So severe is the human plight disclosed by Plato's probing analysis that it remains a fair question whether the *paideusis,* or scheme of education, that he devised as antidote is sufficient to cope with the problem he eventually disclosed.

A contrasting impulse to Plato's brooding social concern in his earlier philosophizing was a personal encounter with a man of extraordinary intellect and monumental character. The near omnipresence of Socrates in the dialogues (he is absent from the *Laws* and takes almost no part in the *Sophist* and the *Timaeus*) is evidence enough that Plato's encounter with Socrates constituted a kind of germinal matrix and continuing inspiration of much of his reflection upon existence. Whatever Socrates' positive teachings were, and that will always be disputed, Plato roamed hardly anywhere in thought without his mentor, as Dante wandered nowhere in Hell without Virgil. Such acknowledgment of indebtedness—primarily to Socrates' spirit and method—has scarcely another example in all literature. We may surmise that it was the man Socrates, not merely speculative genius, which impelled Plato to grapple with ultimate questions related to Being and human destiny. There is even a vantage point from which it is possible to see that the whole massive structure of Plato's thought, his logic as well as his ethic and metaphysic, has its origin in the sublime enigma of Socrates.

If we were governed only by antiquarian interests, we might undertake to describe in detail the doctrinal tenets of Socrates. Such, in a measure, was the penchant of Xenophon; but even he, in his *Memorabilia,* found it natural to display Socratic teaching in the context of occasional conversations between Socrates and a motley crowd of contemporaries. The reason for this is perhaps not on the surface, but Plato was in full possession of it. What Socrates taught was not separable from the impact he had upon his hearers. For Socrates the aim of teaching was not what he could impart of truth but what truth he could induce others to apprehend as their own discovery. In addition, in an unexampled way, certainly for Plato, Socrates was a kind of prism in which the light of truth was broken into its constitutive colors so that men who kept his company discerned what was indiscernible before. In his own person, Socrates embraces, though doubtless with different emphasis, most of the various constructions placed upon him: whether those of Xenophon, Euclides, Antisthenes, or Plato. Plato, by common acknowledgment, gives us the richest account; but variety there must needs have been, since what was basic in Socratism was not spelled out, but of necessity was interpreted and construed. Manifestly, the construction depended upon temperament, perspective, and the measure of sympathy possessed by his various companions.

Nineteenth- and early twentieth-century "historicism" was, we now believe, uncritically self-confident about its ability to recapture the naked truth of history. But history involves interpretation, and every interpreter inevitably intrudes upon the selection, evaluation, and arrangement of his data his own basic sympathies, predisposing interests, and world-view. Therefore anyone who believes today that he can definitively sift and select from the many materials and recompose them into one portrait embracing the irreducible truth about Socrates must certainly be mistaken. At the most, he can succeed in composing only another more or less authentic portrait. Heinrich Maier cherished something of the earlier confidence in historical criticism. With all his remarkable mastery of the materials, however, his picture of Socrates remains a historical construction. His composition is a portrait, an interpretation and not a photograph.[3]

Despite all this, historical scholarship cannot forsake responsibility for discriminating among the ancient interpretations of Socrates. It must render some judgment upon the verisimilitude of the competing portraits. Since, however, the actual Socrates has forever disappeared, the crucial problem centers in the hypothesis from which inference is to proceed. None is certain; yet the following surmise has much to commend it. Plato kept Socrates almost continually in his company along the labyrinthine way of his philosophical pilgrimage and as one controlling influence. It is therefore likely that we have, in Plato, materials for the richest and therefore probably the more authentic portrait of the most provocative teacher of classical antiquity.[4]

When, however, we go to Plato with the question, What exactly did Socrates teach? the question does not elicit Plato's interest. Plato knew better than we that Socrates' concern was not in conveying positive doctrines. Ernest Barker is wholly right in urging that Socrates "never attempted to instil knowledge" and that his prime concern was to "awaken thought."[5] He was bent upon inducing men to become alert to truth as it was dimly or more clearly manifest to them. Furthermore, Plato knew that Socrates made it his principal business to assist, through cross-examination, the clarifying process. It is as R. W. Livingstone has said, in his highly satisfying introductory essay on Socrates, that discussion was the way to knowledge for Socrates—"beating a subject up and down, till the chaff is winnowed from the wheat." And this, on the ground that knowledge "was not an article handed out by those who possessed it to those who did not, but something which men have inside them already."[6] And so every opinion, whether about courage or the end of man, was to be regarded as worthy of examination. Properly sifted and probed, it might contain a germ of validity and even be transformed "into a perception of the genuine truth."[7]

Plato's interest in Socrates and the veneration which he entertained for the master were grounded in the realization that Socrates himself was altogether responsible to truth as it was disclosed to him. The real question, then, for Plato was not the academic one concerning what Socrates taught. Much more pertinent was the question: Who was this Socrates and how was such a man as he possible in view of the decadent state of Athenian society?

We can progress, moreover, in understanding Plato's unconcern for an exact account of Socrates' doctrine by noting that Plato generally avoided didactic presentation of his own teaching, especially where it was concerned with highest reality. Certainly there is little doubt that the dialogue was intended by Plato to preserve in so far as possible the Socratic mode of instruction—not conveying ideas, but supplying an avenue by which earnest participants might stumble upon truth for themselves. Plato's own explanation for the avoidance of dogmatic teaching is his statement in the *Seventh Epistle* that truth will not begin to germinate where men are, by inferior nurture, ill-disposed toward the acknowledgment of truth. Evidently it was Plato's conviction that the intention of Socrates was not to enforce doctrines but to dispose the minds of his respondents toward available reality.

Socrates' conception of philosophic truth, furthermore, was such that it could hardly be conceived as any man's eminent domain. There was a common world of truth which all might share—that is, all who would submit to the discomfiting and rigorous discipline of sifting their first impressions. Accordingly, truth did not depend upon any authorities however venerable. Truth is not the more true because Homer or Solon uttered it.[8] Quite the contrary, even if they should declare it, validation is only by way of the hearer's critical assent or acknowledgment. In the absence of judicious agreement, even a Solon's assertion is only an untested opinion accepted on bare authority. Certainly, some men are wiser than others; but their wisdom is not an exportable commodity. Above all, men of wisdom are regularly those who refrain from dogmatizing, because they perceive that, apart from personal insight, positive declaration is, in any case, nearly useless. There is thus reason to believe that Socrates' immunity to intellectual pride is attributable to his realization that true knowledge is nobody's prerogative to transmit as it is no one's private holding. If, as is indeed the case in the *Republic*, the people and the auxiliaries possess only "right belief" which is engrafted by education and is derivative from the sure knowledge of the guardians, this is something of a departure from Socrates' standpoint.[9] It reflects Plato's more pessimistic conviction that the multitude is incapable of philosophic understanding and must rely upon the superior wisdom of philosophers who are kings.[10]

A deliberate exposition of Socrates' thought, then, would have involved gross insensitivity to the Socratic emphasis upon both universality of truth and knowledge as insight. Plato's restraint in setting forth Socratic doctrine in detail, therefore, is evidence of his tact and fidelity to the mind of Socrates. It is very much as Leonard Nelson argued respecting Socrates: He employed a method of reflection "to lift the knowledge we already possess into consciousness."[11] From all of this, it may be surmised that Socrates' conviction regarding the general accessibility of truth, on condition of the right way of seeking it, in some measure accounts for the fusion of Platonic and Socratic elements in the dialogues. For this unstudied mingling Plato is wholly responsible but without evident embarrassment. Plato indicates his general attitude when, in the *Phaedrus* (275b) he remarks, in connection with rustics who listened to "oaks," that they were wiser than men are now. With them, it made no difference who the speaker was or where he came from; it mattered only that he spoke the truth.

It was as a servant of the truth, not as an oracle of it, that Socrates left his lasting impression upon the mind of Plato. The teacher's role is not that of expositor, but that of *provocateur* and solicitous guide. But Plato's restraint regarding the doctrines of Socrates probably also reflects his conviction that the measure of Socrates' mind could be taken only by direct encounter with the man. As Livingstone has said: "The doctrine is inseparable from the man and the man is even greater than the doctrine."[12] Socrates must be known in his incomparable artistry as a physician of souls.[13] By way of dialogue, therefore, to the limit of his power, Plato perpetuated Socrates in act. In the dialogues we find Socrates in his accustomed role as the skillful surgeon of the mind, at his practice of dialectic. He can be known only as he works—now cutting with surgical skill the cancerous presumption of men by means of *elenchos*, or cross-examination, and then healing with his protreptic or hortatory art of exhortation. The latter serves to shame a man into acknowledgment of truth and goodness of which he feigns to be unaware. Apart from this encounter with the physician in person and with his "living and breathing word,"[14] recapitulation of doctrine seemed wooden and profitless to Plato.

It was, indeed, Socrates the man who was a compelling force of Plato's reflections. To Plato he was the antithesis of the perverted and truncated man whom he saw everywhere about him. Through a debased society, moreover, Socrates moved with an incomprehensible mixture of communal concern and detached serenity. His whimsical, even satirical, exterior, his endless talk of virtue, his seemingly ridiculous analogies drawn from the crafts—smiths, cobblers, and tanners[15]—and his deft confutation of reputable opinions held with distended pride, these things both fascinated and infuriated the Athenians. Whatever measure others might take of Socrates, he was, to Plato's penetrating eye, a person of bewildering complexity whose curious exterior concealed an inward image that was godlike.[16]

To be sure, Plato lets us know that the "divinity" in Socrates is recognizable only to those who, in some measure, have emancipated the divine element which is in themselves. Not all the Athenians felt a tumult of compunction in the presence of the man. Many persons did, among them persons as different as Alcibiades and Plato. Plato was not one to wear his heart on his sleeve. Nevertheless, in the tipsy eulogy of Alcibiades at the banquet of Agathon, he brings us into the presence of Socrates with reverence so masked by wit and humor as to safeguard his own reserve. In the burlesque of Alcibiades, however, Plato allows us a momentary glimpse of his own reaction to Socrates. In his presence, Alcibiades experiences "shame" toward his own trifling and irresponsible living.[17] He is humbled in his own eyes as he confronts the integrity of this enigmatic person. In this respect as in others, Socrates, in Plato's estimate, had no peer either before or in his own time.

Socrates, moving among his fellows, astounded Plato with a serene uprightness which was proof against every solicitation to unprincipled action. By comparison, his integrity simply dwarfed the limping virtues of the many. Sooner or later most men were discovered lending an ear to prudence, as they conceived it, or compromising honesty to the siren voice of self-interest. By the measure of Socrates, the virtues of the many were but "painted imitations." If men appeared temperate and just, a closer inspection usually revealed that their restraint today was only an exchange for larger self-advantage tomorrow.[18] Thus virtue was always a commodity at the bidding of something else. Although for different men the bargain price might vary, it usually came to the right amount of pleasure, prestige, or power.

Socrates embodied virtue. Other men only applauded it. Justice, they agreed, was to be honored; so also courage and temperance. Even the Sophists taught that no civilized man would care to appear other than virtuous.[19] Few, however, seemed to recognize the relevance of these laudable norms in specific application to particular choices. In any case, self-interest cautioned against excessive nicety in their application.

The beloved Crito himself was not above special pleading. He bribed the guard and, in the last hour of possible escape, besought Socrates to come to his senses and make off to Thessaly. Socrates, he urged, was betraying his rightful interests by supine acceptance of the court's sentence. He was abandoning his children to the whims of inscrutable fortune. He was placing his friends in the disgraceful position of seeming indifference to his fate. Altogether, Socrates' action hardly befitted a man of initiative, courage, and good common sense. Crito's arguments, of course, were only commonplace examples of such rationalizations as his contemporaries employed to justify any degree of wrong which ministered to private interest. Socrates knew how the blandishments of self-concern may transform cowardice into seeming courage and how word-jugglery may trans-

mute irresponsibility into integrity.[20]   But it was astonishing to Plato
that, understanding these things, Socrates, unlike most men, profited
by the knowledge.   He did not swerve nor was he deflected from
the course he had chosen.

The marvel of Socrates was that he lived and died by principle.
Even more commanding was the serene composure of his spirit, not
merely at the trial and afterwards in the prison, but in all the vicissi-
tudes of peace and war which had fallen to his lot.   In the last
extremity, as Socrates awaited the return of the ship from Delos and,
therewith, his execution, Crito and his closest associates could neither
altogether credit nor fathom his immunity to the promptings of
natural impulse or the entire poise and equanimity of his mind.
Much less could they conceive that he was happy, for happiness
seemed to Crito and the others inseparable from flight.   Yet Socrates
did not find his imminent execution an occasion for modifying his
principle: It is not living but living well which should command
all of a man's effort.[21]

When the various facets of Socrates' life and person were assessed,
a surprising result became visible.   Plato perceived that the one man
he knew whom people generally regarded as miserable was the only
man he knew who abounded in a consciousness of *eudaimonia*, or
well-being.   Socrates was not merely self-controlled; he was at peace
with himself.   He was faithful to his main purpose, a purpose he
believed every man rightly ought to share, namely, to make his soul
as good as possible.

It was encounter with Socrates, in both his manner of living and
his manner of dying, which convinced Plato that despite appearances,
the man Socrates was evidence enough that virtue and *eudaimonia* are
inseparable.[22]   More than that, Socrates established Plato in the
view that, as virtue is the key to happiness, so happiness is the likeliest
evidence of solid virtue.[23]   For the real nature of virtue is represented
by a mind which is in unison and harmony with itself.[24]   Where
virtue is, the warfare between the conflicting impulses of the soul is
resolved.   The life possesses inner order and harmony because it is
controlled by a true "ruling principle."[25]   Thus the man becomes, as
Plato was to say, a unity, "one man instead of many, self-controlled
and in unison."[26]   All this is, of course, Plato's account of the unified
and just soul in the *Republic*; but that it is Plato's portrait of Socrates,
analyzed into its constituent elements, is forcibly suggested.

In Socrates "self-mastery" was not extirpation of desire or even
subjugation of inclination.   It was something positive.   It was life

controlled both by vision of, and by affection for, superior principles of divine origin.   As the *Apology* shows, Socrates was not only responsible to what he regarded as his divinely authorized vocation and the promptings of the "god" under whose command he served (29d); he found in the fulfillment of responsibility an unfailing sense of well-being.   He was a man in love with truth which somehow his keen vision was able to descry.   The dissension, the warfare that divided the minds of other men, was in the case of Socrates resolved in favor of a higher principle he took to be divine.   Absent was the contradiction in the soul, the turmoil and struggle between antagonistic loyalties.[27]

Thus, for Plato, Socrates was the integral man.   The meaning and import of Socratic integrity and *eudaimonia* became clearer to Plato as he worked out the implications of the fact in his psychology, epistemology, and metaphysics.   Not till the final line of the *Republic* was written did Plato rest content with his portrait of Socrates.   Not till then had he probed sufficiently the enigma of the man.   Up to that period, it may with some measure of truth be said that Plato's philosophy was a strenuous effort to conceive knowledge and Being as of sufficient dimension and depth to account for the uniquely great fact of his experience—the intellectual and moral stature of Socrates.   In this sense Plato's philosophy, through the writing of the *Republic*, is an interpretation of reality on the principle of sufficient reason.   Like the *Apology*, the *Republic* is also an *apologia*, though it is enormously expanded over the earlier work.   The aim of the *Republic* is restated toward its close: "We have proved that justice is the best thing for the soul in itself, and that the soul ought to do justice whether it possess the ring of Gyges or not" (612b).   This was the task of the *Republic*, and by successfully discharging the task Plato also vindicated the life of Socrates.   Of course, in addition, the defense of the life of justice embraced Plato's answer to the political nihilism of his age and his warning against the perennial divisiveness of unprincipled self-seeking.   Plato could see no hope for society unless it could be shown that reality was of such a nature as to justify Socrates in the premise by which he lived and by which also he dared to die.

2. A Revolution of Perspective

In addition to his belief that Socrates' positive doctrines could best be fathomed by understanding the kind of man who propounded them, Plato (absorbing the import of his teacher's word and bearing) recognized with increasing clarity a unique aspect of Socrates' character: It was a living transvaluation of common human standards. Socrates was not merely eccentric to the popular mind; he was in most respects its antithesis. Especially here his greatness was revealed; for unlike the Cynics, who professed to follow him, Socrates displayed none of the proud contempt for human ways and works, none of the arrogant disdain for silly mortals, which marked the figure of Diogenes of Sinope.[28] Socrates' transvaluation of values was evident. He feared least what ordinary men feared and avoided most. And, conversely, Socrates feared most what others feared but little and took small pains to avoid. He cherished the novel opinion that a man's first business is the perfection of his soul—its assimilation in so far as possible to the likeness of "God."[29] Therefore wrong and injustice to another he considered the greatest self-injury.[30] Against Callicles' contemptuous taunts in the *Gorgias,* Socrates is made to reply calmly that righteousness is, in his view, the most effectual self-protection (522d). To Callicles, as to others, this was paradox. Men like Callicles accounted the body of greater importance than the soul and consequently viewed with greatest alarm whatever imperiled the physical man (512d). But Socrates considered the soul man's "dearest possession."[31] However lonely in his judgment, it was thus clear to him "that doing wrong is worse than suffering it, and escaping punishment worse than incurring it."[32]

This lofty ethic was fixed in the ineffaceable substance of Socrates' way of life. Simple as it is, it illustrates the revolution of perspective which Plato attributed to Socrates. Hence everywhere in the earlier dialogues it is customary for Socrates to rebuke his fellows, as in the *Apology,* "for scorning the things that are of the most importance and caring more for what is of less worth" (30a). In making certain discoveries about human nature, Socrates had acquired a new conception of human well-being. If Socrates was right about man; if he was right in making the soul ($\psi\upsilon\chi\dot{\eta}$) primary and regarding it as possessing an affinity with the Divine, then, plainly, the average Athenian's set of values was perverted.

The situation was never more ably described than by the hard-headed Callicles: Either Socrates is joking when he contends that injustice in the soul is the worst evil that can befall a man, or, if it is really true, the life of human beings is turned "upside-down," and most men are doing exactly the opposite of what they ought to be doing.[33] The observation was valid, for the prevailing motivations actuating men in the city-state were based upon the unexamined supposition that the good for men is prescribed by their nature as physical beings. The prevalent success philosophy of the age was nicely rationalized by the teaching of the Sophists. It construed well-being in terms of sensuous satisfactions, together with the largest attainable measure of affluence and personal prerogative. As matters stood, then, the majority of the Athenians had no inclination to luxuriate in Socrates' apparently untenable exhortations. It was by no means clear to them that it is, in no circumstance, right or honorable to do wrong or that, in the so-called legitimate pursuit of one's interest, it is worse to commit than to suffer injury. Glaucon was not misguided in suspecting that, while many honor the word justice, they practice it reluctantly and frequently find themselves constrained, in consideration of their best interests, to defer to expediency. There is, in fact, plenty of indication that Socrates' proscription of all wrong-doing, even retaliation to foes, must have struck his contemporaries with its patent absurdity. According to the persisting "tribal nature of morality," as F. R. Earp has called it, an Athenian "is not restrained from injuring an Athenian by the scruple that he is a fellow citizen. If the man is a stranger, there is no disgrace in injuring him; if he is personally unfriendly, there is even merit in so doing."[34]

If we may take from the *Republic* a word of Plato's about the right kind of statesman and apply it, as Plato would certainly do, to Socrates, he was "the figure of a man 'equilibrated' and 'assimilated' to virtue's self perfectly, so far as may be, in word and deed" (498e). It seemed to Plato that the difference between Socrates and other men was that the latter confounded their true "belongings."[35] Such confusion could occur only if men were ignorant of their essential nature and, therefore, of their true good. Hence fidelity to justice usually came at a price they could ill afford. Strictly speaking, assent to the proposition that it is better to suffer than to commit wrong was, by the standard of existing mores, just short of ridiculous. Socrates' last message to Evenus the Sophist—that if he was indeed a wise man he would make haste to follow Socrates in death—was exactly the kind of *non sequitur* the common man would expect from an eccentric like Socrates.[36] Either Socrates was a buffoon with an uncommon talent for his act, or his madness had a method in it touched with divinity.

The explanation, then, for Socrates' reversal of the prevailing value-scale was his conviction about the *psuchê*. It was the burden of his message to his fellow citizens that they ought, above all things, to seek first after virtue (ἀρετή) and the betterment of their souls, since the soul was man's greatest treasure. This is probably the underlying contention governing the whole of the *Phaedo,* where reasons for the contention are elaborated. According to Socrates, the good or evil destiny of man stands with the state of the soul.[37] But now we must add that the significance of the soul for Socrates is not to be looked for merely in its power to determine the character of private conduct and the aspect of public affairs. Likewise we must not conclude that, when, as in the *Apology* (30b), Socrates speaks of affluence as the result rather than the condition of virtue, he intends to justify goodness and the tendance of the soul by its utility. Its utility, to be sure, is a most acceptable by-product; but care for the soul is urgent for additional reasons. The soul, as "the seat of knowledge and thought,"[38] when fully and earnestly consulted, shows man to be related to a trans-empirical and divine environment with which he may have community. In that community man finds his fullest satisfaction and self-completion and apart from it only self-stultification. The significance of the *psuchê* is for Socrates its provision for access to ultimate reality and thus for a loftier vision of man's *telos* and ultimate good.

Intellectual vision and *koinônia,* or communion with what we may term for the present simply "divine reality," is surely an inexpugnable feature of Socratic experience. This is especially manifest if we allow proper place to what A. K. Rogers rightly insisted are genuine biographical elements in the *Phaedrus* and the *Symposium.*[39] As to the exact object or content of this trans-phenomenal experience, consideration deserves to be given to Rogers' suggestion that although the Forms, as ideals of scientific explanation, may not have been the content, it is still possible that Forms considered as objects of aesthetic contemplation and moral aspiration were intended.[40] This is a plausible hypothesis and a fruitful one in so far as it provides some explanation for the fact, to which Burnet and Taylor always impressively pointed, that Plato distinctly leaves the impression in the *Phaedo* and in the *Parmenides* (129a-130b) that Socrates assumed the existence of Forms as implicates of dialectical inquiry.

The merits of Rogers' theory for the solution of the historical question cannot be settled here, nor is it necessary to do so. But as to religio-mystical experience of which we have sight in the *Phaedo* and the *Symposium* (174d f.), it is hard to imagine, as Burnet maintained, that is is not at least as congenial to the Socratic as to the Platonic temperament. It is true Werner Jaeger reminds us that

Socrates was a "hard, plain thinker." He was indeed. More than that, he had a wry, shrewd sense of realities which would yield no sanctuary to bumbling piety, as in the case of Euthyphro, nor countenance the vagaries of any unexamined orthodoxy. As Xenophon pointed out, Socrates might seek guidance of heaven in matters exceeding human calculation, but he was rigorous in pushing reason to its limits in probing human affairs.[41] It is certain that Socrates had, as Livingstone says, "the scientific habit of mind." We may even agree that "If Reason has ever been incarnate on earth, it was in the person of Socrates. . . ."[42] Nevertheless, the word "rationalist" does not apply to him. As has been rightly said, intelligence was for Socrates "something touched with emotion."[43] And as the reason was as yet undivided into theoretical and practical, so knowledge for Socrates was not attained without vision that welled upward to its objects supported by the lift of a divine eros.

What, then, in Socrates' judgment, gives to ψυχή its great importance? The answer must be sought in its power or function, for what the soul *is* will be judged by what it *does* and is capable of knowing. It is hard to avoid the impression that there is something out of balance in Jaeger's discussion of the Socratic *psuchê*. In his treatment it is safely domiciled in the world of Becoming and only adds a "spiritual" or intellectual dimension to the unity of human nature.[44] Jaeger does not fully succeed in conveying the new significance which Socrates attaches to the *psuchê* when he says: "The old conception of *phusis* which stems from natural philosophy now takes on spirit too, and thereby is essentially changed."[45] It is our contention that the importance Socrates attaches to the soul and its care is inseparable from what may be called its trans-phenomenal reach. In this connection, we cannot lightly dismiss his sense of vocation and responsibility to what he calls the "behest" of the god.[46] In the *Apology*, the word *theos* appears, with its orthodox denotation scarcely modified. Perhaps this is partly explained by the fact that the dialogue is Plato's somewhat over-eager apologetic, for there is much evidence in the *Phaedo* that Socrates had altered his conception of deity as compared with received tradition. Socrates could not, without equivocation, associate his thought of God with inherited mythology, and there is no disputing that in his defense against the charge of impiety he was evasive (27e). But this circumstance did not prevent Socrates from conceiving a power, or a supreme *Nous*—a conception no doubt quite beyond the range of the prevailing orthodoxy—by which all things are ordered according to goodness. And if we may trust the *Phaedo*, especially the "autobiographical passage," it is the conception of such a cosmic Mind toward which his thought is verging. Moreover as we shall see, it is feasible to connect this end-directed *Nous* with the human consciousness of moral obligation of which Socrates was exceptionally sensible.

It was the strength of the soul's reach and what it laid hold of by way of vision which produced the Socratic revolution of values. Anything less than this cannot explain the unperturbed serenity and immovable fidelity of Socrates to principle. Only from this vantage point was it possible for a man to see that wickedness is more to be feared than death because wickedness runs much faster.[47] And aversion to unrighteousness can be understood only if Socrates had, by probing the inwardness of his *psuchê*, discovered therein the indication of a standard, not given by the self but received by it, which measured every human act and sat in judgment upon it.

3. THE PROPHETIC SOUL AND TELEOLOGY

Early Greek reflection, called scientific, was marked by partial abandonment of myth as a method of explanation, and manifested an exteriorization of interest which was mainly directed toward the investigation of *phusis* or nature. The Ionian "physicists" had inclined to take their clue for the understanding of man by analogy from the outward impersonal world. Conversely, it was to be characteristic of the Socratic succession in philosophy to take the measure of the world without by enlarging use of analogy drawn from the world within—from the human *psuchê*. These contrasting, and in some respects antithetical, modes of analogical interpretation have, throughout the history of Western thought, alternately predominated.

Doubtless, every more or less systematic effort to understand the world—to render it intelligible—is inevitably analogical in procedure. Some feature of experience is taken as possessing widest generality and is applied by analogy to the whole. Probably the two modes of analogy, one from the outer and the other from the inner world of experience, ought to be regarded not as antithetical but as complementary. But the human mind, moved by obsessive interests and urged on by an impulse toward unity, is impatient to enthrone some preferred datum as the unique symbol for the comprehension of the whole of reality. Consequently the symbols referred to—the mechanical or quantitative and the humane or axiological—

have tended to succeed each other by periods. Either the one or the other has tended to exclude its opposite in the epoch of its ascendancy and to yield place only when the entirety of human concerns demanded a wider perspective. It was Socrates' discoveries in the sphere of human inwardness which put a period to the exteriorized outlook of the earlier investigation of *phusis* and made room for the inward look from which was to come the axiological and, therefore, the teleological world-view.

If we did not have Xenophon's word for it and Aristotle's well-known reminder, we should still have, in Plato's dialogues, more than sufficient indication that Socrates occupied himself with man and his affairs, rather than with the investigation of nature.[48] The shift to an anthropocentric focus has for long been recognized as marking the real dividing line between pre-Socratic and Socratic epochs in human thought.[49] There is, however, less agreement among experts as to what Socrates, by his keen-eyed probing of the soul, discovered there and what the import was for Plato's teleological conception of the world. With these questions we are now concerned. In seeking answers there is reason to think that we shall be helped by finding out, if we can, what Socrates may have intended by the casual and seemingly whimsical remark to the effect that the soul is prophetic or oracular, *mantikon*.[50] We shall take the view that *nous*—which was for Socrates the principal, perhaps the exclusive, *dunamis* of the *psuchê*, especially if we follow the *Phaedo* —is governed by a controlling consciousness of goodness. This value-awareness may be, and usually is, stifled and inarticulate; but for those to whom it is somehow given to search into the self, as Heracleitus had earlier counseled, *nous* is found to be drawn to a good.[51] It is this constraint from beyond which supplies to man, at one time, his moral calling and, to *nous*, its end-directedness.

Since John Burnet's essay appeared more than thirty years ago, scholarly opinion has conceded that Socrates was spokesman for a new conception of ψυχή. He viewed it not merely as vital principle but as the seat of normal consciousness and intellectual life. Nowhere in prior Greek literature did Burnet find anything resembling the Socratic *psuchê*. In the popular view, the soul had been traditionally understood in one or two ways. It was associated with the "breath" which vivifies the body. Or again, the soul was conceived in Homeric fashion as the "strengthless shade" or ghost. It was not the living man but his surviving wraith or double which, with the dissolution of the body, passed into the dim half-existence of the lower world.

Therefore when Socrates admonished men to tend their souls, as Burnet quaintly observed, it was like saying to an Athenian, "Tend your ghost!"[52]

There are sources upon which Socrates may have drawn in arriving at his novel view of the soul. Among them, the most likely is the Orphic mystery with its dualistic cosmogony. A. E. Taylor, with great skill and erudition, vigorously defended the thesis that the real "impiety" of Socrates—implied in the indictment of Anytus and evaded in the reply of Socrates—was a firm belief in the Orphic-Pythagorean doctrine of the soul.[53]

Our knowledge of Orphism is certainly fragmentary. There is not much doubt, however, that Orphism entertained notions of separability of soul from body and a comparative excellency of the soul. With this went the idea of transmigration or recurrent embodiment. If we may take Plato's word for it, the embodiment was a kind of imprisonment in expiation for some ancient wrong.[54] The soul might be delivered from its cycle of rebirths and reunited to its divine "kin" by means of initiatory rites and ascetical and rigorous moral practice.[55] Recent research in comparative mythology has shown that perhaps the really basic feature of Orphism is a dualistic anthropology rooting in a dualistic cosmogony. According to the Orphic myth of Dionysos-Zagreus, man is of two-fold nature. On the one hand, he springs from the ashes of the Titans, who were destroyed by the wrath of Zeus. But at the same time he partakes of the divine life of the god Zagreus, whom the Titans had torn to pieces and devoured. It is not too much to say that the central theme of Orphism is this: Man is of the earth, earthy and, at the same time, of heaven, heavenly.[56]

We need not settle the question whether or not Socrates' impiety was, as Taylor brilliantly argued, association with Orphic conventicles and therefore fraternization with an alien stream of religious practice. This is subordinate to our interest in Taylor's claim that Orphism was in the very fabric of Socrates' thought. Did Orphism indeed constitute a significant contribution to Socrates' conception of the soul and the unique stress which he laid upon its care?

Attention to the *Phaedo, Gorgias,* and even passages in the *Republic,* suggests numerous points of comparison with what is presumably known of Orphic doctrines. There is, for example, the characteristic Socratic conception of the soul's affinity with the realm of "the good and wise god."[57] There is *katharsis* by which the soul is made pure in order to dwell with the pure.[58] There is the negative attitude toward the body and its desires, because the body serves to imprison the soul and hinders it in its upward course toward loftier being.[59]   And there is the implied dualistic conception of man, with his salvation dependent upon the sloughing off of the earthly admixture.   That which is said of man in the *Timaeus*—that he is "not an earthly but a heavenly plant"—is, judging from the evidence of mythology, Orphic in sentiment.[60]

There are indeed these similarities, but the fact remains that Orphism is vague in what it denotes by *psuchê*.   Although Socrates may have shared with the Orphics a notion of divine derivation and destiny of the soul, his relation to Orphism was ambivalent, whimsical, and soundly critical.   This is evident from the following passage of the *Phaedo* (69c) in which the obliqueness of his relation to Orphism is obvious:

And I fancy that those men who established the mysteries were not unenlightened, but in reality had a hidden meaning when they said long ago that whoever goes uninitiated and unsanctified to the other world will lie in the mire, but he who arrives there initiated and purified will dwell with the gods.   For, as they say in the mysteries, . "the thyrsus-bearers are many, but the mystics few"; and these mystics are, I believe, those who have been true philosophers.   And I in my life have so far as I could, left nothing undone, and have striven in every way to make myself one of them.

It was the "hidden meaning" of the Orphic mysteries which attracted Socrates if, indeed, we may assume that the passage represents his mind.   The dark sayings of the Orphics were riddles upon which Socrates did not hesitate to put his own construction.   And we may be sure he no more abandoned his irony with reference to Orphism than he did with respect to any other orthodoxy.   We may fairly surmise that the moral earnestness of Orphism was attractive and, likewise, its notion of a wider environment of the soul by reference to which its measure was taken.   Judgment there doubtless was for the soul if it was akin to a divine order; for that order was one of sovereign Goodness.[61]   In addition there are some very likely reasons why the Orphic mystery, with its demarcation between the "initiated" and the "uninitiated," should be particularly apt for denoting the difference between the lover of wisdom and the untutored multitude.   For Plato, and we may presume for Socrates before him, the "initiated" is one who has been relieved of the ignorance that is joined to presumption of knowledge.   He is so reoriented in the habitude of his entire mind that he is able to apprehend truth of which he was formerly insensible.

Finally, it may well be that Orphic motifs, among others, appeared in the conversation of Socrates whenever he made those reported shifts from the dialectical to the protreptic or hortatory method. On those occasions, of which we have examples, the *muthos* of Orphism may have offered useful symbolism for the kind of entrancing exhortation of which Socrates was capable. Half revealing and half concealing his meaning, Socrates relied upon suggestion; but to the power of his words, Alcibiades and others stood witness.[62] As Socrates said, words of the right sort are "charms" which heal the soul. He often refers his own most suggestive utterances to some ancient source of quasi-mythical wisdom as, for example, to Zalmoxis, a legendary hero of Thrace.[63] And, if words of the right kind induce wisdom in the soul, Socrates is not averse to being an enchanter, after a fashion. He is prepared to excite a kind of "ravishment," namely, moral sensibility and αἰδώς—shame or reverence for goodness.[64] Whether by cross-examination or by the protreptic art, Socrates' method was always maieutic, that is to say, evocative. The function of speech is to lead souls by persuasion; and the true rhetorician is one who knows the various kinds of soul and suits his discourse to the particular variety.[65] And, if we may judge by Socrates' testimony in the *Theaetetus*, his "art of midwifery," the maieutic art (184b), not only enabled him to be the instrument of many happy deliveries of "fair things" that pregnant minds discover within themselves (150d), but also to sort and sift the issue so as to distinguish the true from the false (150b).

All this is something different from the world-flight of Orphism. Although the dissolution of the body is the imminent expectation of Socrates in the *Phaedo*, his other-worldly look is still restrained by the conviction that responsiveness to the prophetic summons in the soul is quite as much the condition of *eudaimonia* in this as in any other world. And although Socrates may have entertained with the Orphics a notion of man's dire need for *katharsis*, his conception of the nature of that purification was so different as to possess little or no comparability. In this connection, it is of decisive importance that Socrates, probably with a suggestion from Anaxagoras,[66] identified the *psuche* with all the reflective, deliberative, and envisioning powers of *nous*. As we might say, henceforth, man is not to be "saved" without his intelligence; and this alone amounts to a definitive departure from Orphism.[67]

But, now, we have cleared the ground to consider the original question: What was it that Socrates discovered, by attention to the soul's deliverances, to make the soul the object of his principal concern? Why was it a man's most urgent business to know and to examine himself?[68] In what sense was self-knowledge the beginning of wisdom; and why was the unexamined life not worth living? In part the answer was that through self-knowledge a man might be apprised of his own ignorance and thereby disabused of presumption. The Socratic trauma, the induced shock and perplexity, however, was only a means to, not the end of, self-knowledge.

The Socratic program of research is classically stated in the *Phaedrus*. The setting is the pleasant vale of the Ilissus near Athens, with shade of plane trees and clear running water on a summer day. There is the sleep-inviting shrill of the cicadas. Not far off is the altar of Boreas which prompts Socrates to ponder aloud to Phaedrus: whether, as the ancient legend held, Boreas carried off Oreithyia from this place or whether in sober truth, as the rationalizers of the myth maintain, a blast of Boreas, the north wind, swept her off the near-by precipice and so she disappeared. Socrates does not presume to decide such questions, although he suggests that the explanations of the rationalizers strike him as laborious and over-clever and, in any case, never more than probable. Then he adds:

But I have no leisure for them at all; and the reason my friend, is this: I am not yet able, as the Delphic inscription has it, to know myself; so it seems to me ridiculous, when I do not yet know that, to investigate irrelevant things. And so I dismiss these matters, and accepting the customary belief about them, as I was saying just now, I investigate not these things but myself. . . .[69]

To Socrates it was a trifling and empty occupation to vex one's waking thought with these enigmas of a legendary past while there lay so close at hand the enigma of the self which needed opening. It was no doubt a like reflection which, according to the *Phaedo*, diverted Socrates from an examination of physical questions and prompted his reflection, not about the material elements of things, but about an intelligent Cause from which things received their order and structure. Somehow for Socrates all explanation was muddling which did not issue from a prior investigation of the self that knows. And so we find him saying in the *Phaedrus* that he is fond of learning; hence he rarely ventures out of the city into the country, because rural places and trees won't teach him anything while people in the town do (230d).

The "proper study of mankind is man." Socrates evidently believed that it was a study upon which all others depended; but can we recover his reasons? In the famous "autobiographical passage" of the *Phaedo* (96a-101e), Socrates recounts how, as a youth, he was eager for the kind of wisdom which is called "investigation of nature," how exhilarating was the search for the causes of everything: whether heat and cold bring about the structure of animal life and whether it is by blood, air, or fire that men think (96b). But he found that explanation of sensation, of growth, of memory and of thought by way of physiological and physical sub-structures was confusing and in the end concluded that he was totally unfitted for this kind of research. Moreover, Socrates found that he had been so "blinded" by this manner of study that he had lost the knowledge which, before, he had supposed he possessed. Physical investigation became to him, as is so clearly symbolized in the *Phaedrus*, the siren voice of the cicadas inviting him to sleep and to forgetfulness of true reality and the proper approach to it.

According to his testimony in the *Phaedo*, Socrates was suddenly relieved of his befuddlement by hearing the doctrine of Anaxagoras that it is "the mind (νοῦς) that arranges and causes all things" (97c). He immediately concluded that, if this were so, then the mind, in ordering and establishing all things, would necessarily order things in each case as was best and fitting. "For," said Socrates, "I never imagined that when he [Anaxagoras] said they were ordered by intelligence, he would introduce any other cause for these things than that it is best for them to be as they are."[70]

This inference is of capital importance; for, if he indeed made it, as Plato bears witness, Socrates probably deserves to be considered the first serious teleologist; for what Socrates implies, as he in fact declares, is that cosmological explanation can proceed only by reference to a *telos* or Good considered as the controlling referent of intelligence. He assumed, then, that Anaxagoras would go on and explain each thing in terms of a good or a purpose which it both instanced and served. But in this he was disappointed as is well known; for Anaxagoras quickly reverted to explanation in terms of secondary causes, the physical constituents of things, succumbing again to the siren voice of sense.

Socrates himself, however, had taken a momentous step in cosmological explanation. He had accepted from Anaxagoras the dictum that it is *nous* which orders the world; but, to the conception of its distinctive causality, he made his own unprecedented contribution. This conception could only have come to light through his program of self-knowledge.   From self-examination, from the probing of *nous* as the distinctive power of the human *psuchê*, he had made a discovery that is stated clearly enough in the "autobiographical passage": It had become plain to Socrates that *to act according to intelligence is to act from a decision or choice of what is best* (99a).   Accordingly, if it is, as Anaxagoras claims, intelligence which contrives and arranges the cosmic whole, then Socrates suggests that the real cause is a comprehensive Good which informs and therefore comprises the purpose of the cosmic Mind.   It is this Good (τὸ ἀγαθόν) and its power (δύναμις) to which men must finally refer in causal explanation, understanding that it embraces and holds together all things.[71]

It is not explicit in these passages just how Socrates understands the ontal relationship between the cosmic intelligence and the Good with which it is instinct.   Nor is it at all confidently to be urged that the Good has disengaged itself from the cosmic *Nous* and acquired an independent status as in the *Republic* (506-509).   In the passages before us one can only say that it is tending in that direction.   Socrates, in the *Phaedo*, shortly adds that he is at the end of his tether in these matters and would gladly learn from one who would teach him more fully concerning the nature of this Cause (99c).   Perhaps this is the point at which Plato gracefully relieves Socrates of responsibility for such further developments of the Idea of the Good as we see subsequently in the *Republic*.   In any case, it is at this point that the well-known "Second Voyage" of explanation in terms of *logoi*, gets under way.   This, as Burnet says, is no "makeshift."   We are in fact about to be launched into the theory of Forms in real earnest.   But we can leave the matter here with the suggestion that the Forms (*logoi*) were Plato's initial way of establishing *mediating* linkage between the Cause which had emerged and its phenomenal effects. As for the cosmic *Nous*, Plato was for some time to leave it alone; the state of his theology was such as to leave him, for the moment, a little embarrassed about God.[72]

We have now all but accomplished our purpose.   It remains only to answer the question how it was that Socrates arrived at the conviction that, as he says, intelligence is action from a choice of what is best.   This insight is Socrates' major positive contribution to Western thought and culture.   It represents his loftier estimate of man and his evaluation of the resources of the human soul.   By research into himself, by active response to the deliverances of his *psuchê*, Socrates discerned what he took to be a "divine imperative" notifying him of an irreducible difference between right and wrong, good and evil. By such consultation also, as *Phaedo* 100c indicates, Socrates was conscious of irreducible aesthetic distinctions, as between beauty and its opposite. Hence for Socrates the primary data of the human consciousness are ineffaceable axiological distinctions. Plato faithfully reports, in the *Crito*, the axiological criterion in its ethical form as the *archê* or first principle of Socrates' thought. The principle is that "we ought neither to requite wrong with wrong nor to do evil to anyone, no matter what he may have done to us" (49c). And, in the context of the same discussion, we are distinctly informed that *psuchê* is that part of man which is concerned with right and wrong, by its distinctive and inherent aptitude, and that it is benefited by righteousness and injured and ruined by unrighteousness (47d).

Why is the soul ruined by wrong and benefited by the right? Ultimately it is because disvalue denatures the soul and removes it further and further from the province and likeness of "divine reality" with which it has kinship. This is the pervasive message of the *Phaedo* and is re-echoed in a memorable passage of the *Theaetetus* where the end of man is "to become like God," that is, "to become righteous and holy and wise."[73]

Socrates, in examining himself, was not only alerted to a root difference between good and evil but made aware of his responsibility to the good and his obligation to shun its opposite. For Socrates the soul transmitted a moral summons to righteousness. And in this consciousness man became a self-transcending and responsible being, distinct from merely cyclical process. One obvious phase or token of this consciousness is the "familiar" or "divine sign" which Socrates calls the *daimonion* that characteristically restrains from heedless ways.[74] Socrates had just been checked by the "sign" after his "shameless" speech of the *Phaedrus* when he was prompted to observe how "prophetic" the soul is. Ironically, Plato allows Socrates to observe that the "sign" is somewhat exceptional to him,[75] although it was customary with him from childhood.[76] The *daimonion* was certainly nothing so pale and insipid as a kind of "spiritual tact."[77] Likewise it is impossible to consent to Zeller's view that the *daimonion* has nothing to do with conscience, although, admittedly, the word συνείδησις does not occur in Plato.[78] There can be no doubt that the *daimonion* served to notify Socrates of a good with which he was presently out of line. But we are not literally to conclude that this moral datum was really unique with Socrates. So to think would be to divest Socrates of his exemplary and pedagogical role in Plato's thought of him. Plato's word in the *Republic* (440b) concerning a reason which enjoins, "Thou ought not," seems to have general applicability; and the truth really is that the "sign" is exceptional with Socrates precisely because he deliberately heeds and honors it. For himself he can witness to its cautionings within; but it is beyond possibility either to prove or to enforce another's admission of the divine summons. It is possible only to admonish another to attend and to heed for himself.

This was Socrates' problem: the prime datum of the human consciousness (*i.e.*, axiological awareness) cannot be exhibited and demonstrated to all and sundry. It requires "tendance of the soul," alertness to it, and, above all, veracity about its notices; no one of these can be required of any man. Therefore Socratic teaching was, as the opening pages of the *Theaetetus* enforce once again, characteristically an effort to elicit the confession of men to the truth of their own deepest insights and noblest aspirations (150d).

For the subject of teleology, our findings are these. Reality is to be explained in terms of a Good, a *telos*; that is, it is to be referred to intelligent rather than to material causality. The reason is that the root character of *nous*, in man and in the world, is consciousness of Good by which it is solicited and to which it is pledged.[79] A truly intelligible explanation of the world is one that answers to and therefore satisfies the fundamental structure of the mind. It will be, as Plato reaffirms at the very close of his literary career, by way of an intelligent will "aiming at the fulfillment of good."[80] Intelligence was found by Socrates to be inveterately axiological. In the axiological structure of the mind, Socrates not only discovered the distinctive nature and value of the soul of man; he caught sight of the analogy in terms of which the alien outer world might receive a *logos*, an intelligible account, no longer foreign to the human spirit. He put the teleological or humane world-view upon its feet.

Thereafter and for some time to come, Plato was devoted to an interpretation of the world through *logoi*, for it struck him that the Ideas were suitable schematic structures in terms of which the causality of the Good became available to the knowing mind. The Ideas were to be the instruments of the ultimate Causal Principle for a teleological explanation of the world; while, at the same time, and against the Heraclitean flux theory, they were to give structure and knowability to transient things of Becoming. This latter program is almost certainly Plato's and not that of Socrates; and the ontology, whose instruments are the Ideas, is most surely Plato's advance beyond Socrates' epoch-making discrimination between the older "physicalistic" type of causation and Socrates' own teleological interpretation of the world. Thus through his reverence for the soul as man's dearest possession and his probing of it, Socrates opened the way for human thought to pass beyond physicalism as, earlier, physicalism had superceded mythical cosmogony. In this, moreover, Socrates was surely responsible for establishing for the Western world the foundational distinction between nature and culture, that is, between necessity and responsibility.

NOTES

1. *Protag.* 319a; *Meno* 70a, 87b. All references are to the Platonic text contained in the *Loeb Classical Library* edition (London, W. Heinemann and Harvard University Press). The *Loeb*, for the whole Platonic corpus, is generally regarded as the most trustworthy translation for English readers. Therefore I have found it desirable to allow the *Loeb* translation to stand as a norm. Wherever "block" quotations are found they are from the *Loeb* translation.

2. *Laws* 960b-d, 968a; *Protag.* 356d f.; *Polit.* 297b; *Rep.* 429c, 465d.

3. Heinrich Maier, *Socrates; Sein Werk und seine Geschichtliche Stellung* (Tübingen, 1913), 1-2. Even a photograph, of course, does not assure objective reproduction, so that the contrast is not really complete.

4. *Ibid.*, Maier 102-146, took the view that Plato's *Apology* and *Crito*, together with certain of the minor dialogues such as *Euthyphro*, *Laches*, and *Charmides*, provide us most reliably with the historic Socrates. There is very much to commend this judgment, since any reader is struck repeatedly by the biographical intent of the first three dialogues. We simply cannot discard, however, the biographical features in the *Phaedo*, *Phaedrus*, and *Symposium*. When we embrace them, a religious dimension is added to the magisterial moral personality of Socrates. However, Maier rightly accentuated the moral element.

5. Ernest Barker, *Greek Political Theory* (London, 1951), 118.

6. R. W. Livingstone, *Portrait of Socrates* (Oxford, 1938), xix. Cf. *Symp.* 175d. This introductory essay deserves to be required reading for every undergraduate.

7. Cf. E. Barker, *op. cit.*, 119; *Theaet.* 151b-c.

8. *Rep.* 334b, 377d, 379c, 536d.

9. *Rep.* 430a-b. Cf. G. M. A. Grube, *Plato's Thought* (London, 1935), 225.

10. *Rep.* 428e f.

11. Leonard Nelson, *Socratic Method and Critical Philosophy*, trans. T. K. Brown (New Haven, 1949), 16.

12. R. W. Livingstone, *op. cit.*, xli.

13. Cf. *Charm.* 156a f.; *Gorg.* 514d; 521a f.

14. *Phaedr.* 276a. W. Jaeger, *Paideia* (New York, 1943), II, 37, takes note of the twofold nature of Socrates' method involving exhortation (*protreptikos*) and cross-examination (*elenchos*). Xenophon gives explicit warrant for this, *Memorabilia* I, iv, 1. The distinction, however, is fully evident from Plato's dialogues. Cf. *Apol.* 29d-31a.

15. *Symp.* 221e. Cf. Xenophon, *Mem.* I, ii, 37, and *Gorg.* 491a.

16. *Symp.* 215b. A. K. Rogers, *The Socratic Problem* (New Haven, 1933), 125-128, has rightly drawn attention to the full-length portrait of Socrates in the speech of Alcibides (*Symp.* 215a-222b) as an indispensable supplement to the rendering of the *Apology*. We here glimpse Socrates as the seer whose own moral earnestness is an irresistible exhortation to righteousness.

17. *Symp.* 215b-216b.
18. *Phaedo* 68e.
19. *Protag.* 323c, *Cf. Theaet.* 176b.
20. *Cf. Rep.* 560d.
21. *Crito* 48b; *Gorg.* 522e.
22. *Cf. Rep.* 580b-c; *Gorg.* 478e, 493d; *Laws* 662e, 716a.
23. *Rep.* 576b-c.
24. *Rep.* 554d, 441d-444d.
25. *Rep.* 442d.
26. *Rep.* 443e, 554e.
27. *Gorg.* 482b-c. *Cf. Rep.* 443d f., 586e. Here we have the integral man: self-controlled, in unison with himself, and devoid of "inner dissension."
28. For an instructive and balanced presentation of Cynicism, see G. C. Field, *Plato and His Contemporaries* (London, 1930), 119-121, 160 f. Cynicism was an offspring of the rigorous and abstemious Socrates. Diogenes was not gifted enough to perceive that, with Socrates, rigor was a by-product of larger concerns and not an end in itself nor a badge of intellectual superiority.
29. *Apol.* 29e, 36c; *Gorg.* 504e; *Rep.* 591c. *Cf. Rep.* 500c, 501c, 589d; *Theaet.* 176c; *Laws* 716c.
30. *Apol.* 30d; *Rep.* 577d, 588e; *Gorg.* 509a f.
31. *Protag.* 314a. *Cf. Charm.* 154e; *Gorg.* 512a; *Alcib.* I, 132c.
32. *Gorg.* 474b, 480a, 505b.
33. *Gorg.* 481c. For similar usage of ἀνατρέπω, see *Rep.* 389d, 442b, 444a; and, for a classical expression of its ethical and psychological significance, see *Rep.* 489d f.
34. F. R. Earp, *The Way of the Greeks* (London, 1929), 34. In the same place, the author goes on to say that beneficence to friends and deadliness to foes was a recognized principle of Greek morality. *Cf. Rep.* 334b. He adds: "Not unnaturally this principle was criticized by the moral philosopher, but long after Socrates had argued that to injure another is to injure one's own soul, we find orators still appealing to the old doctrine as an accepted principle."
35. For τὸ οἰκεῖον as what belongs or pertains as possessions to soul, see *Lysis* 221e, 222a; *Rep.* 433e, 443e, 586d-e, 611e; *Phaedr.* 248b-c.
36. *Phaedo* 61b.
37. *Charm.* 156e.
38. *Alcib.* I, 133c.
39. A. K. Rogers, *op. cit.*, Ch. V. Rogers' insistence upon the mystical and contemplative side of Socrates is ably presented and must be credited. His position is a necessary corrective to the excessively moralistic presentation of W. Jaeger. *Cf.* J. Burnet, *Plato's Phaedo*, liv-lv.
40. A. K. Rogers, *op. cit.*, 115 f. Rogers' suggestion, as he indicates, was based upon J. A. Stewart's distinction between Forms as instruments of scientific intelligibility, a Platonic contribution, and Forms as ideal paradigms corresponding to an aspiring aesthetic and moral apprehension of reality.
41. *Mem.* I, i, 9.
42. R. W. Livingstone, *op. cit.*, xxxix.
43. E. Barker, *op. cit.*, 91. *Cf.* J. Burnet, *Greek Philosophy* (London, 1950), 168.
44. W. Jaeger, *op. cit.*, II, 43-47.
45. *Ibid.*, 43.
46. *Apol.* 23b. *Cf.* 22a, 28e, 29d, 30a, 33c; *Crito* 54e; *Theaet.* 150c.
47. *Apol.* 39a.
48. Xenophon, *Mem.* I, i, 11 and Aristotle, *Met.* 987 b 1 f. In the *Apology* (19b-d), Socrates denies any investigation of physical questions or any private or

public conversation upon such matters. This is not necessarily contradictory to the statement (*Phaedo* 96a) that when he was young he was eager for the kind of wisdom called "investigation of nature" or that he was early edified by matters he heard another read from a book by Anaxagoras. *Phaedo* 97b.

49. Wm. A. Heidel, Περὶ φύσεως, Proceedings of the American Academy of Arts and Sciences (Vol. XLV, 1910), 95 f. See also F. M. Cornford, *Before and After Socrates* (Cambridge, 1932), Ch. V, and W. Jaeger, *Paideia*, II, 31-32.

50. This remark is apparently casual, but it should be estimated in conjunction with other passages referring to the *daimonion*, as for example *Apology* 40a f. where Socrates' devotion to truth has ended in his condemnation, and his mood is scarcely whimsical. No doubt our passage at 242c needs to be related to eros, the madness which is superior to sanity if it comes from god. *Cf.* 244d, 265a-b. The mantic character of the soul is also to be compared with "pregnancy" of the soul as at *Theaet.* 151b.

51. Kathleen Freeman, *Ancilla to the Pre-Socratic Philosophers* (Oxford, 1952), 31, Frg., 101. Miss Freeman makes it rather clear that, at the least, Heracleitus and Socrates had a common admiration for the Delphic Oracle with its exhortation to self-knowledge. (*Pre-Socratic Philosophers* [Oxford, 1949], 121.) Who knows whether Socrates might have heard Heracleitus' other word: "You could not in your going find the ends of the soul, though you traveled the whole way: so deep is its Law (*Logos*)." Frg. 45 (*op. cit.*, 27). But who doubts that Plato, if not Socrates, held *nous*, in man, cognate with *Nous* in the cosmos by way of a *Logos* common to them both?

52. John Burnet, *Essays and Addresses* (New York, 1916), 126-168. *Cf.* F. M. Cornford, *Before and After Socrates*, 50.

53. *Varia Socratica*, First Series (Oxford, 1911), 17-23.

54. *Cratyl.* 400c; *Phaedo* 82e.

55. See E. Rhode, *Psyche* (New York, 1925), 343-346, and M. P. Nilsson, *A History of Greek Religion* (Oxford, 1949), 220-222.

56. See Jane E. Harrison, *Themis* (Cambridge University Press, 1927), 462-466, especially Nilsson, *op. cit.*, 213-217.

57. *Phaedo* 80d. *Cf.* 79b-d, 80b, 86b; *Laws* 899d, *Phaedr.* 248b; *Tim.* 90a.

58. *Phaedo* 67b.

59. *Phaedo* 82e, 67d, 91e.

60. F. Solmsen (*Plato's Theology* [1942], 125), has a valuable chapter on the nature of the mystery-religions and their influence upon Plato's maturing conception of the soul. He says "the mysteries carried with them a general assurance of the unique worth and the divine or nearly divine quality of ψυχή."

61. *Cf. Phaedo*, 107c, 108a, 113d; *Gorg.* 523a-527e. See also *Epist.* VII, 334e f. Here, as it seems, we have Plato's own confession of faith in the soul's immortality and inevitable judgment.

62. *Symp.* 215d f.

63. *Charm.* 156d. *Cf. Phaedr.* 270b and *Symp.* 186c, for comparable view of the therapeutic function of language of the proper kind. The words of Diotima in the *Symposium* (210d f.) are, of course, also examples of "mantic" wisdom, obviously of mythical and legendary provenance, and suitable to excite in the mind of Socrates' hearers presentiments of reality beyond the reach of sense for which, however, the soul of man possesses a susceptibility and kinship.

64. *Cf. Symp.* 215d-216c. For *aidôs*, see *Phaedr.* 253d, 254b, e.

65. *Phaedr.* 271d.

66. *Phaedo* 97b; *Phaedr.* 270a; *Cratyl.* 400a.

67. See *Alcib.* I, 127e. Socrates' divination, *manteia*, is herein mainly dialectic. This dialogue is not generally regarded as a work of Plato. There is, however,

good reason for considering it a concise and discriminating presentation of authentic Socratism.

68. *Phaedr.* 229e. *Cf. Apol.* 21d, 38a; *Charm.* 167a; *Alcib.* I, 128e, 130e; *Gorg.* 514a.

69. *Phaedr.* 229e.

70. *Phaedo* 98a. R. D. Archer-Hind (*The Phaedo of Plato* [London, 1894], *ad loc.*, 99c, n. 6), seems to be right: "The main fault of Anaxagoras is that the Good is not the ultimate cause in his system."

71. *Phaedo* 99c. In these passages, ἀγαθός is used as a neuter substantive only once. There is, instead, recurrent use of βέλτιστος, the superlative, and frequently as substantive, τὸ βέλτιστον. τὸ ἄμεινον (97e), the irregular comparative of ἀγαθός, is used as substantive. These commonplaces are noteworthy because the employment of the comparative and superlative degrees suggests a tendency toward *substantizing* the Good which is still incomplete; but the Idea of the Good is actually seen in its emergence.

72. See W. H. V. Reade, *The Christian Challenge to Philosophy* (London, 1951), 34-35. *Cf. infra*, Ch. III, n. 9.

73. *Theaet.* 176a-b. *Cf. Phaedo* 79d-81a.

74. *Apol.* 40a-c; *Euthy.* 3b; *Rep.* 496c; *Phaedr.* 242b.

75. *Rep.* 496c.

76. *Apol.* 31d.

77. Paul Shorey, *Republic* (*Loeb*, II, 52, note *a.*), and E. Zeller, *Socrates* (London, 1885), 95.

78. See F. Hiedel, *The Gospel of Hellas* (New York, 1949), 213.

79. E. Barker (*op. cit.*, 189) held that in Plato "there is always implicit a teleological conception of the world, based on a teleological conception of mind." Thus, rational action is always essentially purposive. F. Solmsen (*Plato's Theology*, [1942], 100) says it is unnecessary to prove that whatever Mind does is good "because it works with the good of the Whole in view." He comes closer to the point made by us in saying: "Human actions, characterized as they are by the presence of a purpose, serve as models of a teleological pattern." Our interpretation supplies the simple but missing link, *viz.*, the moral datum as the root datum of the human consciousness. Primarily, it seems, it is this which affords to mind its teleological orientation.

80. *Laws* 967a.

CHAPTER II

The Human Plight and Plato's Task

In our eyes God will be the measure of all things in the highest degree—a degree much higher than is any man they talk of.—Laws 716c

I. THE RATIONALE OF THE IDEAL

NINETEENTH-CENTURY Platonic interpretation was so under the spell of Hegelian idealism that it gave disproportionate stress to the Platonic theory of Forms. It tended to lose sight of the pressing human situation in the light of which the rationale of Plato's metaphysics can best be understood. If it is suitable to speak of Platonism as *philosophia perennis*, it is mainly because it was in origin a diagnosis of and a response to the perennial human plight. The commonplace notion of Plato as architect and builder of a world of ideal objects, a home of the soul, nostalgic for the eternal and indifferent to the exasperations of the temporal, is baseless caricature. It is fitting, then, to draw attention to Plato's own statement that he forsook politics for philosophy, not to find an irrelevant retreat, but, through right education, to create a moral climate from which better politics might come.[1] This was not Plato's only purpose; but it was always his ulterior one. He withdrew from the field in order to return with weapons suitable for an urgently needed moral and intellectual renovation of man.

We are to remember, in the first place, that behind Plato was a popular tradition in "dispraise of learning." Both in the *Gorgias* and in the *Republic* Plato attempted to meet and overthrow the vulgar assumption concerning the irrelevance of theory to life and to show the pertinency of philosophy for human affairs.[2] Against the stream of opinion, he contended in the *Republic* (487c-e) that men are not rendered socially useless by the pursuit of wisdom. On the contrary, he claimed that all existing governments are indicted in so far as their people neither understand nor are able to employ to good effect the philosophic nature (489b). It is a dismal commentary

upon politics that the lover of wisdom, who pursues truth and un-
covers "the painted imitation of virtue" and the evils of existing social
arrangements, is customarily accounted a meddler and a visionary.
He is vilified and persecuted and may expect, as in the case of
Socrates, to come to an untimely end. The truth-seeker is as a man
fallen among wild beasts, unwilling to participate in their misdeeds
and unable to hold out against the prevailing savagery.[3] The example of Socrates enforced upon Plato's consciousness the bitter
observation that, though he may prevent unjust and illegal happenings
in the state, no man will be safe who nobly opposes the pleasure of
the populace.[4] Through the writing of the *Gorgias* and the *Republic*, it is the galling judgment of Plato that the practice of
politics is mainly directed toward the acquisition of power through
connivance with, and flattery of, the public whims. Too often it is
prostitution of honor in the interest of individual prerogative and
partisan advantage. The best politician is he who knows best the
various tempers and moods of Demos, the great beast, and what words
are most soothing for every occasion.[5] It is manifest in the *Gorgias*
(464c-d) that not rhetoric alone but politics, which employs it, is the
craft of flattery practiced by those who care nothing for what is best
but dangle what is most pleasant before the multitude as a "bait to
folly."

Plato countered prevailing political incentives with the startling
claim that the end of political art and the aim of the true politician
is to engender love of virtue and to eliminate injustice—in short, to
make citizens as good as possible.[6] This, moreover, is the same as
securing to the *polis* as a whole the greatest possible measure of
eudaimonia,[7] for it is already an established conviction of Plato that
virtue and real happiness are not separable.[8] If virtue, both in
individual life and in public expression, is the great goal of politics,
then scrutiny of current practice revealed that existing statesmanship
pursued no such end and was, in addition, impotent to achieve it.[9]
From this vantage point, it became obvious to Plato that the only true
politics was the best *paideia* or program of education. And, if that
was true, then, in opposition to the popular prejudice, the best statesman was a *philosophos*, a lover of wisdom.

Now Socrates had been pre-eminently the philosopher. It was
he who had spent his days encouraging men to examine themselves—
to perfect their souls in virtue. More than any man of his generation,
more than Themistocles, Cimon, or Pericles, who were renowned
before or in his own day, Socrates had inculcated good citizenship

(*Gorg.* 519a). Therefore it seemed to Plato no stretching of the truth to affirm that Socrates was one of the few, perhaps the only one, in Athens who undertook the true art of statesmanship and rightly managed affairs of state (*Gorg.* 521d). Assuming, then, that existing politics was bankrupt, the only remaining politics was a *paideusis* or program of training, the rudiments of which Socrates bequeathed as a legacy to Plato—a legacy which, in turn, Plato was to enlarge upon and systematize in the *Republic*.

The important thing in the *Republic* is not the particular shape or contour of the conceptualized state which is fabricated there. The important thing is not whether a republic so conceived could in fact exist. Plato openly and soberly weighed the question of its possibility.[10] It is axiomatic with him that the world of Becoming never admits an undiminished actualization of the ideal. And Plato knew, in any case, that such a society had no possibility of existing unless the philosophic Muse took control of a state, or as he put it, philosophers became kings, or kings philosophers.[11] But even this is somewhat beside the point. It is true that Plato cherished the hope that through the proper *paideusis* the essential state might have greater fulfillment in the actual world. Yet in the *Republic* the center of interest is quite as much or more the definition and vindication of the virtuous life and the delineation of the method of education from whence the good life may come.

In the light of this we are in a position to see the indispensability of the epistemological and metaphysical standpoints which are characteristically Platonic. The theory of Forms, but more especially the metaphysics of the Good, was *sine qua non* for a vindication of Socratic righteousness in defiance of the consequences. This, indeed, was what the program of the *Republic* called for as it was formulated by Glaucon and Adeimantus in the opening pages of the Second Book. They remarked that no one of all the ancients had ever censured injustice or commended justice otherwise than by reference to the imprudence of the former and the prudence of the latter (366e). What is needed is a vindication of goodness without appeal to rewards which, experience shows, are not always assured. It must be shown that justice is good for the soul whether it possess the "ring of Gyges" or not.[12] To personalize the situation, it must be shown that Socrates was not, as many supposed, a fool but sublimely wise in his integrity. Accordingly answer must be made to those who claimed that "the just man will have to endure the lash, the rack, chains, the branding iron in his eyes, and finally after every extremity of suffering, be crucified, and so will learn his lesson that not to be but to seem just is what we ought to desire" (*Rep.*, 361e). It was a clear issue, and Plato saw no means of settling it in favor of justice without reference to a higher norm than any available to historical sight or empirical inspection. The measure, therefore, must be transcendent to the ordinary perspective though nôt inaccessible to the rightly oriented mind.[13]

The measure (τὸ μέτρον), here referred to, came to be called by Plato in the *Republic* the highest object in the "intelligible realm," the Idea of the Good, the supreme *archê*, or first principle in the scale of being. The conception is no doubt considerably developed over the stage at which we left it in treating the "autobiographical passage" of the *Phaedo*. Meanwhile, the *archê* seems to have become disengaged, in Plato's thinking, from the cosmic *Nous* and to have become the proper object of the latter. But at the same time the *archê* has also become the object of man's aspiring mind; and so Plato does not hesitate to make it the standard by which Socrates took his own measure and by which he took the measure of right and wrong. Thus Plato came to hold the Idea of the Good as the source of truth and probity in those who act wisely in private or public life.[14] For Plato such a norm alone afforded escape from social chaos which inevitably resulted when the whims of the multitude or the special interests of man or party were taken as measure of what is just or unjust.[15] Manifestly there could be no stability in government so long as politicians connived at feeling the unstable pulse of the citizenry. Likewise if imperious desire and self-will are the true measures of justice, as both Thrasymachus and Callicles contended, then, in the last analysis, the norm of goodness is the will of that party or individual which, by possessing the greatest power, enforces its decision about the good.[16] In that event, justice becomes synonymous with power, or, as Callicles put it, the right consists in the sway and advantage of the stronger.

The obliteration of moral distinctions either by fawning politicians, catering to the public mind, or sophisticated nihilists was plainly subversive of order and decency. Only men whose real love is focused higher up—men for whom, therefore, rulership is a doubtful privilege and a burden which they accept only reluctantly—can be trusted with the affairs of state.[17] It would be plainly absurd to deny that a main contention of the *Republic* is this: No ruler can be trusted whose vision is not "sighted" upon the eternal *paradeigma* of goodness and whose primary affection is not centered upon the city whose home is the ideal.[18]   In this we come closest to discovering the *raison d'être* for Plato's so-called ideal state.   It is not that he expected its realization; and, certainly, its envisionment is no invitation to world-flight.   It is, rather, that the vision of it and the love of it can alone assure goodwill capable of disinterested administration of justice in the affairs of men.[19]

2. THREE INADEQUATE SOURCES OF VIRTUE

The metaphysics of the Good, then, as we find it in the *Republic*, alerts us to Plato's strenuous effort to exhibit the relevance of the apparently irrelevant.   For certainly the ordinary man of the city-state conceded responsibility to little beyond his own advancement in affluence and such civic duties as convention and immemorial custom imposed.   Doubtless the gods required sacrifice at allotted times and according to ancient usage.   But that men either possessed in fact or had need of a measure of justice not their own was a thought that troubled the consciousness of few.   The earlier piety, which derived civic mores from the gods, was relaxing its hold upon the men of the fifth century.[20]   Periclean democracy had the effect of pointing to the will of the people as the source and norm of both *nomos*, law, and *themis*, custom.[21]   But unfortunately the will of the people, besides being mainly bent upon private satisfactions, was unstable and unpredictable.   It was fractured by party loyalites that resisted subordination to the commonweal.   Beneath the surface of civilized behavior ran a growing suspicion that, although a man ought to appear just and virtuous, greater self-advantage derived from covert injustice.   A few, like Polus, Calliches, and Thrasymachus, openly affirmed that the greatest reward comes from a life of calculated injustice which contrives to appear just.[22]   Plato surmised that this was only an unblushing disclosure of a prevalent, although unexpressed, opinion that it is *pleonexia*, grasping self-advantage, which every man by nature pursues as his real good.[23]   It was an idea which had gained currency in an age of intensifying individualism.   In any case, it was increasingly observed that men practiced justice reluctantly, and scarcely at all beyond certain limits of diminishing returns.[24]

Where was to be found, then, a criterion of virtue which was not susceptible of manipulation?   Where was to be discerned a norm which, by common acknowledgment and valid interpretation, might become the integrating principle of community?   Apart from such a rallying point, society was surely destined to disintegrate under the corrosive force of rampant individualism. In Plato's opinion, there was little to be hoped for by an appeal to the nobler virtues and simpler and more rigorous ways of the ancients.[25] Their virtues rooted in a world outlook which was now vastly altered. The vitality of the older piety had waned. Without that standpoint, which Plato himself believed could no longer be accepted without critical revision, the virtues of the ancients were as cut flowers. They could take no rootage in an alien soil. What is more, judging from the evidence of history, great men, who were themselves renowned for virtue in their time, usually failed to teach or bequeath it to their own children. It was so in the case of Aristeides, Themistocles, and Pericles—memorable for their civic consciousness.[26] It was clear to Plato that virtue could not be "transmitted" to others either by precept or example. Those who possessed it did so because they had a particular perspective not shared by their contemporaries. They might have entertained "true opinions" about the nature of virtue; but, because opinions fall short of knowledge, *epistêmê*, they were unable to share with others what they themselves possessed by way of *theia moira*, or divine good fortune.[27]

If neither the religious past nor the tradition of the elders was able to supply resource for moral nurture, it was next in order to inquire of the Sophists—teachers like Protagoras of Abdera and Gorgias of Leontini. They had no hesitancy in claiming to teach virtue.[28] But Plato considered the Sophists, far from being a healthy influence, a peril to the city-state. His lack of esteem did not arise solely from the fact that iconoclasts, like Thrasymachus, Polus, and Callicles, were among their entourage. As brash shatterers of tradition, these men did not shrink from declaring that accepted ideas of justice were only conventions enforced upon resourceful men by the unresourceful and mediocre majority. Such conventions had no real basis in nature (φύσις) and were obstructions to men of real spirit, manliness, and excellence.[29] Apart, however, from the "cynics" among their profession, there were other considerations, less spectacular but much more fundamental, which disqualified the Sophists as teachers of virtue. Plato is relentless in exhibiting these disqualifications as he permits Socrates to move among them, uncovering the inner workings of their minds and exposing the banality of their eloquence.

In a democracy, where oratory and the deft word paid off in votes of confidence, where skillfulness in debate and persuasiveness in speech and gesture received their reward of a hearing in the assembly or a

favorable judgment in court, there was a secure place for teachers
of rhetoric.   In a society which increasingly calculated the ends of
life in terms of largest exercise of power for the individual, the man
who offered to instruct in skills of speech had many clients.   In such
a society what can be more important than "winning friends and in-
fluencing people?"   The Sophists claimed to impart a skill in doing
just that.   Thus, on examination, the "civic virtue," in which even
so honorable a man as Protagoras claimed to instruct, turned out to be
the art of pursuing what was commonly taken to be the prizes of life
or success.   This included the manner of best managing one's private
affairs and those of one's household.   In the city it embraced the
skills by which one attained the greatest influence in both word and
action.[30]   Plato simply could not go along with the assumption that
such *paideia* made men "good citizens."   Above all, it was clear
that the Sophists had no real notion of what *aretê* was; or, at the
best, they were simply accommodating themselves to the prevailing
notions about it.   They were not interested in questioning the current
fashion of life, only in implementing it.

Plato has profounder observations to make upon the deficiencies
of rhetoric as it was taught, which will be dealt with later on in the
proper place; but in the *Gorgias* he bitterly attacks it, because rhetoric,
as taught and practiced, subordinates truth to mere persuasiveness.
His anger is hardly contained as he has Gorgias, somewhat naïvely,
admit that the aim of rhetoric is to gain conviction irrespective of
truth.   Plato does not intend to attribute outright cynical immoralism
to Gorgias or to the Sophists generally.   He is trying, however, to
indicate the inherent tendency and bearing of their pedagogy.   It
tends, in neglecting prior questions about the aims of life, to en-
trench men in their devotion to unexamined goals by making them all
the more successful in securing them.   As Socrates argued in the
Protagoras, virtue is not teachable by the Sophists, for one reason
at least, namely, that the virtue they inculcate is not virtue at all.   The
aretê taught by the Sophists is a "knack" or "skill" by which men
are equipped to wangle the greatest measure of personal prerogative
without regard to truth or merit.   The *Gorgias* shows that rhetoric
acquires a conviction, secures an advantage, concludes a bargain without attention to the prior question of the real self-advantage in pursuing such a course (522d).   In short, sophistry accommodates itself
to the prevailing *êthos*.   It leaves human life unexamined and un-
changed.

In the judgment of Plato, then, the bearing of the Sophistic teaching—mainly rhetorical in content, for the Sophists codified the art of rhetoric—was that of subordinating the quest for truth to the art of persuasion. It therefore had the effect of canonizing the *status quo*—the existing incentives of civilized man. To persuade is to render plausible, and to render plausible is frequently to render something one believes and desires apparently conformable to what one's hearers also believe and applaud. Persuasion means some measure of accommodation. The rhetorician studies the opinions of the multitude and adjusts his words to suit the prevailing temper—now rousing and now soothing with fitting utterance and tone.[31] Thus the politician, who employs the art of persuasion or practices rhetoric finds himself compelled to give the public what it wants as the price of securing his own ends. But what the multitude desires in its present perverted state is no measure of the good or the excellent. Worst of all, prevailing rhetoric inclines to adapt itself so far in the direction of existing mentality as to call the things which please the public good, and those that vex it evil.[32]

By its inherent nature, then, the rhetorical art is disposed to make the opinions of the average man the measure of right and wrong, of good and evil. The norm is not the noble Aristeides but the man of the prevailing *êthos*, the man bent upon his own largest measure of private good. It is the man who measures *eudaimonia* in terms of uninhibited desire. As Plato described him in the *Republic*, he is the sort of man who says to himself: "For a front and a show I must draw about myself a shadow-outline of virtue, but trail behind me the fox of the most sage Archilochus, shifty and bent on gain" (365c).

In Plato's opinion, the Sophists were, for the most part, conventionalists. Far from upsetting the prevailing mores of cities they visited, they lived prudentially. The political theory of a few, like Callicles and Hippias, may have been potentially subversive. On the whole, the Sophists exercised discretion and temperance and counseled their pupils to observe due restraint as the best policy. *Sophrosunê*, temperance, did not mean to them what it meant to Socrates. It was the *savoir faire* of discreet men who know how to pursue their best interests with resourcefulness, but with proper caution. It was the bearing and import of Sophistic rhetoric which troubled Plato, and he was always exposing it to acute dialectical analysis and critique. He was not misled, however. The real corruptors of young men were not alone the Sophists. A more fundamental and pervasive source of corruption was the dominant public mind which, by censure or praise, molded the young into its own likeness, a likeness unsavory to Plato, since it represented an unsifted and often debased set of values.[33]

Withal, the Sophists were elegant and urbane children of the world, altogether domesticated in and to it. The man they catered to was comfortably domiciled within the tolerably ordered *polis* of the Periclean age. Both he and they were mostly undisturbed by even an occasional look beyond the nicely articulated confines of civilized ways and works. The Sophists were the apostles of existing culture—its smoothest justifiers and advocates. Undoubtedly they were accomplished instructors of those who paid their fees, supplying techniques for reaping the most from the immediate environment. For Plato their whole perspective was flat, not to say vapid. Both the Protagorean man and the Protagorean world had insufficient dimension in depth to afford a realistic account of the evil in human life or to provide resources for combatting it.

3. Man the Measure

Among the Sophists, Protagoras is famous for his dictum: "Man is the measure of all things." Plato's strictures upon the *metron anthrôpos* doctrine are extensive and searching.[34] His criticism of the teaching is well known, but it is not so commonly observed that both Socrates and Plato had something to share with Protagoras in this doctrine. We have already seen that Socrates' distinctive program of study served to occupy him almost exclusively with man; and both Socrates and Plato were in agreement that the likeliest and most promising index to reality was man's *psuchê*. So while they agreed with Protagoras that in a certain sense man is measure, they were wholly at odds with him over two points in particular. First, they repudiated Protagorean sensationalistic "phenomenalism," according to which Protagoras denied an independent self-identical structure to reality and, whereby, man turned out to be a measure only of himself.[35] Secondly, they strenuously dissented from the views of Protagoras respecting the nature of the man who, properly, might serve as measure. We shall consider the views of Protagoras and Plato's objections in this order.

In its origin the *metron anthrôpos* doctrine was calculated to deal constructively with the knowledge-problem which, in the fifth century, as always, was intensified in proportion as alienation between the subject and object of experience came to recognition in thought.

According to Mario Untersteiner, Protagoras formulated his theory of knowledge to cope with an impasse in which, he believed, knowledge found itself because of dialectical or contradictory conception. The contradiction in thought derives from the fact that everything admits of a two-fold account (*logos*) at the same time, the sort of contradiction Plato takes note of at *Republic* 524a and *Theaetetus* 154c. Untersteiner designates this the δισσὸς λόγος doctrine and finds its antecedence for Protagoras in a presumably Pythagorean cosmology according to which all things "are compounded of opposite qualities" and therefore admit of contradictory predicates. Hence nothing is simple and unmixed; and accordingly a concept, which is necessarily unitary, cannot convey the truth about reality any more satisfactorily than its opposite.[36] Untersteiner takes note of the consequent relativity, for instance, in moral judgments—the inevitability of contradictory predicates attributable to the same action, with consequent relativism.[37] Thus was incurred a problem which seemed to Protagoras insoluble so long as knowledge remained on the level of conception; and so he had recourse to immediate experience (αἴσθησις); *viz.*, knowledge is equated with what appears directly to the perceiver at each successive moment.

Untersteiner recognizes also the place of the Heracleitean flux theory, but he allies it with the "Pythagorean" theory of matter with its notion of a continual alternation of "*logoi* in opposition."[38] Hence the distinctive feature, as well as basis, of Protagoras' epistemology is his materialistic "monism" adopted from the Pythagoreans. This "Pythagorean" matter is characterized by periodicity of oscillation in the course of which the *logoi*, resident within, are successively and alternately manifested. Man, with his experiences, is likewise a temporary expression of the substratum and of a piece with it. On the strength of this, Protagoras believed there remains no dualism between knower and known, since human perceptions (τὰ αἰσθητά) are entirely correlated with whatever is becoming, namely, *logoi* surfacing or being manifested. Untersteiner summarizes: "Man, therefore, is matter in flux, together with all the objective world: in the common possession of the attribute 'to flow' (ρεῖν) exists the possibility of a true knowledge. . . ."[39]

This reconstruction of Protagorean theory has considerable plausibility, especially in its ingenious use of the so-called Pythagorean "matter." Possibly this is the hitherto missing link in recovering the rationale of Protagorean phenomenalism; for it supplies a more solid explanation for a theory which, by Plato's account, otherwise verged upon crudity, even naïveté.[40] Untersteiner's reconstruction, moreover, gives to Protagoreanism an astonishingly modern cast by even clearer exhibition of its known affinities with contemporary process philosophy. The doctrine that man's experience and knowledge are themselves the ongoing of the reality-process, that man is therefore master and arbiter of all things, surely must be recognized as the progenitor of the view, expressed by F. C. S. Schiller, that would "utterly debar us from the cognition of Reality as it is in itself and apart from our interests," and which asserts that "if such a thing there were, it could not be known, nor rationally believed in. For our interests impose the conditions under which alone Reality can be revealed."[41]

So according to Untersteiner's account knowledge comes about when man "succeeds in *mastering* things, when, that is, in the course of the states in which his own *fluctuating* existence finds itself he finds in matter, among the various λόγοι which are immanent in it, that which corresponds to his manner of existence."[42] But in Untersteiner's treatment the correspondence is resolved into a monism: what is, is what is perceived. Hence it comes out, as Plato had asserted of Protagoras' doctrine, that nothing "exists by itself" or is possessed of an independent self-identical structure. And, in every case, the things which appear *are*, that is, have existence, to the one to whom they appear.[43] Accordingly the percipient is master, for he is the sole arbiter of the existence or non-existence of the "phenomenon"; indeed, *his perception is the event in which* φύσις *manifests itself.*

Plainly, then, the phenomenalism of Protagoras carried with it a denial of any trans-phenomenal reality on the obvious ground that such reality exceeded the possibility of knowledge. From this the agnosticism of Protagoras about the gods, and his polite dismissal of the question, are as understandable as they are also patently alien to the temper of Socrates.[44] Herein Protagoras made his contribution to the kind of "rationalistic" criticism which in the fifth century was cutting the ground from under the state religion and no doubt arousing the sort of antipathy which is visible in the case of Anytus in the *Meno* (91c).

The reach of man's knowledge did not exceed the limits of sense-perception; indeed, it is more accurate to say that appearance (φάντασμα) was the measure of all the reality there was. Protagoras had, to his satisfaction, solved the vexing problem of correlating subject and object by reducing both to motions of the same "matter" and finding their unity in the moment of experience. On Plato's interpretation, the solution came at the exorbitant price of truth-destroying pluralistic solipsism. It might indeed be a useful account of *perception*, but not of *knowledge*. Every perception was the vector of two continually changing variables, the subject and the object of experience, each changing not only in reference to itself but to the other. Here clearly was a threat to identity and to structure and therefore to the very intelligibility of the world. Not only must the present fleeting appearance be the measure of truth, but so also must its successor, and so on indefinitely, however different among themselves. Furthermore, every percipient occupied his unique, as well as varying, relation to the manifold, with no possibility of checking conflicting experiences by any single standard. On Protagoras' showing, every man was obliged to credit his own "phenomena" as the truth, however eccentric.[45] Hence there was no escape from the solitary world of "seeming true to me" into a world of commonly acknowledged reality.

The result was evident: In Plato's opinion, Protagoras had destroyed science by voiding any real difference between truth and falsity. His phenomenalism really meant pan-subjectivism. With reference to judgments of existence as well as to judgments of worth, all things are to each person as they seem to him; and there is no measure but the man himself, by appeal to which, conflicting claims may be resolved. In Plato's view no one had done more than Protagoras to justify the ascendant and reckless individualism of the age.

We come now to Plato's second point of issue with Protagoras: Plato could not consent to the *metron anthrôpos* doctrine because he could not concede that the man Protagoras described was either the true and essential man or the proper man to be a measure. There could be no agreement between Socrates' account of the ψυχή and that of Protagoras, since, for the latter, "the soul is nothing except the sensations." These include the affective states of pleasure and pain and such emotions and volitions as ensue therefrom.[46] Judging from the Promethean Myth (*Protag.*, 320 d f.), Protagoras was not accustomed even to use the word ψυχή, much less with such meaning as Socrates had come to attach to it. Meanwhile, in his developing conception of man, Plato had made sensible experience subordinate to mind. *Nous*, as the seat of knowledge and intelligent life, provided the avenue to reality; and the reality it descried had nothing in common with matter-in-flux.

The Protagorean man was disqualified from being the measure of truth and reality precisely because he was hedged in and sense-bound. In Plato's view he is the man who makes great the sensible and appetitive part of his total nature and grievously subordinates the superior to the inferior power of the soul. He is the man whose range of interests is defined by the tangible goals of mundane existence. Consequently Socrates' indictment of him remains: He perverts the scale of goods and turns the true order of value upside-down.

To make good his case against the Protagorean man and to prove that not he, but another man, is measure, constituted a sizeable portion of Plato's apologetic for the life of justice. It was also preliminary to formulating his own program of *paideia*. Plato had to delineate the nature of the essential man. He was obliged to widen the human environment, to relate man significantly to a Reality with which man had genuine, if obscured, "kinship."[47] He had to show what faculty (*dunamis*) of the soul had access to the larger environment and on what conditions. Finally, Plato was obliged to offer the best evidence he could supply to show that the essential man, who rightly might be regarded as a measure, was so for no other reason than that he was already measured. As Protagoras left the matter, man was no measure save of his own fleeting impressions and equally fugitive desires. Therefore if there was to be any sense in which man might be taken as a clue to reality, it could be located only at that point where there was actual, as well as potential, *conformity* between the soul of man and an eternal and indefectible order. This conformity ought rightly to manifest itself in human acknowledgment of and responsibility to the Good. It had also to be shown to what extent and why the multitude, unlike Socrates, are ignorant of their maximum and ultimately significant environment.

By his conception of a primordial conformity between the mind of man and an order of Being, unavailable to sensuous preoccupation but available to *nous*, Plato, perhaps Socrates, bequeathed to Western thought a new and enormously influential conception of man. It is precisely at this juncture, moreover, that we may locate the distinguishing difference between Protagorean and Platonic "humanism." Socrates is not the only man of whom Plato may declare, as in the *Symposium* (215b), that he is like a "Silenus-figure" with grotesque exterior but inwardly is possessed of a divine likeness. The same may be said of man generically if, at the same time, it is recognized that there are great variations among men in liveliness of the image. According to the symbolic language of the *Phaedrus* myth (249b, e), the soul which has never seen the truth can never pass into human form. By this Plato doubtless testifies that there is no human soul which is not possessed of intimations of abiding reality, however dimmed, and affinity (τὸ ξυγγενές) for the truth.[48] From birth, however, the vividness of the soul's apprehensions and its fitness for knowledge vary among individuals.[49] Too hastily perhaps, but from sobering experience, Plato declares in the *Republic* that the multitude have little or no aptitude for philosophy (490d). And reluctantly he concedes that the philosophic nature, with aptitude for learning and a lively aspiration for realities which abide beyond the "multiplicities of multifarious things," is exceedingly rare.[50] It is a nature, seemingly, which men have or do not have from birth (490a). Despite all this, there is, in the soul of every man, an *"organon* of knowledge" by the possession of which a man also receives the dignity of being human. Within *nous,* there remain vestigial patterns, *paradeigmata,* after-images of the soul's primordial communion with divine realities. As surviving patterns adumbrating reality, they are *a priori* or antecedent to sensible experience and are, indeed, its "formal" presupposition. As Plato suggests in the *Republic* (589d), they are a "divine" component in man's nature. By possession of them, men are *theoeidês* and *theoeikelon,* deiform and in the likeness of God (501b).

Nevertheless, inherent likeness to the "divine" becomes fractured, obscured, and almost lost. As men become immersed in the life of sense, the intimations of a larger perspective and a nobler calling begin to fade. With the insistent clamor of desire, men grow forgetful of larger loyalties and more chaste incentives. The true good, the proper end of life, is *dislocated.* The native and essential orientation of the soul toward that with which it is "akin" is diverted to alien concerns, properly subordinate and of secondary value.

Plato is prepared to regard man as measure in virtue of his essential kinship, his potential conformity with trans-empirical reality. Judging by the *Republic* especially, we may safely identify this reality with the Idea of the Good. The locus of potential and actual conformity is, of course, to be found in intelligence. To say that deiformity of man centers in the potential and actual conformity of *nous* with *reality* is to say that *nous* is inveterately axiological in its structure, and that its pristine inclination is toward the trans-empirical Good.[51] Although Plato speaks of the "Idea" (ἰδέα) of the Good, the Good is nothing so pale, logical, or psychological, as is connoted by our word idea. It has the character of a pattern (παράδειγμα) or form (εἶδος) (*Rep.* 484c-d). It is objective to the knower and it is ingredient in the Cosmos as its constitution or immutable order. As such, it is the law of the mind's life. Conformation to the law is *aretê*; and virtue and well-being are inseparable. Conformity affords at the same time an inner concord which is described as the soul's agreement with itself.[52] According to the measure of man's conformity to the Good, he becomes himself increasingly a clue to reality. In his response to a divine summons and in the rectitude of his life, there comes to actualization an *analogia entis*, an analogy of being, between the knower and the reality to be known. Plato's ontology is basically theomorphic. Man may be taken as measure of reality only because he is, in fact, measured by reality and may be fashioned after its likeness.

4. Upside-down Existence

Throughout the centuries there has rested upon Plato a heavy burden of proof. Most men presume they are wide awake to the realities of their world. For them, seeing is believing. But Socrates' teaching concerning the *psuchê* had loosed Plato forever from the tyranny of the obvious. For him there is an "organ of knowledge the value of which outweighs ten thousand eyes," because only by it is true Being discerned. He knew that those who shared his viewpoint would agree, but he was fully aware, as he stated in the *Republic* (527e), that those who had no first-hand acquaintance with the powers of *nous* would necessarily regard his sketch of reality as incredible. Plato's task, therefore, was that of bringing men to the point of acknowledging that they were, in fact, asleep to the real nature of their world.

Plato frequently contrasts the waking with the sleeping state— the dreaming with the truly waking life.[53] It is a figure cognate with the better-known myth of the Cave of the *Republic*. In the cavern, men are represented as living their whole lives in chains with their backs to the light. Their glance is always toward the innermost wall and the half-darkness. Oblivious of the outer world, they assume that the shadows cast by passing objects at the cavern's mouth are the only realities. They are fully habituated to the darkness. Most of the prisoners become adept at identifying the shadows which come and go. They honor, as wisest of their number, those who are "quickest to make out the shadows as they pass and best able to remember their customary precedences, sequences, and co-existences" (516c).

Plato's satire upon phenomenalism is here, as elsewhere, mingled with humane concern. He knows that it is next to impossible to convince men by demonstrative argument either that they are dreaming with respect to reality or that they are imprisoned in a cave of ignorance. The illusion is too complete. The system of evident impressions is, taken by itself, adequately coherent. Moreover, the perspective is shared by most; is, indeed, so uniformly entertained as to exclude misgivings—those prickings of doubt which otherwise might precipitate a revision of judgment.[54] In addition Plato was aware of a "habituation" of the mind which enforces ignorance and fixes it as an inverted outlook of the whole soul. Thus it was plain to Plato that *paideia* involved, not so much cogent argument and formal proof, as it did the art of waking men from sleep or turning them around and leading them out into the light of a brighter day. Only immediate acquaintance with reality, as it discloses itself to the rightly oriented mind, is able to convince men of its self-evidencing truth. Apparently, then, the valid political art is not one of conveying truth to man in the form of propositions but rather one of conducting men, by an exacting scrutiny of opinions, into the presence of reality. There they may inspect the Real for themselves and grasp the amplitude of its dimensions. Yet Plato noted well the resistance of the multitude to the awakening art. And at the end of his career, in the *Laws*, he was constrained to say: "Truth is a noble thing . . . and an enduring; yet to persuade men of it seems no easy matter" (663c).

The tragedy of human existence and, therewith, the problem of *philosophia* as a method of education, are signalized in men's contentment with living an "unreal and alien life."[55] This is the melancholy motif which recurs in the writings of Plato. Indeed it is Plato's own version of the *nemesis* theme of traditional Hellenic *muthos*. As Callicles was made to state the matter, the life which men customarily follow is one "turned upside-down."[56] They do not know that they live an inverted existence.

John Wild has rightly called attention to this inversion of life (ἀνατροπή) as the fundamental Platonic diagnosis of the condition of man. Wild understands *anatropism* to be "the miscarriage of human action involving misapprehension of the hierarchical structure of means and ends." It involves, he says, "both theoretical misapprehension and malpractice as they are combined in the actual inversion of the moral order."[57] We shall see that the inversion amounts to a misidentification of true realities and their correlative true goods.

Inversion of reality, as the character both of man's individual and of his social life, is Plato's picture of the "natural man." The conception was possible only on the basis of Socrates' account of the human ψυχή, although Plato's fully developed "tripartite" psychology was able to portray the inversion more graphically. But Socrates had led the way in his conviction that the dignity of man resided, not in his *dunamis* as a sensible being, but in the *dunamis*, or power, of *nous* through which he was related to superior reality and nobler goods. Henceforth the pathway to the good life for individual and society consisted in lifting the veil of man's ignorance about himself to the end of fuller knowledge of his ultimate environment.

But impediments to knowledge were formidable. Ignorance was stubborn and resilient. The anatropic condition was somehow self-confirmatory. Hence Plato's awakening art, dialectic, encountered heavy going. The ignorance (ἀμαθία) of men was not simply want of knowledge; it was the "double" form of ignorance. In the *Apology* (29b), Socrates called it reprehensible in that men presume to know what, in fact, they do not know. Because, however, they do not desire to be deceived about the nature of reality,[58] but are nevertheless in error, double ignorance is called "the involuntary lie in the soul."[59] Because it is a kind of "self-deception," there is nothing more difficult to extirpate, for the self has become identified with, and committed to, its own error.[60] Consequently ignorance takes on a moral dimension because it involves pride. Thus Plato comes to refer to it as a disease, corruption, or vice of the soul; and he subjects it to moral censure, calling it *aphrosunê*, or folly.[61]

In summary, the topsy-turvy state of human existence was manifest in several areas of experience. First, men confounded the realm of Becoming and the objects of *aisthêsis* with the real world of essential Being. Men confused the objects of opinion, *doxa*, which do not admit of stable knowledge, with what is abidingly real.[62] Secondly, in direct consequence, men as "lovers of opinion" set their store upon sensuous goods. They placed higher valuation upon things which support physical life than upon "goods of the soul." And as an unfortunate consequence those who are "lovers of opinion" and sense-bound must necessarily defer to the interests of bodily existence whenever benevolent impulse or non-egoistic loyalties demand such devotion as exceeds the limits of expediency. Thus, in the third place, the inversion of life compels men to honor virtue with their lips while they serve their own desires with might and main. Plato perceived in such a condition the worst form of human bondage, the exact antithesis of real freedom.[63]

Finally, Plato illustrated the inversion of human life by means of his "tripartite" conception of the *psuchê* and its powers. The sensuous impulses which, in the *Phaedo*, were associated with the body, are, in the *Republic*, embraced within the threefold economy of the soul's life.[64] It is well known that, structurally considered, there are three factors in the soul, but functionally speaking, the organization is twofold. First, there is *logistikon*, the rational power. Secondly, there is *thumos*, the spirited part, which expresses a kind of righteous indignation when affronted by the mean and base and which allies itself with the aspirations of reason. The third component of the soul is the appetitive faculty (τὸ ἐπιθυμητικόν). It is the irrational power, and Plato refers to it as the preponderating part of the soul.[65] It is the "multitude in the soul," teeming with desire. The life of man is, therefore, a continual struggle, a contest for supremacy between the rational and the irrational principles. Among the majority, the appetitive power dominates, so that the best is ruled by the worst, the naturally superior by the naturally inferior.[66] When, therefore, Callicles describes *aretê* as uninhibited satisfaction of private desire, he is, in Plato's view, advocating the complete overthrow of the proper order of human life. He is declaring that the man of excellence is the man in whom the "many-headed beast" of passion is unchained and allowed to roam at will. But such a man is, of all men, most miserable; for the true ruling principle of his soul is in abject bondage.

Wild is on solid ground in saying that this "inverted subordination of the higher faculty to the lower is what is meant by being in the cave."[67] Plato's Cave is plainly a symbol of the inverted life of man: its human prisoners cheerfully exchange shadows for reality, oblivious of their own bondage, ignorant of themselves. This, in sum, is the plight of man; and this is the dire condition for which Plato seeks to devise a *therapeia*, a scheme of education adequate to cope with it. Since, according to the *Republic*, the structure of the city-state may be regarded as the soul of man "writ large," the education which Plato prepares for the soul is, at the same time, a contribution to true statesmanship. This was the contribution he hoped to make in forsaking a career of practical politics for philosophy.

NOTES

1. *Epist.* VII, 325b-326b.
2. *Gorg.* 484c-486d. Here we have Callicles' dispraise of philosophy. Philosophy is a charming thing for the young, but it ill fits a man for the hurly-burly of public life and competitive effort. *Cf. Rep.* 499e.
3. *Rep.* 496d-e. *Cf. Rep.* 516e-517a; *Gorg.* 522b-e.
4. *Apol.* 31e.
5. *Rep.* 493a-d. *Cf. Gorg.* 456b-457b, 462c-d, 463d-465c, 502e, 513a-d; *Phaedr.* 267d.
6. *Gorg.* 504e, 513e, 515c. *Cf. Apol.*, 30a, 36c; *Rep.* 345d, 591a; *Polit.* 297b. The term ἡ φυλακική, "guardianship," which Plato employs to indicate the function of the statesman in the *Republic*, intentionally replaces πολιτευτής, "politician." The guardian seeks the good of his charges; the politician is a partisan of his own or party interests.
7. *Rep.* 420b, 519e.
8. *Gorg.* 478e, 507c, 508b; *Rep.* 354a, 580b; *Laws* 664b-c.
9. See *Gorg.* 515d-519d for Plato's unsparing criticism of such eminent leaders as Cimon, Themistocles, Miltiades and Pericles. The heart of it is that these men were successful so long as they gave the people what they wanted; but, not having elevated their wants, they were, in time, repudiated for disappointing them. A good statesman, therefore, will make men better by elevating their desires.
10. *Rep.* 472d-e, 499c, 502c, 540d, 592a
11. *Rep.* 499b, 501e; *Epist.* VII, 326a-b; *Laws* 713e, 875c.
12. *Rep.* 359d-360d. See also *Rep.* 612c.
13. *Cf. Rep.* 518c-519b.
14. *Rep.* 517c. The terminology for the supreme *metron* is Plato's, not that of Socrates. For Socrates, τὸ μέτρον is not finally distinguishable from the mind and will of "the good and wise god" to which we have frequent, if oblique, reference in the *Apology* and *Phaedo*. *Cf. Rep.* 504c, 500c-d.
15. *Gorg.* 486c, 503c.
16. *Cf. Rep.* 338c-d and *Gorg.* 483d.
17. *Rep.* 521a-b. *Cf.* 345e, 520c; *Gorg.* 508a-b.
18. *Rep.* 592a-b. *Cf. Rep.* 484b-d, 485b, 500c-d, 517b, 540a.
19. *Rep.* 520c-521b; *Cf. Laws* 713c. Men are incapable of exercising sovereign rule over affairs without becoming filled with pride, *hubris*, and injustice. Long ago Plato was aware that "power corrupts, and absolute power corrupts absolutely." See *Rep.* 565d-e; *Laws* 691c-692b.
20. F. Solmsen (*Plato's Theology* [1942], Chs. I-III), may be consulted on the integral relation of religion and mores in the earlier city-state. The disintegration of the older religion entailed, in the fifth century, the recession of the prevailing moral sanctions. The emancipated individual became judge of his own good, and individualism, coupled with declining belief in divine providence, led to a critical attitude toward state and religion (17-18, 23-28). "Whether attacked and discussed or not, the gods were losing ground. Thinking in Athens passed through a general process of secularization. . . ." (31).
21. *Gorg.* 512e-513c. Socrates' satirical advice to Callicles to accommodate his words to the temper of *dêmos* if he desires success in politics is stated.
22. *Rep.* 344a-c, 360d, 554c; *Gorg.* 465b, 471a-d, 483c.
23. *Rep.* 359c. The significance of *pleonexia* may, in some measure, be estimated

by the number of times Plato refers to it in the dialogues. See *Rep.* 349c, 344a, 344d, 548e, 590a; *Gorg.* 483e, 491a, 508a; *Gr. Hipp.* 283b; *Symp.* 182d; *Critias* 121b; *Laws* 677b, 727a-b, 731d, 875b, 887a. The importance which Plato attaches to the divisive effect of self-will and egoism upon society has been neglected. See *Rep.* 586c and *Laws* 731e.

24. *Rep.* 358c, 347c; *Gorg.* 511b.

25. *Laws* 853c. The mythical past, a lost golden age, in which a less corrupted humanity was naturally pliant to divine law is not Plato's literal belief. It does, however, signify his recognition that an older era of hardier moral rectitude has passed away.

26. *Meno* 93b-94d. *Cf. Protag.* 319e f.

27. *Meno* 99b-100b. *Theia moira* is a "divine apportionment." The phrase is of more than passing significance as will appear later. At a minimum, it refers to *aidôs*, or reverence for goodness.

28. *Protag.* 319a f; *Meno* 71c.

29. *Gorg.* 482e, 483a-c, 492a-c; *Rep.* 359b. Thrasymachus and Callicles were legal positivists. *Nomos*, law, had no basis except the prevailing will of the "sovereign," in this case, the majority. The rule of the majority is "against nature" and constitutes an unnatural covenant of the many against the excellent few (492c).

30. *Protag.* 319a; *Gorg.* 520e; *Meno* 91a.

31. *Phaedr.* 260c, 267d.

32. *Rep.* 493c.

33. *Rep.* 492a-b.

34. The most important discussions are to be found in *Cratyl.* 386a f. and *Theaet.* 152a f. In the *Cratylus* the Protagorean doctrine, in conjunction with the theory of universal flux, readily solves the question of the "adequacy" of language to reality by denying antecedent reality with which words may correspond. In that case, the "correctness of names" could not properly be a problem. But this cheap solution to the question of "the natural correctness of the name" (391a) carries the liability, in the Protagorean doctrine, of pluralistic solipsism; *viz*, every man's experience is his only measure of truth with the result that *truth* and *falsity* become indistinguishable (386c).

35. For suitability of the term "phenomenalism," see Mario Untersteiner, *The Sophists*, trans. K. Freeman (Oxford, 1954), 48. The clear-headed Schiller fully recognized the real pedigree of pragmatism. Of the *metron anthrôpos* doctrine he said: "Fairly interpreted, this is the truest and most important thing that any thinker has ever propounded." F. C. S. Schiller, *Humanism: Philosophical Essays* (London, 1912), xxi.

36. M. Untersteiner, *op. cit.*, 24-25, 44-45.

37. *Ibid.*, 31-32. *Cf. Protag.* 333e-334c. In this passage Plato does indeed seem to allude to the δισσὸς λόγος problem in having Protagoras affirm that things may be "good" either when profitable (ὠφέλιμος) to man or when not profitable (μὴ ὠφέλιμος); thus, τὸ ἀγαθόν admits of contradictory predicates. Hence, Protagoras asserts "the good" is "an elusive and diverse thing."

38. M. Untersteiner, *op. cit.*, 45-46. *Cf. Theaet.* 152e f.

39. *Op. cit.*, 46.

40. The presence of the so-called Pythagorean matter theory, of which Plato himself was to make enlarging use, plausibly accounts for Plato's acceptance of the theory of perception (*Theaet.*, 156a-157b) recounted by Socrates. There are more reasons than F. M. Cornford submits for his acceptable judgment that Socrates' formulation in this passage is "a satisfactory account of that perception which Theaetetus has identified with knowledge" (*Plato's Theory of Knowledge* [New York, 1935] 51). Plato was obliged to formulate a theory of "knowledge" of Becoming once he had set himself the task of incorporating Becoming within the

totality of Being. The passage at *Theaet.* 156a-157b is really the constructive result of the dialogue. It signifies the kind of "knowledge" suitable to Becoming. The dialogue then proceeds to make plain that this *kind* cannot possibly represent all that is required of knowledge. If will serve tolerably for such "knowledge" (!) as we have by sense-perception.

41. F. C. S. Schiller, *op. cit.*, 9, 10.

42. M. Untersteiner, *op. cit.*, 46.

43. *Theaet.* 153e, 160b-c. Historically considered, methodological anthropocentrism issues in, or else justifies, some form of monism. In the case of Protagoras, it is materialistic. Dewey's pragmatism was a monism of process as Experience. With Berkeley, it was mentalism. There is methodological anthropocentrism in Plato, but it is critical and restricted because of realism respecting antecedent reality. In knowledge, unlike the above monisms for which the subject determines the object, for Plato the subject is *conformed* with the object.

44. K. Freeman, *Ancilla*, 126, Frg. 4. "About the gods, I am not able to know whether they exist or do not exist, nor what they are like in form; for the factors preventing knowledge are many: the obscurity of the subject, and the shortness of human life." We may compare this with Plato's statement (*Theaet.* 162d) ". . . Protagoras, or someone speaking for him, will say, 'Excellent boys and old men, there you sit together declaiming to the people, and you bring in the gods, the question of whose existence or non-existence I exclude from oral and written discussion' . . ." For commentary, see M. Untersteiner, *op. cit.*, 26-28.

45. *Theaet.* 161c-e; *Cratyl.* 386c.

46. *Cf.* M. Untersteiner, *op. cit.*, 46.

47. The idea of the "kinship," ἡ συγγένεια, of *psuchê* with intelligible Being, τὸ νοητὸν ὄν, is a fundamental feature of Plato's epistemology. The concept is omnipresent in the dialogues, *viz.*, *Phaedo* 79d, 80b, 81a; *Phaedr.* 246d, 247d; *Rep.* 490a-b, 487a, 494d, 611e; *Meno* 81d; *Polit.* 309c; *Phileb.* 31a, 65d; *Soph.* 265d; *Tim.* 47c, 90a; *Laws* 716d, 892a, 899d; *Critias* 120b; *Epist.* VII, 342d, 344a. Intelligible reality is accessible to knowledge because of conformity between *nous* and its appropriate objects. The notion of "affinity" is related to the Empedoclean principle Plato uniformly adopts: "like is known only by like." Diels, *Vorsokratiker* (Berlin, 1934), Frg. 22. Aristotle recognized this as fundamental to Plato's epistemology (*De An.* 404 b 17-18). Likewise, Proclus, *in Tim.* 132d 24-25, ed. Diehl, understood it to be integral to Plato's thought. Sextus Empiricus, *Adv. Log.* I, 119, attributes to Plato the view that the faculties are "kindred" to their objects. We do not, however, have to depend upon the ancient commentators; there is evidence enough in the dialogues themselves.

48. *Rep.* 494d; *Cf. Phaedr.* 248b.

49. *Phaedr.* 248d; *Rep.* 487d.

50. *Rep.* 491b, 492a, 495b, 503b.

51. *Rep.* 505e. See also *Rep.* 611e, 534c, 517c.

52. *Rep.* 554d-e. *Cf. Alcib.* I, 126c-d.

53. This contrast is a recurrent theme in the dialogues. It symbolizes the plight of man and specifies the task of *paideia*. See *Rep.* 476c, 520c, 533c, 534c; *Phaedr.* 277d; *Tim.* 52b-c.

54. The salutary function of doubt, ἀπορία, the perplexity which ensues upon the "cracking-up" of presumption, is a necessary stage in the process of education. See *Meno* 80a; *Euthy.* 11b; *Alcib.* I, 116e.

55. *Rep.* 495c.

56. *Gorg.* 481c. *Cf. Rep.* 519b.

57. John Wild, *Plato's Theory of Man* (Cambridge, Mass.: 1949), 36. See pp. 34-44.

58. *Rep.* 413a, 589c; *Gorg.* 488a; *Phaedo* 66b.

59. *Rep.* 535e, 382a-c; *Protag.* 358d; *Laws* 730c.

60. *Cratyl.* 428d. *Cf. Rep.* 382b; *Soph.* 228c; *Laws* 689a. Ἀμαθία usually denotes this double form of ignorance in the dialogues.

61. *Cf. Gorg.* 477b; *Tim.* 88b; *Laws* 888b f. ·

62. For classical statements, see *Rep.* 475e-480a, 508c-511e, 523b-534e, 584d-585d.

63. *Gorg.* 469e f. Real power, i.e., freedom, is capacity to follow the "real wish" of the soul. License is bondage to appetite. Hence, for Plato, freedom is life empowered by the superior affection of the soul.

64. The first explicit presentation of the "tripartite" theory is, of course, found in *Republic*, Bk. IV, xiv-xv.

65. *Rep.* 588d, 580e.

66. *Rep.* 589d-e. See also *Rep.*, 574d, 431a; *Laws* 626d-e, 628e; *Phaedo* 80a.

67. J. Wild, *op. cit.*, 191.

CHAPTER III

Virtue and Knowledge

But it is the methodological study of all these stages, passing in turn from one to another, up and down, which with difficulty implants knowledge, when the man himself, like his object, is of a fine nature; but if his nature is bad—and, in fact, the condition of most men's soul in respect of learning and of what are termed "morals" is either naturally bad or else corrupted—then not even Lynceus himself could make such folk see.—*Epistle* VII, 343e

1. THE AUGUSTINIAN DEDUCTION

IN the history of European thought, there is a philosophic tradition which preserves authentic elements of Plato's philosophy. And one thinker of the Latin West who bulks large in the legitimate succession is Augustine of Hippo. Although Augustine was a Christian, he was also a debtor to the Greeks, and he preferred Plato above all "the philosophers of the Gentiles."[1] Augustine was, however, fully cognizant of the differences between Hellenic philosophy and the Christian faith; and more clearly than any Christian predecessor, he defined the area of discontinuity. With reference to Platonism in particular, he located the differentiating factor at the point of the Incarnation of the eternal Word.[2]

But our concern with Augustine's thought in this context must purposely neglect his discriminating and influential treatment of the faith and reason problem.[3] Rather our interest here is focused upon those references to Socrates which Augustine makes in *The City of God*. Socrates is to be distinguished from his predecessors, according to Augustine, by virtue of the fact that he was the first among Greek thinkers to direct the aims of philosophy toward the improvement and regulation of the moral life, whereas his predecessors had occupied themselves with the investigation of physical processes.[4] Speculating upon possible explanations for this transformation of interest, Augustine suggests that Socrates may have found the investigation of physical questions difficult and their solution obscure and uncertain.

This is a possible explanation, Augustine surmises, but he favors another hypothesis. And he attributes to Socrates the fixed conviction that unpurified minds are disqualified for the investigation of divine reality. Socrates, says Augustine, "was unwilling that minds, defiled by earthly desires, should essay to raise themselves upward to the divine."[5] The worthlessness of investigation of *phusis*, by unpurified minds, inherently incapable of apprehending true Being, is amplified by Augustine:

For he [Socrates] saw that the causes of things were sought for by them, —which causes he believed to be reducible to nothing else than the will of the one true and supreme-God,—and, on this account, he thought they could only be comprehended by a purified mind; and, therefore, that all diligence ought to be given to the purification of the life by good morals, in order that the mind, delivered from the depressing weight of lusts, might raise itself upward by its native vigor to eternal things, and might, with purified understanding, contemplate that nature which is incorporeal and unchanging.[6]

There is nothing novel in Augustine's claim that Socrates distinguished himself from previous thinkers by turning from physical to ethical questions. Classical commentary is fairly unanimous regarding this transference of philosophic interest and effort. If Augustine did not have the word of Plato himself in the *Phaedo*—and there is reason to think he may have had it—then there was the weighty authority of Aristotle on the point. That authority had long since become the common property of interpretation.[7] The distinctive contribution of Augustine to Platonic exegesis is to be found in his *explanation* of the Socratic transference of interest from physical to anthropological and ethical investigation. In this Augustine has no antecedents, and, although he exhibits in this explanation his customary perspicacity, his contribution toward understanding Plato's theory of knowledge has received virtually no attention in modern times.

Augustine's deduction is momentous in its import for our comprehension of *philosophia* as Plato conceives it. It strongly affects our conception of Plato's views concerning the way to knowledge and the nature of education. In Augustine's interpretation of Socrates, the determining factor, conducing either to ignorance or to knowledge of reality, is the moral condition of the whole man. Character, or ἦθος, is decisive either for ignorance or for knowledge of truth about Being. If Augustine is right, virtue is quite as much the condition of knowledge as it is also true, and better known, that knowledge is the condition of virtue. *Philosophia,* as the pursuit of wisdom, is no disinterested intellectual exercise but presupposes a transformation of character. Likewise, *paideia* must be understood as a method by which cognition is redirected through a transformation of affection. In so far as Plato, especially in the *Republic,* identified *phusis* preeminently with the Idea of the Good, there could be no apprehension of *phusis* apart from *katharsis* and amendment of life. All this is implied in Augustine's explanation of Socrates' abandonment of physical questions for anthropological ones. Augustine believed he discerned in this revolution the Socratic conviction that, since "like can only be known by like,"[8] an "ethically" irresponsible mind can have no access to an order of reality which is inherently axiological. To put it in Augustine's own words, the Good can only be known by a "purified mind."

Our task is to acertain whether Augustine's reconstruction of the Socratic viewpoint can stand up in light of the evidence of the dialogues. We may in passing take note of the fact that by current standards Augustine is uncritical in his somewhat easy identification of ultimate *phusis* with "the will of the one true and supreme God." Socrates is not in fact quite so readily placed among monotheists. To be sure, we have observed a movement in Socratic thought toward universalization of deity. For if we may credit the "autobiographical passage" of the *Phaedo* it would appear that Socrates was prepared, if he could see the way, to refer the orderly Cosmos to the energy of a supreme *Nous,* itself axiologically determined.[9]

It is possible, furthermore, to raise another preliminary question, one of "higher criticism." Is Augustine correct in attributing to Socrates, rather than to Plato himself, the content of his important surmise? Is it Socrates or Plato who taught that "purification of the life by good morals" is prerequisite for apprehension of true Being? In reply, it is plain that the critical problem was of small consequence for Augustine. The "Socratic problem" in its modern form was quite unrecognized. Clearly, Augustine's deduction was based upon the general bearing of the literature, either portions of Plato's own writing or such commentary as Augustine may have found in Cicero, Marcus Varro, and possibly in Chalcidius.[10] In like manner we are not to be occupied with the historical problem. Regarding the principle that virtue is a condition of knowledge, our interest centers upon the question whether it is grounded in Plato's writings and, if it is, what difference it makes to his theory of education and his conception of philosophy.[11] It is, however, of first importance that Augustine's deduction implies a certain precedence of the axiological over the ontological problem. The ontological problem concerning the nature of ultimate reality is to be settled by reference to the total spiritual disposition of the knowing subject, a disposition that somehow makes either for knowledge or for ignorance respecting ultimate reality.

2. . *Katharsis:* KNOWLEDGE THROUGH AMENDMENT OF LIFE

In the opening pages of the *Republic* (328d), Plato suggests that there is, as in the case of the venerable Cephalus, an intimate connection between the wisdom of old age and the decline of distracting appetites and passions. The tumultuous emotions of youth decline. No longer do they interfere with the more sober joys of good discourse and amiable reflection. For reasons similar to these, we may presume, Socrates in the *Phaedo* recommends the life of philosophy as the best which human existence affords. It involves a kind of dying to the body and its desires in order that the mind may increasingly dwell alone with itself. At length, when the body is overtaken by death, the lover of wisdom contemplates the separation of the body from the soul and is content.

Death, for the philosopher, is no catastrophe nor its approach a cause for alarm. Long and diligently he has sought to relieve the soul of impediments incident to its embodiment. Bodily cravings have always proven a hindrance to the achievement of wisdom. The involvements of daily life obscure the apprehension of those realities which Plato calls justice-in-itself, beauty-in-itself, and the Good-in-itself.[12] The bodily nature chokes the soul with loves, desires, and fears, oppressing the mind by their continual insistencies and perturbations. Furthermore, the senses are deceptive in so far as men's omnivorous preoccupation with things tends to fix attention exclusively upon the sensible world. To be sure, it is also true that the senses may assist the process of learning, in that under certain conditions they may stimulate "recollection" of abiding realities.[13] By way of association, the senses actually provoke recall of the ideal objects or the real essence (αὐτὴ ἡ οὐσία) of which sensible particulars themselves are but "deficient" or imperfect and fleeting instances.[14] But despite this instrumental value, there is something inherent in sensibility which persistently obstructs the mind's recollection of the reality behind appearances.

Consequently the philosopher will, day by day, bend all his effort to the end of "collecting and concentrating" the soul within itself in order to stabilize its apprehension of essence. Rather than put his confidence in the senses, he will place his trust in "the eye of the soul."[15] Philosophy, therefore, involves a kind of purification. It is a deliverance of the soul from the deceit of sense and from the attendant passions of the body. The philosopher acknowledges that prior to the final release of the soul, some communion, some intercourse, between *nous* and the bodily nature is unavoidable. He concedes that some bodily functions and some sensuous activities and interests are essential to, and inseparable from, mortal existence.[16] Therefore according to Socrates *katharsis* ought to begin now, during the soul's earthly pilgrimage, but it can only approximate completion. Since the apprehension of true Being necessarily waits upon the completion of the purifying process, a full and unclouded vision of reality is unattainable in this life. Such consummation is to be anticipated elsewhere.[17] It is to this happy issue that Socrates looks forward, and in that eventuality he finds sufficient reason for repose in the prospect of death.

Because the wisest and best of men in this mortal life will scarcely, if at all, attain pure and undiluted knowledge of "most real Being," which abides above the perpetual flux of time and place, the philosopher must content himself with the status which his name implies, a lover of wisdom. He will cherish and cultivate every intimation of the truth which he is privileged to receive; but his peculiar excellence or virtue will be found, not in the possession of wisdom, but in the earnest and undeterred pursuit of it.[18]

In spite of the limitations that mortal life imposes upon the fulfillment of knowledge, the philosopher will welcome every opportunity for purging the mind of erroneous opinion. He will not resist deliverance but seek it (82d). In the *Phaedo* (75d-e), as also in the *Meno*, it is taught that learning comes through "recollection" with the assistance of dialectic. But *katharsis* entails more than this. It involves the perfecting of the soul in moral virtue. So, to the utmost of his power, the philosopher will strive to "assimilate" himself to the likeness of abiding reality. Holding his course, he awaits death's beneficent release. Then his immortal nature passes to the realm of "the good and wise god"—to that sphere or order of Being with which, in Socrates' account, the soul has affinity (84b).

Such is Plato's portrait of the philosopher in the *Phaedo* and, we may believe, of Socrates as Plato sees him. Exalted though the picture is, Plato is realistic, for he does not let us forget that the sensate man looks upon the philosopher with an admiration mingled with incredulous contempt. The sense-bound man regards him, while yet living, almost as good as dead (65a); for the philosopher takes slight pleasure in appetitive gratifications. He endures them as "necessary," but he has no craving and is little tempted by their fleeting joys; he is incredibly content and even annoyingly composed.

In order to distinguish the philosopher from *hoi polloi*, the Platonic Socrates calls him an "initiate." By analogy he compares him with those who have been inducted into the Eleusinian Mysteries, or the rites of Orphism.[19] Like the followers of the Mysteries, the philosopher also undergoes cleansing. In his case, however, *katharsis* involves clarification of mind. This is identical with the process of learning, called *anamnêsis* in the *Phaedo* (76a). By means of recollection, true reality begins to be discerned and gradually to unfold itself to the learner's vision.

Do virtue and amendment of morals, as Augustine claims, condition advancing knowledge of reality? Attention to the teaching of the *Phaedo* clearly enforces the view that *katharsis* is more than learning, more than the clarification of the mind to itself. Although *katharsis* requires the articulation of the presentiments of truth which lie as an unexplored deposit in the human soul, it also involves increase in virtue. Additionally, it is purging of unrighteousness from the soul. But *katharsis* is also something positive, namely, replacement of vice by self-restraint, justice, courage, and wisdom.[20] Wisdom replaces "folly" in the soul and is itself the summit of virtue. Thus *katharsis* retains the moral connotation it possessed in the mystery religions; by it the soul is nurtured in righteousness. But this, also, is of special interest, for the cultivation of virtue has a particular and important meaning. It is the conformation or "assimilation" (ἀφομοίωσις) of the *psuchê* to the likeness of that reality which is also the proper object of its thought.[21] It is this reformation of the whole soul and its conformation to divine reality which, both in the *Phaedo* (80e ff.) and elsewhere, is regarded by Plato as the goal of human existence. Whatever may be the penultimate end of human life, the *ne plus ultra* of man's destiny is assimilation to the nature and likeness of divine Being.

In agreement with this positive view of *katharsis*, as assimilation to goodness, we find Plato, in the *Republic*, affirming that virtue consists in being likened to "God" so far as that is possible with man (501b). In a passage of peculiarly Socratic temper from the *Theaetetus* (176b), this view finds classical statement and reiteration. In the *Timaeus* (90c-d), it is said that the proper tendance (θεραπεία) of the immortal part of the soul (*i.e., nous*), is one of conforming its nature, so far as possible, "like unto the object of its thought." There it is added that the attainment of this consummation is achievement of the goal of life. The dialogues clearly indicate that *katharsis* which, on its negative side, is a cleansing and emptying, is, on its positive side, a repletion in goodness or virtue. A prime motif of the *Phaedo* itself is discernible in this: The lover of wisdom is one who exchanges "intercourse and communion" with the body for communion, *koinônia*, with absolute essence or immutable reality.[22] When this exchange is accomplished and stabilized, the ensuing habit or state of the soul is called wisdom (79d).

The implication is plain: for the *Phaedo*, amendment of life and advancement in knowledge of essential reality accompany each other. Plato refuses to sanction the notion that the *visio Dei* is possible without an axiological renovation of the mind. From the *Phaedo's* account of *katharsis*, it is manifest that attainment of knowledge presupposes refashioning of the soul into such a likeness as corresponds with the qualitative excellence of its object (79d ff.). On this point the Platonic Socrates is explicit.

Referring to the philosopher's continuing effort to be freed of sensuous distractions incident to physical existence, purification is said to be necessary, because "it cannot be that the impure attain the pure" (67d). But in the *Phaedo* philosophic discipline will have its ultimate fulfillment only beyond the bounds of death when, purification being perfected, assimilation to the Divine will be realized. So it is added in the same passage: "And in this way, freeing ourselves from the foolishness of the body and being pure, we shall, I think, be with the pure and shall know of ourselves all that is pure,—and that is, perhaps, the truth" (67a).

On the basis of his highly favored epistemological principle that "like is known by like,"[23] Plato is prepared to maintain that "most real Being" is approachable by a cleansed intelligence but that it is fundamentally inaccessible to a perverse and reprobate mind. A similar standpoint is suggested in the *Phaedrus* myth where it is indicated that the moral integrity of the winged intelligences is a condition of their vision of the eternal forms (250c). Knowledge does not depend simply upon the potency of the cognitive faculty but is equally dependent upon the disposition and quality of the whole soul. It is an understatement when G. M. A. Grube observes that Plato "easily passed from the cognitive to the moral aspects of the psyche." He is suitably more emphatic in stating that the "confusion caused by unanalysed perception and that of immorality go together and are corrected at the same time."[24] In the virtuous man "affection" clusters about and centers upon the highest object of knowledge. Hence the consenting together of cognition and affection alone assures knowledge; but it is of the utmost importance to stress the point that the kind of affection presently dominant in the soul largely determines the kind of knowledge attainable. Accordingly, as there can be no virtue without knowledge of a superior kind, so also there can be no such knowledge without virtuous "affections."

3. Ignorance an Affection of the Soul

The recognition of the paradox which we have encountered in Plato's thought is the first step in comprehending it. It is certain that knowledge is the conditioning ground of virtue, while, at the same time, virtue is quite as much the *sine qua non* of knowledge. Plato's teaching on *katharsis* in the *Phaedo* supports the view that knowledge advances *pari passu* with amendment of life. Clearly, in such a case, the kind of knowledge which "saves" is not independent of character. So far, it seems, Augustine's deduction is substantiated. We have now, however, to consider the matter of ignorance. If, indeed, increasing apprehension of truth and reality is dependent upon a morally estimable state of affection, is there some way, however obscure, in which ignorance or misidentification of reality is also assignable to an affectional condition of the soul? If approbative affections are conducive to knowledge, are there reproachable loyalties and inclinations which obstruct it and conduce to ignorance? What, indeed, is the cause of ignorance among men, especially the double ignorance which is conceit of knowledge in the absence of it and which contrives to turn the order of being and value upside-down? The question about ignorance is important, and we have in the *Phaedo* some searching if provisional answers.

It is to be noted, in the first place, that Socrates customarily regarded human wisdom as of little worth (*Apol.* 23a), and Plato shared his opinion. Taken at large, men are in a condition of lamentable ignorance. Their ignorance, however, does not consist in want of information about the things pertaining to their surroundings and the management of affairs. On the contrary, the ignorance of mankind was, in part, illustrated by Sophists whose versatility was notorious. Hippias, in particular, signalized the brimming sophistic repertoire of diversified "knowledges." Stuffed with scientific and historical information, he was ever ready and willing to disgorge his learning in the presence of any group of open-mouthed bystanders.[25] To Plato information without enlightenment was as good as, or worse than, nothing.[26] Technical knowledge, which according to Protagoras was the gift of Prometheus to man (*Protag.* 321c), was no guarantee against ignorance of the worst sort. Like Heracleitus before him,[27] Plato detested trifling knowledge of many things on the part of minds which were, nevertheless, impoverished in respect to wisdom.

Ignorance as "bondage" and imprisonment of the mind is a theme of the *Phaedo* (84a). In that dialogue the familiar Orphic myth is taken as illustrative of the human plight. Ignorance is the "entombment" of the soul in the body.[28] Hence Socrates declares that the philosopher is one who seeks release from the body's "foolishness." He understands this liberation to be a deliverance from the "slough of ignorance" in which the human mind is sunk.[29] But we need to inquire more exactly into the cause and nature of this bondage which is ignorance. Why does Plato regard *amathia*, double ignorance, as a matter for reproach as well as for regret?

In the opening speeches of the *Phaedo* Socrates reminds his hearers that knowledge of the truth must remain imperfect in man's present existence. Regrettable as it may be, the soul cannot evade intercourse or *koinônia* with the body; so long as the body companies with the soul, so long, it is said, the soul is inhibited and prevented from attaining its real "desire," the truth of Being.[30] Something there is, then, about communion of the soul with the body which frustrates the ultimate "wish" of the soul and obstructs knowledge. The obstructive factors shortly are identified with passions or loves and desires and fears. It is the clamorous insistency of these "affections" (παθήματα) which so disturbs the exercise of reason "that it prevents our beholding the truth."[31]

The *Phaedo* reveals that, in Plato's opinion, the multitude is ignorant of reality because of overwhelming "appetite." It is desire, *epithumia,* for the corporeal, that is, for what men "can touch and see and drink and eat and employ in the pleasures of love" (81b). These fascinate the mind and rivet attention upon physical and sensible existence (83c). Attention is so exclusively preoccupied with "things" that its prospect is hedged in, and cognition exhausts its function upon the world of sensible particulars (82e). According to Plato's explicit statement, it is "desire of the corporeal" which fetters cognition to the realm of Becoming and engenders "forgetfulness" of reality, which nevertheless remains accessible to the rightly disposed mind. The cognitive faculty becomes captivated and wholly engrossed (83d), so that, Plato affirms, men come to believe that "nothing is true" which does not answer to sense or affords no pleasure to sensation.[32] Therefore, Socrates declares: "The lovers of knowledge perceive that, when philosophy first takes possession of their soul, it is entirely fastened and welded to the body and is compelled to regard realities through the body as through prison bars, not with its own unhindered vision, and is wallowing in utter ignorance."[33]

Plainly, the mind is in veritable "bondage" to the imperious interests of *epithumia* (84a). In the *Phaedo,* of course, sense and desire are not yet dissociated from the body; and because the mind is thus enslaved it entertains opinions, *doxai,* which are engendered by the appetites. Plato says, "It opines those things to be true which the body affirms to be true" (83c). Dropping the psychology of the *Phaedo* and employing that of the tripartite soul, as in the *Republic* (439d-e), it may be said that those things are presumed to be reality which the appetitive faculty (τὸ ἐπιθυμητικόν) singles out and offers for observation and apprehension.[34] The faculty of cognition is disoriented but not disabled. It is constrained to exercise its powers of cognition at the command of controlling interests. Nevertheless potentialities for truer knowledge remain as the soul's inherent birthright, for, says the Platonic Socrates, let us suppose that the rational power, "the vision of the soul" which is presently "turned downwards," were redirected. In that case the very same faculty would be "keen in its vision of the higher things, just as it is for the things toward which it is now turned" (*Rep.* 519b). The misdirection of affection, together with its attendant cognition, results in the kind of knowledge, namely, *doxa* or opinion, which is characteristic of the prisoners in Plato's cave. The consequence is quite as John Wild affirms: "As a result of this restriction of their opinion-forming faculties, the prisoners will achieve not a wholly false but an al-

together inverted understanding of their environment."[35]   It issues
in a sensationalistic phenomenalism, namely, in the sort of "false
opinion" described in the *Sophist* as thinking what is the opposite of
reality (240d).   It opines that those things which certainly are, are
not at all (240e) and, contrariwise, regards those things which are
deficient realities to be the only order of reality worth contem-
plating.[36]

In the *Phaedo* (82e), Plato declares that "the most terrible thing
about man's imprisonment is the fact that it is caused by the desires
of the body, so that the man in bondage is the accomplice to his own
bondage."   Men are "self-deceived" in the sense that one interest is
so masterful as to obstruct and suppress intrinsically superior inclinations.   So it becomes fully evident that the cave-wisdom of mankind,
which in Plato's view is "false opinion," does not derive from the
simple fact of sense perception.   To be sentient and "sense-bound"
are quite different conditions.   The latter, alone, is the dismal state
of ignorance which Plato encounters in the mass of men.   The words
of the *Phaedo* (83c) best summarize the predicament: "The evil is
that the soul of every man, when it is greatly pleased or pained by
anything, is compelled to believe that the object which caused the
emotion is very distinct and very true; but it is not."

On the strength of this, the conclusion is inescapable: Human
ignorance is, in part, the product, not of the inaccessibility of true
Being, but of a misdirection of the cognitive power.   We arrive at
the consequence that, in Plato's thought, ignorance (and, for that
matter, knowledge) is contingent upon the dynamic balance of the
entire affective life.

Augustine of Hippo claimed that Socrates turned from physical to
anthropological inquiry because he found reality inaccessible to human
apprehension apart from amendment of life.   So far as the Socrates
of the *Phaedo* is concerned, Augustine's interpretation is adequately
substantiated.   As for Plato himself, it will become manifest that
his system of *paideia* is formulated in the light of his conviction that
ignorance is mainly attributable to a "volitional" or affective disorientation of *nous*, the cognitive faculty.

4. Ignorance Is Folly

It is customary with Plato to state in one way or another that
men are ignorant against their will and that they err involuntarily.[37]
Actually this is a paradox that does not, taken by itself, represent
Plato's full meaning.   As it stands, this theme ill-prepares us to

comprehend how ignorance is in a certain way voluntary, and, since it is voluntary, renders the erring mind subject to censure.

There is a kind of ignorance which is benign, and although regrettable is not subject to reproof. This is "simple ignorance," which Plato always distinguished from the "double" variety.[38] Simple ignorance is innocence and lack of information about all manner of things. Plato often styles it the "ignorance of the artisan" or the technician.[39] Secondarily, simple ignorance is lack of knowledge about essential Being, in the absence, however, of the presumption that one's ignorance is knowledge. The case of the unpretentious slave boy in the *Meno* (81c f.), who under Socrates' tutelage "recovered" knowledge, as it were, out of his head, is a good instance of this secondary ignorance. Double ignorance is quite different and poses much more formidable problems. Double ignorance, according to Plato, is a state of "folly." A man possessed of it is "gripped not by ignorance only but also by a conceit of wisdom."[40]

There is an intransigence and willfulness about double ignorance because the "affections" are involved and the ego has become identified with the erroneous judgment in question.[41] The ignorant man is commonly vehement in his wrong-headedness. In the *Cratylus*, Plato observes that the lamentable feature of double ignorance is "self-deception," the worst of all deceptions: "How can it help being terrible, when the deceiver is always present and never stirs from the spot?" (428d.) In point of fact, the cause of ignorance is with the man himself.

We have no difficulty in identifying the nature of this ignorance. Plato describes it as "deception in the soul about realities."[42] It is the old error of turning reality upside-down and identifying the "real" with the objects of Becoming. What is worse, the error is unacknowledged. Instead of conceding possible error, men stubbornly cherish their espoused opinions and blindly affirm them to be the truth. They are wedded to, and affectionally involved in, their own ontological inversion.

How, then, can we square the two orders of fact? On the one hand, Plato everywhere roundly declares that falsehood "no one willingly accepts" and that the soul, if ignorant, is ignorant against its will.[43] On the other hand, it looks very much as though men entertained false opinion with a kind of mulish obstinacy which argues lively self-involvement. As a matter of plain fact, and paradoxical though it may be, both things are true, and there is no real contradiction. But it is impossible to make sense of the paradox until we have it clearly in mind that the soul of man is subject to two ruling and leading affections which, in the non-philosophic nature, are always at odds with each other (*Phaedr.* 237e f.). In addition, it is necessary to understand that both ignorance and knowledge are correlated with contrary appetitions in the soul. We get nowhere in comprehending Plato's psychology unless we understand that the rational and irrational principles of the soul, mentioned at *Republic* 439d f., are both alike animated by and instinct with contrary appetitions or loves.

When Plato declares, then, that men do not err voluntarily and are not willingly ignorant, he presupposes something not on the surface. He presumes a pristine inclination of the rational faculty toward its appropriate intelligible and trans-empirical objects. We noted the formulation of this conception in our earlier treatment of Socrates' doctrine of ψυχή. *Nous* is possessed of an axiological urge (ὁρμή), a hormic movement toward ideal reality, or the Good. Augustine described it as the soul's "native vigor," raising it upward to eternal things. Of these, it has real if obscure and baffling presentiments.[44] This urge certainly expresses for Plato the primordial affection or eros of man.[45] When unencumbered or not otherwise prevented, the rational faculty is impelled toward the realities of which it has "apprehensions" and native, if unfulfilled, community.[46] The "kinship" of the soul with abiding reality, inaccessible to sense but intimated to intelligence, is the cause of an ineluctable, though usually thwarted movement of the soul, a movement of like toward like. There is, however, a contrary impulse in the soul. It also is a hormic movement. It is the stirring of *epithumia*. This is what we have already identified in the *Phaedo* as "desire of the corporeal." In the *Phaedrus* and *Republic*, it is the sensuous eros which waxes great and tyrannizes over the true "ruling principle."[47] It develops the impetus of a "mastering passion," overthrowing the rule of reason and engendering false opinion.[48]

Of the two ruling and determining principles in the soul, one leads through intelligence toward what is best. The other is bent upon pleasurable satisfactions. The two are sometimes in agreement within the individual; but, with most men, they are in perpetual strife.[49] Moreover, sensuous impulse frequently prevails over intelligence so that desire overcomes "true opinion."[50] And, now, without pursuing further this dual-directional appetition in the soul, we are better prepared to understand how men are said to err unwillingly.

When Plato says in the *Republic* (413a) that "men are unwillingly deprived of true opinions," he is to be taken at his word. His meaning, however, can be gathered only from his conception of the internal economy of the psychic powers. Plato means to say that the departure of "true opinion" is involuntary (ἀκούσιος) in the sense that it is contrary to the mind's native and original bent toward true Being. Men unwillingly err, if we view the matter from the perspective of the primitive impulsion of the rational faculty. From this vantage point, ignorance is contrary to the elemental "wish" or preference (βούλησις) of the soul.

If, on the other hand, we take the alternative position and approach ignorance and error from the viewpoint of man's sensuous proclivities, there is, equally, a manner in which men voluntarily (ἐκουσίως) err. It is true that Plato does not explicitly say so. In the *Lesser Hippias* the question is asked whether it is better to err voluntarily or involuntarily, but this means, wittingly or unwittingly. And, while the preference is given to voluntary error, the anomaly is resolved with the recognition that conscious error is either not error at all, and only a pose, or else it is one step above involuntary error because it is not presumption of truth in the absence of it.[51]

The meaning of voluntary error can best be approached by attention to the prisoners in Plato's Cave (*Republic* VII, i-ii). It is true that they are fettered with their backs to the light, but their bondage is self-imposed and their contentment with cave-knowledge is undisturbed, or almost so. They are, as it were, by preference committed to opinion (δόξα) and the objects of opinion and for one reason primarily: The objects of opinion (τὸ δοξαστὸν) correspond to their prevailing aspirations. The objects of opinion are commensurate with the presently ruling, if inferior, passion of their souls.

It is true that elsewhere in the *Republic* (382b) Plato declares "deception *in the soul* about realities, to have been deceived and to be blindly ignorant and to have and to hold falsehood there, is what all men would least of all accept. . . ." But it is shortly stated that, however loath men would be to be deceived (if they were aware of it), this unwitting ignorance is a malign affection (πάθημα) in the soul, a passion, a being affected somehow and by some influence. It is this influence Plato has in mind when he refers to those who "alter their opinions under the spell of pleasure or terrified by some fear."[52] Clearly it is appetite, in the form either of inclination or aversion, which is the "sorcery," as Plato calls it, that "over-persuades" or instils forgetfulness. It works in such a way as to befog and nullify opinions and sounder judgment by a "mixture of persuasion and deceit."[53] All this accords with Plato's already noted assertion that it is tyrannical appetite which misdirects or "turns downward the vision of the soul."[54] When we suggest, therefore, that men are ignorant voluntarily, we mean that their present misidentification of reality results from prevailing preferences for such realities as serve and promote dominant sensuous interests. Because this appetency masters the whole nature, ignorance is stubborn and resists enlightenment and is, of course, self-incurred.

Appetency of varying kinds (corresponding with varying objects of incentive and cognition) very nearly specifies all that we are allowed to mean by volition so far as Plato's writings are concerned. Erich Frank maintained that neither Plato nor, probably, any of the Greeks, attained to the conception of "free will" and that in Plato's case, *volition*, considered as an independent faculty of the soul, is not contemplated.[55] The point is well taken, Plato does not mean by "voluntary" or "involuntary" the spontaneity of a will considered as a power of self-determination. Any conception of autonomy is quite foreign to Plato's understanding of man. Man exists in the context, mainly, of two contrasting orders of reality with two appetencies as well as two modes of cognition appropriate to each order. Just as cognition of the two orders (Becoming and Being) takes, in either case, the form of intuitive apprehension, so, what we denominate volition takes the form of appetency for one or the other or both of these orders. Furthermore, both cognition and appetency, or eros, presuppose a certain inherent commensurability between the human subject and the correlative orders of reality. So there are two dominant loves of the soul, yet these two principal "volitions" are in no sense autoinduced. Rather, they are affective, as distinguished from noetic, responses to the promptings or solicitations of antecedent reality. When, therefore, Plato speaks of the "voluntary" in human experience, he registers a hardly concealed preference for one of the two principal affections of the soul, namely, the felt lure of the higher order of Being. By "voluntary" he specifies an inherent and pristine affection of the *psuchê*, its real eros. By "involuntary" he means the suppression and inhibition of this eros by an encroaching and contrary affection of lower rank.

Therefore the word *boulêsis,* which Plato occasionaly uses, ordinarily signifies the presently controlling preference or dominant affection of the soul. Hence when we say that man errs voluntarily we mean that his present state of ignorance is enforced by and correlated with what Plato recurrently calls in the *Republic* a "ruling passion" (574d f.). As knowledge and true opinion are attended and prompted by a loftier and superior affection, so ignorance is incurred and ingrained by a lower and inferior one. Since the nobler aspiration, which impels *nous* to a vision of reality, is regarded as the true eros (611e), men are deprived of that vision against their essential *boulêsis* or preference. But, since they are governed and enslaved by an inferior preference, they are, so far as ignorance of truth attends that affection, voluntarily ignorant; for preference, however depraved, is still determinative.

Ignorance results, then, whenever *epithumia* exercises sway over the total economy of the soul's powers. The mind consents with desire and comes to believe that "things are true which the body says are true."[56] Evidently, then, the ignorant man errs by preference. He is self-deceived. Since his ignorance is linked with the quality and direction of his appetition, the ignorant man is joined to his own error and pledged to it as to his own inclination. This will be the case unless by good fortune the "habituation" of his affectional bias can be altered.[57] This, then, is what Plato perceived about double ignorance. Because volition is implicated, a man is his own prisoner and the cause of his own blindness.

Understandably Plato regarded ignorance as a morally "reprehensible" condition, subject to censure and reproach (*Apol.* 29b). He was, in fact, accustomed to designate it "folly," *aphrosunê,* in express contrast with *phronêsis.*[58] The latter is "wisdom" and frequently substitutes for the word *sophia.*[59] Recurrently, ignorance in the soul receives reproof as if it denoted, as indeed it does, moral turpitude. Further, error and folly (ἄνοια) are closely associated.[60] In the *Timaeus* (86a), one part of folly is double ignorance; the other is madness. In the *Phaedrus* (270a), *anoia* is represented as the opposite of *nous* or intelligence. This is not surprising, because both possess axiological denotation. Plato declares plainly that injustice is ignorance and that, together, they are "vice" in the soul; but his clear meaning is somehow lost to conventional interpretation.[61] Indeed Plato himself explicitly takes notice of the "unwillingness" of men to concede that ignorance, when it arises in the soul, is evil and vice.[62]   In an important passage of the *Sophist* (228a-e), it is said that there are two species of vice in the soul. The one is commonly designated "unrighteousness," instanced by intemperance or injustice. The other is ignorance, which is a "deformity" or disproportion in the soul. Ignorance is itself the prime unrighteousness of the soul. Its very presence is an indication that the native impulse of the mind, aspiring toward reality, is held down or diverted into another channel. And it is in this context that light is thrown upon Plato's definition of ignorance at *Sophist* 228c: To be ignorant is the aberration of a soul that aims at truth when, somehow, the understanding passes beside the mark. Plainly, the aim, the impulse toward truth, is misdirected by some diversionary factor. Therefore Plato does not hesitate to speak of ignorance as both "disease" and symptom of disease in the soul.[63]   It signifies a "pathological" condition, or more exactly, an evil "habituation" of affection. Ignorance exists when, in the soul, the appetitive faculty "opposes what are by nature the true ruling principles—knowledge, opinion, or reason." Plato adds: "This condition I call folly, whether it be in a state, when the masses disobey the rulers and the laws, or in an individual, when the noble elements of reason existing in the soul produce no good effect, but quite contrary."[64]

5. Truth and Character

From what has been indicated, it is plain why a proper discipline of the appetitive faculty is prerequisite for the attainment of truth about reality. It is said in the *Republic,* that clever men are quick enough to discern things which really command their interest and affection. This is sufficient proof that it is not poor vision which is the cause of ignorance, but, as Plato declares, a vision which is "forcibly enlisted in the service of evil" (519a). This conception of the origin and nature of ignorance is not confined to the earlier period of Plato's thought. In the *Laws* Plato holds that wisdom, intelligence, and opinion are each accompanied and supported by their appropriate affections, i.e., volitions (688b). Each form of cognition is associated with and impelled by its special axiological incentive. Furthermore, there is the plain statement that ignorance is incurred when the cognitive faculty is swept along by the "multitude in the soul." According to the *Timaeus* (42a f.), human birth entails an initial perturbation and disorientation of the *psuchê* as it is beset with violent and unordered affections incident to physical and sensible existence. If the nobler faculty of the soul gains mastery by conforming to the revolution of intelligence within, the man will live justly. But here, as elsewhere, Plato notes that cognition is obstructed by tendentialities of affection; and false opinion and double ignorance are in this manner inculcated and confirmed. Eventually, it is said: "Whoso, then, indulges in lusts or in contentions and devotes himself overmuch thereto must, of necessity, be filled with opinions that are wholly mortal, . . . inasmuch as he has made great his mortal part" (90b).

a. The Worthlessness of Polymathy

For Plato there is no doubt that proper "tendance of the soul" involved, as he said, "making the part that thinks like unto the object of its thought."[65] This is the finally sufficient *therapeia* for double ignorance.[66] By this means alone can reality be brought into focus. Ancillary to this general position there comes into view, threading through the dialogues, a derived but characteristic, twofold insistence: technical knowledge without virtue is worthless; and the best and most righteous man is the surest authority and most reliable guide to truth and reality.

The first of the themes requires only slight attention, since it has already been alluded to. The persistent strictures of Plato against technical competence which is indifferent to the moral uses of knowledge are familiar. Plato's scorn is plainly evident when he notes that the city is full of "many and manifold knowledges or sciences." These include the skills of artisans, builders, and horticulturalists.[67] Men are lovers of spectacles. They delight in information and are always eager to hear some new thing.[68] But this cannot be accounted wisdom. Neither do any of the abstract sciences, such as mathematics or astronomy, qualify for the title. According to the *Lesser Hippias*, the possession of mere tehnical knowledge assures only the doubtful competency of being equally able to instruct or to deceive. As the *Republic*, Book VII, shows, Plato regarded sciences, such as arithmetic, geometry, stereometry, and astronomy, as helpful propaedeutic studies. In his scheme of *paideia*, they have an honorable and integral place. They are liberating in function, facilitating emancipation of *nous* from bondage to sense and Becoming. But learning, even of this sort, is no unmixed blessing. Aptitude in the pursuit of these "knowledges," devoid of moral earnestness, can easily be perverted to uses of social evil. Without virtue and love of the

Good which measures man, the sciences are nothing, or worse than nothing: "And if we do not know it [the Good] then, even if without the knowledge of this we should know all things never so well, you are aware that it would avail us nothing, just as no possession either is of any avail without the possession of the Good."[69]   Later, in the *Laws*, Plato reaffirms his position even more emphatically.   Incapacity for the sciences hardly becomes an intelligent man; yet, he says, "complete and absolute ignorance of them is never alarming, nor is it a very great evil; much more mischievous is a wide variety of knowledge and learning combined with bad training."[70]   From the beginning, in the *Charmides* (174b-c), Plato held that all "knowledges," taken together, avail nothing for man's well-being without knowledge of the Good.   But knowledge of the Good *is* virtue; and just as certainly virtue is a condition of its apprehension.

b. The Best Man Is the Surest Authority

The second corollary now claims attention: It is Plato's rather astonishing conviction that the better man, morally speaking, is the sounder authority in matters of truth.   Incredible as this may appear to those who, since Plato's time, have consented to give a certain self-sufficiency to the "theoretical" by sundering it from the "practical reason," Plato's conviction is already registered in the teaching of the *Crito* and *Gorgias,* namely, that the just man is also the wisest man.[71] He is wise because he is conformed to the paradigm of Goodness which intimates itself to his consciousness and answers to the essential "constitution" of the human soul.   But more especially it was Plato's encounter with Socrates which early enforced upon his mind the realization that the best man he knew was also the wisest.   The undimmed recollection of this concurrence of knowledge and virtue in the person of Socrates remained a guiding principle as Plato wrestled with the problem of knowledge and pondered the enigma of human error.

By the time Plato wrote the *Seventh Epistle* (343e), he was prepared to assert that reality is inaccessible to a morally indifferent or to a reprobate mind.   In both the *Philebus* and the *Laws* it is stated that the judgments of the virtuous regarding justice and truth are superior to those of unjust men.   "Which of the two judgments shall we say is the more authoritative," Plato inquires, "that of the worse soul or that of the better?"   The answer given is, "That of the better, undoubtedly."[72]   This is a prevailing theme, not a formalized doctrine, of Plato. It is a corollary of the more fundamental view that virtue is the condition of knowledge.

There are two passages worthy of special notice which illustrate with particular intensity Plato's conviction that knowledge of reality waits upon amendment of life. The first of these is found in the *Sophist,* where Plato undertakes to show that crude empiricism is in error since it confuses true reality with that which is not true Being. Plato's task is the logical and ontological one of showing that what is not Being is, nevertheless, not unreality but something other than full Being. When the Sophist affirms, therefore, that what is not Being (*i.e.,* Becoming) is reality, it is Plato's intention to show that the Sophist is not talking nonsense but confounding inferior with superior reality (240a-e). He is turning the order of Being upside-down in the Sophists' customary way.

In the course of the dialogue, Plato appraises various ontologies, among them materialism. Only half in earnest, Plato undertakes a preliminary refutation by exhibiting the contradiction implicit in the minds of its proponents. The latter, although they concede the existence of nothing which is not sensible and corporeal, are at a loss what to say about qualities such as justice, wisdom, and virtue. Plato, however, does not in this instance overrate theoretical refutation. He is aware that all logical argument in defense of immaterial reality encounters a non-theoretical barrier more formidable than any merely logical system could interpose. This barrier consists of unexamined pre-possessions which he understands to be judgments engendered by an affectional bias or preference of the entire mind. Sensationalistic materialism is, in the final analysis, a registering of preference. It is an ontological judgment engendered by and conformable to a dominant affective interest. Hence it is a manifestation of character. Accordingly, Plato declares that the really efficacious propaedeutic to any fruitful discussion, as well as the first duty of the pedagogue, is "to make such men better" than they presently are.[73] The meaning of Plato's cryptic utterance is immediately disclosed. Improvement (τὸ βέλτιον) of life is required because "the acknowledgment of any-thing by better men is more valid than if made by worse men" (246d). Here it is clearly implied that, for overcoming ignorance, a purification and renovation of the "entire soul" are necessary. Only in this way, as Plato suggests earlier in the dialogue, can men, be-coming "angry with themselves and gentle toward others," be freed from their "high and obstinate opinions," their double ignorance

(230b-d). It is impossible to displace ignorance and unseat presumption merely by submitting evidence or by logical argumentation. Proverbially there are none so blind as those that will not see. And Plato is fully aware that the volitional indisposition to acknowledge the reality in question must be altered before the intimations of truth can meet with an attitude favorable to their indications.

Turning, finally, from the *Sophist* to Book X of the *Laws*, we find Plato encountering difficulties with the "atheistic" *sophoi*. The "modern scientists," as he calls them, assert that the universe is the product, not of intelligence or art (τέχνη), but of *phusis* and chance.[74] The cosmos is the fortuitous arrangement of irreducible "elements." How, then, shall Plato defend the view that the Cosmos is, on the contrary, the product of *technê* and intelligence aiming at good? How shall men "who desire to be impious" be furnished with an adequate demonstration so as to convert them to a fear of the gods?[75] It is not fitting that they be refuted in a fit of anger and passion but that they be mildly persuaded, because they do not willingly err, but are corrupted in mind. Plato's contention once more finds illustration; for, in his view, materialism, although it produces an impressive theoretical structure for its self-justification, roots in a pre-possession of the soul.[76] What he means, of course, is that predilections of the sensuous nature are exercising such tyranny over the "ruling principle" as to inculcate double ignorance or the "involuntary lie."

Thus it is not formal refutation which is able or fitted to encounter and extirpate the ignorance Plato deplores. Theory runs upon non-theoretical reefs submerged and hidden below the surface of purely inferential discussion. These are the unacknowledged, but decisive, premises of thought. They disclose foundational preferences to which the mind is committed before inference gets under way. There is, therefore, as Plato clearly saw, no definitive refutation of theoretical atheism. It is so because logical inference and deduction ignore the first principles of thought and move unsuspectingly above the level where decision has already been made and both consent and commitment given. Accordingly Plato perceived that a "gentle" transformation of perspective must be induced. For this purpose a new and superior art of persuasion was required, wholly different from the polemical and contentious rhetoric of the Sophists. But, however effective a new method of persuasion may prove to be, no pedagogy for relieving ignorance can finally escape being *ad hominem* in its procedure. From Plato's position it cannot be otherwise, for ignorance is censurable vice in the soul, and what a man knows is dependent upon the kind of man he is. Consequently, as Augustine surmised, ignorance gives way to knowledge in proportion as vice gives way to virtue. For that reason Socrates turned from physical to ethical questions.

NOTES

1. *De Civ. Dei* VII, 4. *Nicene and Post-Nicene Fathers* (ed. P. Schaff, New York, 1886).

2. *Conf.* VII, ix.

3. See the author's essay "Faith and Reason" in *A Companion to St. Augustine* (New York, 1955), XI, 287-314.

4. *De Civ. Dei* VIII, 3.

5. *De Civ. Dei* VIII, 3.

6. *De Civ. Dei* VIII 3.

7. Aristotle, *Met.* 987b 1 f., 1010a 5 f. Cicero, in his *Academica* I, iv, 15 f., expresses the prevailing view about Socrates. He derives it from M. Terentius Varro, the encyclopaedic scholar of the new Academy. *Cf. De Civ. Dei* VI, 2-10; VII 1-22.

8. Refer *supra*, Ch. II, n. 47.

9. *Phaedo* 98a f. W. H. V. Reade (*The Christian Challenge to Philosophy* [London, 1951], 34 f.) made the interesting suggestion that although Plato "is feeling his way toward monotheism," he is impeded by the fact that Greek religion presents "God" in the quasi-historical form of myth. But myth was, to Plato, literally false; and the "historical," moreover, cannot embody the truth of reality. This is a perceptive diagnosis so far as it goes; namely, in so far as it suggests that Plato's mind cannot come to rest in the thought of "God" without creating a new *muthos* as the vehicle. It should be noted, however, that the new *muthos* is to be identified with such cosmological interpretation as we find in the *Timaeus* or in Bk. X of the *Laws*.

10. Augustine was acquainted with Cicero's *De Academica*, see *De Civ. Dei* VI, 2. Undoubtedly Varro is a prime source for Augustine on ancient religion and philosophy. He attributes to Varro forty-one books of antiquities. Varro's enormous erudition was universally esteemed in his age (ne: 116-24 B.C.). See *De Civ. Dei* VI, 3.

11. In the *Phaedo* the relation between ignorance and the state of affection in the *psuchê* is first made explicit. In view of this fact, it is significant that Augustine possessed direct access to the works of Apuleius of Madaura (ne. 124 A.D.), who provided a Latin translation, now lost, of both the *Phaedo* and the *Republic*. Augustine makes numerous and extensive references to the writings of Apuleius, a fellow African and a brilliant rhetorician; see *De. Civ. Dei* VIII, 12-22. It is altogether likely that Augustine had access to the *Phaedo* and the *Republic* in Apuleius' translation. *De Civ. Dei* VIII, 13 shows evident use of detailed data from the *Republic*. In VIII, 15 there is a passage referring to the ordering of the "elements," suggesting accurate knowledge of Plato's treatment of physical bodies in the *Timaeus*. Consideration should be given to the fact that Chalcidius annexed a partial Latin translation of the *Timaeus* to his commentary on the same. The version of Chalcidius was available by the final quarter of the fourth century and may well have come into Augustine's hands.

12. *Phaedo* 65c; *Symp.* 211d.

13. *Phaedo* 75e. *Cf. Phaedr.* 250d for the instrumental value of ·the senses in the process of recollection of formal reality.

14. *Phaedo* 74d-76a. The "deficient" (ἔνδεια) is that which alerted Plato to the difference between Being and Becoming and, among other things, caused him to investigate the ground of deficiency and locate it in a "material principle."

15. *Phaedo* 66d, 83a. *Cf. Rep.* 527d, 533d.

16. *Phaedo* 64d-e.

17. *Phaedo* 66d, 68b.

18. *Cf. Phaedo* 85c-d, and especially *Phaedr.* 278d, where Plato offers a definitive judgment on this subject.

19. *Phaedo* 69c, 81a. Plato frequently borrows from the Mysteries the contrast between the *ateletai*, "uninitiated," and the *teletai*, the "initiated." In Plato's meaning, of course, the initiate is the philosopher, who is able to distinguish between true reality and the realm of sensible particulars. *Cf. Gorg.* 493b; *Phaedr.* 249c, 250c, 253c; *Theaet.* 155e.

20. *Phaedo* 69b-c and 78d.

21. This is the import of the Socratic vocation. *Apol.* 36c, 41c-d; *Gorg.* 522d. The view is fully implied in *Phaedo* 67a and 79d. In the *Republic* 500c, αφομοιοῦσϑαι, "assimilate," is specifically used to describe the endeavor of the *philosophos*. In *Rep.* 613b, *Theaet.* 176c, and *Tim.* 90d, forms of the verb ὁμοιάω are employed. The soul is "made like" the object of its thought.

22. *Phaedo* 67a and 80d-e.

23. *Cf.* John I. Beare, *Greek Theories of Elementary Cognition* (Oxford, 1906), 14, 45.

24. G. M. A. Grube, *Plato's Thought*, 137.

25. *Less. Hipp.* 368b f.

26. *Euthyd.* 293b.

27. K. Freeman, *Ancilla*, Frg. 40, 27.

28. *Phaedo* 69c, 82e. *Cf. Cratyl.* 400b-c.

29. *Phaedo* 82e. In the *Republic* 533d and 535e, Plato employs Orphic myth to symbolize the condition of human ignorance. Men wallow in the mud of ignorance, insensibly as pigs.

30. *Phaedo* 66b. *Cf. Rep.* 611e.

31. *Phaedo* 66d. The explicit source for the ensuing interpretation, apart from the passages here referred to, is to be found at pages 80a-84b of the *Phaedo*.

32. *Phaedo* 81b. *Cf. Theaet.* 155e; *Soph.* 247c-d.

33. *Phaedo* 82d f. Plato signifies a real fettering of the mind by the verb ἀναγκάζω. That Plato seriously means to indicate a genuine "bondage" of the soul can be seen by comparing use of ἀναγκάζω at *Rep.* 524e, 525d, 526b, 529a. The image of the Cave in the *Republic* is obviously a graphic symbol that enlarges upon the already fully developed theme of bondage as we find it in *Phaedo* 80d-84b. Plato means what he says. The minds of men are shackled in bonds, ἐν δεσμοῖς. *Rep.* 514a, 515c, 516c, 519b.

34. See the clear indication that the tyrannizing appetitive faculty, *to epithume-tikon*, determines "opinion" and what is taken to be reality. *Rep.* 382b, 553d, 581c-d, 586a f.

35. *Plato's Theory of Man*, 193. See also 162.

36. *Soph.* 240b; *Cf. Rep.* 476b-478b.

37. *Cf.* the following passages: *Gorg.* 488a; *Protag.* 345d, 358d; *Rep.* 382a-c, 413a, 589c; *Soph.* 228c. Error as involuntary corresponds with the idea that men do not voluntarily do wrong. *Symp.* 205a; *Rep.* 505d, 438a, 577e; *Gorg.* 468c; *Meno* 77c; *Tim.* 86d; *Laws* 731c f., 860d.

38. At *Laws* 863c we have the most explicit treatment of this distinction to be

found in the dialogues. However, see also *Apol.* 21d, 22e, 29b; *Meno* 84a; *Symp.* 204a; *Soph.* 229b.

39. *Laws* 689c. *Cf. Apol.* 22d f.

40. *Laws* 863c. *Cf. Apol.* 29b; *Meno* 84a-b; *Soph.* 229c.

41. *Laws* 732a. Here Plato clearly attributes intransigent "opinion" to pride, *hubris*, and intrenched ignorance to the fact that, since men have attached their own egos to their opinions, they cannot alter their views without depreciating themselves.

42. *Rep.* 382b.

43. *Rep.* 382a, 413a f.; *Soph.* 228c.

44. *Rep.* 505e and 581b. *Cf. Laws* 950b; *Phaedo* 79d; *Rep.* 475b, 485b, 490b, 517b; *Phaedr.* 247d, 248b.

45. *Cf. Phaedr.* 266a-b. It will be plain to the reader that the author fully subscribes to what Wild suitably calls "the intentional structure of psychic action" in Plato's theory of cognition (*op. cit.*, 151). Wild is wholly correct in urging (*ad loc.*) that the rational power of the φυχή, as in *Rep.* Bk. IV, is possessed of an aspiring eros which he, suggestively, regards as the efficient cause of insight. His useful formula is: "Aspiration is the efficient cause of insight, while insight is the formal and final cause of aspiration" (149).

46. *Rep.* 611e.

47. *Phaedr.* 238a f., and *Rep.* 573b-e.

48. *Rep.* 574d. *Cf. Rep.* 442b; *Laws* 863c-e.

49. *Phaedr.* 237d, and *Laws*, 689b. *Cf. Rep.* 439c, 440e. The famous *Republic* passage on the "powers" of the soul exhibits a "functional" division of the soul into two portions: the rational, τὸ λογιστικόν, and the appetitive or irrational power τὸ αλογιστόν. The latter is τὸ ἐπιθυμητικόν, *Rep.* 580e. The whole result is a two-directional orientation of the soul characterized by dynamic tension. There are two contrary affectional or volitional tendencies. The tension is not finally resoluble. In the *Timaeus* the measured movement of the superior part imposes its rhythm upon the "unorderly" movement. Symmetry and harmony result, as in the *Republic* 441d-e, 443e, 444d, but nice équilibrium is always precarious.

50. *Phaedr.* 238b-c.

51. *Less. Hipp.* 373c f.

52. *Rep.* 413c.

53. *Rep.* 413b; *Cf. Gorg.* 493a.

54. *Rep.* 519b; *Cf.* 586a f.

55. Erich Frank, *Philosophical Understanding and Religious Truth* (Oxford: New York, 1945), 174. Frank holds, with great plausibility, that the concept of free will is Hebraic-Christian in origin and has first full development in the Church Fathers. He thinks Aristotle's *proairesis* or "free choice" is not truly a free will. It is pretty clear that free will arises in the context of prophetic religion where the Divine command lays upon man a responsibility which, at the same time, discovers him as a center of independence and contrariety. Plato's conception of volition, however, survives in a complex with other ingredients in Augustine's *voluntas*. *Voluntas* is exercise of *amor, dilectio* or *caritas*. A good will is *bonus amor*, a rightly directed love; an evil will is *malus amor*, a base or misdirected affection. As for Plato, so for Augustine, a man is "free" in so far as the *bonus amor*, i.e., love of God, controls him. (*De Civ. Dei* XIV, vii.) For further treatment, see *infra*, Ch. VIII, n. 1.

56. *Phaedo* 83d.

57. *Cf. Rep.* 516a, 517a, d, 518e, 520e.

58. *Protag.* 332a f. For our word "folly," which does in part convey the connotation of moral disrepute. Plato customarily employs two words ἀφροσύνη and ἄνοια.

59. *Phaedo* 79d; *Phaedr.* 250d; *Cratyl.* 411d; *Phileb.* 21a.
60. *Phaedo* 81a.
61. *Gorg.* 477b.   Cf. *Soph.* 228b f.
62. *Soph.* 228d f.   Cf. *Laws* 863e f.
63. See *Phaedr.* 238e; *Tim.* 86b; *Laws* 886b, 888a.
64. *Laws* 689b.   For Plato's characteristic view that the "epithymetic" faculty constitutes the "mass" or "multitude" in the soul and is greatest by mere bulk, see *Rep.* 431a, 442a, 580e, 588c-d.
65. Tim. 90c.   Cf. *Phaedr.* 248b, 250b.
66. *Tim.* 90c.
67. *Rep.* 428b f.   Plato's use of the plural, *epistêmai,* "knowledges," stands for "knowledge so-called," truths of the crafts and arts.
68. *Rep.* 475b.
69. *Rep.* 505a.   Brackets are mine.
70. *Laws* 819a.   See *Epist.* VII, 343c.
71. *Crito* 47c f. and *Gorg.* 507e, 522d.
72. *Laws* 663c; *Phileb.* 40b.
73. *Soph.* 246d.   Of course, βελτίων, the comparative of ἀγαθός, suggests "better," morally speaking.
74. *Laws* 889a f.
75. *Laws* 887a.   The use of ἐπιθυμοῦσιν ασεβεῖν, "desire to be impious," is intentional. It accords with Plato's judgment that error results from the bias of desire.
76. *Laws* 888b.   Plato in this case calls it a disease of the *psuchê.* Cf. *Rep.* 439d; *Tim.* 86b.

CHAPTER IV

Knowledge As Re-cognition

Then if this is true, our view of these matters must be this, that education is not in reality what some people proclaim it to be in their professions. What they aver is that they can put true knowledge into a soul that does not possess it, as if they were inserting vision into blind eyes.—Republic 518b

1. KNOWLEDGE IS NOT TRANSMISSIBLE

EVERY reader of the *Protagoras* is aware of the contradictory position in which Socrates seems to place himself in the course of the dialogue. Entering upon the discussion in skeptical mood, Socrates openly doubts that virtue can be taught.[1] As the interchange between him and Protagoras proceeds, however, Socrates gradually moves toward the position that moral excellencies are either derivatives of knowledge or forms of wisdom.[2] Indeed, the tenor of discussion leads toward the well-known Socratic dictum that courage, justice, temperance and so on, are really knowledge (ἐπιστήμη) or modes of it. It is suggested that virtue is wisdom and that one who possesses knowledge of goodness will not be diverted from a righteous course.[3] At the end of the conversation, Socrates has apparently reversed himself. In maintaining that virtue is knowledge of some sort, he is evidently making the best case possible for the claim that virtue is teachable; for nothing is more teachable than knowledge.[4]

The contradiction is actually more apparent than real. This is manifest on three grounds. First, in the course of the dialogue, it should be noted that the conception of virtue has been enlarged and completely, though unobtrusively, altered. Virtue is no longer the *aretê* Protagoras had proposed to teach. In the second place, the "knowledge" of which virtue is comprised also becomes entirely transformed and redefined. It is in no sense the kind of knowledge which Protagoras claimed to convey, a variety of techniques which Socrates, in any case, never really doubted Protagoras was fully able to transmit. In the third place, throughout the dialogue, Plato is suggesting that the prevailing conception of teaching (*didachê*), as giving out information, is wholly unsuited to the nature of real knowledge and the reality it embraces. In short, virtue as Plato defines it is knowledge of such a kind that it is not teachable in the manner of Protagoras. When, therefore, Socrates began the discussion, doubting that virtue could be taught, he was really only declaring that virtue, as he conceived it, was not teachable as Protagoras understood teaching. It is now desirable to clarify these points for the purpose of showing why, in Plato's opinion, *epistême* is not transmissible.

If virtue is, as Protagoras assumes, competence in the management of one's domestic business and rhetorical skill for attaining influence in public affairs, then Plato does not doubt that such virtue can be taught. Virtue, so conceived, is a kind of technique. And although Protagoras poses as an instructor in civic science, *politikê techne* (319a), his curriculum, in Socrates' view, supplies only a sort of practical "know how." Protagoras was ready to claim that its possession made men "better."[5] To Plato the claim was extravagant, but he was willing to grant that "skills" could be both taught and learned.

To state the matter in Plato's distinctive way, if virtue is *technê* rather than, as he believed, some sort of *epistême*, it has both instructors and learners; and the Sophists are without peers in the teaching profession. As practitioners and trainers in forensic arts, they were unsurpassed. To be sure, Plato harbored the suspicion, to which he gave occasional utterance, that this "art" in which the Sophists were versed hardly deserved the name *technê*. It was something inferior to art—a kind of "knack" or "skill"—really devoid of true art.[6] But in any case Plato did not dispute the point that it could be taught in the sense of being "transmitted" (παραδίδωμι) to others and engrafted by practice and experience.[7]

Plato, however, was altogether of a different mind from Protagoras. He did not believe that the knowledge which constituted virtue was *technê* in the sense in which the Sophists understood the word. He did not believe that it could be acquired by practice or impartation. And this disagreement is a clue to the significance both of the *Protagoras* and the *Meno*. The latter dialogue is best understood as a further development of the issues brought to focus by the argument of the *Protagoras*. In both dialogues Plato undertakes to redefine *aretê* and to indicate the kind of knowledge which it presupposes.

In order to convey his meaning and insinuate it effectively—for his method is regularly evocative rather than didactic—Plato takes up the matter of instruction in virtue. Between him and the Sophists there is, to be sure, initial agreement. Both sides concede that virtue involves some sort of knowledge and, therefore, is capable of being taught. This is about as far as agreement goes. Thereafter, in order to open a way for the development of his distinctive views, Plato introduces a problem of historic fact.

Socrates is made to refer to a notable failure on the part of many eminent men of the past—a failure to impart effectually their own moral excellence to others. Most remarkable was their inability, judged by the evidence, to instruct their children in virtue and so bequeath to them a measure of their own rectitude.[8] Themistocles, of high public spirit and devotion, put his son Cleophantus under good instructors so that the youth became truly wonderful in feats of skill, such as javelin throwing while standing upright on horseback.[9] Aristeides and Thucydides, of noble fame, each put his sons under proficient masters and made the youths extraordinary in physical skill, but no one of these great men succeeded in passing on to his sons his own excellence of character. Since it is inconceivable that Themistocles and the others actually refused "to impart" (παραδιδόναι) the quality of their own goodness to their sons, there seems to be a real question whether virtue can after all be taught.[10] The *Protagoras* arrives at the conclusion that if virtue is indeed knowledge, it ought, on every count, to be teachable. Yet Socrates does not neglect historical evidence to the contrary. In the *Meno*, similarly, the position is reached that virtue is indeed knowledge; therefore it ought to be teachable. The plain fact seems to be, however, that there are neither teachers nor learners of virtue.[11] The impasse suggests the presence of some concealed inconsequence or ambiguity of thought. Upon this the discussion founders as upon a hidden shoal. The ensuing "perplexity," however, may have a salutary effect. Characteristically, Plato regards the moment of doubt or bewilderment, *aporia*, as valuable for alerting the inquirer to the presence of faulty assumptions and uncritical language which lead to real or apparent contradictions or to a stalemate in the argument.[12]

There is, in point of fact, throughout the lively interchange of both the *Protagoras* and the *Meno*, an ambiguity in words, which is mainly responsible for the difficuty we have been noting. Unobtrusively, Plato has all the time been pointing to equivocation in the word *didachê*, instruction. It is this which is giving all the trouble. In his initial demurrer to Protagoras regarding the teachability of virtue, Socrates had said he did not believe that virtue could be taught. But he had also casually defined the word in passing without calling attention to it. He did not believe virtue could be taught in the sense of being procured by some men for other men (319b). Plato recurrently dwells upon this point. He is perfectly sure that virtue is of such a nature that it is quite incapable of being "transmitted" from one man to another by either precept or practice. Socrates, therefore, doubts with good reason that Protagoras, provident as he may be, or Pericles, or any other worthy, can convey his own virtue to others, or, by the same token, make men good citizens (319a).

In the *Meno* Plato neatly summarizes the issues distilled in these companion dialogues:

Our inquiry into this problem resolves itself into the question: Did the good men of our own time and of former times know how to transmit to another man the virtue in respect of which they were good, or is it something non-transmissible nor taken over from one human being to another? That is the question I and Meno have been discussing all this time.[13]

Knowledge which makes for virtue apparently is not transmissible. But transmission is the prevailing connotation of the verb "teach" (διδάσκω) and the noun "instruction" (διδαχή). There is no disputing that Aristeides and Themistocles were exceptional for virtue. But there is no denying, either, that they failed to provide for their offspring a comparable excellence.

The point is now reached where it is possible to see that the underlying problems are two in number and closely related. The first question is, then: What is this knowledge upon which virtue depends and why is it not transmissible? Secondly, what is the nature of the knowledge, if it be such, by possession of which men of the past were exemplary for virtue? There is, of course, the possibility that good men are so "by nature," by some happy circumstance of disposition or aptitude.[14] This suggestion, however, is put aside with the observation that it is not by nature that the good are virtuous but by some form of learning.[15] This is to remain faithful to the agreed premise of the discussion; namely, that virtue is a matter of knowledge of some sort even if it is not yet apparent what it is. Plato was aware, furthermore, that if men are virtuous "by nature," that is, by some inscrutable good fortune, then the hope that virtue may be teachable is empty. In that case, any expectation of human betterment through the right *paideia* or true political art (*Gorgias* 521d) must be abandoned.

What is the knowledge, then, that constitutes virtue and is, at the same time, not susceptible of transmission? Plato's answer is not hard to find; the knowledge in question is "recollection" or *anamnêsis*. All true inquiry and learning, it is said, are wholly recollection.[16] This "learning" secures the kind of knowledge of which virtue consists. It is an immediate apprehension of reality, a direct acquaintance. In the *Republic* Plato frequently designates it "intellection" (νόησις) as distinguished from discursive reason or understanding (διάνοια) which proceeds through deduction or inference.[17] Knowledge is characterized by presentational immediacy and dawns after the manner of illumination. "All nature is akin," says Socrates in the *Meno* (81d); and he suggests that knowledge obtains when there is conformity or *koinônia* of the mind with intelligible Being. The latter is always available, but its apprehension requires suitable accommodation on the part of the knower toward reality to be known. For Plato knowledge by way of recollection means, for one thing, that the precondition of knowing is the pre-possession of the signatures or Forms by which all "particulars" of the sense world are known and known as instances.[18] Although fuller treatment must be deferred, *anamnêsis* is to be understood as signifying a firm repossession of truth and reality. It is a certain recapturing of truth with which every human intelligence has natural conversancy, but which, through inattention, desuetude, or some "forgetfulness," has been obscured and lost to direct awareness.[19] With most men, the "belongings" of the mind are unexplored and unreclaimed. *Anamnêsis* is the reclaiming.[20] Learning, then, is something like recovering knowledge out of oneself, as Plato says in the *Meno*. This recovery of knowledge under the stimulus of dialectical examination is a case of recollection.[21]

Under these circumstances its becomes fully evident that there is no instruction in the sense of handing over or transmitting the kind of knowledge upon which virtue depends. "There is not teaching but only recollection," declares Socrates.[22] This is the explanation of the riddle which Plato does not hesitate to propound: that, of the knowledge which effects virtue, there are neither teachers nor learners.[23] Hence the prevailing conception of teaching cannot possibly provide the sort of knowledge which, in Plato's view, is in-dispensable for the virtuous life.

2. From Cognition to Re-cognition through Dialectic

Preceptual teaching which relies upon transmission of rules of prudence is nothing more than the dissemination of proverbial opinions. True or false, in any case they are unsifted. As Plato states at *Sophist* 229e, the admonitory and preceptual method is not wholly ineffectual or worthless, but the efficacy of moral precepts, if that is what Protagoras enjoined, is limited to that margin of diminishing returns where self-interest whispers caution. The knowledge which constitutes real virtue—justice that does not succumb to expediency when the going gets rough—derives from another source. A man must look for it elsewhere: from the sure deliverances of his own mind—a mind which is presently reclaiming its truest "belongings." What is required, therefore, is a different kind of instructor. The true pedagogue is a dialectician. In the first place, he knows how to induce "perplexity" where ignorance is joined with conceit of knowledge. By plying the mind of his pupil with appropriate questions, he invites a reconsideration of conventional and engrafted opinion. He engages in "joint-inquiry" with his pupil.[24] He does not prematurely intrude solutions. He solicits response and cross-examines each answer with a view to its implications. In this way he clears up the false assumptions of deposited opinion. He opens a path for the mind to move gradually in the direction of truth, which is the objective of its native propensity. By letting the discussion have its head, being sure to divide and classify things according to their real similarities and differences,[25] the teacher helps to dispose the learner's mind in the direction of reality so that the latter may discern for himself.

Something like this is the content and nature of the Socratic "dialectic process of questions and answers."[26] Plato affords us a memorable exhibition of the method in the case of Meno's slave-boy. Upon careful cross-examination, the lad was found, without having formally learned, to possess unwittingly the "true opinion" that the double of any square surface is the square of its diagonal.[27] In the sphere of the "sciences," men are not commonly so presumptuous as they are in matters relating to virtue. In any case, the facility with which the *elenchos,* the cross-examination, under the skillful management of Socrates, achieved its end was directly proportionate to the absence of presumption in the mind of the slave boy.

It was the powerful employment of the dialectical method which, in Plato's eyes, made Socrates the true instructor in knowledge and virtue. In morals every man presumes to be an authority; and Protagoras went so far as to condone and rationalize the presumption.[28] Hence the fruitfulness of the Socratic *elenchos* is, initially, its power to disperse conceit by astonishing the presumptuous mind with self-contradiction among its unexamined notions. Thus, as Meno testifies, Socrates is like the "torpedo sea-fish." He numbs men's minds by reducing them to a healthful perplexity.[29] But Meno urgently needed to be reduced to doubt, before his mind could be rightly disposed toward truth (80a). In this way erroneous opinions are pruned away. The *elenchos* has the faculty of dispersing them as mists which obstruct vision or insight. In this way, as is so well said in the *Sophist*, a man comes to "think that he knows only what he knows and no more."[30] Or, as stated in the *Meno* (84a), a person "feels the difficulty he is in, and besides not knowing does not think that he knows." Then and only then, says Plato, does he feel a craving to find out. Then only does a new appetite for truth arise sufficient to counter-balance the old affectional bias in favor of cherished suppositions (84c). Now at length he is disposed to follow the argument without resistance.[31]

With the onset of this condition, the instructor or dialectician has already begun, in Plato's figure, to act the part of the "mid-wife." According to the *Symposium* (209a), there is a "pregnancy of soul," a "conceiving" of those things which are proper for the soul to conceive and bring to birth. In the *Theaetetus*, in similar vein, the dialectician is one who, by cross-examination, assists those who accompany him in discourse to bring forth many fair things, sometimes knowledge itself.[32] In the metaphor, dialectic has nothing to do with insemination. It has to do only with delivery and happy issue by assisting the mind to clarify its own apprehensions of truth.[33] In short, the true pedagogue and teacher, by discriminating questions and acute analysis of answers, as stated at *Phaedo* 73a, contrives to elicit recollection of realities. Evidently some awareness of these realities slumbers in the human soul.

Plato's epistemology as well as his ethics heavily depends upon a fundamental Socratic conviction; namely, that the mind of man is cognate with reality; that reality is, in some sense, already a datum.

However disoriented the soul may be, *nous* retains intimations and presentiments of the supreme *metron* of virtue, which in the *Republic* is called the Idea of the Good. It is this, it must be stressed again, "which every soul pursues and for its sake does all that it does, with a prophetic foregleam of its reality, but yet baffled and unable to apprehend its nature adequately" (505e). But by way of opinion as distinguished from the way of knowledge through dialectic, the mind "does not really know the good-in-itself or any particular good; but if it apprehends any adumbration of it, its contact is by way of opinion rather than knowledge" (534c). In this way, a man goes "dreaming and dozing" through this present life, possessed and yet dispossessed of the knowledge which is requisite for virtue.[34]

The condition of men generally, therefore, is like that of legatees who have not troubled to claim their inheritance. Men are indigent, not because they are without riches, but because they are strangely self-dispossessed of them. Taking a suggestion from the *Theaetetus*, men as a whole are somewhat like the owner of an aviary whose cage is amply stocked with an assortment of birds. Though the birds are his rightful possession, he must acquire control over them by learning to catch whichever bird he pleases and, at will, to let it go.[35] Only then has he such command over them that he may be said to "have" them.

According to the chariot-myth of the *Phaedrus*, there is no human mind which has not come in sight of divine reality. In this myth Plato seems plainly to assert that no one's mind is devoid of lingering apprehensions of truth. Indeed, he seems to consider this to be the universal condition of humanity; for "every soul of man has by the law of nature beheld the realities."[36] Accordingly it appears that dialectic is the art of repossessing knowledge which, in some sense, is already possessed or is connatural with the mind.[37] If there is any question about the identity of this knowledge, there is Plato's word that it is knowledge of "the absolute essence, which we, in our dialectic process of question and answer, call true being."[38]

Man, then, is a dispossessed possessor of truth about Being. He is half-blind to his own legacy. Although awareness of reality and truth is the mark of his humanity, awareness commonly fails to crystallize and formulate itself into articulate comprehension. Many admit nothing to be real and true which is not prescribed by the interests of sensibility.[39] Prompted by sensuous incentives, like Callicles, men redefine virtue as satisfaction of private desire.[40] Per-

versely they rename reverence, folly, and moderation, rusticity.[41] In
their frenzy, some go the whole limit of excess and identify the good
with self-advantage (*pleonexia*) and justify it as a law of nature.[42]
Yet they cannot completely dispossess themselves of every solicitation
of the Good or of all responsiveness to truth; and in the *Gorgias*
(474b), Socrates insists, despite their protests, that they really believe
with him that "doing wrong is worse than suffering it, and escaping
punishment worse than incurring it." So men cannot altogether repudiate their origin or cast aside what, for both the *Phaedrus* (249c)
and the *Republic* (589d), is the hallmark of their humanity. They
may even attempt to suppress their conversancy with superior values,
but the awareness is irrepressible; and its indications, however feeble,
now and again erupt to unsettle the even tenor of their way. This
unsettlement is itself a kind of *aporia*.

Considering the intention of Plato, there is substantial justification
for regarding *aporia* as a kind of medium-point in the struggle between contrary affections, each seeking, as at *Republic* 587, to exercise
mastery over the entire soul. *Aporia* serves as an interval of neutral-
ity in which the hitherto prevailing momentum of the whole soul
is suspended. Its onset affords opportunity for the mind to rectify
its perspective, assisted by a redistribution of the affective impulses.
Then it is that the pristine nisus or "urge" of the soul, which we
noted in the previous chapter, may resume its rightful leadership of
the mind. The cognitive powers may be redirected by a transformation of interest. In such a case the obscure awareness of reality may
reshape itself into explicit comprehension and acknowledgment.
Actually, as will later become apparent, dialectic in the hands of the
artful pedagogue does count upon the native impulsion of the
soul toward truth. The salutary interval of doubt, then, is not merely
a moment when hitherto entrenched opinions subside and revision of
judgment becomes possible. It is also a moment of affectional
suspense in which the superior appetition of the mind is given an
opportunity to reassert its native vigor and reinforce the cognitive
faculty as the latter is renewing its apprehension of essential Being.

By now it is sufficiently evident why Socrates introduced his exchange with Protagoras in avowed disbelief that virtue could be
taught. If, contrary to his conviction, virtue were simply action from
maxims of prudence or the adroit manipulation of public affairs and
men's opinions through the adept use of words, then indeed virtue
might in some measure be conveyed from teacher to pupil. For

Plato neither of these is virtue, only its "painted imitation." The knowledge, which both makes for and is virtue, is not won so cheaply. It cannot, as he asserts in the notable *Republic* passage, 518c, be inserted as vision into blind eyes. Far from being anything like furnishing minds, as empty containers, with information,[43] it is a calling to remembrance something which has been forgotten.

It is hardly possible to exaggerate the vigor of Plato's rejection of the container-filling theory of education or the significance of his denial that knowledge can be put "into a soul that does not possess it" (518c). In Plato's view, knowledge does not begin with a blank slate. His conception of the soul, derived from Socrates, with its aboriginal apprehensions of abiding truth, excludes this possibility. Yet neither can it be said that among actual human beings the pre-possession of truth amounts to knowledge. Whatever it is, it is only the raw material of *epistêmê*. The latter is distinguished partly by the method or methods through which it is attained. Nevertheless the conception of pre-possession is incontestably a basic premise of Plato's theory of knowledge as well as of his theory of *paideia*. On its objective side, as everyone recognizes, the *a priori* factor in knowledge finds its characteristic expression in the so-called theory of Forms or ideal essences. But this metempirical symbolism for denoting the *a priori* ought not to obscure the equally important subjective co-implicate, namely, the inarticulate, inchoate, and antecedent awareness of intelligible reality. Where and when *epistêmê* is in process of stabilization, its precondition is an obscure and faltering presentiment of the Truth. Thus in the oft noted passage, *Phaedo* 73-76, the precondition of ascertaining empirical "equality" is a sort of spontaneous recollection of absolute equality (75a); and this circumstance is extended to other "absolutes" such as justice, goodness, beauty and holiness (75c). In this regard, the pre-possession of truth is the condition, not only of articulate knowledge, *epistêmê*, but of empirical cognition, which Plato usually terms *doxa*.

In the *Phaedrus* at 250b as well as at *Phaedo* 74a and 75e, the complementary position is stated, namely, that sense experience may serve to prompt and stimulate the process of recapturing. But the presentiment is given; and the statement, for example, at *Gorgias* 468a about man's always desiring "the good," while confounding apparent with real good, is illuminated by what is said at *Republic* 505e, where the real is distinguished from the apparent. Thus the prior awareness Plato alludes to is in no way to be identified with *epistêmê*.

Nevertheless it is plainly presupposed as the precondition of both *doxa* and *epistêmê*. Knowledge will be seen to consist in a transformation of potentiality into actuality.

Plato's avowed position that the possibility of any kind of knowing, whether *doxa* or *epistêmê*, rests upon the fact of already having known plainly suggests that all cognition is fundamentally re-cognition, a view which is as congenial to the *Theaetetus* as to the *Phaedo* and *Phaedrus*.[44] Among other things, knowledge as re-cognition implies that the criterion of truth in judgments will be self-evidence. Self-evidence would exist if and when agreement or coincidence obtains between the mind that knows and the known—between the intelligence and the appropriate intelligible objects. There is strong reason for believing that when Plato insists that knowledge cannot be intruded upon a mind which does not possess it, he is urging that knowledge is possible only between a knower cognate with the known or, conversely, a known cognate (συγγενής) with the knower.[45] The doctrine of *anamnêsis* can scarcely mean anything other than that learning, as is evident from *Meno* 85c-d, is essentially a renewal of prior awareness. It seems to entail re-establishment of conformity, not between "alien," but between cognate realities, *nous* and its object. Learning, then, is quite as Socrates describes the process in *Phaedo* 75e; it is really "recovering knowledge which is our own." In like manner, at *Meno* 85d, the slave boy under cross-questioning is said to recover knowledge, as it were, out of himself, a conception which is reaffirmed in a quite different but, as we shall see, significant context at *Theaetetus* 198d-e.[46] In all, there seems ample ground for the conclusion that the knowledge which is virtue cannot possibly come by way of transmission but, so far as the *Meno* and *Phaedo* testify, must be very like restoration. It is thus apparent that the only possible teacher of virtue, whether we speak of the *Phaedo* (73a) or the *Theaetetus* (150 b f.), is one who assists the process of restoration.

This, in the main, may stand for the meaning of Socrates' denial in the *Protagoras* that virtue can be taught. At the same time, it affords an answer to our first question: What is the knowledge which makes for virtue and why is it not transmissible? There is in addition a kind of corollary. It will be obvious that if learning is altogether *anamnêsis* (*Meno* 81d) and thus arousal of dormant awareness (86a), *epistêmê* necessarily will have the character of something like immediate and personal discovery of truth and reality. Discovery (τὸ εὐρίσκειν), indeed, is a favorite word of Plato's. Learning is discovery and the result of dialectical inquiry.[47]

But however much discovery is the fruition of joint inquiry, as declared at *Meno* 86c and 84c, and however capable it is of being shared, the appropriation of its distinctive content is a personal acquisition and takes the form of private insight. The soul, as Burnet has said, "must see the light for itself."[48] Accordingly the pedagogue who knows his function seeks only to arouse and arrest, not to impart, as Socrates regularly insisted.[49] The rationale of the matter is plainly stated at *Phaedo* 73a: "When people are questioned, if you put the questions well, they answer correctly of themselves about everything; and yet if they had not within them some knowledge and right reason, they could not do this."[50] The succeeding assertion that this is most clearly demonstrated by taking persons to *diagrammata* for interpretation strongly suggests a direct reference to Socrates' examination of the slave boy in the *Meno* (85c), where it is affirmed that, by suitable questions, "true opinions" are stirred up out of slumber into waking consciousness.[51] The nature of these "true opinions" we must examine. Evidently, they have some affinity with the *orthos logos* of the *Phaedo* passage, just noted. Meanwhile we may confidently assert that the conception of knowledge which we have been reviewing carries with it a distinctive notion of the role of the teacher and the nature of *paideia*. If knowledge, in the last resort, is insight, it manifestly cannot be conveyed even if its conditions may be induced. The conventional notion of instruction had to be replaced by a new and more suitable *paideusis* which would make room for "recovery" of knowledge out of the self.[52] For such knowledge alone is virtue.

3. *Doxa Alêthês*: THE *A Priori* IN KNOWING

If knowledge, by aid of the *elenchos*, entails something like revivification of dormant awareness, it is, nevertheless, to be acknowledged that among all sorts and conditions of men this awareness will exhibit degrees of liveliness. It is commonplace, for instance, that in the *Republic* Plato ranks the citizenry according to a threefold scale with the truth-loving group a very small minority, though alone suited to rule (428e). A somewhat larger group is possessed from youth of "high spirit," which eventually may warrant placing its members in the class of "helpers" to the guardians. But as to "reasoning," it is acknowledged that "some of them never participate in it" (*Rep.* 441a). And as for the "multitude," Plato soberly concedes that they are quite incapable of philosophy (493e). Degrees of vitality of what *Phaedo* 73a termed *orthos logos*, right reason, may also be inferred from the hierarchical ordering of souls at *Phaedrus* 248d-e. There, a connection seems intended between the measure of previous conversancy with the Forms and present aptitude of the soul for recollection.

It is now to be our claim that the more or less lively condition of awareness is what supplies to Plato the possibility of using and developing the companion categories of *doxa alêthês*, "true opinion," and *orthê doxa*, "right opinion." These terms we shall find prominent in the *Meno* and the *Republic* as elsewhere. In the measure that this thesis is defensible, we shall incidentally find an answer to the second of the two questions we have been considering: What is the source and nature of that knowledge by possession of which some men have been distinguished for virtue?

Turning our attention once again to the *Meno*, we should note that the discussion is inaugurated by Meno's question about the teachability of virtue (70a). Thereupon Socrates ironically reproaches himself for utter ignorance respecting virtue. Manifestly, he observes, if he has no knowledge of virtue, he will be unable to specify its nature or declare whether it can be taught (71b). Thereafter we have Meno's four brash attempts to define virtue. Under the scrutiny of Socrates, each is found to be abortive because self-contradictory. By this time Meno is properly disabused of his easy assurance concerning the nature of virtue and is reduced to healthy perplexity (80a). Thereupon, in chastened temper, he hits upon a riddle which he puts in the form of a question to Socrates. The question is itself a sign that Meno is beginning to substitute candid inquiry for ill-considered opinions hastily improvised. He recalls that Socrates professes ignorance of virtue. On sudden illumination, he now inquires of Socrates: "Why, on what lines will you look, Socrates, for a thing of whose nature you know nothing at all? Pray, what sort of thing, amongst those that you know not, will you treat us to as the object of your search? Or, even supposing, at the best, that you hit upon it, how will you know it is the thing you did not know?" (80d)

In his honest perplexity, Meno, it may be, is stumbling upon the core of Platonic insight concerning knowledge. How is it possible, he asks, to inquire concerning the nature of something of which one possesses no previous insight? This problem was already mentioned by Socrates in his initial response to Meno at the very beginning of their conversation.[53]   It recalls the kind of difficulty Socrates alluded to at 169b of the *Charmides*: How could it be determined whether *sophrosunê*, as a kind of knowledge of oneself, was also a virtue? How could this be decided apart from a prior knowledge of the qualities of temperance?   Thereafter Socrates stated that he had a "presentiment" that temperance is something beneficial or good even though he was so far unsuccessful in articulating the grounds of his judgment.

Meno's second question is an elaboration of the first.   How is it possible, he asks, for research even to get under way if that for which we inquire is among the things altogether not known?   Clearly we do not inquire after what is unknown but after that of which we have some ill-defined, however vague, awareness, either directly or through its effects.

The third question, makes an advance over the two previous ones.   Suppose that, while seeking for the unknown, one should chance to stumble upon it, how would it be recognizable as that which initially prompted the search?   How is it possible to know the unknown, that is, to identify it with that for which one seeks when as yet one is ignorant of that for which one seeks?   For Plato, who propounds this puzzle again at *Theaetetus* 191c with serious intent, this is really reducing to absurdity any assumption that, in the process of learning, one proceeds from the literally unknown to the known. All advancement in knowledge presupposes an act of *identification* or, what is the same thing, re-cognition.   The prior condition of knowledge, therefore, is some elusive pre-possession of its constituents which, however, requires examination and analysis.

The import of Meno's question is right-headed: It seems evident that knowledge of reality has no absolute beginning where it was not before.   A word of caution is, however, in order: Plato is not in this context primarily concerned with knowledge of the sensible world of Becoming, although as we shall discover in due course *doxa*, the mode of apprehension suitable to the sense world, also admits of clarification unto knowledge of a certain kind.   Here, however, the discussion is limited to knowledge of "most real Being."   We are occupied exclusively with the knowledge of reality upon which true virtue depends—the "cause," of which virtue is the effect.   With this qualification firmly stated, it is now permissible to add that knowledge which has to do with intelligible Being, is essentially analytical in nature. "Analytical" is used here according to Kant's description of analytical propositions.[54]   In knowledge of the kind Plato has in mind, we might say that the predicate of a proposition contains explicitly nothing more than is implicit in the subject term.   In other words, in the "noumenal" realm where, according to Plato, we speak of knowledge in the strict sense,[55] advancement in knowledge is a gradual unfolding and elaboration of the inarticulate content of the subject or the known. It remains to be seen, however, in what form the subject term is already present and given to consciousness.

Meno's threefold question seems to be much more than a "sophistic puzzle" of which Plato has left us examples in the *Euthydemus*.[56] The problem posed by Meno arises from "perplexity" and a chastened temper, and, even if it had prototypes in the eristic jousting of the day, Plato intends to turn it to good use in uncovering a crucial aspect of the problem of knowledge.   This aspect is dealt with at length in the *Meno* more positively than in any previous dialogue.   Socrates' rejoinder that Meno's query is something of an "eristic argument" is not to be stressed unduly (81d), for he goes on directly to concede its real implication; namely, that knowledge does indeed presuppose prior acquaintance.   Socrates immediately adopts the view that antecedent acquaintance is attributable to immortality of the soul (81b). In virtue of its undying existence, he posits its "cognizance throughout all time" of verities of which present learning is but recovery (86a).   Accordingly, knowledge as the fruit of inquiry is not something acquired *de novo*, since "the soul was always in a state of knowing" (85d).   Hence Socrates observes that, if this is the truth about the soul, then Meno's problem is overcome.   If learning is a kind of remembering or recollecting—being alerted to what has been known but is presently lost to mind—then the paradox is resolved, and inquiry and learning are exclusively *anamnêsis*.[57]   In that case, however, learning is essentially proper identification.

Since we now have before us the doctrine of the *Meno* that, as Plato puts it, "the truth of all things is always in our soul" (86a), presumably we are better prepared to take up the question of the nature of "true opinion," eventually to distinguish it from *epistêmê* or *gnôsis*, and to learn the nature of its inferiority to the latter.   So once more we return to our recurring question: If, as Socrates asserts in the *Phaedo* (75c), we are born "knowing" the absolute equal, good, just, and holy—knowing yet not knowing through some strange forgetfulness—what is the import of this condition for understanding the moral rectitude and true opinions about righteousness of great men to whom both the *Protagoras* and the *Meno* bear testimony?   Or if, as is asserted of the slave boy at *Meno* 86a, his soul had cognizance of truth through all time, and true opinions had only "to be awakened by questioning to become knowledge," what does this suggest regarding the condition of some men in respect of knowledge? Is there not a true sense in which, according to the varying quality of men's minds or vitality of awareness, they are in a state of potential knowing but know it not? Plato is fond of this paradox and, as we shall see, returns to it in the *Theaetetus*.

The *Meno* offers the proper starting-point for discussion of Plato's conception of *doxa alêthês*, for it is in this dialogue that it appears for the first time along with its companion term *orthê doxa*. As already noted, it is in the *Meno* (93b-94d) that Plato singles out virtuous men of the past like Aristeides, Themistocles, and Thucydides as illustrious, each in his way, for uprightness. No one of these men, however, succeeded in instructing his children in virtue. Nevertheless Plato is fully prepared to assert: that good men have existed and do exist (96d); that virtue is not a natural disposition;[58] and that where it exists it is the resultant either of knowledge or of right opinion (98c). Wherever, says Plato, we find a man who is a guide to what is right, we find one of two conditions, *viz.*, either true opinion or knowledge (99a). But the men in question were virtuous not by knowledge but by right or "good opinion."[59] Plato's reasons for this judgment are as interesting as they are important for distinguishing between the two. That true opinion and knowledge are different is not something Socrates conjectures but something he is willing to affirm that he knows—a commitment, incidentally, well beyond Socrates' accustomed range (98b).

In point of efficacy, true opinion is as good a guide to the virtuous life as is knowledge. A man who possessed a valid but unverified opinion about the road from Athens to Larisa is as certain to arrive there as one who has actual knowledge of the way. In terms, then, of usefulness for life, right opinion is not inferior to knowledge.[60] But that is the extent of their equality. The man of right opinion may have acquired it in many ways. But however it may have been acquired, he can give no definite explanation of his reckoning. Admittedly, he has a true opinion, and that is commendable; but he cannot account for it, which is to say that he has no mental landmarks by which to retrace his way if he should lose it. By the same token, he is no guide to others in matters of virtue. Although he rightly estimates what is noble and good and honors them in his actions, he can give no reasoned explanation of his judgments. He can only reiterate that things look this way to him, that justice is better than injustice, and that self-restraint is better than excess, and act accordingly. We may admire his uprightness; but that does not assist us in adopting his ways, because he is quite unable to share the perspective which fosters his own virtue. Therefore, says Plato, because his excellence is not the fruit of knowledge but only of right opinion, he is powerless to direct others in the way (99b). In short, true opinions regarding virtue are beneficial for no one but the possessor. They are private and incommunicable. Men who possess them are, as it were, inspired, enraptured, and possessed of a "divine dispensation" (99d-e). They are analogous to soothsayers and diviners who utter noble things in transports of frenzy; but they are incapable of justifying their insights (99c).

In contrast with true opinion, there are two important characteristics of knowledge. The first is communicability. Knowledge must admit of mutual corroboration. The second characteristic of knowledge is an articulate account of any judgment entertained as true. Plato was fully aware that some measure of communal, as distinguished from private, authentication is a necessary criterion of knowledge in contrast with opinion. If there is to be knowledge, there must be escape from the solitary assertion: "It is so, according as it seems to me." It was this sort of pluralistic solipsism which Protagorean sensationalism incurred. Plato perceived that it guaranteed many private worlds but no knowledge.[61] Hence, at *Protagoras* 348d, Plato took the view that "if one observes something alone, forthwith one has to go about searching until one discovers somebody to whom one can show it off and who can corroborate it." However valid, therefore, true opinion may be, *epistêmê* requires a community of kindred minds wherein truth is jointly acknowledged and so is removed from the closet of merely private surmise. However, this does not obviate the fact that every man must apprehend reality for himself. Knowledge is still direct acquaintance and personal vision; nevertheless, the "vision" is possessed in common because some men occupy a similar vantage point and a comparable perspective.

This affords us one important reason why dialectic is the superior method of teaching. Plato often referred to it as a "joint-inquiry" which proceeds, through a series of joint-agreements, to some culminating common acknowledgment (ὁμολογία).[62] The dialogue itself, which Plato consistently employed as a vehicle of expression, points to his undeviating conviction that nothing can be called knowledge which is not wrought out step-by-step in mutual interchange, cross-examination, and joint-corroboration. So-called Platonic friendship is a joint-pursuance of truth. It is inspired by common devotion to truth and presumes goodwill, *eunoia*, among partners who share the enterprise.[63] Knowledge, then, in contrast with true opinion, is a social, not a solitary attainment, as is indeed brilliantly illustrated in the *Phaedrus* myth, 252c-257b.

The second criterion of knowledge, furthermore, requires that a reasoned account shall be given, or the stages exhibited, by which an eventuating judgment has been achieved. It was on this score also that virtuous men defaulted as teachers of their own excellence. They possessed no communicable *logos* of their own moral insights. Their judgments were true, but true opinions, although fine possessions and exceedingly useful so long as they stay fixed, are shifty and fugitive. Plato is fond of the analogy taken from the legend of Daedalus, for he several times refers to it.[64] The images fashioned by the mythical sculptor reputedly became animate and took to their heels, evading their owners. So opinions, even true ones, are elusive, play truant, and run away (97e). Thus Plato asserts at *Meno* 98a: So long as they stay with us true opinions "are a fine possession, and effect all that is good; but they do not care to stay for long, and run away out of the human soul, and thus are of no great value until one makes them fast with causal reasoning (αἰτίας λογισμῷ)."

This estimate of opinion is not peculiar to the *Meno*. A glance at the *Republic* and the *Gorgias* finds Plato complaining that men shift their opinions according to solicitations of desire and the urgencies of the moment. Under the spell of fear or pleasure, as if by sorcery, true opinions or beliefs are filched from men, although unwillingly.[65] And where there is want of knowledge, it is Plato's persisting indictment of sophistic rhetoric that it induces men to alter their opinions, whether true or false, to suit the designs of partisan speech.[66] This sort of persuasion is only possible where men entertain beliefs without knowledge. In the sphere of sensible experience also, where *epistêmê* has not come to the assistance of mere "appearance," things seem now one way and now another and continually equivocate.[67] Therefore, laudable as *doxa alêthês* may be, and even though it is "as good a guide to rightness of action as knowledge" (97b), it partakes of the same disabilities which attend *doxa* of every kind as contrasted with *epistêmê*. Accordingly Plato indicates that true opinion must be stabilized by being "turned into knowledge" (98a).

Concerning the nature of this transformation, Plato says but little in the *Meno* except that true opinions may be made fast by "causal reasoning" or reasoning according to principle. We have, perhaps, an example of this procedure at *Phaedo* 99d-e. There, instead of seeking to understand realities by way of perception and *doxa*, which is the sort of investigation he abandoned, Socrates has recourse to *logoi* to ascertain in them the truth of realities. In the *Meno* passage presently being considered, however, Plato explains his reference to "causal reasoning" by associating this process with *anamnêsis* as the way in which true opinion is transformed into knowledge. Furthermore it is to be remembered that the principal instrument for assisting recollection has already been shown to be dialectic (84d). Recollection is not something begun by dialectic but something presupposed and advanced by dialectic. And thus the likeliest interpretation of the associative process at *Phaedo* 73c-75e rather clearly suggests Plato's conviction that some recollection is the indispensable condition of empirical cognition (i.e., *doxa*) of particular instances of equality, justice, and beauty. The business of dialectic is to discriminate fully the *logos* implied, but not truly discerned, in ordinary experience.

The transformation of true opinions into knowledge through implementing the recollective process by dialectic was strikingly illustrated in the case of Meno's slave boy. By the skillful use of *elenchos*, Socrates was able to show that, quite unwittingly, the lad entertained true opinions concerning the square of the diagonal. At first, says Plato, true opinions were "stirred up in him, like a dream" (85c). As suitable questions were directed to him, he came to an exact understanding of the import of each one. At length he attained an articulate grasp of their comprehensive bearing.

In this fashion an incoherent apprehension was transformed little by little, into articulate comprehension, and, finally as a summation, into an unhesitating admission or concurrence (85b). The concluding pages of the *Meno* make it plain that Plato regards the knowledge upon which virtue depends to be attainable in a similar way. Furthermore, judging from *Meno* 99b and following, it is surely Plato's view that in the ethical sphere, quite as much as in the "scientific," men are also prepossessed of true opinions about justice and righteousness relating both to private and public *praxis* (98c). He is at pains to show that it is this which distinguished certain great Athenians for virtue. In them, we may suppose, there was a larger share of sensitivity or "respect" (αἰδώς) for justice. This, in his myth of Prometheus, Protagoras had declared to be the gift of Zeus to all men as the means of their social preservation.[68]   To this sort of right or true opinion, remarkable for vitality and clarity among a few but not altogether wanting among the many, Plato alludes frequently.[69] Even in souls corrupted by vice and wickedness there survives a divine and correct "intuition" of the difference between better and worse, together with a sorely embattled inclination toward the better[70]—a factor which caused Plato characteristically to affirm, as at *Republic* 589c, that even the brutalized man does not willingly err.   This surviving discernment does indeed become cloudy and dull through "corruption of morals," as Plato recurrently insists from the writing of the *Phaedo* through the *Laws*.[71]   Plato sometimes alludes to the possibility of its complete extinction but never enforces the point.[72] On the whole, he retains confidence in that which he variously designates as "the touch of the god-like" in man's nature or "divine kinship" (θεία συγγένεια);[73] and we have fairly sound reasons for supposing that this dignity registers itself, among other ways, in a capacity for *doxa alêthês* respecting the real Good and *aidôs* or reverence for it.

Perhaps this is why Plato suggests that when men are born, they are ordinarily full of zeal for truth and goodness.   Righteous indignation burns within them.   They follow the foregleams of goodness which come to them.[74]   Their "shame" or "reverence" has not yet waned and lost its keenness—that "reverence" for goodness which, we may believe, Socrates, in the *Protagoras*, took to be a divine endowment of the human soul.[75]   Nevertheless, wherever it chances to appear and win ascendancy, true opinion about the Good is vulnerable because of its unstable nature.   Under the force of criticism, of public censure or applause, a man's heart is moved.   True opinion becomes darkened within him as he gradually accommodates nobler discernments to prevailing sentiment.[76]   Even dialectic unskillfully applied and wrongly understood as the art of confutation unsettles young minds in respect to earlier convictions about the just and the noble.   And so a youth comes to believe that acquired and traditional beliefs in these matters are "dated" and no longer binding.[77]

The value of dialectic, properly understood and employed, becomes manifest.   Its work is arousement, purification, and quickening. It aims at recovering and renewing knowledge which is man's own.[78] It is a refining process, as we are reminded in the *Phaedo* and again in the *Sophist*.[79]   The fruit of dialectic is knowledge, for dialectic is a kind of alchemy capable of transmuting true opinions into defensible judgments.   It begins with what Plato sometimes intimates is a "divine apportionment." All the language of Plato suggests that it is a presentiment of the Good and a consciousness of responsibility to it. It is exactly this, seemingly, of which virtuous men, past or present, are recipients.[80] *Theia moira* is apprehension of the Good entertained in the form of true opinion and manifested in conduct. *Theia moira* is, as was intimated in the Promethean myth of *Protagoras* 322c, a divine gift to men. However, unlike Protagoras, Plato took the symbolism in earnest (361d). It does not perhaps exceed the bounds of probability to suggest that this *theia moira*, this *doxa alêthês*, may be understandable as the content of those notices of the Good to which Socrates alluded and on account of which he reckoned the *psuchê* to be prophetic. There is here, it seems, even some connection with his *daimonion* whose admonitions are not so exceptional as his ironical utterances in the *Republic* (496c) might suggest, at least not so exceptional for those who give heed. This divine apportionment signifies, perhaps, the aegis of the Good under which Socrates lived and by which, in the hour of inadvertency, as at *Apology* 33c, he was prevented from wrong-doing. At many points the instinctual cautionings of true opinion regarding right and wrong provided guidance where knowledge had as yet not found its way.

NOTES

1. *Protag.* 319a-b.
2. *Protag.* 333b, 357d, 360d. Cf. *Phaedo* 69b; *Charm.* 174c; *Meno* 88c.
3. *Protag.* 352c.
4. *Protag.* 361a-b. Cf. *Meno* 89c.
5. *Protag.* 318a, 319a.
6. *Gorg.* 463b and *Phaedr.* 260e.
7. Cf. *Euthyd.* 273d; *Gr. Hipp.* 284a; *Phaedr.* 268d. For the use of "experience," ἐμπειρία, in this denotation, see *Gorg.* 462c and 463b.
8. Cf. *Protag.* 319e f.; *Meno* 94a f.; *Alcib.* I, 119a.
9. *Meno* 93d.
10. *Meno* 93c, 94e.
11. *Meno* 89d-e.
12. *Meno* 80a. Cf. *Gorg.* 457c; *Rep.* 487b. In the case of those inexperienced in dialectic, the argument is led astray little by little until it accumulates in a contradiction.
13. *Meno* 93b.
14. *Meno* 70a, 89a f.
15. *Meno* 89b.
16. *Meno* 81d. Cf. *Phaedo* 72e, 76a.
17. *Rep.* 511d, 534a. The ontal correlates of νόησις, in numerous places of the *Republic*, are τὰ νοητά, the intelligibles, and, sometimes, αὐτὴ ἡ οὐσία. See *Rep.* 478a-b, 509d, 511a-c, 532b, 534c.
18. *Phaedo* 74a-75b. This passage is especially useful in exhibiting the *a priori* factor in knowledge. By means of the antecedent formal content of *nous*, the particulars are recognized as exemplars or deficient participants in the *eidos*. This is

the solution to the problem of "correctness of names" acutely examined in the *Cratylus*. The correctness of nomenclature depends upon the antecedent apprehension of the Form in which the particular "participates." See *Cratyl.* 439 a f.

19. *Phaedo* 73e, 75d; *Phaedr.* 248c, 250a; *Rep.* 621a.

20. *Phaedo* 73b-c; *Meno* 85c-d; *Phaedr.* 249c; *Theaet.* 198d-e. From the *Phaedo* and *Phaedrus* it appears that the *a priori* factor in knowledge is associated with the soul's pre-existence or its immortality. However, in such dialogues as the *Cratylus*, *Republic*, and *Theaetetus*, the *a priori* factor is not especially conjoined with transmigratory symbolism. The emphasis is upon native endowment of *nous* for "apprehension" and "presentiment" of intelligible objects. See n. 78 below for "belongings" of the soul; see especially *Alcib.* I, 133d; *Lysis* 221e.

21. *Meno* 85d; Cf. *Phaedo* 75d.

22. *Meno* 81e; *Phaedo,* 75e-76a.

23. *Meno* 89e. Cf. *Protag.* 327b, e.

24. *Meno* 84c, 86c; *Protag.* 333c, 336b.

25. *Phaedr.* 265d, 273e, 277b; *Cratyl.* 388b-c.

26. *Phaedo* 75d.

27. *Meno* 85b.

28. For Socrates' complaint on this point, see *Protag.* 319c-d. For Protagoras' justification, see *Protag.* 322c-323a and 325c f. The "civic consciousness" which, according to Protogoras, is common to men, we have already found to be prudential regard for custom and statutory law.

29. For the function of *aporia*, see *Meno* 80a, 84a; *Rep.* 487b, 538e; *Apol.* 23a-c; *Theaet.* 151d; *Soph.* 230b; *Alcib.* I, 116e.

30. *Soph.* 230d. Cf. *Alcib.* I, 117b-c.

31. See *Phaedo* 82d, 83b; *Rep.,* 498e; *Protag.* 333e; *Gorg.* 474b, 505b-c.

32. *Theaet.* 149a-151d. Cf. *Gorg.* 472b; 487e.

33. *Theaet.* 150d, 210b-c. Cf. *Symp.* 210a-e.

34. *Rep.* 534c. For Plato's comparison of opinion with dream consciousness as contrasted with waking thought, see *Rep.* 476c, 520c-d; *Apol.* 31a; *Polit.* 277d.

35. *Theaet.* 197c f.

36. *Phaedr.* 249e. Cf. *Phaedo* 75d. Socrates says, "we must always be born knowing these things, and must know them throughout our life." Also *Meno* 85d-86b.

37. Cf. *Meno* 81c-d; *Phaedo* 75e, 80d; *Phaedr.* 249c; *Rep.* 486d; *Phileb.* 65c.

38. *Phaedo* 78d. Cf. *Rep.* 534b. "And do you not also give the name dialectician to the man who is able to exact an account of the essence of each thing?" See definition of *anamιêsis, Phaedr.* 249b.

39. *Phaedo* 81d, 82e, 83c-d; *Rep.* 586a.

40. *Gorg.* 503c.

41. *Rep.* 560d. Cf. *Laws,* 732a.

42. *Rep.* 359c.

43. Cf. *Meno* 86a and *Theaet.* 148e.

44. *Theaet.* 193c, 198d-e. Cf. *Phaedo* 74a; *Phaedr.* 250d.

45. Cf. *Phaedo* 79d, 80b; *Rep.* 487a, 494d; *Epist.* VII, 344a.

46. Cf. *Phaedr.* 278a, and *Theaet.* 150d.

47. For the correlation of learning and discovery, see *Lach.* 186c-e; *Alcib.* I, 114a; *Phaedo* 85c; *Cratyl.* 438b; *Theaet.* 150d. For discovery as the fruition of dialectical inquiry, see *Alcib.* I, 129b; *Meno* 81d, 84c; *Cratyl.* 436a; *Phaedr.* 278a; *Rep.* 392c, 412b, 429a, 472b.

48. J. Burnet, *Greek Philosophy* (London, 1950), 222. Also A. E. Taylor, *Plato* (New York, 1936), 136-137.

49. *Meno* 84c-d; *Theaet.* 151d, 210c.

50. For comparable instances of the power of proper questioning, see *Meno* 84d;

85c; *Phaedr.* 276e; *Theaet.* 150c; *Soph.* 265d. The phrase *orthos logos* occurs rarely in the dialogues. The one instance that approximates in meaning is *Laws* 696c, where the man of cultivation is described as he whose feeling of pleasure and pain are in accord with "right reason." He is obviously the antithesis of the man of greatest ignorance, *Laws* 689a, whose feelings are not in accord with "rational judgment." This latter conception of ignorance recalls *Phaedr.* 238b and *Soph.* 228b. The *orthos logos* of *Epist.* VII, 327c seems to suggest the introduction of formal instruction like the *orthê trophê* of *Tim.* 44c. But in the latter place, *Tim.* 44b, we do get an indication of what *orthos logos* really means. It is accurate identification and discrimination between the Same and the Other, *viz.*, between true and deficient reality; see *Tim.* 51d. In short, *orthos logos* is the opposite of *doxa pseudês*, *Soph.* 240d. It is therefore almost certainly associated with *doxa alêthês*, as superior to mere *doxa*, but not necessarily always equivalent to knowledge for which Plato regularly reserves the word *epistêmê*.

51. See *supra*, n. 34.

52. *Meno* 85d, 81e; *Lach.* 186e; *Gorg.* 486e. For ἀναλαμβάνειν as recovery of knowledge, see *Phaedo* 75e; *Theaet.* 198d; *Phileb.* 34c.

53. *Meno* 71b. *Cf. Theaet.* 165b, 191c.

54. *Cf.* N. K. Smith, *Immanuel Kant's Critique of Pure Reason* (London, 1929), 47-48. Kant makes the following statement: "This analysis supplies us with a considerable body of knowledge, which, while nothing but explanation or elucidation of what has already been thought in our concepts, though in a confused manner, is yet prized as being, at least as regards its form, new insight." Without the "matter" of sense-perception, theoretical knowledge was not one whit advanced, however, it might be refined by analysis. Whether Plato or Kant is finally correct, it should be clear that "knowledge" means something quite different for each of them; *viz.*, it has different objects. For Kant, its objects are phenomena; for Plato, noumena. *Cf. Tim.* 52c.

55. *Rep.* 509e, 511d, 533c; *Meno* 98c; *Tim.* 51d. The term noumenon is probably Plato's coinage. It stands for the realm of intelligible objects, τὰ νοητά which are identified with τὸ παντελῶς ὄν, or most real Being. *Rep.* 477a. It is, of course, very interesting that Kant should regard the phenomenal sphere as the locus of "veridical knowledge," whereas, for Plato, it is in relation to the noumenal alone that "accurate" knowledge is possible. See *Rep.* 533d; *Phileb.* 59c; *Tim.* 29b-c. This is not merely because of Kant's empiricism, but because both Kant and his contemporaries were not aware that physical reality does not admit of *exhaustive* rational analysis. Unlike Plato, they confound the ideal and the actual.

56. *Cf. Euthyd.* 276b f. See A. E. Taylor, *Plato* (New York, 1936), 136-137. Taylor, I think, takes the *eristicos logos* too seriously and unnecessarily begins looking for comparisons.

57. We thus come in *Meno* 81d upon Plato's distinctive doctrine of learning as *anamnêsis*. *Cf. Phaedo* 72e, *Phaedrus* 249e. Here, as at *Phaedrus* 249b-251a, *anamnêsis* presupposes the pre-existence of the soul. In the companion *Phaedo* passage (72e-76e), the argument is reversed, and the truth of immortality is inferred from the pre-possession of truth, unaccountable save on the hypothesis of previous existence (76d-e). There is not much doubt that Plato took seriously the mutuality of *anamnêsis* and prior existence of the soul, although apart from a possible oblique reference at *Republic* 610e-611e, it is not elsewhere stressed. Thus, the testimony of the *Timaeus* on the immortality of the individual soul and dependence of learning upon it is ambiguous. To be sure, there man as microcosm partakes of the World Soul and of its movement and rationality. He learns and becomes intelligent in so far as "the circle of the same" is dominant within him (44a-c). However, *Timaeus* 90a-d obviously revives the standpoint of the *Phaedo* and *Phaedrus*. Thus, while we can agree with A. E. Taylor (*Plato*, 136), that the

philosophic importance of the doctrine of *anamnêsis* is its indication "that the acquisition of knowledge is not a matter of passively receiving instruction," we need not discount with him the close association of the doctrine with the continuous existence of the soul. *Cf.* F. M. Cornford, "The Division of the Soul," *Hibbert Journal,* XXIII (1929-30), 209. To overly domesticate the *psuchê* within the world, is to deprive Plato of his customary way of accounting for the *a priori* factor in knowing. All the same, it must also be said that it is the essential "kinship" (συγγένεια) of the soul with intelligible reality or the conformity (*i.e.,* ξυγγενὴς ἀληθείας, *Rep.* 487a) between *nous* and *noumena* which is also required, along with prior existence of the soul, to grasp the meaning of *anamnêsis.*

58. *Meno* 98d, 99e. *Phusis* is contrasted, presumably, with *technê.* *Cf. Laws* 889a f.

59. *Meno* 99b. The word *eudoxia,* as a synonym for true opinion, has, so far as I can tell, no other instance in the dialogues.

60. *Meno* 98c, 97b. *Cf. Theaet.* 200e.

61. *Cratyl.* 385e-386c. "Do you think this is true of the real things, that their reality is a separate one for each person, as Protagoras said with his doctrine that man is the measure of all things?" See *Theaet.,* 160c.

62. For dialectic as a process of "joint-inquiry" and "agreement," see *Protag.* 333c, 336a-b; *Meno* 86c, 84c. The reason for Plato's use of the dialogue form is to be located here. Dialogue stands for a common undertaking in pursuance of truth at the start of which common "consent" in its pursuit is pledged. See *Gorg.* 457c; *Crito* 49d. For this reason also Socrates consistently objects to long and solitary harangues in which the speaker pours out his unexamined prejudgments. The Academy was the logical expression of Plato's conviction that knowledge is attainable only in community. See *Soph.* 218b.

63. *Gorg.* 487a; *Phaedr.* 255b, 241c; *Theaet.* 151c; *Protag.* 337b; *Polit.* 262c.

64. *Meno* 97d. *Cf. Euthy.* 11c; *Rep.* 529e.

65. *Rep.* 413a-b; *Gorg.* 493a. *Cf. Rep.* 508d.

66. *Gorg.* 455a, 458e-459d; *Phaedr.* 260c-263b.

67. *Rep.* 479a-c, 524d. *Cf. Phaedo* 99e, and *Phaedr.* 263b.

68. *Cf. Protag.* 322c-d.

69. *Meno* 99b. *Cf. Rep.* 368a, 485c, 505e, 534c, 585b; *Gorg.* 474b; *Phaedo* 73a; *Phaedr.* 237d, 250a; *Polit.* 309c.

70. *Cf. Laws* 950b-c and *Meno* 99b-c. See also *Phaedr.* 237d; *Rep.* 440a-b, 611b f.

71. *Epist.* VII, 343e; *Phaedo* 81b, 82e f.; *Phaedr.* 247a-b; *Theaet.* 176e f.; *Soph.* 253e; *Laws* 888a *et al.*

72. *Cf. Rep.* 410a; *Protag.* 325a; *Gorg.* 525c; *Phaedo* 113e.

73. *Cf. Rep.* 368a; *Laws* 899e; *Rep.* 501e; *Polit.* 309c; *Tim.* 90a.

74. *Rep.* 441a-b. Here true opinion and the "spirited" faculty are, seemingly, rather closely associated. The question, however, should be weighed in the light of the *Phaedrus,* centering around 253d.

75. *Cf. Protag.* 361d with 322a-c. See also *Phaedr.* 253d, 254b. At *Rep.* 560a Plato describes the restoration of "awe and reverence" when order and reason are re-introduced into the "divided man."

76. *Rep.* 492c.

77. *Rep.* 538c-539a.

78. *Phaedo* 75e. *Cf. Lysis,* 222a; *Rep.* 504c, 586e; *Phaedr.* 248b; *Tim.* 90c.

79. *Phaedo* 82d, and *Soph.* 230d.

80. *Meno* 99a, 99e, 100b.

CHAPTER V

True Opinion Examined

I mean that the really true and assured opinion about honour, justice, goodness and their opposites is divine, and when it arises in men's souls, it arises in a godlike race.—*Politicus* 309c

1. *Doxa Alêthês*

AMONG the terms which recur in Plato's epistemological vocabulary perhaps the most elusive is "true opinion." In the *Meno* (97b-c, 99a), Plato seems to use either *doxa alêthês*, true opinion, or *orthê doxa*, right opinion, indiscriminately and with approximate meaning. If there is the slightest variance between them, it is that *orthê doxa* possesses a connotation more narrowly ethical, while *doxa alêthês* has relevance to any mode of apprehension of Ideal reality that falls short of knowledge, *epistêmê*. Either, however, seems to entail assured personal but unreasoned and therefore as yet obscure presentiment of abiding truth—the kind of thing that must be presupposed for the onset of "recollection" as described in *Phaedo* 75 and *Phaedrus* 250.[1] The *Meno* seems to presume that either term may refer to such truth as is in fact acknowledged by men and finds real if precarious embodiment in traditional and conventional morality, the signal representatives of which are given prominence in the dialogue.

That traditional and even prevailing mores do embody some truth and goodness, Plato surely allows for, in the *Meno* as elsewhere.[2] Socrates defends this notion in the *Gorgias* (488d); and in the *Republic* we are alerted to the value of *dogmata* about the just and the excellent, inculcated from childhood, which may be perniciously relativized by unprincipled disputation or overpowered by newer opinions engendered by the tyranny of inferior passions.[3] There are, moreover, "the many conventions of the many" about the excellent and the honorable.[4] These, though unstable and midway between truth and falsity, are entertained by *doxa* and are not wholly devoid of intelligibility. Plato is here beginning to depend upon the pervasive principle so clearly stated in the *Philebus*: "That in which there is no admixture of truth can never truly come into being or exist."[5]

Socrates had customarily insisted that virtue was to be looked for only in company with knowledge or wisdom.[6] In both the *Protagoras* and the *Meno* (96e), Plato is showing signs of uneasiness in the recognition that there is, as a matter of fact, a considerable amount of virtue without benefit of *epistêmê*. And so he is obliged to consider on what basis it may be accounted for. That knowledge is superior to true opinion is, for him, not a conjecture but a certainty.[7] But, modifying the stricter Socratic standpoint, he is constrained to admit that in point of usefulness (for those who have it) true opinion is not inferior to knowledge for attainment of moral excellence.[8] However, the analogy of Daedalus (*Meno* 97d) teaches that, although righteousness and the proper opinion of its nature are not altogether wanting among men, there is nevertheless needed a *paideusis* capable of transforming the exceptional, incommunicable, and uncertain into a greater surety. Thus, although strictly inferior, *doxa* is not wholly discontinuous with knowledge. Indeed, it even provides a point of beginning from which advance to knowledge may be made.

In the *Republic* (534b) we have confirmation on this point. Here Plato seems to speak of any respectable citizen who, whatever the probity of his life, if his excellence rests only upon *doxa* is said to dream and doze περὶ τοῦ ἀγαθοῦ, concerning the Good. His condition corresponds with that of the exemplary and renowned men of the *Meno*:

[If he is] unable to define in his discourse and distinguish and abstract from all other things the aspect or idea of the good, and who cannot, as it were in battle, running the gauntlet of all tests, and striving to examine everything by essential reality and not by opinion, hold his way through all this without tripping in his reasoning—the man who lacks this power, you will say, does not really know the good itself or any particular good; but if he apprehends any adumbration of it, his contact with it is by opinion not by knowledge. . . .[9]

This passage and *Meno* 99b-c mutually supplement and illuminate each other. In the *Meno*, the *aretê* of Themistocles and the rest is not an effect of knowledge, and so must be referred to the alternative cause, *doxa alêthês*. Thus, none of the venerable men is able to instruct others in virtue or give an account, *logos*, of its principle and nature. It can scarcely be more plain that dialectic is, in the *Republic*, that which Plato now holds to be the real meaning of αἰτίας λογισμός. By way of dialectic, as at *Meno* 98a, true opinions, presently unaccountable and fugitive, are stabilized and rendered communicable and knowable. E. S. Thompson's assertion seems justified: "It appears in the *Meno* (85c) that δόξαι arise in the individual soul, and that it is by dialectic, by friction with other minds, that these become converted into matters of knowledge."[10] In like manner Shorey says: "Practically knowledge is true opinion, sifted and tested by dialectic, and fixed by causal reasoning."[11] Shorey alludes to a difference between "causal reasoning" and dialectic. This cannot be. *Republic* 534b, set within the full-scale treatment of dialectic, disproves it; for dialectic is shown to be the supreme instrument of *epistêmê* in the attainment of highest principles. But the bearing of the evidence seems clear enough: The "material content" of *doxa alêthês* is inseparably connected with an *a priori* apprehension or presentiment of truth and goodness which Plato takes to be somehow congenital with the human mind. It bespeaks the soul's conversancy with the intelligible Forms, and this attenuated familiarity is the presupposition of *anamnêsis*.

So far, we have sought to explain how or why it is *true* opinion with which we deal. It remains to be shown why, on the other hand, it is also true *opinion*, that is, why this mode of apprehension is closely associated, at least initially, with *doxa* rather than with *epistêmê*. Meanwhile our passage *Republic* 534b is important because it, along with 506c, represents perhaps the most evident allusion in the *Republic* to the *doxa alêthês* of the *Meno*. In 506c we are again apprised of a δόξα περὶ τοῦ ἀγαθοῦ. And, there, true opinion of the Good is depreciated in comparison with *epistêmê*. This is because, recalling *Meno* 97c, true opinion "without *nous*" is said scarcely to differ from the case of the blind man who chances to go the right way. But neither passage intends to depreciate altogether the worth of true opinion. They only forcefully suggest, as E. S. Thompson noted, that "the good is the enemy of the best" in this case as in others.[12]

Other references to *doxa alêthês* as related to ideal insight are to be found at *Symposium* 202a f. and perhaps at *Phaedrus* 237d. Since these are to be evaluated in Chapter VIII, we refer here only to instances in the *Philebus* and the *Politicus*. The true opinion of *Phileblus* 11b and 60d, regularly associated with *nous*, can, rather assuredly, be related to true opinion περὶ τοῦ ἀγαθοῦ—the kind we have been closely associating with the prominent *Meno* passages. Its antecedent in the dialogue is probably 37e ff. Pleasure is being discussed—pleasures associated with *doxa alêthês* and *epistême* or, by contrast, those associated with *doxa pseudês* and ignorance. It is the preferability of the former which is to be argued, and eventually, in 64c and 66b, they do find a place in the "mixed life." But the nature of true opinion and its difference from or likeness to *epistême* is not at issue nor is it illuminated. It is, however, noteworthy that here, as in the *Seventh Epistle* (342c), *nous*, *epistême*, and *doxa alêthês* are closely linked with one another in the same "class" as if they are in some way complementary.[13] If our previous analysis is sound, then the complementary relation should consist in the fact that *doxa alêthês* stands to *nous* and *epistême* in the relation of potentiality to actuality; for knowledge comes to exist in the transformation of true opinion into stable and communicable judgments.

There are two places in the *Politicus* that apparently hark back to the true opinion of the *Republic* and the *Meno*. *Politicus* 277d-278e should be compared with 390c-e. In addition to the dictum that no one can ever attain even to a small part of truth or wisdom if he starts from false opinion (278d), there is the implication that he may so attain if he starts with its opposite, namely, true opinion. Both 277d and 309c rather easily suggest something like the spontaneous *doxa alêthês* of the *Meno*. And the contrast between "waking" and "dream" states of the mind suggests the difference between true opinion and knowledge at *Republic* 534c. The passage 309c-d seems to reassert the main views of the *Republic*. On the one hand, there is reference to the really true and assured *doxa* about the just and the good which is "divine" and arises in a godlike race, we may suppose, somewhat spontaneously (309c). On the other hand, there is also such true opinion as is implanted (ἐμποιεῖν) by rightly received education (309d). The latter corresponds with Plato's statement in the *Republic* respecting the kind of "knowledge" held by the subordinate classes as compared with the *epistême* of the philosophic guardians. A brief consideration of this form of true opinion is now in order and will conclude this present phase of our investigation.

Republic 428e-431c leaves no suspicion of a doubt that the class of guardians who partake of knowledge, though few in number, are to lead and rule the many who do not. But it is equally clear that this leadership is not to be arbitrary. If it is not to be so, however, then the subordinate classes must in some measure share in the knowledge of the guardians, but this can only be in the form of *orthê doxa* (430b, 431c). Therefore it is the business of popular *paideusis* to find every means possible to convince the citizenry of the rightness of the laws and to instill in them an abiding *doxa* of their validity (430a). The opinion will assuredly be *alêthês* in so far as it derives from superior knowledge of the guardians. Thus we have an inculcated or implanted true opinion in addition to the spontaneous and fortuitous variety.[14] It is further indicated that courage in the timocratic class is the unfailing conservation of *orthê doxa* and lawful belief.[15] To what extent Plato means to stress "conservation," as distinct from "inculcation," in the engendering of true opinion is not really clear. It seems likely, however, that true opinion has identical or nearly identical function whether he is thinking of it as a stage preparatory and antecedent to *epistêmê* or as a consequent and derivative of education in the hands of those who know. In either case, what he says of it in the *Meno* will hold true. It is as useful a guide to righteous action, for those who have it, as is knowledge.

2. *Doxa* AND *Doxa Alêthês*

Our inquiry concerning *doxa alêthês* has so far led to the result that we can say it is a condition of knowing in which there is no want of *truth* but want of *knowledge*. It is true, no doubt, but not known to be true; so in this respect it remains short of knowledge, as yet with the same defect as *doxa*. Furthermore, there is here registered Plato's conviction that, whatever the method of verification, the method does not turn *true* opinion into truth; rather, it turns true *opinion* into knowledge. Already in the *Laches* (194b-c) the need to transform something like true opinion into knowledge is recognized as Laches stumbles in his effort to articulate his thought, to which presently he cannot give "the stability of speech." This is comparable with the "perplexity" in which, according to *Meno* 99b-d, men distinguished for virtue find themselves when attempting vainly to communicate the basis of their laudable convictions. So for Plato truth does not consist in verification, even that of dialectic; but it is surely exhibited and communicated by dialectic. To this extent and in this manner, knowledge is the conservation or repristination of what is given for recollection. And the *given* rests upon a prior conversancy of *nous* with superior reality. It is not exceptional but characteristic with Plato to hold, as stated in the *Philebus*, "that mind is either identical with truth or of all things most like it and truest."[16]

But now we must acknowledge that the foregoing excursis on true opinion is complicated by a seemingly disparate usage of *doxa* in prominent passages of the *Republic* and elsewhere. In these, *doxa* acquires rather technical significance and is juxtaposed to *gnôsis* or *epistêmê* as a mode of cognition that at first seems to have little to do with the *a priori* in experience. To begin with, *Republic* 476b-478e is certainly a momentous step forward in Plato's formulation of theory of knowledge. The view taken is seemingly comprehensive enough to allow room for the kind of "investigation of nature" which Socrates, according to his word at *Phaedo* 83a-b, had abandoned. It also makes a place for the kind of inquiry that he subsequently espoused and which investigates reality through *logoi*.[17] In the *Republic* passage, Plato distinguishes a noetic capacity (*dunamis*) called *doxa*, and marks it off from another power of cognition called *gnôsis*. These powers, as is well known, Plato correlated with their appropriate ontological referents. *Gnôsis* is correlated with τὸ γνωστόν, namely, with what is at once "most real" being (τὸ παντελῶς ὄν) and "most knowable" being (τὸ παντελῶς γνωστόν). On the other hand, *doxa* is correlated with what stands "between" (τὸ μεταξύ) that reality which completely is and τὸ μὴ ὄν, or what completely is not. Both *doxa* and its objective referent, "the opinable," have less clearness (σαφήνεια) than has *gnôsis* together with its intelligible object. But *doxa* has greater clearness then "nescience" (ἄγνοια), the latter being correlated with not-Being (478c).

In what follows, 478e-479e, it is scarcely doubtful that τὸ δοξαστόν, the ontal referent of *doxa*, is identified with the particular things of the sensible world. At the very least it is closely associated with sensible experience. This is surely confirmed in the figure of the "Divided Line," *Republic* 509d-510b, and is seconded by the familiar distinction between "the visible" and "the invisible" at *Phaedo* 79a, with which *Timaeus* 52a also is to be compared. The definitive confirmation is supplied at *Republic* 534a, where *doxa* is taken to be the mode of cognition suitable to the whole range of Becoming.[18] *Genesis* is, of course, the sphere of continual physical change and is contrasted by Plato with that realm of Being which ever remains the same.[19] This contraposition of knowledge and reality in correlation is too familiar to require further elaboration or support. It is manifestly presupposed by *Phaedrus* 248b ff. and is given late illustration and reaffirmation in both the *Timaeus* and the *Philebus*.[20]

At *Philebus* 61d, knowledge is said to consist of two kinds. The one "turns its eyes toward transitory things, the other toward things which neither come into being nor pass away, but are the same and immutable forever." In the *Timaeus*, 28a and 52b, Becoming is said to be the object of *doxa*, the latter operative with the aid of "unreasoning sensation." And once again the objective referent of *nous* is "the self-identical Form" (52a). *Nous*, as we should expect, is said to be stable and immovable by persuasion and is always "in company with true reasoning" (51e). By way of contrast, *doxa*, and here the term *doxa alêthês* reappears in 51d, is said to attain only "likelihood" or probability and is entirely movable by persuasion and arises in us also by instruction.[21] In sum, we have herein a recurrence of Plato's insistence upon the inferiority of *doxa*, even of true opinion, in comparison with *epistêmê* or *gnôsis*. We have, in addition, a fuller account of the "fallibility" of *doxa* as contrasted with the "infallibility" of *gnôsis*, such as is asserted, for instance, at *Republic* 477e.

Quite plainly now, our question is how we shall conceive the relation of the kind of *doxa* which Plato evidently correlates with the particulars of Becoming to the *true* opinion of *Meno* 97b and other passages we have been discussing. While the former *doxa* seems to represent phenomenal knowledge, true opinion seems to imply a trans-phenomenal content.

We can begin by agreeing with N. R. Murphy that although *doxa* is difficult to define it seems, especially in certain *Republic* passages, to remain close to the perception of the senses. We may further agree that the word "acquaintance" is possibly a suitable indication of its cognitive mode or, in Murphy's words, "getting acquainted with objects otherwise than by understanding their nature."[22] It may be argued, for example, that men possess *doxa* rather than *gnôsis* who, as Plato says at *Republic* 479e, apprehend "sounds and sights" and delight in beautiful tones, colors, and figures but whose thought is incapable of apprehending αὐτὸ τὸ καλόν, that is, the essence or self-identical Form of Beauty. A similar statement is made concerning opining of justice, and the whole condition here described is said to characterize the *philodoxoi* (480a). These latter are surely akin to the cave-dwellers of 514a whose state of mind is evidently *doxa* and whose avenue of cognition is pretty exclusively *aisthêsis* or sense-perception. For on this point we must concur with Shorey's view that "sense-perception is rightly said to involve judgment and so issues in δόξα, opinion or belief."[23] We do not get anything like a fuller development of the "judgment," however, until *Theaetetus* 190a. There, as well as in *Philebus* 38d and *Sophist* 263e, *doxa* is the resulting affirmation or denial which follows the reflection of thought. Outwardly expressed, it is speech or proposition, *logos*, and it may have the further quality of being true or false. In the light of this,

Shorey's interpretation seems all the more justified that for Plato the
"senses are the organs through which, not the faculties by which,
we know."[24]

All this does well enough for *doxa,* taken alone; but the *doxa
alêthês,* with which we are concerned, is not only said to be *true,* but,
in addition, we have seen that it implies some immediate acquaintance
with ideal realities which cannot be attributed to mere sensible experience. Is it possible that while *doxa alêthês* is not wholly dependent
upon sensible experience it is regularly possessed in company with
sensible experience? We must explore this possibility.

N. R. Murphy seems in some measure to account for the ambiguity within the single concept of *doxa* when he says: "Apparently,
the word refers to the kind of intellectual acquaintance we get with
an object which we have seen and touched (if it is thus sensible) or
have felt and are familiar with, but have not thought out or explained
to ourselves."[25] Murphy appears to suggest that, apart from sensibility, there may be apprehension which is not sensuous, and this, indeed, seems to be a presupposition of the "learning" which Plato says
is wholly *anamnêsis.*[26] As a matter of fact, it is with such "recollection" that true opinion is from the first most closely associated,
beginning at *Meno* 85c. Thereby, we are first alerted to a certain
trans-phenomenal reference belonging to it. But even if we should
make the above inference on the strength of Murphy's somewhat
vague suggestion, we still would not have answered the question why
Plato does call our state of knowing *doxa,* however true it may be.
We shall now propose that, while true opinion is not *explainable* by
reference to sense experience, it is regularly entertained in conjunction
with sense experience.

A fuller answer to our question, then, requires that we take explicitly into account the positive contribution of the senses in assisting
the process of *anamnêsis.* We first clearly encounter mention of
this contribution at *Phaedo* 73c-76a, though it may have been implied
in the instance of the slave boy in the *Meno.* In any case, at *Phaedo*
76a it is stated "that it is possible, on perceiving a thing by sight or
hearing or any other sense, to call to mind from that perception
another thing which had been forgotten, which was associated with
the thing perceived. . . ." A principle of "association" is suggested
here as at 73c f., and the context, of course, makes it plain that what
has been "forgotten" are the ideal Forms which sensible particulars,
being "deficient" likenesses, serve to call to mind. Especially, it is
the "deficient" character of sensible particulars, *i.e.,* their like-unlike-

ness,[27] which serves to provoke recall, not only of absolute equality, but of other absolute "essences" such as the Beautiful and the Good.[28] From this we are led naturally to the view that, ordinarily, *doxa* will not be merely the "knowledge" of particulars; it will be "knowledge" of particulars as-informed-by-the-Ideas, so that really there will be no apprehension of particulars which is not implicitly and potentially apprehension of the Ideas in which they participate. Even cognition of particulars, then, in the mode of *doxa,* assisted by "unreasoning sensation," is *de facto* apprehension of the Ideas, though only unwitting and implicit. In order for *doxa* to become *epistêmê* it is necessary that the Idea implied, and constituting the formal content of *doxa,* be descried, that is, be isolated by dialectic and an account or *logos* be rendered.[29] In this methodical way a true opinion may become known as true—what is implicit rendered explicit.

Such an intimate connection between *aisthêsis* and *doxa,* as is suggested in the *Phaedo* passage, seems equally manifest in *Republic* 478a and 479d. Nothing, admittedly, is said there about men's *doxai* being true. It is only said that they do have opinions about the Just and the Beautiful *as these Ideas mingle* (i.e., have *koinônia*) *with actions and bodies and present themselves under a multiplicity of aspects.* This, it would seem, is analogous with the condition of *virtuous* men of the *Meno* who are loyal to such goodness as they opine, but can give no account of it either to themselves or to others. The *Republic* passages here mentioned further indicate the close relation between sense-perception and *doxa.* They appear also further to illustrate the instrumental value of the senses in recollection. This instrumentality is subsequently reaffirmed in *Phaedrus* 249d and made the basis for the assertion that the philosopher is one who, seeing beauty on earth, is thereby prompted to recollect true Beauty in heaven and is stricken with love and aspiration. But it is also said that only "a few, approaching the images through the darkling organs of sense, behold *in them* the nature of that which they imitate [*i.e.,* the Forms], and these few do this with difficulty" (250b). The many resign the quest or, rather, never begin it, and feed upon *doxa* (248b).

The point seems to be that most men do not pierce through to the essence αὐτὴ ἡ οὐσία, which gives structure to the particular.[30] They are preoccupied with the particular. They do perceive the particular and so they cannot help apprehending it as "informed" by the Ideas; but, as Plato suggests at *Phaedrus* 250e and *Republic* 493e, they do not disengage the essence from the thing. Accordingly, their state of mind is *doxa*, hardly true opinion and in no sense moving in the direction of *epistêmê*. There is want of clearness, definition, and *logos*. The same obstacle to the attainment of truth is mentioned by Plato in the *Seventh Epistle* (343c). In methodical advance toward the real essence, the ultimate object, "cognizable and true," is always given in company with distracting quality (τὸ ποῖον) with the result that men are confused and settle for "images," without trying to search beyond the appearance for the nature of "the Fifth," or real Being.

Do we not see the following indications? First, that *doxa* is a state of knowing with twofold content: there is the datum of sensation but accompanying it, and "peering through," as we might say, is the trans-phenomenal Ideal content. Consequently, *doxa* is, necessarily, unwitting apprehension of Ideal realities in so far as particulars partake of them, or, conversely, in so far as the Forms are instanced by the particulars. In this, we seem to have come within reach of a solution to the problem noted earlier: *Doxa* seemed to denote phenomenal knowledge only, while *doxa alêthês* implied a trans-phenomenal content. The truth seems to be that all *doxa* carries an Ideal content whether discerned or not. *Doxa* veers in the direction of true opinion in the measure that the Ideal content is recognized and acknowledged though as yet it is not systematically disengaged from the carrier. In proportion as this tendency is being accentuated Plato seems inclined to class *doxa alêthês* with *nous* and *epistêmê*.[31]

Again, in the second place, *doxa* is an incompleted mode of cognition—the state of "knowing" where *nous* has as yet not pressed through or behind the instances to Ideal objects. It has not discriminated the One in the Many.[32] Yet *doxa* would not be "knowing" at all did it not entertain the Ideal content even though unawares. Thirdly, because *doxa* does not discriminate the Form *in* or *with* the particular, it cannot give an account of the truth of its judgments. Already we have seen at *Phaedo* 76b that *epistêmê* entails being able "to give an account," the *logos* of the matter. And this, indeed, is what Socrates undertakes to delineate in the famous "Second Voyage" passage of *Phaedo* 99d. Inability to give an "account" is the defect in men of true opinion at *Meno* 98a. But to be able to give an "account" is to stabilize opinion with "causal reasoning." Until this is done, however true opinion may be, it is not known to be true, nor is its truth in any sense enforceable. Fourthly, may we not say that *doxa* is, so to speak, the minimum stage of cognition? As such it is the apprehension of Becoming, a world-in-change, which is structured or informed by and is *representative* of the Ideal in so far as the Forms mingle with actions and bodies, as Plato clearly indicates not only at *Republic* 476b but later and more definitively at *Politicus* 278d and *Timaeus* 50c. Furthermore, it appears in most respects likely that, since the Forms, whether discriminated or not, are obliquely apprehended in a blend with the data of sense, the content of *doxa* will be a twofold admixture: The Ideal Structure will be given *in* and *with* the complex of what may be called sense qualities. It does not appear that Plato devised a name to distinguish this complex as apprehended from the Ideal content until, in the *Theaetetus* and the *Sophist,* the word φαντασία came to serve something of this purpose.[33] *Phantasia* seems closely related with the subjective content of *aisthêsis* and dependent upon sense alone as at *Sophist* 264a.

It is now quite possible to understand how, from a certain vantage point, *doxa* and *doxa alêthês* are inseparably related and difficult to differentiate one from the other. We have seen that *doxa* is the *more-or-less* unwitting apprehension of Becoming as structured. And so we are forced back again to our original question. We have to ask in what respect *doxa* acquires the added "quality" of being either true or false. The answer seems to be that it will tend to be true in so far as the mind is in process of awakening, through "recollection" as described in the *Phaedrus* (250a, 251d), to renewed discrimination of the Forms. Or, short of this, it will tend to be *true* opinion in so far as the ideal Forms, as instanced by the particulars of sense, receive the approbation and consent of the whole mind. On the other side, *doxa* will tend to take on the "quality" of falsity in so far as the mind is content to remain with the particulars *as informed,* and, like the prisoners of the Cave, stubbornly mistake these "shadows," as Plato parabolically terms them, for the whole of the real.[34] The condition of the Cave dwellers is δοξάζειν as at 516e, but its falsity must be referred to "affection." It is, indeed, the affection of the "lovers of spectacles."[35] Or, again, with equal correctness, we may say that false opinion and *philodoxia* go together.[36] *Philodoxia* is not only apprehension of Becoming but contentment with it together with the ensuing "judgment" that takes the phenomenal to be the real. False opinion is precisely double ignorance (*amathia*) which, to the awareness of Becoming, adds the judgment: It is real Being. It is precisely the benighted condition of the people in the Cave. It is the *doxa pseudês* which Plato undertook to refute definitively in the *Sophist* (240d); it is misidentification of true Being. Withal, Plato is fully aware that, in the absence of a valid method for isolating and identifying the Ideal content of *doxa*, a reliable method through dialectic, it remains a "divine dispensation" if some men entertain true rather than false opinion, if conventional morality embodies some verity, and if anything at all turns out well in the state.

We evidently arrive at the result that *doxa* is something like a neutral minimum state of cognition which is potentially true or false by the addition of what we may, with some justification, call a "judgment" (κρίσις). Admittedly it is not until the *Theaetetus* and the *Sophist* that Plato articulates the concept of the judgment. In the later writings, with a few earlier exceptions, *viz.*, *Republic* 582d, *krisis* is the agreement and decision of the mind with itself. In the *Theaetetus*, a judgment is said to issue in *doxa* and is verbalized in statement or proposition.[37] It involves affirmation or denial.[38] But, now, already in the *Republic*, *doxa* implies decision or judgment, and the differential between true or false opinion depends, as already suggested, on the bent of affection (*pathêma*). Plato asserts there are those "who view many beautiful things but do not see the beautiful itself and are unable to follow another's guidance to it, and many just things, but not justice itself, and so in all cases. . . ."[39] Apprehension takes in the particulars as "informed" but does not discriminate the Forms in which the particulars participate. Such men are said "to opine" rather than "to know." All this is as we should expect: Those who merely opine do not identify the Forms peering through the *sensum*. Now follows the interesting statement: "Shall we not also say that the one welcomes (ἀσπάζεσθαι) and loves (φιλεῖν) the things subject to knowledge and the other those subject to opinion?"[40] What is it, then, that aids and encourages true opinion as contrasted with mere *doxa*? Evidently, it is a certain "spirit of truthfulness" (ἀψεύδεια), a disinclination to "falsity," an affinity for truth which, at *Republic* 485c, Plato describes as the trait of the philosophic nature. On the other hand, it is plain that the affection and, therefore, the interests of the *philodoxoi* are focussed upon things and have not been transferred to the "realities," by participation in which, things have their deficient goodness, truth, and beauty. Accordingly thought becomes fixated in the false assumption or judgment that the many sensible things are reality. By contrast it is averred at 490a that it is the nature of the lover of learning "to strive emulously for true being and that he would not linger over many particulars that are opined to be real but would hold in his way, and the edge of his passion would not be blunted nor would his desire (ἔρως) fail till he came into touch with the nature of each thing in itself by that part of his soul to which it belongs to lay hold on that kind of reality."[41] The sequel to this sort of view is manifestly the whole treatment of the role of love or "divine madness" in knowledge, which is a central concern of the *Phaedrus*. There, at 250d, we are told how the Forms, pre-eminently, Beauty-in-itself, shining through things of sense, arouse a terrible love or yearning for the Real.[42]

The outcome is that *doxa* will be true, or tend to be, in so far as Formal or essential reality, *given in* the complex of sensible qualities, is honored and approved even though it is not methodically identified as true Being. *Doxa* will tend to be true in so far as the philosophic mind makes it, not the stopping-point, but the starting-point of a truth-enamored quest. True opinion represents a mind on-the-way-to-truth through honoring such intimations of it as it presently has. Such is the philosopher.[43] *Philodoxia*, on the contrary, is a state of mind always verging toward false opinion and ignorance. It arrives there in so far as it mistakes "resemblance for identity," that is, the particulars for the essence.[44] In such a state, a man is "asleep" and "dreaming" in respect of reality.[45] Our study has provided a basis for understanding the superiority of true opinion to mere *doxa* and why Plato always ranked it closer to knowledge but always inferior.

3. *Doxa Alêthês* in the Later Dialogues

Numerous references have already been made to passages of the post-*Republic* dialogues where Plato mentions true opinion. In most cases, with the prominent exception of *Timaeus* 51d-52b, treatment is incidental and no elaboration of the conception is attempted. Even in the *Timaeus* passage there seems to be no perceptible development beyond what we have associated with the *Republic*. The *Sophist* and the *Theaetetus*, however, present a different aspect, although even here, as may be shown, no important advance over the position reached earlier seems contemplated. The *Sophist* itself does not overtly treat *doxa alêthês* but rather its opposite, *doxa pseudês*, with a view to demonstrating the ground of its possibility. It is, of course, true that Plato had for long assumed the existence of both true and false opinion. But the assumption of false opinion required vindication. In the *Sophist*, therefore, he was pledged to the task of showing in what sense the phenomenalism of the Sophists, their identification of sensible particulars with true reality, was false. This entailed proof that *doxa*, which we have described as the minimum stage of cognition, becomes false in so far as Becoming, its ontal correlative, is mistaken for true Being. For when the appropriate object of *doxa* is erroneously judged to possess ultimate ontological status, then *doxa* becomes, by Plato's reckoning, false. But there was a long-standing obstacle to his claim. He could not vindicate it until he refuted the Parmenidean dictum that "is not" cannot be the subject of intelligible discourse.[46]

By implication and according to his own ontology, Plato was asserting that what the Sophist, notably Protagoras, identified with Being, in fact was not Being. But, on Parmenides' ground, Plato's denial was unintelligible nonsense. Hence Plato was obliged to show that what the Sophist denominated reality was not the unreal, the nothing-at-all, but rather a kind of deficient being midway between not-Being and true and essential Being.[47] In this manner Plato was eventually able to show that the Sophist's judgment concerning reality was not nonsense but mistaken identity; and this he had already prepared for in the important *Republic* passages following 476. There, at 477a, he had specifically indicated that *doxa* has to do with the sort of reality which stands "between" (μεταξύ) what completely and absolutely is and that which completely is not. And accordingly Plato was already prepared to understand false opinion as the misidentification of τὸ μεταξύ with τὸ παντελῶς ὄν. It was, as he affirmed, the mistaking of "resemblance for identity," that is, the sensible appearance for the true reality of the intelligible Forms.[48] Now, further, if true opinion, as is suggested at *Sophist* 240b, is the "opposite" of false opinion, then we should expect to find that true opinion, however unreliable and unstable, is veridical identification of ideal Being. This as we have already seen is the case in the earlier dialogues. It now remains to be seen whether this position persists and is reaffirmed by the evidence of the *Theaetetus* where true opinion does receive some attention.

The endless resourcefulness of argument in the *Theaetetus*, culminating however in failure to grasp and define *epistêmê*, should warn us that Plato, most probably, was exposing the futility of attempting to ground knowledge upon an empirical basis alone. To some considerable extent, the foregoing investigation of *doxa* and *doxa alêthês* justifies the presumption that Plato could not possibly in company with Protagoras look to *aisthêsis* as source of knowledge, however much he might acknowledge, as he did, the instrumental value of sense-experience. However true it indeed was that the

Formal content of *epistêmê* was given in and with the *sensa*, knowledge in the privileged sense required renewal of what, in the *Republic* and the *Phaedrus*, Plato commonly referred to as μνήμη or memory.[49]

Refutation of the Protagorean phenomenalism and sensationalism is well understood, but comprehension of what is going on in the latter portions of the *Theaetetus* depends, we believe, upon crediting the general estimate of F. M. Cornford. It is that the "discussion still proceeds . . . on certain assumptions of the refuted theory, namely, that the only things to be known are concrete individual things, and that knowledge accordingly must consist in giving some account of such things. This limitation is in accordance with the scope of the whole dialogue, which asks whether knowledge can be extracted from the world of concrete natural things, yielding perceptions and complex notions, without invoking other factors."[50] It is, of course, the implication of our whole discussion, and Cornford would not disagree, that the "other factors" which must be invoked are the Forms or Ideal content of both *doxa* and *doxa alêthês;* and, further, that *epistêmê,* as in the *Republic,* must derive from the proper method of discernment and identification. The resulting knowledge will have for its ontological referents, as at *Republic* 479e, *Timaeus* 52a, *Politicus* 286a, and *Philebus* 59c, the intelligible, ever-abiding, and self-identical Forms.

a. Doxa and Critical Doxa

The import of this last statement has been challenged, notably by Stenzel, who sees in the *Theaetetus,* as well as in the *Phaedrus* and the *Sophist,* signs of Plato's rather marked and permanent departure from the envisioned or "intuited" Form to the "concept" or universal, understood as the content of thought, *dianoia.* The concept or *logos* is isolated by the combined processes of "division" (διαίρεσις) and "composition" (συναγωγή) exercised upon the particulars of sense to the end of discovering the essence (τί ἔστιν) of things. This development Stenzel mainly attributes to abatement of Plato's concern with the moral problem and to the intensification of an empirical interest which forces Plato to face "the question of knowledge in its whole extent, including even empirical knowledge."[51] One is quite ready to grant that the *Theaetetus,* along with certain other dialogues such as the *Parmenides,* the *Sophist,* and the *Politicus,* does exhibit a marked but not, however, a new interest in the status and nature of empirical knowledge. We can agree that "Plato has to decide how we grasp the essence of things that cannot be known *a priori*,"[52] but we can and indeed must do so without banishing the *a priori* from Plato's total conception of knowledge. But in so far as Stenzel, in making the concept the definitive "culmination" of Plato's development, accepts a reduction of knowledge to something like critical *doxa* and so, by implication, voids most of Plato's metaphysical interest, he takes a step which can hardly square with the epistemology of the *Philebus*, the *Timaeus*, or the *Seventh Epistle* (342b-e). Stenzel's thesis that the "knowledge" deriving from the "new" dialectic of "division" consists of *logos*, definition, concept, or "atomic form" is partially true but also highly misleading in so far as this *logos*, considered as the content of *doxa* (now duly critical), is to be equated with the sum total of what Plato now intends to mean by *epistémé*.[53] It is one thing to claim that Plato is obliged seriously to reconsider the status of empirical knowledge, and quite another to say that, henceforth, his dialectic aims at no other end. It is one thing to say that Plato is bent upon doing greater justice to *doxa* as a grade of knowledge (which it had always been), and to say that all other interests are subordinated to this one.

Stenzel's general view strongly commends itself, however, in so far as the joint-method of "division" and "composition" (*Phaedrus*, 265e-266b) occurred to Plato as a highly useful procedure for discriminating Forms in "their communion with actions and bodies" in that most confusing way which Plato noted in the *Republic*.[54] This was, indeed, a task postponed from the time of its first deferment at *Phaedo* 100d, and yet was especially pressing upon Plato even after he described the ontal status of "things" as "between" what perfectly is and what completely is not (*Republic* 477a). We judge that certain of the dialogues following the *Parmenides*, especially the *Sophist* and the *Philebus*, do truly mark Plato's effort to relate effectually "particulars" to their participant Forms, Becoming to Formal Being, in such a way as to embrace the sensible realm within an enlarged conception of the totality of Being. This, to be sure, did involve both epistemological and ontological development in Plato's thought. On the ontological side, the expansion referred to was definitively accomplished in that important section of the *Sophist* (254a-259b) devoted to the deduction of not-Being. Thereby room was made within the sum of Being, not only for Becoming, but also for Plato's "material principle" which later reappears in figurative guise as the Receptacle of the *Timaeus*.

On the side of epistemological development, we may suggest that the same movement of thought which accords to Becoming an unambiguous and secure place within the scale of Being involves, quite evidently, the need further to clarify the status of knowledge correlative with this order of sensible reality. Accordingly, we do have in the later dialogues an accentuation of empirical interest. While, then, we must accept the view that division of things according to classes belongs, as Plato distinctly says, to the science of dialectic,[55] it is quite unnecessary to concede the extreme position that "definition is made the whole purpose of the dialectical method."[56] On the contrary, jûdging from *Sophist* 226d and following, dialectic is enlarged in conception to embrace both the method of division and the older method of *elenchos*.[57] Furthermore, neither may we grant the result of Stenzel's unnecessary restriction of the method; namely, that the *logos*-concept, as the fruit of such a method, all but exclusively replaces the function of the trans-empirical Form, while Plato, hereafter, is to be cast in the role of a lover of spectacles, essentially empiricist in orientation and, suddenly, naturalistic in sentiment.[58] By way of rejoinder, it may be contended that a main premise of Stenzel's one-sided interpretation is the gratuitous view of Edward Zeller and Paul Natorp, *viz.*, that the earlier Plato completely divorces Being and Becoming and practically voids the latter of all reality. Stenzel perpetuates the notion that, for the Plato of the *Republic*, the Forms are totally remote from things, with the consequence that *doxa* in the *Phaedo* and the *Republic* is held to be the complete "opposite of knowledge," so that opinion and knowledge belong "to quite separate worlds."[59] Our study of *doxa* in connection with the *Republic* should indicate that this interpretation, no doubt of time-worn respectability, if not entirely false, is an over-simplification. In the foregoing analysis of *doxa* and *doxa alêthês*, there is adequate ground for regarding *doxa* as a state of indiscriminating cognition embracing in a complex the sensible qualities of a given "particular" together with the Ideal Structure instanced in its existing constitution. From this unanalysed amalgam as starting-point, the *Republic* represents *epistêmê* as attainable by the exercise of dialectic leading up to an ultimate First Principle.[60] This ascent will be fully discussed in Chapter VII. Here, it suffices to say that the upward course represents the "metaphysical" movement of Plato's thought which remains to the end integral with the whole.

But *doxa* can quite as easily admit of other treatment, and, on this other side, the instrumental value of division and composition seems to be that of providing for *doxa*—having to do with particularity or Becoming—a methodology for stabilizing empirical knowledge by supplying a way (μέθοδος) to differentiate haphazard from critical observation.[61] From what may probably be regarded as its earliest systematic exposition in the *Phaedrus*, as also in the *Sophist* and the *Politicus*, the method of division is calculated for differentiating among empirical realities which are of "doubtful," obscure, and disputed nature.[62] There is reason enough to suppose that these are precisely the objects of *doxa* which "equivocate," as Plato noted at *Republic* 479b-d, appearing now one way and now another. Clarification is to be accomplished by dichotomy (*Polit.* 262b). As Plato occasionally describes the procedure, it is a way of cutting things naturally "according to the joints."[63] In this manner, the distinctive character of a thing is identified, and definition, through differentiation, is accomplished, thus locating both "common qualities" and decisive differences.[64] Division is then, as Plato declares at *Sophist* 226d, a method of discrimination (διάκρισις). Apparently, it is a process of discriminating the *ousia* of the thing.[65] Or it is the procedure by which phenomenal realities are comprehended χατ' εἴδη, that is, according to Form or class.[66]

With this understanding of the joint-method of division and composition, or more broadly, the method of "discrimination," we are ready to concede to Stenzel that the fruitful bearing of his study is the indication that, in this mode, dialectic is able, by suitable isolation of the Formal element, to articulate the cognizable structure of things. We say cognizable, for it is not able to grasp the "material" factor. Thus Plato is devising a method calculated to enhance the knowledge-value of *doxa*. Therewith, he doubtless set the stage for Aristotle's development of the classificatory sciences. It cannot however be conceded to Stenzel that the μία ἰδέα,[67] resulting from the joint-method, has only the status of a concept of thought, a *logos* devoid now of transcendental reference. This cannot be squared with the plain statement at *Phaedrus* 249b that the synoptic *eidos*, "formed by collecting into a unity by means of reason the many perceptions of the senses," is in fact *anamnêsis* of the ever-abiding Forms—a view also strongly implied by the treatment of the μία ἰδέα at *Republic* 507b. Quite the contrary, on the basis of this prominent and unmistakable assertion we are impelled to take the view that, in Plato's intention, the *logos* or so-called "conception" deriving from the joint-method looks, so to speak, in two directions at once. It is not engendered by *dianoia* looking solely toward particular things afforded to sensation, although it is very likely true that Aristotle utilized this aspect of the matter in his "abstractionism." It is true that *Theaetetus* 185-187 supplies some ambiguous support for this interpretation. But it is also to be said that this passage is noteworthy for its rather sharp demarcation between the roles of perception and reflection (ἀναλογισμός). Here Plato evidently wished to affirm once for all that empirical knowing is (1) not "by" *aisthêsis* but with its assistance and "through" it, (2) that such knowledge is not in "sensations" but in reasoning (συλλογισμός) about them, adding (3) that apprehension of οὐσία and ἀλήθεια is by way of reasoning not by way of sensation.

It is further to be noted at 185a, e, as at 189e, that thought (*dianoia*) is construed as a power or *dunamis* in a way somewhat novel for Plato. Thought is "the *logos* which the soul has with itself."[68] As conversation of the soul with itself, *dianoia* is the faculty which entertains the conceptions of discriminating reflection. This might easily foster the impression that "thought" or ideation supplies to the *logoi* their ground and sole status in being. If this were Plato's intention, contrary to the indication of *Phaedrus* 249b and contrary to the ontology of both the *Philebus* and the *Timaeus*,[69] then indeed conceptualism would be the culmination of Plato's epistemological development, as Stenzel argued.

As the case stands, however, the likelier interpretation is otherwise, and concepts are regulative for knowledge of things precisely because they are, as it were, the epistemic correlatives of the still immutable Forms. The articulated *logos* is, with some propriety, to be regarded as *doxa* crystallized and critical, defined through the application of the joint-method of *diakritikê*. The discriminated *logos* (which may, indeed must, embrace genus, species, and differentia) looks, on the one hand, in the direction of the sensible particular offered by *aisthêsis*; and, on the other hand, it looks in the direction of the intelligible Forms supplied by *anamnêsis* or memory and is firmly grasped at last by intellection (νόησις). This latter direction, which is causally primary, seems to be fully implied, as Cornford suggested, if not explicitly avowed in the *Theaetetus*, and, one may add, is implied in the *Cratylus* also, where "names" are examined with a view to assessing their capacity to convey truth about reality.[70]

The case for the two-directionality of the *logos*-concept, however, may be allowed to rest upon evidence of the *Philebus*, especially 16c-17c. There we have important exposition of the diacritical method. There it is indicated why the *logos* or μία ἰδέα (16d), must be both one and many and, thus, distinct from the self-identical Forms while at the same time representative of them in principle. Since "all the things which are ever said to exist are begotten from the one and many," that is, from the Form-conferring Limit (τὸ πέρας) and the uninformed Unlimited (τὸ ἄπειρον), both elements are inherent in the particulars. Consequently, critical understanding of the particulars of Becoming, the class of the "mixed," will neither settle for one predicate about anything, nor, on the other hand, for an infinite number (16e). The first is the Parmenidean error, the second that of Protagorean relativism refuted in the *Theaetetus*. The one destroys empirical knowledge by asserting only "unity," the other by asserting only "difference." But in contrast to this careless procedure, critical reflection will seek to isolate the essential character, μία ἰδέα, and then proceed to break it down as a species into its differentia or distinctive differences (16d). Plato's notion, couched here in mathematical language, is that any *actual* quantity is neither abstract unity nor abstract plurality,[71] but some "whole number" between the two (16d). So an actual entity is not infinite plurality (unlikeness); nor is it ideal unity or self-identity of the Forms (likeness). As being distinguishable entity, it derives its unity from τὸ πέρας, the ideal Limit. As being different and distinct, it derives the aspect of its multiplicity from τὸ ἄπειρον, the Unlimited. But it is the business of applied mathematics to find out "just how many it is" (16d). This, incidentally, is what from the time of *Phaedo* 74d and *Republic* 477a the particular had been, namely, a like-unlikeness "between" Being and Not-being.[72]

Now, however, it is apparently the business of the diacritical method to ascertain the Form or Limit under which the particular may be primarily classed. After the genus is identified it is then necessary faithfully to delineate the differences, which are partly attributable to the pluralization of the genus or Form by the Unlimited considered as the complementary constituent of the "mixture." In this fashion Plato sought a way to grasp more accurately the Ideal unity as it has *koinônia* with actions and bodies. The resulting *logos* discriminates the μία ἰδέα as it is "inherent" in things, thus, as altered by the pluralizing "material principle." It is not the Limit as it is in itself, but as it is in the mixture combined with the Unlimited. All the same, the *logos* descries and identifies the Limit or Formal factor as it is differentiated in the actual particular. Thus, in the *logos*-concept, experience both sensible and intellectual is unified in such a fashion that *doxa*, primitive empirical knowing, is rendered intelligible, and classificatory empirical science becomes possible. This, surely, is part of Plato's profound effort to bring greater unity to his conception both of knowledge and of reality.

It must now be added, however, that this result is not *epistême* in Plato's privileged and ultimate sense. The highest form of knowledge still requires another use of dialectic, such as is described at *Republic* 511b as "the way up" to a First Principle without any supposition, and is reaffirmed at *Sophist* 226d f., and continues to find illustration both in that dialogue and in the *Philebus* as well as significant formulation in the *Seventh Epistle* (342a-344b). These issues are to be attended to in sequence. We may conclude this portion of our study with the following observation: In what we have been discussing there is ample evidence that in the *Theaetetus* and elsewhere Plato has been enlarging his conception of *dianoia* as a mode of knowledge inferior to intellection,[73] to include systematized reflection of the diacritical art. Perhaps there is sufficient indication that *dianoia*, which, in the *Republic*, embraced only the abstract sciences and was subordinate to νόησις, is now enlarged to include critical empirical observation.

If the method of classification is essentially deductive, at least for good or ill it makes way for Aristotle's primary method in empirical science. One may judge that Aristotle seized upon it and upon the *logos*-concept, not caring to observe that the concept may be treated in two ways corresponding to its two-directional reference. It may be taken as the universal or genus from which to deduce the species or it may be used as a "starting-point" for dialectical analysis of another sort—an analysis in which the *elenchos* assists the mind "upward" to the ultimate metaphysical principle, the ἀνυπόθετος ἀρχή.[74] What is firmly to be asserted is that the fruits of the diacritical method are to be ranked as *dianoia*, along with the abstract sciences of the *Republic*, and as inferior to the highest order of knowledge. And this is indeed what we should expect of *doxa* even when it has become critical.

b. Doxa Alêthês in the Theaetetus

The evidence surveyed enforces the need to side with Cornford as against Stenzel's claim that the *Theaetetus* represents a sharp transition in Plato's standpoint; namely, that he is now intent upon eliminating the hiatus hitherto prevailing between *doxa* and *epistême* and that he is coming to hold that "it is sensation which now appears as the principal source of knowledge" so that he no longer has any need of *anamnêsis*.[75] We have seen that the alleged hiatus in fact can scarcely be said to have existed and that *doxa* was, even in the *Phaedo*, a degree or measure of knowing. As for the *Theaetetus* itself, our contention now must be the more customary one that, in the course of the dialogue, sense-perception, true opinion, and true opinion with rational explanation are successively examined and eliminated as candidates for the title of *epistême*. While we learn this, it is only incidentally, if at all, that we learn anything further concerning the nature of true opinion, which has been the main concern of our inquiry. Points with which we are familiar from previous references are reaffirmed; namely, that if true opinion and knowledge were the same thing in law courts, the best judges could never have true opinion without knowledge, which is plainly contrary to fact (201c). We are reminded again, as at *Gorgias* 454e, that true opinion may be fostered by persuasion as belief without knowledge (201b).

Now the question posed in *Theaetetus* 187-201 is the suitability of *doxa alêthês* to qualify for the title of knowledge. The inquiry is complicated at the start by the evident fact that not all opinion is true but some is false (187c), and complicated, too, by the ensuing question how false opinion is possible. Clearly we are not in a position to evaluate the claim of true opinion to be true and so, presumably, to be knowledge, until we have ascertained the ground on which some opinion is false and hence the opposite of knowledge. This task was not accomplished until the *Sophist*; and accordingly we shall expect only tentative results from the present investigation. The question about the possibility of false opinion is tied up with the Parmenidean puzzle as to how anyone can opine or speak about what is not.[76] This was to be faced in the *Sophist* not only by showing that "significant negative predication" is possible but by showing that false opinion, identified by Plato with sophistic phenomenalism, is in fact misidentification of true Being with mere Becoming.[77]

Meanwhile, in *Theaetetus* 187-201, the first two efforts to define false opinion prove unsatisfactory. On the supposition that true opinion is knowledge, false opinion would be some sort of ignorance. Three possible kinds are mentioned: It would be not knowing the things which one knows, confounding one thing which is known with another also known, or confusing what is known with what is not known or *vice versa*. But these alternatives are taken to be absurd on the face of it, and the effort is made to define false opinion, not in reference to knowing or not knowing, but in reference to "being" and "not-being" (188c). Here we run into the result that he who holds an opinion holds opinion of *something* and not nothing, or else he holds no opinion at all (189a). Consequently, false opinion must be different from holding an opinion of that which is not (189b), an important inference later fully established in the *Sophist* and indeed already anticipated in the *Republic*.[78]

Up to this point the effort to determine the nature and possibility of false opinion is beset by a vitiating ambiguity expressly noted by Socrates both at 196e and 200c. Since "knowing" and "not-knowing" have not been defined, we have had no warrant in repeatedly using these terms to grasp the meaning of either false or true opinion. The same ambiguity persists in the subsequent section (189c-200c), although in this third and final effort to define false opinion some problematical but constructive advances seem fairly perceptible.

At 189e we have the interesting development in Plato's language about *doxa* already referred to in an earlier context: δοξάζειν is identified with a moment of thought (διάνοια), a culmination of thought in affirmation or denial, thus, a judgment. This is significant, however, only when seen in the context of the third hypothesis, about to be examined; namely, that false opinion is "interchanged opinion," ἀλλοδοξία (189a) or ἑτεροδοξία (193d). *Dianoia* or thought now becomes necessary as the *responsible subject* of this confusion or interchange. The interchange itself is the mismating of memory-image and present perception.

The suggestion that false opinion may be interchanged opinion at first stumbles over the absurdity that one who possesses differentiated opinion about two matters will hardly confound them. He will scarcely persuade himself that one thing he opines is another thing he also opines. He will scarcely confound the beautiful with the ugly, or right with wrong, and so on. It would seem, then, that there cannot be false opinion on this ground either, or else we have not rightly understood what interchanged opinion really involves. The latter proves to be the case, but in order to make this clear, another supposition must be introduced. It comes in the form of a question: "Can a man who did not know a thing at one time learn it later?" (191c) This recalls the problems stated at *Meno* 80d-e. It was the apparent necessity of prior acquaintance to account for present or eventual recognition—a puzzle Socrates thereafter suitably resolved with the theory of *anamnêsis*. Now, here in the *Theaetetus* in an analogous way it is to be suggested that false opinion can exist only by the conjunction of present with past experience retained in memory, that is, in "the combination of perception and thought."[79]

But to make this plain Plato resorts to the simile of the "wax block" in the soul, which is surely nothing else than μνήμη, memory (191d). Upon the wax, which, among men, is of varying quality and susceptibility of impression and retention (194c-195a), there have been imprinted "perceptions and thoughts" presumably of earlier experiences (191d). False opinion occurs in those instances where a present perception is mismated with an existing imprint (193c). The result is "missing the mark" (ἁμαρτεῖν) or misidentification.[80] It is, moreover, of first importance to note that thought is, as it were, bent upon a proper mating of percept and imprint in order to effect present "re-cognition," ἀναγνώρισις (193c). When the conjugation of imprint and percept is real or apropos, there exists veridical "re-cognition," and this is true opinion (194b, d). When, on the contrary, there is no coincidence or true mating, the result is false opinion. *Doxa* is then either true or false depending upon the suitability or unsuitability of present perception to an antecedent memorial impression (μνημεῖον).[81] Accordingly, true opinion is an occasion of "re-cognition" in which some prior acquaintancy is recognized as instanced in present experience. Or, conversely, true opinion obtains when a present percept is recognized as conforming with some antecedent deposit. In the analogy of the "wax block" the express nature of the antecedent deposit is quite uncertain. We might suppose that Plato is approximating the natural concept or "universal." But the context supplies no indication of the nature of the antecedent factor save the suggestion that memory retains both perceptions and thoughts (191d). It may be noted in passing, however, that Plato is anticipating the Aristotelian dictum that the particular is known only through the universal.[82]

It is now proper to return to the question: Can one who does not know a thing learn it later? Patently, the answer is that, unless some prior acquaintancy is preserved in memory, there can be no subsequent learning, which is to say, no "re-cognition." Learning here, quite as much as in the *Meno*, is proper identification. But in the present context, this learning (μαθεῖν) is not other than δοξάζειν and has, therefore, only the rank of *doxa*. If, however, there is a proper coincidence of percept and antecedent deposit, this opinion will also be *doxa alêthês*. But, as in the case of true opinion, we must now add that, apart from erroneous conjugation of percept and imprint, false opinion is equally impossible. Thus Plato asserts false opinion is impossible "in relation to things which one does not know and has never perceived; but it is precisely in relation to things we know and

perceive that opinion turns and twists, becoming false and true . . ."
(194b).   Opinion is true when, in the conjugation, percept coincides
with the memory deposit; but opinion is false when the conjugation
is not a true union.   In short, false opinion here in the *Theaetetus*,
as we have been led to believe earlier, is misidentification;[83] and now
the misidentification is more precisely defined.

Meanwhile it must be recalled again that the whole discussion has
advanced upon the premise of empiricism.   Doubtless the whole of
the *Theaetetus* is seriously concerned with the question regarding the
nature and validity of our "knowledge" of Becoming, the realm "between," and the right of this cognition to the title of knowledge.
The persisting empirical standpoint, however, now runs head on into
a problem serious enough to inspire doubt once more that we have
indeed attained a reliable view of false and true opinion.   What, for
example, shall we make of the fact of false opinion in abstract ideas
where no perception is involved, such as the erroneous judgment that
seven and five are eleven rather than twelve (196a)?   In such a case
a person imagines that one thing he knows is another thing he knows
and so confounds them.[84]   Perception does not figure here, only
dianoia, and it looks as if either false opinion is not the faulty
interchange of thought and perception, or it is possible, paradoxically,
for a man not to know that which he knows, *viz.*, to know twelve and
not apply it in the instance, still abstract, of five and seven.[85]

At this critical juncture Plato introduces the figure of the Aviary.
It is unnecessary, as it is here impossible, to extend exposition of the
Aviary analogy beyond suggesting that it seems entirely plausible
that the simile, whimsical and even bizarre as it is, does succeed in
resolving somewhat the dilemma we have noted with its attendant
impasse in the conception of true and false opinion.   The working
distinction between merely "possessing" (τὸ κεκτῆσθαι) and "having"
(τὸ ἔχειν) seems to be the difference, figuratively, between some antecedent conversancy with Ideal truth and ascertaining it discrimi-
natingly in the form of stable knowledge.   It is true that in the context
of our passages this interpretation is not enforceable, because the
meaning of *epistêmê* remains to the end entirely ambiguous.   Nevertheless, the use of mathematics as the type of "knowing" in question
strongly recalls Plato's earlier distinction between *doxa* and *epistêmê*.
We seem once more in sight of the difference between true opinion,
as understood in the *Meno* and the *Republic*, and *epistêmê*, where
the differentia of the latter is ability to give a reasoned account, muster
it out at will, and communicate it on demand.

The false opinion of the calculator who "counts" eleven rather than twelve, in the instance of five and seven, is the error of one who reckons without principle and cannot, therefore, have his "knowledge" of number at his unerring disposal but is sometimes right and sometimes wrong.[86] We have seen that this sort of fallibility regularly attends *doxa* and is quite plainly alluded to again at 208a-b. The result is, manifestly, that in this kind of arithmetical practice sums may easily be either true or false, because the calculator is not truly possessed of knowledge and remains in the condition of *doxa*.[87]

Now it is in the light of this circumstance that the impasse stated at 196c is quite possibly resolved. In the manner just described, and paradoxical as it may seem, it is possible for a reckoner not to know that which he knows, *viz.*, not to be master of what he possesses. It is said that knowledge of all number is embraced in his mind but, we may presume, not in such a way that he is able to command it in the form of reliable and stable judgments (198b). And, in the absence of command or control (ὑποχείριος), calculation may quite as readily be erroneous as true; and so, in the course of things, false opinion arises. On the other hand, one who achieves "control" over what he possesses is said, in a sense, "to learn again from himself that which he knows"—undoubtedly a half-disguised reference to *anamnêsis*.[88] This condition is analogous to knowledge. True opinion, finally then, is the fortuitous alternative to false opinion and obtains when the individual, according to the figure of the Aviary, "catches the knowledge he intends to catch" (199b). Hence the way is prepared for a reiteration of the view of the *Meno*, but now much later at *Theaetetus* 200e, namely, that "true opinion is surely free from error and all its results are fine and good." But the old disability remains: It is unstable and cannot secure its own tenure.

Because of the prevailing empirical standpoint and the conspicuous absence of any overt reference to the transcendental factors in knowledge, the outcome of discussion of *doxa alêthês* in the *Theaetetus*, must admittedly remain ambiguous. If we assume, for example, that neither memory, in the case of the *tabula rasa* (191d), nor knowledge pre-possessed, in the case of the Aviary (197e), embraces anything but the deposit of previous sensible experience, then it would be unlikely that we are dealing with the kind of *doxa alêthês* we meet with in the *Republic* and *Meno*. On this point, decision will rest with our over-all estimate of what Plato is intending to do in the dialogue. We have taken the position that Plato's purpose is twofold at least: To show (1) that unmitigated empiricism leads to insoluble difficulties; but (2) that he is seriously engaged in assessing the nature and status of our knowledge of Becoming to the end of ascertaining its measure of validity.

In view of the fact that Plato had much earlier correlated *doxa* with Becoming, it would not be at all strange if, after disposing of the uncritical Protagorean phenomenalism in the earlier portion of the *Theaetetus*, he should successively explore the propriety of "true opinion" and then "true opinion accompanied by rational explanation" as claimants to the title of *epistêmê*. But, on the basis of our understanding of *epistêmê* in the *Republic* and elsewhere, it would be unthinkable that any *doxa*, even true *doxa*, could measure up to that stature. *Doxa* can be assimilated to *epistêmê* only because, as we saw earlier, it embraces within an undifferentiated amalgam the Ideal content along with the *sensum*. For it is the Form or Idea in the complex, though as yet undiscriminated, which supplies to *doxa* its continuity with the Intelligible order and, therefore, its potential assimilability to superior levels of knowledge. There has been the strong indication that some *degree* of knowledge will be ascribable to *doxa* in the measure that the Ideal content is discriminated by the joint-method of division and composition, on the one hand, or by the *elenchos* on the other.

Now it is necessary to emphasize a further point. If, as we have argued, *doxa* does embrace not only the *sensum* but also the Form proffered with the complex impression, then we may readily see that the same two-directional reference (*i.e.*, to particulars and to Forms) which we have discovered to belong to the *logos*-concept belongs properly also to *doxa*. Hence the two-directionality of both strongly confirms the required assimilability to each other. For we have already sought to show that the *logos*-concept, as the resultant of *diakrisis*, is precisely *doxa* or empirical acquaintance rendered critical. In this event, the *logos*-concept, or any system of concepts, will be, as already suggested, the primitive cognition of *doxa* now transmuted into a higher level of knowledge. It will be precisely the level of *dianoia* and will be "stable" in so far as critical empirical classification admits of "exactitude."[89]

Despite the exasperating inconclusiveness of discussion in the *Theaetetus*, there are certain features which contribute to the understanding of true and false opinion and, indeed, are suggestive of continuity with Plato's earlier treatment of the subject. To see the continuity, however, it is necessary to supply a "missing link." That is, the *tabula rasa* and the Aviary must be taken literally as parables and as so intended. When this is done, almost everything said about true or false opinion is paralleled by what we know of them elsewhere, whether earlier in the *Republic* or later in the *Sophist* and the *Politicus*. First, however, we may say with some confidence that, as nowhere prior to the *Theaetetus*, Plato has hit upon an analogy in the *tabula rasa* which illuminates the nature of false opinion. The mismating of percept and antecedently established impression, called ἀλλοδοξία or interchanged opinion, serves rather well to describe in a figure what is involved in the case of *doxa pseudês*. And, conversely, the proper dovetailing of percept and previous impression graphically symbolizes *doxa alêthês*.[90]

It is with no great difficulty that we observe a similarity between this characterization of false opinion and that described at *Republic* 476c as "the mistaking of resemblance for identity."[91] Here, however, in the *Theaetetus* the factor that is misidentified is not the Form or Ideal content given in and with the complex of the *sensum*. On the contrary, no Ideal content is overtly mentioned. Thus, instead of false opinion misidentifying reality, *i.e.*, accepting the sensible particular in place of the Form it purveys, in the *tabula rasa* figure false opinion fails to mate a present percept with a previous deposit. If now, however, into the power of memory we introduce what is missing, namely, *a priori* awareness of the Forms, then false opinion becomes once again what it was in the *Republic*, namely, identification of reality, not with the Form, but with the *sensum*. Or it is failure to discriminate in the present impression the *ousia* with which the mind is antecedently conversant, however dimly. It is failure to recollect—a condition which, in the *Republic*, the *Phaedo*, and the *Phaedrus*, characterizes those who do not "re-cognize" the Ideal content instanced in and peering through the sensible configuration.[92] Doubtless some method of discrimination is a suitable corrective.

When we turn to the parable of the Aviary the supposition that something is missing and has to be introduced is even more forcibly suggested. Manifestly the Aviary is calculated to account for error in mathematical judgments where sense-perception is explicitly excluded (196a). Here, therefore, the difference between "possessing" and "having" or commanding cannot be explained by a μνήμη that has been stocked only with sensible impressions. Accordingly it must be considered a deliberate irony when Socrates "presumes" that the receptacle is originally empty in childhood (197e). Such "radical empiricism" has no other foundation but itself in all of Plato's utterances and no scrap of support outside the *Theaetetus*. The alternative must rather be that here an *a priori* content is required for memory such as is in fact accorded it in multiple instances elsewhere, especially in the *Phaedrus*.[93] If this is done, then false opinion becomes that unfortunate but always possible alternative to true opinion. For we have seen that *doxa*, as the minimum state of cognition and as contrasted with the stability of *epistêmê*, embraces the precarious and equal potentiality of becoming either true or false by the addition of a judgment prompted, perhaps, by interest or affection. If opinion is true, it is a happy fortuity, a *theia moira*. If false, then it is what Plato is inclined to regard, as at *Sophist* 228e, as deformity in the soul, indeed, double ignorance, which knows not but presumes to know. Its chief instance is still what it was in the *Republic*, namely, the Sophistic phenomenalism which "supposes that things which certainly are, are not at all," *viz.*, ideal Being.[94] On the other side, true opinion is still mainly what it was: the highly fortunate but unreliable identification of essential Being, barely discernible and almost obscured in the texture of multifarious experience.

Modern scientific interest has rightly perceived something congenial with its temper in the later dialogues. But this interest is unduly coercive when, from its own contempt of metaphysics, it thinks to divine Plato's also. Plato's own philosophic course is testimony enough that the starting-point of metaphysics is never physical nature but man on the side of his axiological consciousness. But Plato intended to do justice to both.

NOTES

1. *Cf. Rep.* 534c, 611e.
2. Paul Shorey held that, according to Plato's thinking, "the traditional morality is substantially sound." "The Idea of the Good in Plato's Republic," *Studies in Classical Philology* (Chicago, 1895), 215. This judgment needs no revision.
3. *Rep.* 538c-e and 574d.
4. *Rep.* 479d. Plato's favorable estimate of law and custom may be gathered by reference to *Gorg.* 504d and *Rep.* 589c-d. Whatever its positive derivation, it contributes to order and subordinates the irrational to the rational in human nature. See *Rep.* 590e; *Phileb.* 26b. The fuller development of Plato's reliance upon law is indicated at *Polit.* 301d. Here, however, the laws are not traditional customs "without knowledge," but the product of reason and critical *technê*. In every case, custom requires criticism; and in some instances emancipation from inferior convention is sorely needed. See *Phaedr.* 252a, 265a.
5. *Phileb.* 64b. *Cf. Rep.* 585c for Plato's question: "And if a thing has less of truth has it not also less of real essence or existence?"
6. *Laches* 194d; *Crito* 47c; *Phaedo* 69b.
7. *Meno* 98b. *Cf. Theaet.* 201c.
8. *Meno*, 98c. *Cf. Theaet.* 200e.
9. *Rep.* 534b-c. See *Polit.* 278a-e.
10. E. S. Thompson, *The Meno of Plato* (London, 1901), 305.

11. P. Shorey, *What Plato Said* (Chicago, 1933), 517.

12. Thompson, *op. cit.*, 301.

13. The close association of *doxa alêthês* with *epistêmê* and *nous* is plain at *Rep.* 585b. These together constitute one "class" (τὸ γένος) that most fully participates in "pure essence." Together, they are opposed to the "class" of sensible pleasure and appetite. This classification is identical with that stated in *Epist.* VII, 342c where the class as a whole constitutes the "Fourth" phase in the advance of the *logos alêthês* (342a). This strongly suggests that it cannot be accidental when, in *Laws* 689b, the three again appear together, as the better elements in the soul, and once more at *Phileb.* 60d, where true opinion is placed in the same "class" with wisdom, knowledge, and memory. *Cf. Phileb.* 64a, 66b. The evidence is strong that, whatever *doxa alêthês* is, it is clearly intended to rank above mere *doxa*. It is evidently a form of cognition on the way to becoming knowledge.

14. *Rep.* 429c, 602a. *Cf. Laws* 632c.

15. *Cf. Rep.* 430b; *Laws* 633c f.

16. *Phileb.* 65c. *Cf. Phaedo* 79b-d; *Rep.* 585d; *Tim.* 90d. It is defensible to suggest that the correlation of *gnôsis* with "most real Being" at *Rep.* 477a-478a and 585d is simply a rendering explicit of the primordial conformity between man's *nous* and intelligible Being. In the condition of *epistêmê* or *gnôsis*, this conformity has become consciously, because methodologically, established; true opinion has given way to "science." The agency is, of course, mainly dialectic.

17. *Cf. Phaedo* 98d-e and 83a-b.

18. *Cf.* the well known formulas *Rep.* 534a and 508c, also 585b-d.

19. *Cf. Rep.* 478e, 585c; *Phaedo* 80b; *Phileb.* 59a-c.

20. See especially *Tim.* 28a, 29c, 51d and *Phileb.* 58a, 59a-c, 61d-e.

21. *Tim.* 51e, 29c. *Cf. Meno*, 98a; *Gorg.* 455a; *Phaedr.* 260a, 272e.

22. N. R. Murphy, *The Interpretation of Plato's Republic* (Oxford, 1951), 103.

23. P. Shorey, *The Unity of Plato's Thought*, Univ. of Chicago Decennial Publications (Chicago, 1904), 47. *Cf.* Rep. 523b.

24. *Ibid.*, 45.

25. Murphy, *op. cit.*, 103.

26. *Phaedo* 72e, 73c, 75e; *Meno* 81d.

27. It is precisely Plato's willingness in the *Parmenides* (127e) to accept the "absurdity" of contradictory predicates attaching to particulars which signalizes his challenge to and repudiation of Eleatic monism. A particular is both like and unlike (129a-b). But it is so in a variety of respects. It is both like the Form in which it participates, but, being deficiently representative, unlike it too. It is both like and unlike in the sense also that it has identity, a unitary character, but it possesses this unity in multiplicity, that is, as possesed of a plurality of aspects (129d). So that the particular is both one and an indefinite plurality in combination. This is the class of the "mixture" in the *Philebus* (23c, 25d).

28. *Phaedo* 75c-d.

29. *Rep.* 507b affords a good instance of what is suggested. As at 479e, the many particulars of sense are presupposed. Their character as "beautiful" or "equal" (*Phaedo* 74c) is a judgment of *doxa*. Knowledge supervenes upon true opinion, when in place of the many beautiful or equal things the Beautiful-in-itself or the Equal-in-itself is discriminated out of the midst of the manifold. Thus, the One *in* the Many is located or "posited," the μία ἰδέα. This is the object not of "sight" but of *nous*, and so the distinction between the "visible" and "invisible" emerges, the correlates of opinion and knowledge. *Cf. Tim.*, 51d. *Republic* 507b may be compared instructively with the bearing of *Phaedo* 65e-66a. In the latter passage it seems clear that the function of *logismos* is to disengage the essence, which is obscure so long as reliance is upon the bodily senses. At *Rep.* 493e the failure of the "multitude" to discriminate the Form, as unity, from the multiplicity of par-

ticulars bearing its image is noted as the basis of the incapacity of the "multitude" for philosophy.

30. *Phaedo* 78c, 101c; *Phaedr.* 237c.
31. See *supra*, n. 13.
32. See *supra*, n. 29.
33. *Theaet.* 152c; *Soph.* 263d, 265a.
34. *Rep.* 515c.
35. *Rep.* 475d, 479a.
36. *Rep.* 480a.
37. *Theaet.* 190a. Cf. 170d; *Soph.* 263e; *Phileb.* 27c.
38. Cf. *Theaet.* 190a; *Soph.* 263e; *Phileb.* 38d.
39. *Rep.* 479d-e.
40. *Rep.* 480a.
41. Cf. *Phileb.* 58d and *Rep.* 505e.
42. Cf. *Phaedr.* 251d-e.
43. *Phaedr.* 278d. Cf. *Rep.* 475b-d.
44. *Rep.* 476c. This is the "deceit" of the senses, so prominent in *Phaedo* 83a, 66a. It consists in confounding the visible and sensible with reality. Reality is rather to be identified with *ousia* and is invisible and apprehended by reason alone. *Phaedo* 83b. Cf. *Rep.* 524c, 527b, 532a. *Republic* 520c makes it clear that the *eidôla* of the Cave, *viz.*, the particulars of sense, will be known by the emancipated mind, not as reality, but only as "semblances" of the same. Thus, with the enlightened, mis-identification is overcome.
45. *Rep.* 476c. For further use of this analogy, see *Rep.* 520c, 534c; *Polit.* 277d, 278e.
46. *Soph.* 241d f.
47. This interpretation of the aims of the *Sophist* the author has set forth as part of an unpublished doctoral dissertation: "Not-Being and the Problem of Evil in Plato" (Yale University, 1942), 195-260. The study is occupied with exposition of the fundamental concepts of Plato's physical theory and completed ontology.
48. *Rep.* 476c. Cf. *Soph.* 240a f.; *Theaet.* 195a. See *supra*, n. 44.
49. Cf. *Rep.* 486c-d, 487a, 490c; *Phaedr.* 249c, 250a, c, 253c, 254b, 275a; *Theaet.* 191d f., 209c; *Phileb.* 38b, 39a, 60d, 64a. Plato's use of *mnêmê* is not consistent. In the *Republic* and *Phaedrus* it is manifestly possessed of transcendental content and reference. In the *Theaetetus* memory has apparently only empirical content. There is the clear assertion of *Philebus* 34a that *mnêmê* is properly defined as the preservation of sense perception, and yet at 11b and 60d *mnêmê* is closely associated and ranked with *phronêsis* and *noêsis*. If there is any explanation for these variations it may be that, in the later dialogues, Plato is not occupied strictly with the metaphysical problem and therefore is not interested, save incidentally, in the metaphysical reference of *mnêmê*. See *infra*, n. 93.
50. F. M. Cornford, *Plato's Theory of Knowledge*, 154.
51. J. Stenzel, *Plato's Method of Dialectic*, trans. D. J. Allan (Oxford, 1940), 56.
52. *Ibid.*, 55.
53. *Ibid.*, 70, 78, 90, 117.
54. *Rep.* 476a. Cf. 479a, 524a-c; *Polit.* 278d.
55. Cf. *Soph.* 253d; *Phaedr.* 273d-e.
56. Stenzel, *op. cit.*, 96.
57. See *infra*, Ch. VII, sec. 2, a.
58. Stenzel, *op. cit.*, 87.
59. *Ibid.*, 81-82, 88.
60. *Rep.* 510b.

61. For the prominence of μέφοδος see *Phaedr.* 266b, 269d, 270d; *Soph.* 218d, 219a, 235c; *Polit.* 260e, 266d, 286d.

62. *Phaedr.* 263b; *Soph.* 218d, 231b-c; *Polit.* 258c.

63. *Phaedr.* 265e; *Polit.* 259d, 287c; *Cratyl.* 387a.

64. *Cf. Polit.* 285b; *Phaedr.* 273e; *Theaet.* 208d.

65. *Polit.* 285b. *Cf. Cratyl.* 388c.

66. *Phaedr.* 273e, 277b; *Soph.* 226c, d; *Polit.* 286d.

67. *Phaedr.* 273e; *Soph.* 253d; *Polit.* 278c; *Phileb.* 16d. These instances are to be contrasted with *Rep.* 507b where the μία ἰδέα clearly stands for the "transcendent" Form.

68. *Cf. Soph.* 263e; *Phileb.* 38c.

69. *Phileb.* 23c-27b. Here is set forth the four great classes of Being in their reciprocal relations. The class of the "Limit" (τὸ πέρας) constitutes the Formal ingredient of the Mixed class (τὸ μιχτόν). Of this latter, the Unlimited (τὸ ἄπειρον) is the "material" constituent. The Mixed class, of course, represents the sphere of Becoming. It is comparable with and has the same status as τὸ μεταξύ at *Republic* 477a, *viz.*, that which stands "between" Being and Not-Being. *Cf. Phileb.* 16e. At *Philebus* 59a-c it is manifest that the "sciences" of Becoming, or the "Mixture," do not attain to the most perfect truth; and this truth, quite as at *Republic* 585b-d, "has to do with the things which are eternally the same without change or mixture" (59c). *Cf. Tim.* 28d, 29a, 52a. Also, at *Philebus* 61d, the knowledge which has to do with things that neither come into being nor pass away is, quite as at *Phaedo* 79a-d, exalted above the kind which occupies itself with the transitory. All this cannot be squared with Stenzel's conceptualistic interpretation of Plato's late epistemology.

70. *Cf. Theaet.* 185d, e. The soul is said to apprehend the factor, "common to all things" (185c) directly "by itself." This factor is the οὐσία (186a) which earlier, at *Rep.* 511a, represents such realities as are grasped (ἰδεῖν) only by *dianoia*, presumably, in its function as νόησις (511d). The same direct relation of mind to the "immaterial realities" is rather plainly suggested at *Polit.* 286a. In that place it is clear that we are dealing with the resultants of classification, but the resultant *logoi*, while they enable us to organize the empirical manifold κατ' εἴδη (285b) retain ambiguous reference to something transcendent. A comparable ambiguity pertains to the ὄνομα in the *Cratylus*. The "name" is in the "middle" referring at once to the thing named and to the ideal essence (*Cratyl.* 389d, 432e, 433d-e). And 439a-d indicates strongly that the reliable knowledge of the "thing" is not to be in the possession of its "name," but is apprehension of the self-identical Form which in some measure the name conveys and denotes, that is, if it is a suitable name. For a comparable line of thought, see *Tim.* 48b-c.

71. *Cf. Rep.* 524e-525b.

72. *Cf. Parm.* 129a-b. See *supra*, n. 27.

73. *Rep.* 511d, 533e. *Cf. Phileb.* 59a-d.

74. *Rep.* 510b. For further treatment, see *infra*, Ch. VII, sec. 2, b.

75. Stenzel, *op. cit.*, 64. See *infra*, n. 93.

76. *Cf. Theaet.* 188d f., and *Soph.* 237e f.

77. *Soph.* 240d-e.

78. *Cf. Soph.* 257b and *Rep.* 478b.

79. *Theaet.* 195d. *Cf.* 165b.

80. *Theaet.* 194a. *Cf. Soph.* 228c-d; *Phileb.* 37d-e.

81. *Cf. Theaet.* 209c.

82. These passages of the *Theaetetus* highlight the persisting problem of Aristotelian conceptualism: the particular cannot be known save through the universal. But, since the universal derives from experience, its real priority cannot be secured *a posteriori*. It conforms with our interpretation of Plato to remark

that he anticipated the difficulty and therefore retained the universal, *a priori*. This is to say in other language that he retained the two directional reference of the *logos*-concept.

83. See *supra*, n. 44.

84. *Theaet.* 196b. For comparable instances, see *Soph.* 263b and *Phileb.* 40c.

85. *Cf. Polit.* 277e f. for a comparable instance of the difficulty. Examination of what is said about *arithmêtikê*, 198a-c, strongly suggests that Plato has in no way modified the kind of autonomy which is accorded it at *Rep.* 525a ff. The "science of all numbers" (198b) is quite evidently *a priori* knowledge independent of sensible experience. Page 196a shows the familiar correlation between abstract number and particulars instancing it. The distinction between applied and pure mathematics is strikingly reasserted at *Phileb.* 56d. *Cf. Polit.* 258d-e.

86. *Cf. Theaet.* 198b-c.

87. So Cornford, *op. cit.* 135.

88. *Theaet.* 198e. *Cf.* 209c and *Phileb.* 66b-c.

89. The limits of this exactitude are clearly discussed and demarked by Plato. *Cf. Tim.* 52c, 53d, 56c, 59c, and *Phileb.* 57b-59c.

90. *Cf. Phileb.* 38b-d.

91. *Cf. Phaedr.* 250e; *Rep.* 585b; *Phileb.* 38d-39d. The misidentification of truth and being is already implicit in Socrates' rebuke to his contemporaries at *Apol.* 30a. It is presupposed as the error of the sensualist at *Phaedo* 81b and is graphically represented in the false opinion of the Cave prisoners at *Rep.* 515b f. and 520c.

92. *Cf. Phaedr.* 250b-e; *Rep.* 479e, 493e; *Phaedo* 65e-66b.

93. See *Phaedr.* 249c, 250a, 253a, 254b, 275a. From *Phaedrus* 248c to 250c the power and significance of *mnêmê* is expounded; indeed the dialogue itself is concerned to identify the best method for awakening memory. That method is dialectic. *Anamnêsis* is the awakening of memory; the latter, plainly, is possessed of transcendental reference. Already in the *Phaedrus* it is *mnêmê* which is fundamental; *anamnêsis* is the process of repossessing what is "forgotten" but is prepossessed. *Cf. Phaedo* 73e.

It is easy to misinterpret the nearly complete absence of *anamnêsis* in the later dialogues. In the first place, *anamnêsis* appears scarcely at all in the *Republic*. In the one instance it does occur, 604d, it has a wholly non-technical meaning. The technical use of *anamnêsis* is confined to the *Meno*, *Phaedo*, and *Phaedrus*; and in these dialogues metaphysical interest predominates. The only technical uses of the verb ἀναμιμνήσχειν are found likewise only in these three dialogues. But the *Republic* is a full-scale example of the fact that Plato found it possible to develop his theory of Forms, with the accompanying theory of knowledge, without any explicit use of *anamnêsis*. Of course, dialectic is the instrument of *anamnêsis*, that is, of the "waking" as opposed to the "dream" condition of the mind. *Rep.* 476c, 534c. And this same analogy is perpetuated in the *Politicus* (277d), and in the *Timaeus* (52b-c).

The only explicit reference to *anamnêsis* in the later dialogues is *Philebus* 34b f. There *anamnêsis* is supplied a twofold definition. In contrast with memory, defined now as "the preservation of perception," recollection obtains either (1) when the soul "alone by itself, apart from the body," recalls experience it has had in company with the body, or (2) when the soul has lost memory of a perception or "*of something it has learned* (μαθήματος)" and alone by itself regains this. Results must be inconclusive here; but μαθήματος recalls the famous *Phaedo* dictum, μάθησις ἀνάμνησίς ἐστιν (73b). *Cf. Meno* 81d. Recollection, in the first place, is a work of the soul by itself. Furthermore, there would seem to be no point in the second phase of the definition unless it is intended to make place for data other than that dependent upon bodily experience. Moreover, if we ascribe to the second part of the definition a denotation suitable to the earlier meaning of *anamnêsis*, we have ground for understanding why at 11b and 60d memory is ranked with wisdom, knowledge and true opinion; otherwise we have no sure indication at all. Finally, if we accredit a real distinction between the two parts of the definition, we are in a position to see that *mnêmê* is conceived by Plato as having both empirical and transcendental reference and employment. In that event, we can square both the teaching of the *Phaedrus* about *mnêmê* with that of *Theaetetus* 191d, and *Philebus* 34a, because memory may have both empirical and transcendental content. This, indeed, we take to be Plato's intention.

There is a final consideration in interpreting rightly the notable absence of *anamnêsis* in the late dialogues. In them Plato is admittedly interested in rounding out his ontology which is to include Becoming. The metaphysical quest which reaches its high tide in the *Republic*, *Symposium*, and *Phaedrus* recedes from the center. As illustrated by the *Philebus* as well as the *Timaeus*, the starting-point of the ontological problem is shifted from the moral consciousness to the actuality of cosmic experience. So the *Philebus* is not concerned with knowledge of the Formal as such but with its contribution to the constitution of actual nature. This remains, with occasional reversions to the earlier standpoint (*cf. Theaet.* 176; *Polit.* 286a; *Phileb.* 59, 61; *Tim.*, 90), the dominant consideration. One can only speculate what would have been the impression if Plato had written the *Philosophos* (*Theaet.* 254a-b), but he never did. There, once more, *anamnêsis* might have had revival as integral with the strictly metaphysical task. But Plato had really already completed this task. To have taken it up again may well have seemed unnecessary.

94. *Soph.* 240e.

CHAPTER VI

Knowledge Through Conversion

Of this very thing, then, I said, there might be an art, an art of the speediest and most effective shifting or conversion of the soul, not an art of producing vision in it, but on the assumption that it possesses vision but does not rightly direct it and does not look where it should, an art of bringing this about.—Republic 518d

1. THE STRUCTURE OF KNOWLEDGE

NOWHERE has Plato supplied a more concise statement of his conception of education than in the words quoted above. Here he plainly declares that knowledge depends upon the proper orientation of the cognitive faculty, upon the right direction of vision, and the key word is conversion or *metastrophê*. Both education and wisdom, the fruit of education, require the turning around of the "*organon* of knowledge" together with the entire soul. In Book VII of the *Republic*, where Plato systematically expounds his educational theory, it is shown to be impossible to impart information to a soul which has no inkling of the truth. Vision cannot be inserted into blind eyes.[1]

When, however, it is indicated that education does not begin with a state of unknowing or with some *tabula rasa* upon which sense impresses its characters, it is, of course, to be added that education does not, in any case, consist of experience, *empeiria*.[2] Plato had been engaged in banishing this misconception long before he undertook its systematic rejection in *Republic* VII.[3] To be sure, Plato points out that the rightly educated man will not be deficient in experience. He expressly declares at *Republic* 484d that persons suited for philosophic training, when educated, will be "those who have learned to know the ideal reality of things and who do not fall short of others in experience." Plato not only concedes the place but insists upon the need of practical mundane knowledge on the part of the philosophic guardians. A man of culture shares with the mass of men the life of sense, and he, no less than they, can evade practical action; but he will keep this aspect of existence under the guidance of a superior insight, to the end that, accepting his peculiar responsibility, he may reorder existing arrangements according to a higher perspective. Because exact knowledge (*epistêmê*) must find pertinent application to the shifting corrugations of human existence in time, the educated man must be thoroughly conversant with the multiplicity of events. Although in the *Philebus*, as in the *Republic*, knowledge of true Being is exalted above knowledge of various and transient "becomings,"[4] nevertheless, Plato observes that it would be "a ridiculous state of intellect in a man, which concerned itself only with divine knowledge" and was ignorant of the human sphere.[5] This is not a new note, for in the *Republic* Plato is continually stressing the need of familiarity with existential and political actualities in order that the truths of superior knowledge may be applied remedially to the human situation.[6]

Nevertheless, education is not increment of experience or multiplication of "knowledges"—the sort of thing Plato ridicules among the "lovers of spectacles" and "practitioners of the minor arts."[7]   In the symbolism of the *Protagoras* (321d), this *empeiria* was the gift of Prometheus; whereas "civic wisdom" was the divine apportionment of Zeus and conferred upon man "kinship" with deity (322a). In this latter sphere, knowledge does not have a beginning where there was none before, while in the former it does. In the case of *empeiria*, everything is dependent upon *aisthêsis*, which has a beginning in time. Sensation may come upon its data, or the data may intrude themselves upon the senses (*Rep.* 507c); but there is no sheer beginning for the sort of knowledge whereby a man is properly said to be educated. The "many arts," says Polus in the *Gorgias*, "have been discovered experimentally as the result of experiences." Moreover, their importance is in no way minor, for they enable us to conduct our work-a-day life according to "art," whereas "inexperience" leaves us at the mercy of chance.[8]

But sensible experience, entertained as *doxa* and generally classifiable as *empeiria*, is possible because the things with which it is occupied show forth the structure of the Formal realities in which those same things "participate." Also this experience is possible because already the experiencing subject has prior and independent conversancy with the Forms. Hence empirical knowledge presupposes a threefold union or concurrence: To use the language of a later time, there is, first, the implicit identity of the self-identical Form with the Form as apprehended *a priori* (*i.e., ante rem*) by the knowing subject. Secondly, there is an identity of the self-identical

Form with the Form *in re*. Otherwise stated, the Form, by participation or ingression, contributes the intelligible structure of the particular thing. In the third place, there is the concurrence of the
Form *in re* with the Form as apprehended by the knowing subject
(*ante rem*) independently of all sensible experience; and it is this
latter concurrence which constitutes the moment of empirical knowledge. In Plato's view, this moment would be impossible without the
simultaneous presence (*koinônia*) of the self-identical Form, both *a
priori* to the experiencing subject (*i.e., ante rem*) and also to the
thing being cognized (*i.e., in re*). Thus there comes to be a sort of
triangular structure of Plato's intelligible world. Manifestly, empirical knowledge is possible because the self-existent Form, which
gives structure to the thing, is identical with the Form that, antecedently, "informs" the knowing mind. The Form is the common
term or unifying medium of noetic union, either in the empirical or
in the transcendental dimension of cognition.

In terms of this schematic arrangement, there is doubtless to be
found, on the one hand, the real import and basis of *anamnêsis*, when
"demythologized," and, at the same time, on the other, the possibility
of *doxa alêthês*. For true opinion becomes possible, as we have
seen, in the measure that the self-identical Form (the One in the
midst of the many) is discriminated in conjunction with empirical
or "aesthetic" intuition; while it is equally true that the implicit *a
priori* concurrence of the mind with the intelligible Forms makes
possible the kind of "recollection" and identification of the Form-in-
itself which, as in the *Phaedo* and the *Republic*, may, with the aid of
dialectic, lead to the apprehension of essential reality, the cognition of
which is *gnôsis*. Of course the Form is deficiently represented in the
particular; and, as the *Phaedo* makes plain in a passage of prime importance (74d-e), it is this "falling short" or deficiency (ἔνδεια) of
the particular, in contrast with the already known "absolute," which
alerts the mind to the independent reality of the Form, as well as to
the difference between the particular thing and the αὐτὴ ἡ οὐσία in
which it participates. It is this deficiency of the particular that caused
Plato, subsequently in the *Republic* (477a), to place it "between"
Being and not-Being; and "deficiency" itself became the characteristic
mark of all actual changing realities. Thereafter it became a major
objective of Plato's researches in ontology, as he indicates in the
Republic, to give a more adequate account of the particular, *viz.*, of
that which partakes at once of both "to be and not to be" (478e).

It is appropriate for our purpose to note briefly the manner in which Aristotle diverges from Plato in these matters. There is no disagreement between them on the view that knowledge, as such, is concerned with the Form or the "universal" and not with sensible particulars. On this they agree. For Aristotle, *empeiria* has to do with particulars of sense, while knowledge is of the Form or the universal (τὸ καθόλου).[9] Sense-experience by itself would never constitute knowledge. What is more, Aristotle agrees with Plato that particulars of sense are known, *i.e.*, are intelligible, only by benefit of the universal.[10] So there is a vast difference between mere experience of a thing and knowledge of it. The latter is the mind's entertainment of and "agreement with" the Form of the thing.[11] But here agreement with Plato comes nearly to an end, not because Aristotle denies the reality of the Forms, but because the Forms or universals are apprehended *exclusively* in conjunction with *empeiria* and the operation of the senses. The universal is really *in* the particular substance which is perceived; and when the mind is "active," the universal is really embraced by the "active intellect." The coalescence or agreement of the two in one, the Form in the thing and the Form in the mind, is the actuality of knowledge.[12] However, in Aristotle's opinion, no Forms are given to the mind *a priori,* that is, antecedent to experience. This restriction is not mitigated by the fact that the particulars are "known" only by means of the universals. The latter is what Aristole signifies in the assertion that "universals are prior in formula, but particulars in perception."[13] All knowledge is inaugurated with perception; and, although knowledge is not perception, yet, without its data, there would be no universals in the mind and no theoretical understanding of anything.[14]

It is clear, then, that Aristotle will have nothing to do with *a priori* apprehension of Being such as Plato held to be possessed unawares by the man of "true opinion." Speaking quite as though he had the teaching of the *Meno* specifically in mind, Aristotle declares that there is no "prior" or antecedent knowledge of anything. A beginner in geometry has no previous knowledge of the principles of that science, says Aristotle. Moreover, this is true of all other branches of knowledge.[15] With Aristotle, in opposition to Plato, there is no cognizance of "ideal" realities throughout all time.[16] The prepossession of truth is in no sense a condition of knowledge. It follows, therefore, that knowledge may be said to begin and to be where it was not before.[17] And, finally, with Plato directly in mind, Aristotle completes his refutation with the following observation: Assuming that there is such a thing as inborn or "innate" knowledge, "it is astonishing that we should possess unawares the most important of the sciences."[18]

It should now be fully manifest that the availability of truth or the immediate accessibility of reality is a basic principle of Plato's theory of knowing. If Aristotle, therefore, remarks "it is astonishing that we should possess unawares the most important of the sciences," Plato's rejoinder is: Astonishing or not, something like that is the case! The incredibility of Plato's view is, perhaps, to be closely associated with a faulty understanding of his teaching concerning the nature of human ignorance (*i.e.*, *doxa pseudês*) and the determinative influence of affection upon the cognitive function. In subsequent treatment it will be shown that, in Aristotle's view, the intellect is emptied of all conative features and is axiologically disinterested. With Plato, on the contrary, intelligence is inherently axiological and is decisively influenced, either for knowledge or for ignorance, by the direction of interest or affection. If Aristotle understood this at all, it was anathema; because, for him, the ideal of knowledge was irrefragable demonstration.[19] His aspiration for "scientific knowledge" would be jeopardized, as he perceived, if the premises of syllogism, however valid the inference itself, were susceptible to non-theoretical influences. Hence he restricted the *a priori* in experience to the "laws of thought," especially to that of non-contradiction,[20] and confined the "material" of logical inference to universal concepts "inducted" from sense-experience. With Plato, as we might say, the premises of thought or the data of syllogism are conditioned upon the prevailing orientation of intelligence, expressive of the dominant affectional focus of the entire soul.

2. OF HUMAN BONDAGE

The great importance of conversion in Plato's conception of education is easily missed if we disregard the fact that, in his judgment, human life is turned "upside-down." This *anatropê* manifests itself in a variety of forms. It is flagrantly apparent in those who, like Callicles, pursue their own desires as the sovereign good (*Gorg.* 503c). But pre-eminently it is expressed in the false opinion, enforced by sensuous proclivities, that reality is what is specified by sense and appetite. It was this which we found Plato protesting against in the *Phaedo*.[21] And in the *Republic* (485d), we find him accounting for the differences between the lover of wisdom and the lover of falsehood partly by the observation "that when in a man the desires incline strongly to any one thing, they are weakened for other things. It is as if the stream had been diverted into another channel."[22] Or, as Plato observes elsewhere, they are "overpersuaded" by the urgings of desire and so are self-deprived of truer opinions.[23]

In Book VII of the *Republic*, Plato undertakes to sketch his theory of education. We may assume from the start that his *paideia* will be designed to encounter and overcome the characteristic inversion of human life and valuation that mislocates reality and misidentifies the true goods of life. We may assume, further, that Plato's conception of education will be suited to deal effectively with double ignorance, the ignorance which is self-deceit and which is "reprehensible" because it is enforced by inferior affections, as at *Phaedo* 83d. These assumptions are so far confirmed by the manner in which Plato introduces his views on education. He begins with a restatement of the prevailing human condition respecting *paideia* and its lack (*apaideusia*) (514a). He does so by introducing the famous analogy of the Cave. Here men live in semi-darkness from childhood, a fettered existence, unable to move or turn their heads, and are continually preoccupied with shadows projected by objects of all kinds, moving against exterior light across the aperture of the Cave.

Manifestly it is not the bodies of men which are in bonds but their minds. On this point there can be no disputing Plato's meaning. The nature of their bondage is the ingrained and false opinion that the "real" is nothing else than the shadows which pass before their eyes.[24] The condition is one of abject folly, *aphrosunê* (515c); but it is perceived as such only when one of the prisoners is freed from his bonds and is "compelled to stand up suddenly and turn his head around and walk and to lift up his eyes to the light" (515c). Only then, and for him alone, is the illusion banished that the shadows are reality. As for the other prisoners, their eyes are so inured to the half-light by long habituation that nothing intervenes to disturb their communal folly. Only the man who has been liberated (515e), whose gaze has been turned toward the light, to the real objects outside the Cave, is able to perceive that what passes for wisdom among his fellow bondsmen is cheat and delusion.[25] Meanwhile the rest remain intransigent in their corporate ignorance and "legislate" what reality shall be according to the common mind, the "idols of the tribe."[26]

There are three features of this bondage which deserve attention. In the first place, Plato is aware of the influence of environment upon ontological judgment. He recognizes that the character of human thought concerning reality is powerfully conditioned by the climate of opinion, the prevailing mind-set, in which the individual participates from childhood. It contributes those fundamental viewpoints that, in turn, constitute the unexamined premises of thought. No one escapes the influence of the presiding human perspective. On the other hand, no man is educated, nor has he even begun his education, who has not undertaken critically to examine the reigning dogmas and assumptions of his age and place.

To the end of his career, Plato served notice that the pursuit of "science" by minds which had not themselves been renovated and purged of presumption, could and did result in a grievous unwisdom, although reputed to be the height of sagacity.[27] In the passages we are considering, Plato cannot withhold a few words of gentle satire for the "experts" among the prisoners in the Cave. Like their less talented fellows, they share a cave-existence, but they are distinguished because they "are quickest to make out the shadows as they pass and best able to remember their customary precedences, sequences and co-existences."[28] This is the *techné* which is acquired experimentally "out of experiences," according to *Gorgias* 448c; and since, apparently, it is as yet not assisted by the art of measurement, it remains, as we have noted, merely conjecture. It is only a "skill," as the *Philebus* puts it (55e), or, as in the *Sophist* (254a), only a groping along in the darkness by practice. Nevertheless these "phenomenalists," with their companions, persist as dealers in shadows; while all the time, in Plato's view, the normal sequences which they regard as the "laws" of phenomenal change are about as remote from true causes as are the shadows from the source of light.[29] The phenomenalistic savant is no more enlightened than his fellow-prisoners. If anything, he is in deeper ignorance, because he has made a coherent system of sensible experience and rendered its schema all the more plausible and self-sufficing. Its utility even helps, we may suppose, to confirm its apparent validity, because, by continual collation of sequences, recurrent patterns of change become discernible, so that the expert is better able to predict what will come next (516d). Successful prediction is taken to be the sufficient warranty of truth and reality. In all of this Plato is to be credited with perceiving that education runs head-on into a problem little dreamed of by his contemporaries. He perceived that premises of thought and discussion are determinations of the prevailing interests and the ingrained mentality of a people at a given time.

There is a second aspect of human bondage for which effectual education must provide an antidote or therapy: Plato discerned that there is no cure for not seeing except seeing. Adopting the analogy of the Cave, we may say that there is no way to overcome cave-blindness unless the prisoners be unfettered, turned about to the light, and ushered into the brightness of the outer day. For Plato the best analogy of knowledge is immediate vision.[30] It is for this reason that he frequently employs the simile of the "eye" or "vision" of the soul.[31] Knowledge replaces ignorance when the "eye of the mind" is "converted to the light from the darkness" (518c), and possesses a direct apprehension of Being. This apprehension is not achieved without the aid of dialectic; nevertheless the process of thought has its own natural fruition in a direct "waking vision" of reality.[32]

Knowledge exists not merely in the truth of judgments but primarily in immediate acquaintance with realities. If they are sensible, then they must be immediately given in sensation. If they are "intelligible realities," then they must be directly available to apprehension analogous to sight (532c). Accordingly, truth does not consist primarily in the validity of syllogism culminating in a necessary conclusion. The latter, indeed, was the conception of truth which Aristotle largely adopted, because it assured him of apodictic certainty within a limited province of investigation where the premises could be taken for granted.[33] Plato, however, takes the position that there are various possible premises of thought because there are differing orders of reality with appropriately diverse avenues of apprehension.[34] Therefore what a man knows, what he judges to be "real" is determined by which avenue he customarily employs and what data he usually accredits as actually "given" for reflection (511a). If he is indisposed to attend to one avenue of possible apprehension, for instance, his axiological awareness, he is necessarily deprived of data which might ultimately afford him a conception of Being different from that derived solely from the manifold of sense. It is not that his thought is any less "logical" within its own empirical frame of reference. But it is a fact that it is less true. Taken by itself, his reflection may easily constitute a coherent system; but it has simply ignored other premises which are entertained or not, quite independently of purely logical considerations. Hence for Plato the truth or falsity of a world view cannot be determined solely by consideration of logical cogency or incogency. Truth is not alone assured by the

"tightness" of discursive reasoning by which a world-view is articulated. It is not sufficient, therefore, to say with Aristotle that "a
man knows a thing scientifically when he possesses a conviction arrived
at in a certain way," the way of valid inference.[35] The more important question is: Whence did he derive the assumptions with which,
as Aristotle knew, the chain of inference begins?[36] For Plato the
latter issue is the decisive one, though the way in which conclusions
are derived from premises is by no means unimportant.[37]

In the analogy of the Cave, the prisoners are those who derive
the premises of thought exclusively from the sense-world through
the faculty of *aisthêsis*. They presume that there are no realities
other than the "shadows" or things of sense. Knowledge they take
to be, first, the proper identification of the particulars of the manifold
(515c), and secondly, the ascertainment of their normal sequences
(516c). There is no doubt that the prisoners see shadows. There
is no doubt, either, that particular sensibles in their normal succession
comprise the milieu of their reflection. But, on the other hand, it is
just as true that a sensate world view can be transcended only by
direct apprehension of another "given," the realm of essential reality
in which the ultimate object is the Idea of the Good.

Now Plato's point is that a loftier order of Being, or the intimation and awareness of it, is not wholly missing from the consciousness
of every intelligent soul. But men, as we find them, are so habituated
to their cave-like existence and so fettered to the senses and their
insistent clamor that the cognition of superior reality, though implicit, is inhibited and suppressed. Granted that the higher reality
continues to solicit their acknowledgment, and granted that many
evince this fact in their possession of *doxa alêthês*, there is yet no
strictly argumentative way to dislodge them from their *doxa pseudês*
or to evoke their awareness. For there is lacking both the incentive
and the disposition to pursue the Ideal realities which are presently
veiled amidst the appearances, as Plato notes in *Republic* 479e. Like
the true geometer (510d), they must somehow acquire an interest in
searching for the essential triangle rather than remaining content
with the perceptible image. In this way alone they may be brought
around to apprehend truth for themselves. According to *Republic*
518c, they must have the *organon* of knowledge, the eye of the soul,
turned round until it "is able to endure the contemplation of essence
and the brightest region of being." This, says Plato (521c), really
involves "a conversion and turning about of the soul from a day
whose light is darkness to the veritable day—that ascension to reality

of our parable which we will affirm to be true philosophy." Only with this revolution (περιαγωγή) will men, hitherto intrenched in false opinion, be open to the perspective which allows the premises (*viz.*, δόξαι ἀληθεῖς) of another and superior world-view to be seriously entertained and then adequately proved by the method of *elenchos* (515c).

There is a third aspect of the bondage of the human mind to which our attention is drawn by the graphic imagery of the Cave: Evidently it is impossible to grasp the deeper meaning in Plato's conception of education through conversion unless we are alert to the obdurate character of human ignorance and, therefore, to its gravity. Faulty interpretation at this point has been responsible for the comparative neglect of the place and role of conversion in Plato's educational therapy.[38] It is because the volitional or affective powers of the soul are implicated in the condition of *amathia* and false opinion that Plato looks for no corrective short of radical transformation of affection. Thus the symbolism of the Cave is Plato's way of calling attention to an inveterate habituation (συνήθεια) in which the whole *psuchê* is involved (517a). Jaeger observes that few commentaries see the image of the Cave as it relates to *paideia* and to the want of *paideia* and as it contrasts the present condition of men with the goal of education. This is plainly the case; but, in addition, the figure of the Cave forcefully conveys Plato's conviction of the radical enslavement of the entire human nature.

Plato's tripartite psychology, already fully elaborated in *Republic* IV, should prepare us to recognize in what special manner the prisoners are bound and fettered in the Cave. Their bondage is not simply want of enlightenment. Their condition is one of false opinion and double ignorance. These we have already found in Chapter III to be attributable to a disorientation of *nous* through the overwhelming urgencies of desire or the domineering of the irrational appetitive power. In this way, men were found to be deprived, as if by "sorcery" or "theft," of varying degrees of true opinion.[39] The latter, as a native endowment, might be a guide to life and, in fact, is such in a few exemplary cases. Among the young, as in *Republic* VI, true incentives are often given spirited support prior to the onset of evil nurture and corrupting influence. Gradually, however, loftier vision becomes obscured and languishes as expediency prompts the mature man to resign himself to commonplace aspirations and to adopt the ordinary fashion and goals of life. Thus, never having been really established in truth, even the more gifted natures may easily, as Plato notes at 492a, be profoundly corrupted by the existing environment and may thus adopt the mentality of the Cave as their "primary habitation." In many instances, indeed in most, the light in the soul is all but quenched in old age (498a). Moreover, men lately perverted shortly conspire with others, already inured to the half-darkness, to deal in shadows as if they were true realities (515c).

Judging from *Republic* 516c, Plato regards the Cave, along with what passes there for wisdom, as the initial condition of man's mind and, ordinarily, his first habitation (πρώτη οἴκησις). This initial habitation—a state of false opinion—is, perhaps, to be associated with the ordinary "human preoccupations" of souls newly embodied after their "fall," as in *Phaedrus* 249d. For the most part, these souls are the victims of *lethe* (248c); and, not honoring reality veiled in the particulars of sense but turning away (250e), the great majority feed upon *doxa* (248b), and do not hesitate to ridicule anyone who turns his attention in the direction of divine rather than human concerns.[40] Or, again, the mind state of those who inhabit the "prison" is suggestively like the "human wisdom" of *Apology* 23a, which is said to be of little or no value—indeed, is scarcely to be distinguished from the censurable ignorance of 29b; and is doubtless the same kind of ignorance which, according to *Theaetetus* 176c, is reputed by the many to be "cleverness," whereas to Plato it is in fact "folly and manifest wickedness."

This pristine ignorance or, more accurately, *doxa pseudês,* is attributable, of course, to a failure to pierce through the appearances to what we have described earlier as the Ideal content. As to the cause of this failure, *Timaeus* 41e-42d throws some light upon it and recalls in some measure what is suggested at *Phaedrus* 248c. According to the *Timaeus,* the first birth (πρώτη γένεσις) subjects the "immortal" part of the soul (72d) to violent affections which initially derange and distort its orderly rational motion and impede knowledge and virtue until the rational power yields itself "to the revolution of the Same and the Similar that is within. . . ."[41] This is the revolution of intelligence in the soul which is "akin" to the revolution of Intelligence in the Cosmos. It is worthy of remarking that this perturbation of the soul, incident to its embodiment, was indicated in *Phaedo* 81b and, continuing through the *Republic* and the *Phaedrus,* finds renewed expression in the *Timaeus* and the *Laws.*[42]

There is every indication, then, that the ignorance of the cave-dwellers is attributable to an imbalanced but arthritic condition of the entire *psuchê*. The delusion of the prisoners is a stabilized condition, *hexis*,[43] not of an autonomous reason, but of the whole man. Man is a "unity" of rational and affective powers,[44] and neither may operate independently of the influence of the other. The habitude of the prisoners is symbolized by the fetters or bonds which always oblige them to look away from the light (519a). This lamentable "habituation" of mind is by Plato attributed to the influence of the appetitive faculty which "turns downwards the vision of the soul" (519b). Repeatedly, Plato speaks of "the eye of the soul" as wrongly directed earthward so that it is sunk in ignorance.[45] This is its *anatropê*. The baneful power of the appetitive faculty to produce this total disorientation of life and thought is summarily described in the *Republic* (586a-b):

Then those who have no experience of wisdom and virtue but are ever devoted to feastings and that sort of thing are swept downward, it seems, and back again to the center, and so sway and roam to and fro throughout their lives, but they have never transcended all this and turned their eyes to the upper region nor been wafted there, nor ever been really filled with real things, nor ever tasted stable and pure pleasure, but with eyes bent upon the earth and heads bowed over their tables like cattle, grazing and copulating, ever greedy for more of these delights . . . . because they are vainly striving to satisfy with things that are not real the unreal and incontinent part of their souls.

The imagery of the Cave is, quite evidently, symbolic enlargement upon the theme of the *Phaedo* (82e), the imprisonment of the mind through sensuous desire. It presupposes, however, Plato's now elaborated tripartite psychology. The rational faculty is no longer enslaved by the body, *soma*, but by the appetitive *dunamis* which is the "main mass" or "multitude" of the soul.[46] This dynamism "sweeps downward" and thereby overpowers the native up-reach and aspiring inclination of the intellectual faculty (517c). Therefore men live with their backs to the light, yet not literally in darkness. Actually they are suffused with light but do not know it. The light, the true realities, are the causes of such cognition as they have; and the Forms of which they are ignorant, are in fact the "real causes" of the shadows with which they are content to spend their days. Thus Plato notes how quick and how eager men of inverted vision are to discern the things which command their interest and how obtuse with respect to true realities. "Have you never observed," he asks, "in those who are popularly spoken of as bad, but smart men, how keen is the vision of the little soul, how quick it is to discern the things that interest it?" Then he adds, "a proof that it is not poor vision which it has, but one forcibly enlisted in the service of evil" (519a). *Nous* is not inherently disqualified for apprehension of truth, but it is forcibly misdirected. Therefore education is not the art of "producing" vision, but of "converting to right use from uselessness that natural indwelling intelligence of the soul" (530c).

3. THE NATURE OF CONVERSION

Once Plato's diagnosis of the human situation is understood, the way is rightly prepared for approaching his conception of the proper therapy. If existing cultural incentives are predicated upon an inverted and, hence, perverted estimate of Value and Being, it follows that it is the function of education to correct this inversion. Therefore Plato taught that *metastrophê* or *periagogê* is required as an antidote to counteract the distortion which presently warps and misdirects the soul's vision. The words for "conversion" or "to convert" appear at least twenty-one times in Book VII.[47] It is a momentous revolution which Plato has in mind; and there is little possibility of understanding Plato's *therapeia* without full assessment of its meaning, for *metastrophê* is the heart of the matter.

Education, as revolution of the "entire soul" (518c), presupposes the accessibility of reality to the knowing mind. The faculty of cognition is designated the "*organon* of knowledge."[48] As an instrument, it is conceived after the analogy of the eye. Plato speaks of *nous* as "the eye of the soul" (533d); and he apparently conceives the knowledge process after the analogy of direct sensible intuition. He observes, however, that in the case of the eye, vision is not inserted into it, for according to the then existing "physiology" of sight, vision occurs when the fire in the organ of sight coalesces with light from outside the organ.[49] Likewise, in the case of *nous*, "the eye of the soul," it is equally true that vision is neither inserted nor conveyed. The light is already in it, but the event of knowledge has subjective conditions which are not satisfied merely by the presence of available reality. In terms of Plato's analogy (*Republic* 518c-d), we are prepared to see that knowledge is an *event* which takes place in the mind when certain inward as well as outward conditions prevail or, what is the same thing, when the total orientation of the soul is right with respect to available reality. But the orientation in question is only figuratively "directional." Fundamentally, it has to do with the inner balance of affective forces.

Reverting for a moment to the imagery of the Cave, which prefaces Plato's teaching about conversion, we observed that the eyes of the prisoners cannot embrace the outward light because their backs are toward it; and they are restrained from doing so because of their fetters. According to the figure, then, knowledge cannot take place in "the eye of the soul" apart from a release from bonds and a turning about. In the event that a revolution is accomplished— always bearing in mind that it is assisted by the application of the sciences and dialectic—knowledge takes place in the mind; for knowledge is an occurrence. It is an event which signifies the transformation of implicit into explicit awareness—the metamorphosis of true opinion into stable and articulate awareness. But, according to the analogy of the eye, knowledge takes place because the light of "the eye of the mind" (*i.e.,* the pre-possession of truth, sometimes in the form of true opinion) meets and unites with its counterpart in antecedent reality. It is thus an instance of *anamnêsis* and re-cognition. It is also the realization of conformity between the knowing mind and the reality known. The event is the proper coalescence or coincidence of the light within with the light without.[50] It presupposes, furthermore, a purification (*katharsis*) of the inward light because, as is clearly suggested by *Phaedo* 67b and *Phaedrus* 250c, it is only those purified in mind who may apprehend divine realities. Indeed, we may suggest that the *metastrophê* of the *Republic* is a more advanced and articulate version of the *katharsis* of the *Phaedo*.

The conventional interpretation of the Cave symbolism has not failed to observe that the minds of men are darkened and need enlightenment; but that is only half of the truth and, when over-emphasized, tends to obscure the reasons for the benighted condition. The cognitive organ is only one power of the integral soul, and it is the entire *psuchê* which is in darkness and bondage. *Nous* participates in and is a victim of that bondage. More precisely, the *organon* of knowledge is in bondage to the rest of the soul and is thus obstructed in its function. Hence, as we have already noted, the bondage of the mind is a kind of self-imprisonment, the distinctive characteristic of double-ignorance. The self-imposed bondage of the noetic power has its analogue in the bondage of the Cave. Accordingly, Plato means to suggest that the imperious preferences of the appetitive faculty, *to epithumêtikon*, illicitly control the direction of the mind's gaze.

Now, from this circumstance, nothing is plainer than that ignorance, or false opinion, suggests an undesirable condition of moral character, that is, it indicates a nature in which the "irrational faculty" is the illegitimate but nevertheless controlling and tyrannizing principle.[51]   Therefore there can be no enlightenment of the "rational faculty" without an alteration or revolution of character or *êthos*. *Êthos* stands for the individual soul considered in its totality—man in his integrity of cognition and volition. It signifies a man's basic moral disposition and temper.[52]   Cave existence is one of faulty and reprobate "habituation." *Sunêtheia* is a word Plato frequently employs in Book VII to indicate that the condition of double ignorance is firmly allied with a defective moral state.   It is, as we have seen, vice in the soul and a condition of folly. *Sunêtheia*, therefore, is precisely that balance in the affective powers of the soul which makes for ignorance.   Accordingly the rule of the "epithumetic" faculty must be replaced by "right reason," and that means by an intelligence which has had its superior affection emancipated.[53] Thus in the analogy of the Cave we have no difficulty associating faulty moral habituation with the fetters which bind the prisoners in the direction of the shadows.

The direction of the mind's attention is, therefore, a function of the whole person, his disposition and perspective. Nothing can be plainer than that the eye of the soul is not, in Plato's view, autonomous and independent of the momentum of the affective nature. Accordingly we find Plato saying that the faculty of cognition never loses its potency, that is, its power of knowing; but everything depends upon "the direction of its conversion" (518e). The intellect does not lose all its capacity for cognition when it becomes fixed in the direction of Becoming, for minds engrossed with the sense world are, nevertheless, alert to explore, identify, and compare the constituents of that world (508d). If, however, the vision of the soul, which has been swept downward, should suffer "a conversion in the direction of the things that are real and true," then a different and superior learning can begin to take place. And, in proportion as dialectic is employed as the instrument of conversion, it will take place. On condition of such a revolution, Plato continues, the "same faculty of the same men would have been most keen in its vision of higher things, just as it is for the things toward which it is now turned" (519b). Plato contends that the reality, which overarches human experience and to which thought and aspiration ultimately are akin, is just out of sight, behind our backs or over our heads, because of an indisposition to give heed. The organ or instrument of knowledge is, in this manner, blinded and misdirected by "ordinary pursuits" and must be "purified and kindled afresh" (527d).

But now it is to be noted further that either the "way up" from darkness to light, or the "way down" from light to darkness, involves its own peculiar "disturbance" of the eyes (518a). Passage either way requires a period of adjustment and appropriate "habituation" (517a). Both alterations involve a revolution, since there is no passage from the one condition to the other without a transformation of *êthos*. Knowledge of superior reality requires a new moral disposition; and this, perhaps, is what Plato calls "the possession and habit of the Good" (509a). So it is not exceptional, but quite in harmony with Plato's regular teaching, when he asserts in the *Seventh Epistle* (343e) that the strict employment of his scientific method "with difficulty implants knowledge, when the man himself, like his object, is of fine nature; but if his nature is bad—and, in fact, the condition (*hexis*) of most men's souls in respect of learning and what are termed 'morals' is either naturally bad or else corrupted—then not even Lynceus himself could make such folk see."

This insistence upon transformation of character, and the dependency of "noumenal" knowledge upon it, is in no sense to be construed as making dialectic and scientific method superfluous. In the next chapter we shall be concerned to show in what way *methodos* is an instrument of conversion and consequent knowledge. But Plato's indication is clear enough that method will not avail in the absence of a moral temper congenial with the Truth. As Professor Grube has well said, "Truth cannot be discovered unless the main stream of desire be directed towards it."[54] In the absence of suitable temper, the final event of knowledge is inhibited and even the best instrument of knowledge, dialectic, as Callicles illustrates well enough, will be frustrated in its performance (*Gorg.* 501c). This discloses perhaps the weak link in Plato's *therapeia*; namely, that dialectic, the principal instrument of conversion, at one and the same time is designed to induce and yet itself presupposes a suitable condition of character.

4. THE HABIT OF THE GOOD

It is now desirable, though admittedly hazardous, to inquire whether these findings concerning conversion and a new *sunêtheia* in *Republic* VII have any bearing upon the parable of the Idea of the Good that shortly preceded in the famous passage of Book VI,

506b-509b. From 518c-d we have seen the indication that knowledge is an *event* occurring when, according to the analogy of vision, light within coalesces with irradiation from outward objects.[55] Conversion assured concurrence by providing a proper orientation of the knowing subject. But we found directionality to be only a simile for suitable *êthos* or moral disposition.

Now what can Plato mean by the remarkable statement that the Idea of the Good "gives their truth to the objects of knowledge and the power of knowing to the knower," or, further, that the Good is "the cause of knowledge and of truth in so far as known" (508e)? On this subject, it is rather late in the day not to presume that everything has been said; nevertheless, it is here suggested that there may be some point in approaching the problem by closely attending to the analogy in terms of which the Idea of the Good is expounded—especially to the mechanism of vision upon which Plato regularly depended.[56] According to the figure employed, the outward light of the sun affords the medium by which the "effluences" from a particular sensible are irradiated and thus are made commensurate with the visual stream emanating from the organ of vision.[57] Because both the inner light of the eye and "color" of the sensible thing together participate in the light emitted by the sun, the eye sees or is possessed of vision, and the particular thing becomes visible (508a).

Now translating the figure, presumably the Forms are symbolized by the common φῶς. In exactly the same way as the sunlight, the Forms are common both to sensible particulars, "participating" in them, and to the knowing mind, which latter, according to the analogy, receives an "influx" of the common light (508b). In consequence, the particular becomes cognizable and the subject is possessed of cognition, though initially only in the form of *doxa*. So, just as sensible things receive the power of being visible (509b), the particulars receive the power of being knowable. That is to say, by "participation" in the Formal realities or Ideal structures, particulars acquire structure and so become cognizable and are provided with their truth (508e). But, by the same token, they are also accorded existence (τὸ εἶναι) and essence (οὐσία) as stated at 509b. The reason for this is that Truth, Being, and Essence are not finally distinct for Plato, since it is Form, supplying intelligibility to particulars, which differentiates them from not-Being, although the latter is not nothing at all but, rather, is Plato's material principle.[58]

So far our interpretation has taken the analogy of the sun to invoke and involve the Forms quite as suitably as the Idea of the

Good itself. This is due to the fact that the analogy is properly to be interpreted in conjunction with the mechanism of vision. But now, in terms of this mechanism, how are we to understand the supremacy of the Good, not merely among, but even over, the rest of the Forms? For the Good is said not to be *ousia* but to transcend it "in dignity and surpassing power" (509b). In like manner, it is also said to be sovereign over "the intelligible order and region" as the sun is, in its province, sovereign over the visible sphere (509d). We get some clue to Plato's meaning if we duly observe the caution stated at 509a. Both "light" and "vision" are said to be "sunlike," but we are never to think of them as identical with the sun. Both the light and the vision it engenders are derivative, although the light is causally primary by being the medium of vision in the eye and of visibility in the illuminated object.

In a wholly comparable way, neither truth (*i.e.*, the Forms-in-themselves) nor knowledge (*i.e.*, the Forms *as* cognized) is to be identified with the Idea of the Good. Or, according to the parable, the "light," that is the Forms, is not to be identified with the Good; nor is the knowledge it invokes to be so identified. However, still keeping to his analogy, Plato asserts that they (*i.e.*, both knowledge and Forms) are "boniform"; thus, like the Good but derivative (509a).

In what sense the Forms are like the Good although not to be identified with it and also surpassed by it in dignity and power is certainly a disputable question. Is the relationship causal? If causal, is it teleological so that the Good is *telos*? It has been objected that we can hardly conceive "the Ideas as having a nisus towards good" or that the Ideas admit of change.[59] We may, however, conceive *telos*, not ontologically, but logically. In this sense the Forms may be referred to the Good as that which "justifies" them, as the *Metron* by reference to which, and as reflecting its light, intelligibility is to be ascribed to them.[60] If, as Ritter has suggested, the Good is "the significance of Being,"[61] then the Forms are causally dependent upon the Good in so far as they are partial expressions of a comprehensive Significance in which their "portions" are embraced and from which, by derivation (*viz.*, logical dependency), they have intelligibility or a place in the total economy of the Good. The relation between the Idea of the Good and the Forms is, perhaps, illustrated by the relation between a genus and its many species: the species presuppose the genus and are rendered intelligible only by reference to it. Since, however, the relation between them is a-symmetrical, the Good remains prior and has supremacy. In this sense it is suggested that the Good is the cause of "being" in respect to the Forms, namely, as cause of their intelligibility. It is the entirety in which their partial "lights" are embraced and fulfilled.

Truth and knowledge having been distinguished from the Good and subordinated to it, Plato intrudes the somewhat surprising statement: "Still higher honor belongs to the habit of the Good" (509a). Shorey translates, "possession (κτῆσις) and habit (ἕξις)."' This is doubtless justified by reference to 505b, where it is averred that all other knowledge or possession is of no avail without knowledge and possession of the Good. But what is meant by possession and habit of the Good, and why should this matter be raised at all when, presumably, we are concerned with the Good as antecedent reality and cause? Shorey says of the "habit of the Good" that Plato "may have chosen ἕξις here to suggest the ethical aspect of the Good as a habit or possession of the soul."[62] In view of 505b, there can scarcely be any doubt of it. Furthermore, in view of the fact that *metastrophê* and a new *sunêtheia* are required for attainment of knowledge, it appears all but certain. This is further reinforced by attention to the figure at 508d, where the orientation of the knower is made integral to the discussion of the ultimate object of knowledge. There it is indicated that when the soul is "firmly fixed upon the domain where truth and reality shine resplendent it apprehends and knows them and appears to possess reason; but when it inclines to that region which is mingled with darkness, the world of becoming and passing away, it opines only and its edge is blunted, and it shifts its opinions hither and thither, and again seems as if it lacked reason."[63]

In this figure one would judge that "truth and reality" are symbolized by the "light," and the "light" is not the sun but is "sunlike." But the sun, of course, symbolizes the Idea of the Good. Therefore a man is said to possess intelligence when he is oriented toward the Good, that is, when the Good is the bent and habit of his soul. This is strikingly similar to what we are told in *Phaedo* 99b; namely, that to act with intelligence is to act with a choice of what is best. It likewise is related to what is said of Anaxagoras at 98a, that if reference is made to *nous* as the cause of the Cosmos, then *eo ipso* it must be to the Good as the *telos* which actuates intelligence as final cause.[64] The relation between the Good and *nous* is both polar and symmetrical. We can only say what intelligence is by saying that the Good is its object; and, conversely, we can only indicate what the Good is by saying that intelligence is fulfilled in its

apprehension.   In the Idea of the Good the proportioned and intelligible structure of reality becomes transparent to the knowing
mind; what *is* (τὸ ὄν) and what is known and loved (τὸ γνωστόν)
become one.

It is now permissible to assert that in proportion as the axiological
bent of the soul, its aspiration for reality, is emancipated, *i.e.*, in so
far as the Good becomes the lodestone of the soul, knowledge and
intelligence may be begotten in it.   Thus the Good becomes the final
cause of knowledge or "the power of knowing to the knower" (508e).
In this sense, "the habit of the Good" specifies the entire subjective
condition, the *êthos*, which assures the commensurability of the knowing subject with Reality.   The habit of the Good *is* the Good participated in according to the manner possible to man, that is, with
his intelligent nature.   Involved here also is the pervasive principle
of Plato's epistemology: like is known by like.   In so far as there
is conformity between subject and objective reality, there can be
knowledge.   If truth and reality are "boniform," then knowledge
can ensue on the condition that the soul is "purified" and made
"boniform."[65]

Knowledge through conformation of subject with object is further
suggested by Plato's description of the mechanism of vision at
Timaeus 45b-d, a passage that only elaborates the theory which almost
certainly was presupposed by *Meno* 74b-76d.   There, vision results
from the confluence of "the pure fire within us, which is akin to that
of day," with the kindred fire without.   Sight occurs when the
"stream of vision" is surrounded by midday light.   It then "flows
out like unto like, and coalescing therewith it forms one kindred
substance along the path of the eye's vision" (45c).   But when the
kindred fire, the light of day, "vanishes into night, the inner fire is
cut off; for when it issues forth into what is dissimilar it becomes
altered in itself and is quenched . . ." (45d).   It is in the combination or coalescence of the inner and outer light—the outer making
surfaces luminous—that vision occurs.   Thus, according to the parable
of the Good, that Idea becomes the "power" which "yokes" the
faculty of knowledge with the intelligible Forms in a fashion quite
analogous to the way in which the light of the sun constitutes the
common medium between vision and what is visible.   In the main,
then, this is the mechanism of vision presupposed and employed by
both *Republic* 518c-d and 507a f.   If so, it is according to this
analogy that we are to understand "the habit of the Good."   It
signifies a condition of the "whole soul" in which the controlling

sunêtheia is one that is conformed to the *archê* of all thought and Being. It is a condition indispensable to education as it is also the chief aim and accomplishment of conversion. To discover what further Plato has to say concerning transformation of *êthos,* we shall eventually have to consult the *Phaedrus* and *Symposium* with their common theme of eros.

NOTES

1. *Rep.* 518b-c. *Cf.* 508c.

2. *Gorg.* 462c, e, 463b, 465e; *Phaedr.* 270b; *Rep.* 422c, 467a; *Phileb.* 55e.

3. See the characterization of the *philotheamones* at *Rep.* 475d and compare with *Gorg.,* 448c and *Rep.* 516c. *Empeiria* represents the practical "know-how" of those whose main source of knowledge is *aisthêsis* and whose cognition has not been systematized nor made exact, for instance, by the application of "measurement." *Cf. Protag.* 356d and *Phileb.* 55e. *Empeiria* is the trial and error practice (πεῖρα) of those whose *doxa* has as yet not been transformed into something more critical, *viz., technê.* See *infra* n. 8. *Cf. Soph.* 254a with *Rep.* 522b f.; *Epist.* VII, 342c.

4. *Phileb.* 58a-59d, 61d-e.

5. *Phileb.* 62a. A man, however learned, says Protarchus humorously, must be able to find his way home. It is perhaps permissible to say, however, that this passage of the *Philebus* does reflect some variation from the *Republic* standpoint. There, Plato was bent upon making good his case, first, that there is a true knowledge of superior realities in addition to *doxa* and, secondly, that political life is chaotic for the want of it. The *Philebus* presupposes and employs Plato's ontological advances, as in the *Sophist* especially. These embrace Becoming, as the Mixed class, within the totality of Being along with the Limit and the Unlimited. Therefore, however necessary "divine knowledge" may be, its sphere of application is the realm of the Mixture, *viz.,* actuality. There, absolute truth will never have undiminished representation either "naturally" or by human application, *technê.* This finding is not new (*Rep.* 473a), but, whereas the *Republic* is concerned to vindicate the higher knowledge primarily, the *Philebus* is primarily concerned with its application. This latter distinction is necessary to understand the difference between the two dialogues in their common effort to define the good life. See *infra,* Ch. VII, n. 15.

6. *Rep.* 539e, 484c-d, 500d f., 540a, 592a-b.

7. *Less. Hipp.* 368b f.; *Rep.* 475d, 476b; *Phileb.* 56a.

8. *Gorg.* 448c. Without the application of arithmetic and the sciences of measurement (μετρητική) and weighing (στατική) the πολλαὶ τέχναι remain trial and error efforts, conjectural, and matters of τριβή, skill and guesswork. *Phileb.* 55e, 56b; *Euthy.* 7c. In short, Plato held that *empeiria* could receive a measure of exactitude in so far as mathematical measurement was applied to casual observation and practice. *Cf. Rep.* 522c, 527c-d, *Phileb.* 57c. Perhaps he thus stated the rationale of physical science *vs.* Aristotle, who said: "Mathematical accuracy is not to be demanded in everything, but only in things which do not contain matter. Hence this method is not that of physical science, because presumably all nature is concerned with matter." *Met.* 995 a 15. Plato, of course, recognized that "materiality" did set an ultimate and insurmountable obstacle to complete mathematical analysis of actual structures. *Rep.* 530a; *Tim.* 48e, 53b. In any case, there are two sorts of *empeiria*: the trial-and-error variety, and that rendered more "exact" by the application of measurement. Correspondingly, there are two forms of *technê*: the one is mere practical "know-how"; the other proceeds by the application of rule and *logos.* This is not fully clarified, perhaps, until the *Philebus.* In the sphere

of rhetoric, *Phaedrus* 271d indicates in what way, as contrasted with *Gorgias* 463b, the practice is transformed from a *tribê* into a true *technê*. In addition, of course, the method of "division" must be employed. *Phaedr.* 265e f.

9. *Met.* 981a 1. All references to Aristotle are to the *Loeb* edition. *Cf. Met.* 999 b 1-4. Here Aristotle says: "If nothing exists apart from individual things, nothing will be intelligible; everything will be sensible, and there will be no knowledge of anything—unless it be maintained that sense-perception is knowledge." *Cf. Met.* 1003 a 12, 1059 b 25 f., 1086 b 33 f. While the "universal" serves to translate the Platonic εἶδος, Aristotle, of course, denies separability of the Form in such a way as to constitute it an individual substance. *Met.* 997 b 1 f.

10. *Met.* 982 b 3.

11. *De An.* 429 a 15-18.

12. *De An.* 430 a 20. "But knowledge, when acting, is identical with its object." Aristotle's view is a critical epistemological monism. Not everything belonging to the particular is "possessed" in knowledge. *Met.* 1031 a 15 f. The Form, however, is "possessed"; and, through the Form there is identity between the knower and the substance known. *Cf. De An.* 431 a 1-5, 432 a 2-4.

13. *Met.* 1018 b 32-34.

14. *De An.* 432 a 9.

15. *Met.* 992 b 26-30.

16. *Meno* 86a.

17. *De An.* 429 a 21-22. This is a clear implication of the view that "the mind itself can have no characteristic except its capacity to receive." The "laws of thought" are exceptions; non-contradiction is a non-examinable principle. *Met.* 1005 b 30 f.

18. *Met.* 993 a 1-3. *Cf. Post. Anal.* 71 a 28 and 99 b 26-27.

19. *Nic. Eth.* VI, iii, 2-4. *Cf.* W. Windelband, *History of Ancient Philosophy* (New York, 1906), 249-250.

20. *Met.* 1005 b 9-34.

21. *Phaedo* 81b, 82e-83b; *Phaedr.* 238a-c.

22. *Cf. Laws* 643c; *Phaedo* 83a.

23. *Rep.* 413a-b. *Cf. Gorg.* 493a.

24. *Rep.* 515c. *Cf.* the nature of δόξα ψευδής, *Soph.* 240d, as that which thinks the opposite of reality. *Soph.* 239c and 254a find Plato alluding to the Sophist as a denizen of the cave-darkness.

25. *Rep.* 516c. For the recurrent theme of bondage: *Rep.* 515b-c, 516c-d, 517b, 519d, 577c.

26. *Rep.* 515c. Plato employs νομίζω here to indicate opinion dictated by communal usage or custom. F. Bacon's "idols" of the cave and tribe, etc., derive, of course, from Plato's famed simile. *Cf. Novum Organum, Works*, ed. Spedding (Boston, 1863), VIII, 77f., with *Rep.* 520c.

27. *Laws* 886b, 819a.

28. *Rep.* 516c. *Cf. Phileb.*, 56a f.

29. *Rep.* 517b. *Cf. Phaedo* 99b. In the simile of the Cave, the sun is doubtless the source of light. But in this passage and at *Rep.* 506e, where Plato refers to the "offspring of the Good," the sun is taken as analogous with the Idea of the Good. As the sun is the highest causal reality in the visible realm, so the Good is the supreme causal reality in the intelligible realm. 508c and 517b. For the nature of real causality, *cf. Phaedo* 97c-99c and *Rep.* 508e.

30. *Rep.* 508c f. *Cf. Rep.* 517b-c. Plato continually employs the verb ὁράω to describe reason's apprehension of the intelligible realm and, with reference to the Idea of the Good, he describes it as a vision analogous to the sight of the sun in the visible world. Intellection is said to be an imitation, μίμησις, of the faculty of sensible vision, ὄψις. *Rep.* 532a. *Cf. Phaedo* 66d, 83b; *Phaedr.* 247c-d, 250d.

In the famous passage of the *Symposium* where apprehension of absolute Beauty is finally achieved after successive stages, knowledge is described as vision. *Symp.* 210e f.

31. *Rep.* 533d. Here Plato employs τὸ τῆς ψυχῆς ὄμμα, the eye of the soul. At 519b we find the alternate usage: ἡ τῆς ψυχῆς ὄψις, the vision of the soul. This is the function, *dunamis*, of the *organon* of knowledge. *Rep.* 527d. For comparable usage of the metaphor, see *Rep.* 518c, *Phaedo* 66d; *Symp.* 219a.

32. *Rep.* 533c. Cf. *Rep.* 486e, 519d, 520c, 526e.

33. Truth and falsehood, for Aristotle, are qualities of discursive reasoning. Judgments are formed by compounding terms according to the rules of valid syllogism. *De An.* 430 a 27 f. There is no truth or falsity in direct sensuous apprehension. *De An.* 427 b 13. There may be "false opinion" through misidentification. *De An.* 428 b 2. Windelband says, "Aristotle sought truth and error only in the union of concepts in so far as such a union is asserted or denied." *Op. cit.,* 251. This would seem to make truth consist merely in the truth of the *system*. This estimate is too severe, for Aristotle required an agreement between the system of concepts and the system of things, as W. D. Ross maintains. *Aristotle* (London, 1923), 26. Nevertheless there is a radical difference between Plato and Aristotle in that, for the former, truth is always wider and more inclusive than the certainty of logical system and cogent inference.

34. This is the general meaning of the "Divided Line," *Rep.* 509d f. The two principal divisions of the line, the "opinable" and the "intelligible," have their appropriate cognitive faculties or avenues of cognition. That of the opinable is sense-perception or *aisthêsis*. That of the intelligible is *nous* which has two distinguishable functions: the understanding, *dianoia*, and intellection, *noêsis*. Cf. James Adam's exposition, *The Republic of Plato* (Cambridge, 1929), 156-163.

35. *Nic. Eth.* VI, iii, 4.

36. *An. Prior* 24 b 10-19.

37. *Rep.* 510b, 511b-c.

38. W. Jaeger, *Paideia*, II, 295-300. He expresses the conviction of this writer in saying: "Therefore the essence of philosophical education is conversion, which literally means turning round. Conversion is a specific term of Platonic *paideia*, and indeed an epoch-making one." But Jaeger does not really develop the theme or connect it with the nature of ignorance for which, in Plato's view, it is calculated. It is surprising to find neither J. Burnet nor A. E. Taylor taking any special note of "conversion" at the appropriate places in their respective writings. James Adam does give perfunctory attention to "the Platonic revolution." He says that although it applies to the intellect primarily, it "effects a moral no less than an intellectual revolution." This seems to misplace the emphasis so that the real nature of Platonic conversion is obscured in that the intellectual is not seen to depend upon the moral. *Op. cit.*, II, 98.

39. *Rep.*, 413a-e. Cf. *Gorg.* 493a.

40. Cf. *Phaedr.* 249d with *Rep.* 517a; *Apol.* 31b; *Gorg.* 521e.

41. *Tim.* 42c. Cf. 44a-b. "Hence it comes about that, because of all these affections, now as in the beginning, so often as the Soul is bound within a mortal body it becomes at first irrational." Cf. *Tim.* 86c. See also *Phileb.* 29b-31a where, for the first time in the dialogues, the mind of man is expressly related to mind in the Cosmos as microcosm to macrocosm.

42. *Rep.* 519b. See especially *Laws* 626e-627d, 634a, 635d, 653d-654d, 660a. In the *Laws* a basic motif of Plato's theory of education is the imposition of the ordered and rhythmic motion of rationality upon the unordered and irrational motion of eruptive and disruptive appetite.

43. Cf. *Rep.* 618d, 435b, 511d, 509a. *Hexis* is a condition of soul more or less fixed, presumably by a good or ill concert of the constitutive powers, therefore in-

volving the affections. *Cf. Protag.* 244b, *Cratyl.* 415d; *Phileb.* 11d, 48c; *Rep.* 591b, 592b.

44. *Rep.* 443d-e, 586e, 588b f.

45. *Rep.* 533d. *Cf. Rep.* 526b, 526e, 527b, 529b.

46. *Rep.* 431a-b, 442a, 580e, 588c-d; *Laws* 689b.

47. On a rough count, Plato uses the term "conversion" twenty-one times in Book VII. He employs a number of different words which all mean "turn about" or "convert." περιαγωγή or the verb περιάγω is used five time, 515c, 518d, 518e, 521c, 533d. Μεταστροφή and μεταστρέφω appear ten times, 518d, 525a, 525c, 526e, 527b, 529a, 532b, 540c. Περιστρέφω appears three times, 519b, 521c, 526e, and στρέφω twice, 518c and 532c. Without having made an exhaustive word-study, this writer is not aware of any technical employment of *metastrophe* elsewhere in the dialogues. It does appear very nearly in the technical sense at *Laws* 887a, where Plato speaks of converting the impious to fear of the gods. This passage, pages 886-889, clearly returns to the perversity in human ignorance as the problem of education. Indeed, one can cite more passages in the *Laws* respecting the volitional factor in knowledge and ignorance than in any other work except the *Republic*. Plato's attempt to meet the problem in the *Laws* is different from that in the *Republic*. In the former, his aims are much more modest. He does not seek to educate "guardians" but the whole of the citizenry. He is content with a less rigorous therapy, which includes "conditioning" from childhood (631e, 639d). Plato's aim is not society under insight of guardian-philosophers, but society "under law." *Cf. Laws* 875a-d, and *Polit.* 301d-e.

48. *Rep.* 518c, 527d.

49. *Cf. Rep.* 508c-d. A theory of visual mechanism is assumed here. Vision does not consist merely in the inflow of light from without but a qualitatively commensurate outflow of light from the eyes. The coalescence is vision. *Cf.* J. I. Beare, *Greek Theories of Elementary Cognition*, 10-14, 43-47. Beare attributes the origin of this theory to Empedocles. Of this there is no doubt. *Cf. Frgs.* 84, 89. K. Freeman, *Ancilla*; and *The Presocratic Philosophers*, 197-199. Beare regards Plato as adopting and employing the main features of the theory. Of this there can be no doubt either, as comparison of the following passages will indicate: *Meno* 76a-d; *Rep.* 507d-508d; *Tim.* 45b-46c, 67c-68d. See *infra*, n. 55.

50. *Phaedr.* 250b alludes to the outward light, which of course is only symbolic or figurative. We understand somewhat more literally what is meant by reference to *Rep.* 478e, 479e; namely, that, for the many, the Forms are not descried through the particulars of sense. Or the particulars are not diaphanous to the Forms, *viz.*, the "light" is not "recollected" through them. In the figure of 508c, the particulars are not sufficiently irradiated by the outward light and also, 508d, the organ of knowledge is wrongly inclined toward the region of darkness, the Cave.

51. *Phaedr.* 237d. See the two leading and ruling principles. *Cf. Rep.* 442a-b, 589d f.

52. In Plato's usage, *ethos* sometimes denotes mores or habits: *Rep.* 541a; *Symp.* 207e; *Epist.* VII, 344a. It may refer to natural disposition of animals, *Rep.* 375e, or to native disposition and temper of men: *Gorg.* 513c; *Rep.*, 401a, 424d, 535b, 577a, 604e; *Symp.*, 195e; *Lys.* 222a; *Laws* 650a, 793e. In the preponderance of cases, *ethos* denotes character, that is, a moral condition of the soul, better or worse. *Cf. Gorg.*, 484d; *Crat.* 406a, 407b; *Rep.* 400d-e, 496b, 501a, 544d; *Symp.* 183e; *Phaedr.* 243c, 279a; *Polit.* 308e, 310c; *Laws*, 741e, 862b. It is in this sense that *tropos* is occasionally made coördinate with *ethos*, *Lys.* 222a; *Epist.* VII, 330a.

53. *Cf. Rep.* 591b with *Phaedr.*, 265a; *Rep.* 515c. There must be λύσις, a release, from the fetters which bind the eye of the mind. *Cf. Phaedo*, 82d, 83d.

54. G. M. A. Grube, *Plato's Thought*, 137. This important observation does not seem to be developed; but Grube is throughout clear enough in support of the general

view that the cognitive and moral aspects of the *psuchê* involve and imply each other. This emphasis has also been made by John Wild in developing his formula, "the intentional structure of psychic action." By this he means to assert, and correctly, that the rational faculty (*logistikon*) involves both "rational apprehension" and "rational aspiration" (eros). *Plato's Theory of Man*, 151, 152. See also Taylor, *Plato*, 282, where it is recognized that the "judgments" of the *logistikon* are tendentialized by appetite, superior or inferior.

55. The mechanism of vision, as conceived by Plato, evidently involves three factors: (1) the outward light of day (*Tim.* 45b; *Rep.* 507e); (2) the inward fire, light, or "visual stream" of the eye itself (*Tim.* 45c, 67c; *Rep.* 508c); and (3) color ($\chi\rho\tilde{\omega}\mu\alpha$) which, after Empedocles, is associated with "effluences" ($\dot{\alpha}\pi o\rho\rho o\alpha\acute{\iota}$) given off by particular sensibles (*Meno* 76c; *Tim.* 67c-d). Plato evidently takes the view that the sunlight must irradiate "the effluences" streaming from the object if it is to be colored and visible (*Rep.* 507e; *Tim.* 46b). But, in addition, visibility is dependent upon the coalescence of the light from within the eye with the light stream from the irradiated effluences without. Thus the definition of color at *Meno* 76d exactly conforms to the prescription: ". . . colour is an effluence of figures, commensurate with sight and sensible." It is of the greatest importance to recognize the parallels between this theory of the mechanism of vision and Plato's theory of knowledge. In particular, there are three things to observe. (1) That light of the sun in general symbolizes the Forms by participation in which particulars are rendered intelligible. This corresponds to the fact that, without illumination, the "effluences" do not constitute a colored surface. (2) That, as vision and visibility depend upon the coalescence of qualitatively identical (*Tim.* 45b) inward and outward light, so in the case of cognition, which initially is *doxa*, there is agreement or coincidence of Form given to the mind with Form partcipated in by the thing. Thus, cognition is conformation or coincidence of like with like. Cf. *Tim.* 45c. (3) That vision, and therefore knowledge also, according to the analogy, is vitiated if the organs of sight are not turned toward objects upon whose "colors" the light of day falls. This is shortly symbolized by the Cave. In that event, the eyes appear blind, "as if pure vision did not dwell in them." *Rep.* 508c. Cf. *Tim.* 45d. Pure vision does actually remain (518c), but Plato believes it has to be "purified and kindled afresh" (527d) after being "blinded" by cave-dwelling (527e).

56. Sir David Ross (*Plato's Theory of Ideas* [Oxford, 1951], 40-41) has recognized the place of the mechanism of vision in the analogy. It is not clear that its full import is developed.

57. *Rep.* 507e; *Tim.* 67c.

58. Without undertaking to develop this subject here, reference may be made to *Phileb.* 23c ff. where Plato clearly sets forth his theory of the Mixture as the combination of the Limit (the Formal) with the Unlimited (indefinite duality) or the material principle. This is the articulation of what was begun at *Rep.* 477a-b. See *infra*, Ch. VII, nn. 13, 15.

59. *Cf.* Sir David Ross, *op. cit.*, 41.

60. *Rep.* 504c, 486d; *Phileb.* 66a. A principal difficulty in denoting the meaning of the Good is due, perhaps, to the fact that it stands in reciprocal or wholly symmetrical relation with the concept of orderliness and that, in turn, with intelligence. This is signified in the *Phaedo* by the view that if the world is orderly— the work of Intelligence—it is good. It is an axiom with Plato, as at *Tim.* 30a, that order ($\tau\acute{\alpha}\xi\iota\varsigma$) is better than disorder. Cf. *Phileb.* 26b. This is axiomatic because the judgment is required by the very constitution of intelligence as axiological. The Good, then, is the objective reality of the intelligible structure of the world. But conversely, human intelligence exists in the measure that the objective intelligible Order is recognized and concurred with. Thus, for Plato, there can be no demonstration of the existence of the Good, or of Order as good, but only acknowledg-

ment of it. If it is not admitted that order is better than disorder, all argument is at an end and, presumably, Titanism must prevail. This is noted by Shorey; see "The Idea of the Good in Plato's Republic," *Studies in Classical Philology* (Chicago, 1895), 231. Acknowledgment of the Good is, initially at least, consent to the constitution of one's own mind. Acknowledgment of its sovereignty rests upon "proper" self-knowledge. Nothing less will avail. Now, an important consequence of this co-implication between the Good (as objective Order or Intelligibility) and *Nous* (intelligence) is that, with greatest difficulty and strain does Plato avoid uniting them. *Cf. Phileb.* 22c, 65d. This accounts for the mooted question concerning God and the Good. Since the Idea of the Good (Objective Order) stands in a wholly symmetrical relation with any and every intelligence, they presuppose one another and, therefore, tend to merge into one another as Constantine Ritter has argued; and, as he has also suggested, Idea tends to become content of divine thought. *The Essence of Plato's Philosophy* (New York, 1933), 374-376. This is not, however, the whole story, we believe; and for a corrective view see Burnet, *Greek Philosophy* (London, 1950), 169 n. 1, 336. The truth seems to be that Plato himself never came to rest in giving primacy either to Idea or Intelligent Cause. The Idea of the Good is the Order and Proportion which "suits" axiological intelligence; and, conversely, intelligence exists in acknowledgment of the Good. It therefore knows reality by knowing itself as axiologically engaged; and it would be absurd to require it to apprehend Reality otherwise than through itself, for it has no other way. Intelligence and the Good mutually "define" one another. No other standpoint is available outside this polarity.

61. C. Ritter, *op. cit.*, 131.

62. *The Republic* II, 105, n. f. In his essay on "The Idea of the Good in Plato's Republic" (234), Shorey understands *hexis* to signify the Good "methodologically" considered as "the habit of flexible disciplined intelligence." C. Ritter (*op. cit.*, 82) held that in one respect at least the Idea of the Good "is interchangeably used with essence (ἕξις) of the good. . . ." This latter interpretation of *hexis* seems forced and unnatural. The meaning of *hexis* in this passage evidently requires understanding of the place of *êthos* and *sunêtheia* in knowledge. An important usage of *hexis* in conjunction with *diathesis*, as states of soul, appears at *Phileb.* 11d and admits of interpretation at least commensurate with the one here given.

63. This statement is a clear anticipation of the parable of the Cave; see *Rep.* 516d f. Also observe the parallel condition with respect to vision at *Tim.* 45d.

64. *Cf. Laws* 967a. See *supra*, Ch. I, sec. 3.

65. *Rep.* 527d. *Cf. Phaedo* 67a, c, 79d; *Phaedr.* 250c; *Phileb.* 59c.

CHAPTER VII

The Means of Conversion

And it is literally true that when the eye of the soul is sunk in the barbaric slough of the Orphic myth, dialectic gently draws it forth and leads it up, employing as helpers and co-operators in this conversion the studies and sciences which we enumerated, which we called sciences often from customary usage, though they really need some other designation, connoting more clearness than opinion and more obscurity than knowledge.—*Republic* 533d

I. THE PROPAEDEUTIC STUDIES

PLATO'S conception of conversion and its role in the attainment of knowledge embodies his own important development of the idea of *katharsis*. It offers a distinctive interpretation of the therapeutic principle which had long been current among Pythagorean and Orphic sects. *Paideia* calls for more than repletion of knowledge. A moral renovation is required if truth is to replace "the involuntary lie" in the soul.[1] This species of error was still referred to in the *Laws* as the extreme and "greatest" form of ignorance. It is "want of accord, on the part of the feelings of pain and pleasure, with the rational judgment" so that a man cherishes what he really judges to be inferior. It is the "greatest" ignorance because it is enforced by and belongs to "the main mass of the soul."[2] In this predicament, a man is not only deprived of truth and reality, he is also at odds with himself. Hence, intelligence must be liberated from base subservience to the passions, freed to attain ends commensurate with its inherent potency.

If conversion is the crux of education, its occurrence cannot be left to happy circumstance and good fortune. Some instrumentalities must be available to promote it, but they ought to be employed in the case of persons who have by nature an aptitude for philosophy, for not all men are suited for learning proper to the philosophic life. This fact gave Plato pause, and over it he truly agonized.[3] Indeed, the long career of Plato as a thinker was overcast by the somber realization, enforced by experience, that the philosophic nature is a rare growth among men. Wherever found, it is especially subject to corruption. Neither arrogantly nor with condescension, but reluctantly, Plato conceded that *philosophia* is impossible for the multitude.⁴ They are too securely fettered in the Cave and too captivated by their *eidola*. So uniform and preponderant is the presiding *êthos*, so powerful to induce conformity, it seemed truly amazing that the philosophic nature should survive at all.⁵ In the light of experience, it was all the more astonishing to come upon a man of the character and perceptiveness of Socrates. For that historical actuality Plato always felt respectful wonder.

Conversion, then, which is imperative for all, Plato anticipates will be accomplished only in the case of a few. The prospect was sobering. It clipped the wings of expectation, and by the time of the writing of the *Laws*, Plato had made his peace with "Necessity" and had found a compensating alternative which doubtless mitigated the frustration of loftier hopes. In the longest and latest of his dialogues, Plato conceived a comprehensive system of societal *paideia* under the sovereign principle of law. It was a society whose sanctions were legal and religious. By inducements and right "conditioning" from childhood, respect for law was to be inculcated; and, where dissent remained, force was to be enlisted when persuasion failed.⁶

In Book VII of the *Republic*, Plato describes two different but related instrumentalities for renewing man's knowledge of reality. If education is the end, these disciplines are the means. Plato first outlines the introductory studies. These are only the "preamble" to dialectic (531d). Each study has one basic purpose and effect: to "draw the soul away from the world of becoming to the world of being" (521d). The mind is presently under ignoble constraints; hence the studies are calculated to "force the soul to turn its vision around to the region where dwells the most blessed part of reality" (526e). The result, Plato anticipates, will be knowledge. It will not be that so-called knowledge which Plato calls opinion, *doxa*.⁷ It will be *epistêmê*: "It is knowledge of that which always is, and not of something which at some time comes into being and passes away."⁸

Every commentary on the *Republic* includes exposition and examination of the propaedeutic studies. Our interest in them here is primarily directed, not to their nature, but to their efficacy for the conversion of the soul. Plato mentions five, but he really discusses only four. The five are arithmetic, geometry, solid geometry or stereometry, astronomy, and harmonics. It is Plato's claim that these studies possess the power to "convert to right use from uselessness the natural indwelling intelligence of the soul" (530c). But the efficacy of these studies or *mathêmata* depends upon Plato's conviction that each of them treats not of particular things but of pure numbers and figures separable from visible and tangible bodies (525d) and by means of pure thought (525c). The studies tend, therefore, to disengage the mind from preoccupation with sensibles and to provoke awareness of the intelligible essence.[9] In this way, Plato believes, the mind first comes to make the necessary distinction between "the visible" and "the intelligible."[10]

This process may be illustrated with reference to astronomy. The objects of astronomy are only in a proximate sense the visible objects, the revolving lights of heaven. Even the fixed stars, which exhibit the most perfect order among all sensible things and the greatest exactitude in their imperturbable regularity, are not the real objects of the study of astronomy.[11] The real objects are "movements of real speed and real slowness in true number and in all true figures" (529d). Whatever Plato means by this in detail, he seems to be identifying the study of astronomy with a rational delineation of an order of geometric figures in motion according to perfect mathematical ratios. It is at this point, in reducing the concrete science of physical motions to an abstract science of number and figure, that Plato has offended the practicing physical scientist; and it is this reduction of the concrete to the abstract against which Aristotle always protested.[12]

There is considerable reason to doubt, however, that Plato was finally content, like Descartes much later, to exhaust the concrete data of astronomy in a pure geometrical or mathematical account. Plato accepted a material principle, constitutive of sensible reality, which defied and imposed limits to exhaustive rationalization of phenomena.[13] When, however, objection is made to Plato's mathematical treatment of physical being, one thing should be remembered. His quantitative analysis of physical bodies and his concept of inertia in the *Timaeus* were the gateway through which physics, from Galilei to Planck, proceeded to its astonishing, if ominous, successes of the twentieth century.[14]

Plato's treatment of astronomy in the *Republic* passages is perhaps unfortunate; but it serves to illustrate his intention. He is proposing this study, among others, because it assists the mind to distinguish between the sensible particulars and Forms in which the former participate. The very irregularities and deviations in the movements of the heavenly bodies serve to call attention to the deficiency and imperfection that characterizes them (529d), and to stimulate awareness of the ideal symmetries and ratios in which, presumably, they participate. Plato's thought at this point is consonant with his observations elsewhere that sensible realities "fall short" and uniformly fail to embody the perfection of the intelligible world of ideal objects.[15] It is, in fact, this awareness of deficiency (τὸ ἐνδεές) which alerts the mind and provokes recollection of true and undiminished realities.

There is opportunity to refer to only one more of the preliminary studies, *arithmêtikê*. Here Plato's case is still cogent and plausible to those who are patient enough to find his meaning. Arithmetic is a study which, in the broadest terms, deals with unity and plurality, the one and the many. As Plato treats it in Book VII, it is concerned mainly with the theory of number. In Plato's opinion arithmetic is especially suited to "provoke thought" and to move and convert the soul to a comprehension of true Being.[16]

To put the matter as plainly as space permits, Plato holds that number and the theory of number are not derived from sense experience of unitary, discrete particulars. Rather, numbers are considered rational concepts, perhaps *logoi*, with the ontological status of Forms, though intermediate between Forms and things. They are antecedent to experience of things and are, indeed, the notation, presupposed, for arranging and ordering particular items of the sense world. For example, one does not attain to the whole-number concepts, 1, 2, 3, etc., by bringing sticks, stones, or apples near to each other in the perceptual field. On the contrary, by means of the first principles of number, *viz.*, unity and plurality,[17] we are able to specify any particular number, thus, any given number of stones, which come before us. But even the perception of "one stone" presupposes the already operative logical principle of identity. The number "one" is the mathematical equivalent of the logical *a priori*, unity or identity. The specific whole numbers of any series are conceived by Plato as the "limitation" of unlimited possibility which exists between "unity" and "indefinite plurality."[18] A given number is the specification of a definite sum between one and infinity. Plato abandoned the empirical derivation of number when, among other things, he observed that contrary operations, for example, dividing an apple or juxtaposing two apples, were opposing causes with identical effects.[19]

But there is an additional and even more decisive aspect of the matter. According to sense-perception, some things, though not all, equivocate and seem to partake of opposite predicates at one and the same time.[20] For example, some objects seem to be in a certain respect both one and many. We may take any number of instances, but consider, for illustration, three books of different dimensions. They are all alike and equal in so far as they are books. But in respect to dimensions, such as length, breadth, and depth, any one of them, at the very same moment, will be longer than the first and shorter than the third, deeper than the first and more shallow than the third, wider than the first and narrower than the third. Reckoning may also be made according to other qualities of other senses, such as hearing and taste, so that the "equivocation" can be multiplied in numerous respects. Plato acutely observed, then, that any given particular in certain relations is, *so far as sense-perception is concerned*, both one and many, like and unlike itself at one and the same time. Consequently, if *aisthêsis*, or sensation, is the sole avenue of cognition, a particular is not any more one thing than another and no more a unity than a multiplicity. And, just because it "equivocates" in this way, sensible experience provokes reflection in an effort to overcome manifest confusion and contradiction.[21]

Strange as this phenomenon may appear at first sight, a little reflection upon Plato's acute analysis of the *sensum* will presently indicate its plausibility. The multiple, and even contradictory, character of sensible particulars does not constitute merely a curious verbal puzzle. It must, however, be remembered that the phenomenon of equivocation obtains for sense-experience only when an object stands in certain relations with three or more objects of a comparable nature. The difficulty is not manifest to mature experience, however, because we have already solved the problem of equivocation by reflection (524b). It is quite possible, therefore, to ignore the problem unless sense-perception is taken in strict isolation from the adjustments which reason and reflection actually introduce. This last observation really indicates the whole point that Plato is propounding and desires to clarify. Because of the confusion or equivocation in which sense-experience is involved, taken in isolation, resort must be had, and actually is, to the power of thought and intelligence to resolve the contradictions. Therefore, Plato calls our attention to a specific need. He declares that "for the clarification of this [equivocation] the intelligence is compelled to contemplate the great and small, not thus confounded but as distinct entities, in the opposite way from sensation."[22]   It is at this juncture that the mind becomes alert to the difference between the sensible and intelligible orders of reality —between τὸ ὁρατόν, the visible, and τὸ νοητόν, the intelligible.

In all this we seem to be remote indeed from *arithmêtikê*. But despite appearances, we are, nevertheless, occupied with the first principles of number. These are unity and indefinite plurality (525a). From the standpoint of sense-perception, a particular is not a unity at all, but an indefinite plurality. This fact Plato believed he had demonstrated by analysis. For sensation, no particular is any more one than many. Plato believed it was this eventuality which forces acknowledgment that number and integer are not derivable from things through sensation.[23]   Number must belong among the Formal realities which are antecedents to, and presuppositions of, experience of sensible particulars. Therefore number is best understood as among the *logoi* by which, according to his own account, Socrates undertook to examine the truth of realities.[24] When reference is made to numbers as formal realities, we are able to restore unity to things and to overcome the indefinite plurality which destroys the integrity of any given sensible.

It is in some such way as this that the study of numbers helps to reawaken knowledge in the slumbering organ of cognition and constrains it in the direction of Formal Being. When, through analysis, there comes the awareness of the confusion in which sense-perception is involved respecting unity, then the soul is strongly directed upward, thinks Plato, and is compelled to discourse about pure or abstract numbers.[25] The element of counter-constraint is not to be passed by casually. The fetters which bind the mind are not easily burst asunder. Arithmetic and the other propaedeutic studies supply a counter-compulsion, which is essential to overcome the former habituation of the soul, its engrossment with Becoming.[26] Taken together, these studies provide the introductory discipline required for the emancipation of the mind and its conversion toward true Being.

2. The Power of Dialectic

Judging from Plato's remarks in his *Seventh Epistle* (340c), the preliminary studies which he recommends and describes in the *Republic* were routine preparations for the main business of philosophy. They are valuable because, in the pursuit of them, a man becomes accustomed to making the all-important distinction between sensation and thought (*Rep.* 524c), together with their respective objects. This is a good and necessary discipline of the mind (533a); but Plato believed it did not carry a man much beyond the vestibule of truth (532d). The really powerful instrument of education and the principal tool of philosophy is dialectic.

In examining the role of dialectic for conversion of the soul, some light will be shed upon the difference between the sciences and philosophy. Some explanation may also be gathered for Plato's subordination of deductive logic to dialectic and science to philosophy or wisdom. This subordination has always aroused interest and, sometimes, a measure of ill-informed speculation. In a day such as ours, when, in the prevailing opinion, philosophy is rightly subordinated to science, it may be interesting to discover why Plato held a dissenting opinion. Perhaps it is not out of place here to offer a tentative explanation for the privileged position of dialectic as compared with the method of the sciences in Plato's thought. The suggestion is offered as a hypothesis to be tested by the evidence. The superiority of dialectic, then, as the prime instrument of *philosophia* is attributable to its unequalled capacity to implement the native axiological impulse of intelligence toward that *archê* or First Principle with which *nous* has primordial affinity. The superior utility of dialectic is, then, to be explained in relation to the peculiar endowments of the human soul.

To begin with, we may as well have it from Plato's own mouth that he understands dialectic to be a means of "release from bonds" and a "conversion from the shadows" of the Cave to the region of truth above.[27] When, in the *Republic*, the question is asked, "What is the peculiar power of dialectic?" (532d), Plato's immediate answer is the one expected: Dialectic possesses the power of disclosing truth itself. In the first instance, this seems to refer to its capacity to give an exact account of the essence or *ousia* of each thing,[28] or to determine systematically what each thing really is (533b). Manifestly Plato means to say that dialectic is a method by which the Forms, in which particulars participate, are descried and apprehended by intelligence (507b). This is the sort of thing which was implied in the *Phaedo* (99e), where Socrates set forth his method of inquiring into reality by means of *logoi*. At the very least, we can admit that the characteristic function of dialectic is to assist the mind in discriminating and in identifying the Forms.

From certain of Plato's remarks it appears that this power is something which exceeds the capacity of the propaedeutic studies (534e). In any case, he says that experts in the sciences are not

necessarily reasoners and dialecticians.[29]   At the same time, Plato
has already indicated that the task of the sciences is, mainly, to
purify the mind and to afford it some measure of knowledge of
abiding reality and so wean it from exclusive preoccupation with
Becoming.[30] There is no doubt that the real object of arithmetic and
geometry is "pure knowledge," that is, of Forms.[31]   In practice,
however, the investigators of these subjects may not attain the
vantage point from which they firmly distinguish between the *pure*
and *applied* objects of their sciences.   While this is much less true
in arithmetic, it obtains in the other sciences.   Geometry and astronomy are each, according to their true nature and purpose, sciences of
"the eternally existent."[32]   But the practitioners of these disciplines
may never, and frequently do not, attain to pure knowledge of the
objects of their respective sciences.[33] Accordingly, Plato believed
that dialectic must come to the assistance of the sciences in order to
aid their practitioners in acquiring a firmer grasp upon the ideal objects
vaguely descried but too ill-defined to qualify as knowledge.   In the
Euthydemus, it is expressly stated that geometers, astronomers, and
calculators do "discover the realities of things"; but, not knowing
what use to make of their findings, hand them over to the dialecticians.[34] Presumably, Plato means that the dialectician alone is able
to exploit the metaphysical import of the discoveries.

Another, and second, difference between the preliminary studies
and dialectic is that the former take their start from sensible experience.   They may thereafter leave sense behind and rise toward an
apprehension of intelligible objects; nevertheless they originate in
the intercourse of sense with the world.   In the *Republic,* on the
other hand, dialectic is described as "discourse of reason apart from
all perceptions of sense" (532a).   In short, as we are already aware
from the *Phaedo,* dialectic approaches reality through *logoi* alone,
or through the medium of intelligible objects, and this is no impedi-
ment, but an asset (99e-100a).

Is dialectic, then, entirely independent of the sensible foundations
of experience?   In answer, we must say that it is not at all necessary
to suppose so.   The positive value and efficacy of sense-perception in
awakening recollection, to which Plato frequently refers, militates
against such a supposition.[35]   In the *Phaedo* and the *Phaedrus,* we
are specifically informed that the learning process may, and does, get
under way and receive its stimulation through the suggestive power
of sense-perception.   Sense-experience may induce re-cognition of
the Forms, under which, as species, the particulars of sense may be

subsumed.[36]   But dialectic deals, presumably, with the "species" alone and, therewith, by rightly dividing and synthesizing, provides us with an articulated grasp of essential Being.   Somewhat in this fashion, according to the *Republic,* the dialectician is said "to find his way to the very essence of each thing and does not desist till he apprehends by thought itself the nature of the Good in itself" (532a). At that point, he has arrived at the limit of the intelligible sphere.

The fact that the power and function of dialectic affords, at the end of the course, knowledge of the Idea of the Good is its third distinguishing difference from the propaedeutic studies.[37]   In developing this theme, Plato endeavors to make plain the irreducible difference between the method of the sciences and that of dialectic.   At the same time, he is incidentally locating the difference between knowledge as "understanding" ($\delta\iota\acute{\alpha}\nu o\iota\alpha$) and knowledge as wisdom. It is upon this important distinction that our interest is focused, because it supplies us with the sought-for explanation of the superiority of wisdom to science and demonstration in Plato's thought.

Nothing less than the power of dialectic is able to yield apprehension of the ultimate object of knowledge.   However, dialectic stands on the base of the sciences.   Upon this, in Book VII, Plato recurrently insists (533b).   But, on examination, he finds that the special sciences are deductive in procedure.   With regard to them, inference is occupied with assumptions—we may call them judgments —from which it proceeds "down" to a conclusion ($\tau\varepsilon\lambda\varepsilon\upsilon\tau\acute{\eta}$) (510b). Plato terms these assumptions "starting-points" of thought, *archai* or *hypotheseis.*[38]

The sciences treat their particular hypotheses, or points of origination, as if they were granted by all concerned.   They are generally conceded; but, since they are left unexamined, Plato describes them as "absolute assumptions" and as "arbirtary" (511c).   It is not that they are imposed, but that consent to them is gained without examination or any effort at verification.[39]   Examples of such arbitrary hypotheses Plato identifies with what, for example, after Euclid, have commonly been termed postulates of geometry such as the shortest line between two points or the three kinds of angles (510c).   From "starting-points" like these, there is a leading-out or application of consequences (510b).   The resulting body of knowledge deduced from any given set of premises undoubtedly assures demonstration ($\dot{\alpha}\pi\acute{o}\delta\varepsilon\iota\xi\iota\varsigma$).   Taken as a system of defined meaning, it may be possessed of cogent connections between the initial assumptions and the derived conclusion.   It is irrefragable, perhaps, with respect to connection; but it is, as Burnet said, "established only by the consistency of its consequences."[40]　　Accordingly it is no more true than the truth of its initial assumptions.　Therefore Plato noted that all which intervenes between the starting-point and the conclusion, together with the conclusion itself, is not really a matter of knowledge because the initial premise was, to begin with, not a matter of certainty (533c).　Thus it seemed likely to Plato that the abstract sciences only afford greater clarity than opinion (*doxa*), but more obscurity than knowledge (*epistêmê*).[41]　This medium state of knowledge Plato distinguishes with the term *dianoia* or "understanding" (533d).

In contrast with the abstract sciences, it is the characteristic of dialectic, not to proceed down from a hypothesis to a conclusion, but to make its initial stand upon a hypothesis, as upon a foothold, and to rise up from thence "to that which requires no assumption and is the starting-point of all."[42]　The assumptions are left behind, and thought attains to that which is a "principle-in-itself," requiring no assumption, but transcending assumption.　In this principle, we are prepared, of course, to locate the supreme intelligible object, namely, the Good.　In bringing the mind to a knowledge of the *archê* of all thought, dialectic is, therewith, shown to be the most powerful instrument for the revolution of the soul and for turning "the eye of the mind" toward real Being.　But is this more than a claim?　If dialectic, starting from certain hypotheses and leaving them behind, conveys the mind upward to the First Principle, by what staging does it rise through the insubstantial air?

Elsewhere in the dialogues, apart from the *Republic*, Plato refers to the kind of hypothesis from which dialectic makes its ascent.　In the *Phaedo* (100a), Socrates describes the dialectical use of hypothesis: "I assume in each case some principle which I consider strongest, and whatever seems to me to agree with this, whether relating to cause or anything else, I regard as true, and whatever disagrees with it, as untrue."　That which Socrates describes in this passage is not simply, as Burnet once suggested, the method of deduction, *viz.*, the way down from a hypothesis to a conclusion.[43] If that only were meant, then Socrates' method would be indistinguishable from the method of the propaedeutic sciences of the *Republic*, not the method of dialectic at all.　On the contrary, Socrates' description of his method in the *Phaedo* has much greater affinity with the kind of hypothesis with which dialectic works, as this is described in the *Meno* (86e-87b).　There it is indicated that dialectic employs hypotheses and that, in the case of dialectic, knowledge advances, not by deducing consequences rigorously from premises, but by exploring, through careful scrutiny, the implications of some antecedently acknowledged principle for the illumination of cognate problems. When, however, in the *Republic* Plato describes the method of the sciences as moving down from a starting-point to a conclusion, he signifies the application of a general principle to less generalized particulars (510d). In the sciences, Plato signifies that knowledge is enlarged in so far as specific facts or relations are shown to be instances of an accredited and more generalized concept. Veridical deduction is the right method of relating the unknown to the already known, but it is not the way of dialectical discrimination of the known, that is, the known in the form of *doxa alêthês*. The validity of deductive science depends upon exhibiting real, rather than spurious, relations between the already known (*i.e.*, an assumed hypothesis) and something else. To this latter purpose, of course, Aristotle codified the rules of syllogism and the canons of legitimate inference in his *Prior Analytics*.

This, however, is not the use which dialectic makes of hypotheses. Dialectic, as described in Book VII of the *Republic*, is essentially the same process which was sketched in an earlier context.[44] It is for the most part the familiar procedure of Socrates, widely illustrated in the pre-*Republic* dialogues. It is the method of searching scrutiny and cross-questioning or *elenchos*. It confronts vacillating opinion[45] and regularly proceeds by exposing and eliminating contradictions hidden in uncritical thinking.[46] Through clarification of thought to itself, dialectic has the effect of rendering explicit and, therefore, stabilizing "true opinions" which, in varying degree, men do entertain regarding truth and reality. As *elenchos*, dialectic does not proceed "down" to conclusions (510b), although dialectic in its other form, as "division," may in a sense do so. Rather, by exploring the import of already acknowledged principles, it is described as proceeding continually "upward" to principles of even greater generality. It is the business of *elenchos* to move among concepts,[47] and to arrange them according to their real affinities and differences. In short, that which the *Republic* mainly understands by "dialectic" articulates the given manifold of intelligible objects, embedded as it were in the matter of *doxa*, and which, collectively, constitute the unexplored but, somehow, given deposit of human intelligence. Hence, dialectic probes the implications of such presagements of intelligible reality as are already apprehended; and, therefore, the presupposition of the independent "upward" movement of dialectic is the universal pre-possession of the ingredients of knowledge present in the form of true opinion. As has already been stressed earlier, this pre-possession, constituted by the fragments of true opinion, is as yet untransformed into the clarity and reliability of stable knowledge. Plato describes such an imperfect state of knowledge as midway between wisdom, *phronêsis,* and false opinion or ignorance.[48] It is the role of dialectic to effect the necessary transformation and clarification.

a. Two Forms of Dialectic

But, now, with what justification may we distinguish between two forms or branches of dialectic: the one, *elenchos,* taking a kind of upward way; the other, "division," proceeding in some sense downward? It is not at all clear that this distinction was articulate in Plato's thought in the period when he composed the *Republic;* so there is no intention here of accenting this differentiation, which really comes later, save in so far as it may assist in understanding the "upward" movement of dialectic in the *Republic* passages under consideration.

Before the composition of the *Phaedrus* and the *Sophist,* Plato seems to have associated dialectic largely with the Socratic *elenchos,* although it was regarded by him as a discriminatory method, as reference especially to *Republic* 454a will show.[49] It therefore implied "division" or separation in its procedure, though not strictly "dichotomy" which was a subsequent development;[50] and Socrates, as Stenzel claimed, is not usually represented as employing it.[51] Nevertheless, it is the purpose of *elenchos* to resolve confusion and contradiction among espoused opinions and to separate out the true from the false. In similar fashion, as stated at *Republic* 532a, the "essence" is extracted, presumably, from what was merely an opinion of it.[52] In the *Phaedrus,* however, Plato set forth the joint-method of division and composition which, thereafter, he was widely to employ.[53] So when we come to the *Sophist* (226c-231b), we find a distinct development in which dialectic seems to acquire broader denotation and stands for intellectual inquiry with two main divisions. As a matter of fact, the method of division is itself employed to differentiate the one from the other. At one point (226c), the word *diakritikê,* the art of discrimination, is used seemingly as a covering term for all discriminatory method, although it has no recurrence in the dialogues. However, it seems to embrace practically all which thereafter Plato is to understand as dialectic.

Looking more closely into the passage of the *Sophist* referred to, it appears that *diakritikê* is divided into two forms only one of which Plato is at the moment concerned to identify. It is the art of the soul's purification and the instrument thereof. Nevertheless, the two are initially distinguished as species of the art of discrimination, the latter serving as genus. The one method separates "like from like" (226d), and is rather obviously to be identified with the method of division, which regularly is employed to make suitable distinctions where "resemblances" between things are so close and instances so "doubtful" as to make accurate reckoning and exact predication difficult.[54] The other method of discrimination separates "the better from the worse." Plato then says that while there is in currency no name for the first, the second sort of discrimination, which "retains the better and throws away the worse" (226d), may be called *katharmos*, a sort of purification.

Then follows another dichotomy in which purification of the body by gymnastics and medicine is separated from purification of the soul. Meanwhile, two sorts of evil in the soul are specified. For one of them, presumably, purification is suited. The one evil is "disease" in the soul, which is disagreement within it of factors that by nature are related and akin.[55] The other is "deformity," which is a disproportion (ἀμετρία) on account of which the soul, in seeking to know, hits beside the mark. Consequently it is ignorant, supposing itself to be wise (229c); and this is "folly" or double ignorance and false opinion.[56] For disease in the soul or "wickedness," the political art is suggested as the proper therapy (229a); but, for disproportion and ignorance, it is the second form of *diakritikê* which is offered as the suitable corrective (231b). But this is immediately identified with the *elenchos*. Its function, first of all, is to expose the contradictions prevailing in the mind "about the same things, in relation to the same things, and in respect to the same things"; and so it emancipates that mind from "high and obstinate opinions." In so doing, it encourages and promotes inquiry in place of presumption (230b). The *elenchos* has much the same role as was ascribed to it in the *Meno* (84a-c), and it is now, once more, affirmed to be "the greatest and most efficacious of all purifications" (230d).

Summarizing the matter, it is of exceptional importance to note the following points. First, that the *elenchos* is conceived as analogous with *katharmos*, which "retains the better and throws away the worse." This perpetuates a thought very similar to that of the *Phaedo* (82d), where the dialectic method of questions and answers is the prime instrument of philosophy for the purgation of the soul.[57] Secondly, *elenchos* is a method employed upon the subject of knowledge or, rather, upon the content of his thought, with a view to enlightenment through clarification. Nowhere, either earlier or here in the *Sophist*, is it a method for knowing the outer world of Becoming; and this, perhaps, explains in part Plato's indication in the *Republic* that dialectic is independent of the data of sense in its operations and aims.[58] Thirdly, the method of purification described in the *Sophist* is identical with the method of dialectic as employed in the *Meno* and *Republic*. It is thus reaffirmed as part of the dialectical art and in no sense resigns its function in favor of the method of division. According to the evidence of the *Sophist*, it is most plausibly to be regarded as one half of the dialectical or diacritical art.

Finally, in the fourth place, the method of division, separating "like from like" by the principle of dichotomy, may be understood as a way of "descent" from the genus to the individual of the species. We start with an espoused general conception and then, by the joint-method of dichotomy and composition, isolate and identify the sought-for phenomenon which falls under the genus. As in the case of "deduction" in the abstract sciences (*Rep.* 510b), the individual, eventually identified, is logically determined by the genus under which it falls; but, since we are dealing with empirical realities rather than abstractions, we must first locate it before we can say so. Hence the determination remains only logical and not actual. This is one reason why, for Plato, empirical knowledge of classificatory science never exceeds probability.

It is, however, by benefit of the genus that we can eventually identify and know the individual, that is, as a species with differentia. But it now must be emphasized that the general conception from which we start in the process of division is *assumed* and, hence, somewhat "arbitrary" in a manner comparable with the arbitrary hypotheses of the pure or abstract sciences of the *Republic* (511c).[59] This is exhibited in the fact that the effort to define the "sophist" and the "true statesman," in the *Sophist* and the *Politicus* respectively, begins in each case with the selection of an "example," pattern, or *paradeigma* which supplies a postulated analogy or assumed general conception from which dichotomy then proceeds.[60] The result will be that the eventuating definition, resulting from "composition" of the isolated differentia, will have reliability proportionate to the actual suitability of the *paradeigma* adopted at the beginning. But the suitability must always remain problematic, with the consequence that the resulting "knowledge" will be problematic also. And this is comparable to the situation in the abstract sciences: As remarked in the *Republic,* the "conclusions," however rigorously deduced, remain merely hypothetical because the postulates are assumed rather than known to be true (533c, 511d). This would seem to enforce the view, taken earlier,[61] that knowledge by way of division rightly pertains to the subordinate sphere of *dianoia* rather than to that of *epistêmê.*

b. The Ascent of Dialectic

In the light of the foregoing, we are in a better position to understand the *ascending* character of dialectical logic as contrasted with the *descending* nature of deductive logic in the abstract sciences. Dialectic, as *elenchos,* examines its own assumptions or hypotheses, a procedure illustrated in every dialogue where Socrates is shown appraising and sifting the well or ill-considered opinions of men respecting courage, justice, holiness, or virtue, as the case may be. The sciences, on the contrary, take assumptions for granted as methodological absolutes (511c). Each branch of science regards its special postulates as understood within its own limited frame of reference. No effort is made to render fuller account of them. To be sure, that which a science such as geometry seeks to know is not particular embodiments of squares or diagonals (527c). What it really seeks is "sight of those realities which can be seen only by the mind" (510e). Thus the sciences do seek and, indeed, find the "intelligible" rather than merely the "visible" (509d); but the sciences employ their postulates, never questioning their validity, with a view to logical operation within the restricted domain specified by the range and pertinency of the postulates themselves. There is no thought of going beyond them in pursuit of prior and superior principles, with the result that the knowledge attained belongs to the subordinate sector of the intelligible portion of the Divided Line—the sector which is correlated with *dianoia,* or understanding, rather than with *epistêmê* (533e).

By contrast, it is the function of dialectic to grasp the other and superior section of the intelligible portion of the Divided Line (511b). To this end dialectic examines its hypotheses rather than takes them for granted. Plato apparently implies, that to examine these initial premises is really to refer them to some higher principle as their necessary justification. Perhaps the most readily available example of this is the *prôton philon* of the *Lysis:* As medicine is justified, *i.e.,* is a good, for the sake of health, so many things are instrumental to the well-being of something else and are justified by the good they serve. In an intelligible or orderly world, there must be a good in relation to which and for the sake of which whatever is good finds its justification, that is, *its reason for being*. Since the final good justifies all else, it itself requires no justification. It is, to snatch Emerson's words from an alien context, "its own excuse for being." And, in the *Lysis* (219c), Plato was already referring to this *prôton philon* as an *archê* or first principle.

It is against such a background that we may partly understand Plato's expressed view in the *Republic* that the hypotheses of dialectic are "underpinnings" and "springboards" from which the mind is able to rise to a principle that requires no assumption at all and which may be regarded, therefore, as a true First Principle.[62] As to the express character of these "underpinnings," enough has hitherto been said to suggest rather forcibly that they pertain to the province of uncritical *doxa*. They are not, however, to be identified with just any opinion, true or false; for Plato asserts in the *Politicus*, as we should expect, that one who begins with "false opinion" can never attain even to a small part of truth (278e). For the attainment of knowledge, it is evidently necessary to begin with "true opinions." It is a boon when these are found already alive and vigorous in such men as Plato points to in the *Protagoras* and the *Meno*. In such a case, all that is called for is to make them fast by "causal reasoning," which we have no difficulty in identifying with dialectic as described in the *Republic*.[63] But when "false opinion" is the prevailing condition of the soul, then, from *Alcibiades I* through the *Sophist*, it is Plato's consistent word that the *elenchos* must first reduce the mind to "perplexity" by admission of contradiction among espoused opinions and to the end that desire of learning may replace obstinate presumption. Where, however, as in the *Meno* (97b), there are men who cherish true opinions, or as in the *Republic* (479e), there are those who honor many beautiful things and many just things but have no comprehension as yet of beauty-in-itself or justice-in-itself, then dialectic goes to work to the end of clarifying and stabilizing true opinion by inducing apprehension of the "one" in the "many" (507c), or of the "essence" of each thing (532a). When this is accomplished, the mind is working up to pitch and is related to reality, not "according to opinion," but "according to essence" (κατ' οὐσίαν).[64]

So far, our finding is that the upward movement of dialectic in the form of *elenchos* is partially explained by the fact that dialectic *refers* the mind to the *import* of truer opinions. It refers the mind to something "higher up," to a superior principle which is implied by a principle or hypothesis "lower down." In this manner, in its power to lead the mind up in the direction of superior reality, dialectic is incomparably the best means for the conversion of the soul (533d). But, in addition, it is in its power to refer the mind to the higher principle implied in the lower that dialectic, in its operation, is said to "do away with" or "destroy" assumptions (533c). The starting-points are left behind in an upward course which continually relinquishes the lower for the higher until an *archê* or principle devoid of all supposition is attained, the ἀνυπόθετος ἀρχή (510b). It is here that we may discern the cogency of Plato's comparison of *elenchos* with purification in both the *Phaedo* and the *Sophist*. In the latter dialogue, we found the *elenchos* identified with that branch of the discriminatory art which "retains the better and throws away the worse" (226d). This is close enough symbolism for the function of *elenchos* in the *Republic*. Probably it was in this parallelism that Plato found an analogy between Orphic religious tradition and his own conception of conversion through dialectic and revolution of *êthos*.[65]

3. Ascent to the First Principle

There remains, however, one more step to be taken in order to render a full account of the power of dialectic. Plato indicates that dialectic, aided and supported by the sciences as helpers (533d), assists the mind to apprehend the ultimate principle of all thought and the supreme object in the intelligible realm. This is an amazing assertion; but Plato is prepared to elaborate his meaning. Dialectic actually advances through the stageless air, as it were, leaving behind or "doing away with hypotheses" (533c). The eye of the mind is raised up to a first principle where it finds the final confirmation of thought (533c). By "confirmation" Plato seemingly means that the mind comes upon a principle that requires justification and explanation by reference to nothing besides itself. In this manner, such a principle "transcends," or requires no assumption whatever.[66] It is of the utmost importance to understand what Plato may mean by a principle which transcends assumption. We already know what that principle is; it is the Idea of the Good (532b). But we have yet to understand why it is the true First Principle without any supposition or arbitrariness.

Functionally considered, there are other first principles both in the sciences and in dialectic. In the nature of things, all knowledge proceeds in a specific direction, *viz.*, from the known to the as yet unknown. Thus, to reiterate, the postulates of geometry are first principles from which theorems are subsequently deduced (511b). Likewise, "unity" and "indefinite plurality" are the first principles of arithmetic (525a). Among the sciences, learning advances in so far as something unknown can be referred to the known by showing that it has implicative relations of some kind with the latter. It is the nature of the "understanding," *i.e.*, discursive reasoning, to progress by admitting to the circle of the known whatever may be safely deduced or inferred from the known. Knowledge takes the form of step-by-step justification of something more by reference to assumed principles. It is extension of application. But, in the sciences, Plato alleges that such premises are arbitrary assumptions, even though they receive the consensus of accreditation. Their sufficient validation consists in the fact that they are "obvious to everybody." If a man is unable to concur regarding their self-evidence, he, rather than the principles, must be regarded as eccentric. No argument is available to disperse his blindness. The premises of the sciences, as points of departure for inquiry, however, are self-evident only *within a defined and limited frame of reference and for the purposes which are prescribed by that same framework, and to which purposes, the postulates are servants.* The man who does not gather the self-evidence of the principles is, doubtless, insufficiently adapted to the frame of meaning within which the postulates have their relevance and, therefore, their self-evident truth. The arbitrariness of the hypotheses of the sciences is a consequence of the partiality and delimited frame of meaning within which they operate.

Plato, therefore, finds no alternative save to locate the ultimate First Principle within an all-embracing frame of meaning which commends itself as the maximum reference-point of human thought. In the hypotheses of the sciences, Plato observed a deficiency of self-evidence. The deficiency he attributed to their partiality and limited denotation as contrasted with the richness of total human experience. The latter is possessed of far wider and more foundational meanings than those defined by the sciences of arithmetic, geometry, or astronomy. Neither the One-and-Indefinite Plurality of arithmetic nor the postulates of geometry could exhaust the quest of the human mind

for significance. There were larger perspectives and more fundamental values; and nothing could be ultimately self-evident which
was too narrow to embrace them.

Like the sciences, as already noted, dialectic starts with assumptions or hypotheses. These hypotheses, as the content of *doxa alêthês,*
likewise possess a more or less limited denotation; but when they are
sifted and examined, they are seen to point beyond themselves
to something else. Whether we consider beauty, or knowledge,
or the parts of virtue—such as justice, courage, or wisdom—in
every case something "higher up" is implicated. Knowledge, for
example, is not beneficial but may be harmful, unless it is knowledge
of the Good.[67] In the light of these considerations, what can be
clearer than that the *archê* which "destroys" or does away with all
supposition is one in which the fundamental interest of the human
mind finds its complete fulfillment and satisfaction? Plato's distinction between a Principle devoid of supposition and the hypotheses
of the sciences is to be looked for here. The moderate arbitrariness
of the latter derives from the fact that they do not answer to the
mind's demand for ultimate significance. Nothing, in fact, does,
except that reality which Plato calls the Idea of the Good. This
circumstance, this fact of human experience, is but a corollary of
what we have called the inexpugnable axiological bent of *nous,* of
human intelligence, or of Intelligence in general.

The true First Principle, the absolutely self-authenticating hypothesis, which has no supposition and "destroys" all supposition, is
exactly what we might expect it to be if we attend to Socrates' words
in the *Phaedo*: To act with intelligence is to act with a choice of
what is best (99b). Intelligence is axiologically determined. Reason
is solicited by, and precipitated toward, the Good. Nothing, therefore, is intrinsically intelligible or is self-evident with crystalline
clarity except the Good to which human reason is essentially conformed. In Plato's view, to deny this is man's repudiation of man
and the subversion of his own nature. To be dissatisfied with this
outcome is to require the impossible—a vantage point for the interpretation of existence other than the one man is given in virtue of his
inherent intellectual constitution.

By this analysis we approximate to a comprehension of the
supremacy of the Idea of the Good in Plato's philosophy. At the
same time, we are in a position to understand the reasons for his
subordination of "understanding" to epistêmê and of the sciences
to *philosophia.* Philosophy, employing dialectic, is able to assist the

mind to lay hold of the Good by which human intelligence is already laid hold. The Good is the *ne plus ultra* of intelligibility, because, with it alone, is there a complete and exhaustive mutuality between the Known and the human knower. Mutuality is only partial and incomplete in the case of the *initial* hypotheses either of the sciences or of dialectic. Their denotation is limited; therefore, their self-evidence is partial. In the case of the supreme intelligible object, the Good, there is such conformity between *nous* and its Object that all further questions are rendered meaningless in the perfected meaningfulness of this coalescence. The true First Principle of thought is at length descried. It is truly an *archê*, because all arbitrariness is resolved. William Temple, conveying his own viewpoint, succeeds very well in indicating Plato's in his suggestive remark: "When Mind, determined by Good as apprehended, initiates activity, no further explanation is necessary. The inquiring mind, confronted with an example of what it perfectly understands as the essential characteristic of its own being, is completely satisfied."[68]

It is the principle that Temple states which is important: Intelligibility obtains where the human mind encounters reality congruent with its own essential nature. Then it is, as noted in the preceding chapter, that knowledge is perfected in the *event* of that mutuality. Temple goes on to say, in the same passage, that knowledge is present when the "mind has recognized itself and is satisfied." This last statement, however, is less suitable to Plato's meaning. *Nous*, "the indwelling power of the soul," is not satisfied because it finds itself again in its Object. Rather, it finds complete intelligibility in its Object because the Good is that antecedent reality with which, in its essential nature, the mind of man is akin.[69] As we have already seen in an earlier connection, the possibility of knowledge depends upon the primordial conformity or "kinship" of the faculty of knowledge with its correlative object. In the ultimate sense, that "kinship" is defined and specified in the concept of the Good. It seems to be true, therefore, as was suggested at the start of this discussion, that the power of dialectic lies in its capacity to implement the native axiological impulse of the mind. The "logic" of dialectic is therefore shown to be inseparable from Plato's conception of essential humanity. This conception perhaps discloses the ultimate faith of Platonism: that the soul of man is related to ultimate reality as microcosm to macrocosm.[70] Did Plato take this from the axiological consciousness of Socrates? There is some reason to think so.

NOTES

1. *Rep.* 535e. Cf. *Alcib.* I, 117a; *Laws* 730c, 731c; *Protag.* 358c; *Soph.* 228c.
2. *Laws* 689a-b, Cf. *Rep.* 431a-b, 442a.
3. Cf. *Rep.* 499c, 502a, 503b-c.
4. *Rep.* 494a; *Polit.* 300e.
5. *Rep.* 496b, 498a.
6. The rationale of the *Laws* is forthrightly stated at 874e-875d. It is probably to be admitted that law, as "second best," replaces the "insight" of the guardians in the *Republic* as the basis of polity. Insight is still indirectly normative, but law has become directly normative. Cf. *Polit.* 301d-e. It ought to be added that an important reason for this is Plato's gradually formulated conviction that even the best men are corrupted by *pleonexia*. Cf. *Laws*, 713c, 731e f., 646b f., 687c f. Also, Plato was early aware that power corrupts. *Rep.* 565d; *Laws* 691c. After the rebuffs of experience, especially with Dionysius of Syracuse, Plato was chastened in his anticipations of the good society through the rule of a king-philosopher. A man "competent by nature and by a birthright of *theia moira*" fitted to assume rulership, Plato did not find existing anywhere, though he might, conceivably, arise. *Laws* 875c-d. However, the rule of law as "second best" is already anticipated in *Republic* 590d-591a. It is not purely a sorry alternative forced upon him in his later days.
7. *Rep.* 509e f. In the widest sense, according to Plato's usage, *epistêmê* embraces both the findings of the "sciences" and those of dialectic. It includes, then, the functions of both *dianoia*, understanding, and *noêsis*, intellectual insight. Its highest stage, however, is *noêsis*, attained only through dialectic.
8. *Rep.* 527b. Cf. *Rep.* 585c-d; *Phaedo* 78d-79a.
9. *Rep.* 525a-c.
10. *Rep.* 524c. Cf. *Phaedo* 79a; *Tim.* 27d-28a.
11. *Rep.* 529c. Cf. *Epist.* VII, 343a-c.
12. One will reasonably concur with Adam's judgment: "Plato's error lies in an undue extension of the method of pure mathematics to Astronomy and Harmonics." *Republic of Plato*, II, 167.
13. Cf. *Rep.* 530a and *Tim.* 53b f. The material principle in Plato's ontology may be variously viewed. Logically considered, it is indefinite plurality, which, in the case of number, is the possibility of any definite sum when "limited" by unity. In another sense, as in the case of the Receptacle of the *Timaeus*, it is the "necessity" which gives temporary fixity to any ingression of Form (*Tim.* 50c), and, therefore, constitutes the particularity of any particular. It is, in short, what makes the difference between ideal possibility and actuality. *Tim.* 50b-c, 52b-c. The actual is always deficient by the standard of the ideal, and so is regularly said to be "as good as possible." *Tim.* 30a, 53b, 56c.
14. Cf. C. Singer, *A Short History of Science* (Oxford, 1941), 194 ff., and Damphier-Whetham, *A History of Science* (Cambridge, 1929), 144, 190. It is now commonly granted by historians of the subject that sixteenth- and seventeenth-century science took its clue, not from Aristotle's qualitative treatment of physical bodies, but referred all "secondary qualities" to the subject of experience, leaving "primary qualities" to the object. The object becomes thereby a magnitude to be known *quantitatively* in terms of extension and force or inertia. Plato's mathematical treatment of physical *stoicheia* becomes, therefore, the pattern of physical investigation. Even F. Bacon recognized that his "experimental method" required "counting, measuring, and weighing." *Novum Organum, Works*, ed. Spedding, VIII, 134. He was willing to state that "inquiries into nature have the best result, when they begin with physics and end in mathematics." *Loc. cit.*, 177. *Timaeus* 56c ought to make it plain that Plato did not regard the mathematical account of bodies to be the whole or exhaustive account; for actual existences are constituted

of absurd or irrational constituent, *viz.*, "matter," but this is not "stuff." The application of mathematics was Plato's method of giving *empeiria* a greater measure of exactitude by the application of *metrêtikê*. Thus empirical observation and trial-and-error practice, *tribê*, were converted into *technê*. For Plato physical science, as in *Tim.* 53c f., is only more or less exact *technê*, never more than a probable account.

15. Cf. *Phaedo* 73d-75b and *Rep.* 476a. The concept of aspiring but "falling short" in the *Phaedo* may well be the antecedent to Plato's placing particulars "between" Being and not-Being, *Rep.* 477a, and probably led eventually to the concept of the Mixture, such as we find in the *Philebus* (27d). Meanwhile, it is interesting to note at *Rep.* 619a that, in the moral sphere, the good life becomes the "mean" (τὸ μέσον) between excess-and-defect, the latter duality being an analogue of the material principle. This pattern is obviously elaborated in the *Philebus* 27c-28a. See also *Polit.* 283e.

16. *Rep.* 523d, 525d.

17. *Rep.* 524e-525a.

18. Plato's theory of number has been the subject of much commentary in recent years. Here the reader is referred to Aristotle's statement that Plato derived number from the dyad of the Great-and-Small, by participation in unity. *Met.* 987 b 21. Aristotle says that number is engendered out of the "material principle" by the introduction of unity as πέρας, or "limit." Consideration of *Philebus* 25a f., indicates the essential correctness of Aristotle's statement.

19. Cf. *Phaedo* 96b-c, 101a f., and *Rep.* 479b, 524b.

20. Cf. *Rep.* 479b, 523b, 524a.

21. *Rep.* 523a-526b. J. Adam, *op. cit.*, II, 110, has indicated an understanding of the dyadic character of perception discernible in the equivocation of sensible particulars. The capacity of sensible particulars to admit of contradictory predication is explicitly recognized in the *Parmenides* at 129a ff. At 129d the young Socrates affirms there is nothing strange in the fact that sensible things may be regarded as both *one* and *many* at the same time. It would only be astonishing if τὰ γένη and τὰ εἴδη admitted of contradictory predication. It is precisely this willingness of Socrates to assert the *difference* between the Forms and the particulars in this respect that makes him an asserter of the reality of the physical world which Zeno's puzzle would deny. According to *Rep.* 524d, "provocative" things are said to be those sensibles which "impinge upon the senses together with their opposites."

22. *Rep.* 524c.

23. *Rep.* 524c.

24. *Phaedo* 99e. Careful examination of *Phaedo* 97a-b will show that Plato was there already posing problems which made the empirical derivation of mathematical concepts difficult, if not impossible. In his treatment of arithmetic in Book VII of the *Republic*, we are allowed a glimpse of his further analysis and its solution.

25. *Rep.* 525d. Cf. *Polit.* 258d.

26. The force of ἀναγκάζειν is not to be ignored in the following passages: *Rep.* 524c, 525d, 526e, 529a. Education proceeds against a powerful lag and spiritual inertia and must introduce a counter-constraint.

27. *Rep.* 532b-c.

28. *Rep.* 534b, 532b.

29. *Rep.* 531d-e.

30. *Rep.* 527b, d. Cf. 521d, 523a.

31. Cf. *Rep.* 525d, 526a-b, 527b.

32. *Rep.* 527e, 530b.

33. *Rep.* 527a and 529a-e. We have here further evidence of Plato's pardonable error with reference to empirical science. His distinction between pure and applied knowledge in sciences other than *arithmêtikê* and *geometrikê*, is arbitrary and probably illegitimate. Plato ought to have recognized, even on his own principles

(*Phaedo* 74a-d; *Tim.* 48b, 52c, 53b, d), that astronomy and harmonics are necessarily concrete. This is so because none of them can finally be divorced from the materio-spatial continuum. Undoubtedly, their phenomena may be rendered intelligible by mathematical notation. The notation is, however, not "pure" but is governed by the given determinations of the material continuum. Thus, only arbitrarily is the notation severable from the phenomena. For example, these sciences cannot operate apart from the "unit" measured, but the "unit" is a unit of something; and the "something" is "given." In other words, the "material principle" is "refractory" in all the sciences other than pure mathematics. Concerning geometry, the fact that physical magnitudes do not perfectly comply with the postulates and theorems of the science indicated to Plato that geometrical theory could find no real counterpart in nature. In nature, there are no straight or parallel lines and no equal angles and no true squares, only approximations. (*Epist.* VII, 343a.) This caused Plato to postulate an ideal science. It caused Aristotle, on the contrary, to deny that mathematics had applicability to things which contained "matter." But modern physical theory, ignoring the difference between pure mathematical structures and *actuality*, has contrived a mathematical physics whose relation to the actual world is an unresolved mystery.

34. *Euthyd.* 290b-d.

35. Sense-perception may provoke the process of learning by *anamnêsis*. Especially important passages are: *Phaedo* 73c-d, 74c-d, 75e, and *Phaedr.* 249b-c, 249e-250a, 265d, 273e; *Rep.* 523b.

36. Cf. *Phaedr.* 265d, *Rep.* 596a.

37. *Rep.* 534b-c.

38. Cf. *Rep.* 510a-c; 511a-c; 533c.

39. It should be noted that the following interpretation is mainly based upon two passages, *Rep.* 510a-511e and 533b-534a.

40. *Greek Philosophy*, Pt. I, 229.

41. *Rep.* 533d. Cf. 509d, 511c, 478c; *Phileb.* 57c.

42. *Rep.* 511b. Cf. 510b, 533c.

43. J. Burnet, *Plato's Phaedo*, 109.

44. See *supra*, Ch. IV, sec. 2.

45. Cf. *Rep.* 508d; *Meno* 98a.

46. Cf. *Gorg.* 460e, 462a; *Alcib.* I, 112a, 117a; *Protag.* 355a; *Charm.* 160b.

47. Cf. *Rep.* 511c-d, 478c-d; *Phaedo* 99e, 79d, 80e, 83b.

48. *Symp.* 202a. Cf. *Meno* 99a-c; *Rep.* 578a, 506d.

49. Cf. *Rep.* 476d and 532c. For the function of discrimination, see *Charm.* 170e, 171c; *Lach.* 184c, 186e; *Ion* 539e; *Hipp. Min.* 364c; *Alcib.* I, 114b; *Gorg.* 465b ff.; *Rep.* 348b; *Theaet.* 150b-c.

50. Cf. *Polit.* 262b, 258e, 259d. See also *Cratyl.* 388b-c; *Soph.* 219d-e. The explicit use of "division" in the *Cratylus* almost certainly places it in the post-Republic period, possibly as successor to the *Phaedrus*. It is the developed concept of dichotomy in the *Sophist* and, more especially, in the *Politicus* that differentiates "division" from the dialectic of *elenchos*. Division, *viz.*, discrimination, is not new.

51. J. Stenzel, *op. cit.*, 18-21. The virtual absence of Socrates from the *Sophist* and *Politicus* is doubtless congruent with historical fact, but it is plain misrepresentation to say, with Stenzel that Socrates was uninterested in discriminatory analysis of concepts in the early phase (p. 36). This subverts conflicting evidence in the interest of theory (*Rep.* 454a-d). However, Socrates' admission that he cuts a ridiculous figure when he attempts "a division into classes" and their combination, at *Philebus* 23d, may well be Plato's tactful and artful way of conceding that this later portion of the "diacritical art" is his own subsequent development rather than Socrates' accustomed method in dialectic.

52. *Rep.* 534c, 476d, 479e.

53. *Phaedr.* 265d-266b. See Ch. V, sec. 3, a, where this subject has received attention.

54. Cf. *Phaedr.* 263b, c, 271a; *Soph.* 218d, 231c; *Polit.* 261d, 278d.

55. *Soph.* 228a. For the nature of this disagreement and its resolution, see *Alcib.* I, 126c ff.; *Rep.* 442d, 443e; *Tim.* 86b.

56. *Soph.* 228d-e, 240c-d.

57. Cf. *Phaedo*, 75d, 73a; also *Gorg.* 462a; *Protag.* 338d; *Rep.* 534d. Cf. *Rep.* 532b where dialectic has a liberating and purifying effect comparable to *Phaedo* 83d, 84a.

58. *Rep.* 532a, 537d, 511c, 476c-d.

59. Cf. *Phaedr.* 265e, also *Soph.* 218d-e, *Polit.* 259e.

60. Cf. *Soph.* 218d, 221c, 233d; *Polit.* 277e, 278a-e, 279a-b. In the *Phaedrus*, the effort to isolate and identify the aspiration in the soul for divine reality is attained by first recognizing that this *himerôs* belongs to the general classification of eros. But eros is complex and among "doubtful things" (263c); therefore, the process of discrimination must be invoked by which, eventually, the "divine" sort of madness (266b) is separated from cognate varieties. But *mania* and eros together constitute the *paradeigmata* or general conceptions (249b), upon which, then, division goes to work (263b, 265b).

61. See *supra*, Ch. V, sec. 3, b.

62. *Rep.* 511b, 533c. Shorey's translation of ἐπιβάσεις, "underpinnings," and ὁρμάς, "footings," in the sense of points for springing up is most suitable.

63. *Meno* 98a. Cf. *Rep.* 476d, 479e, 507b, 511b, 532a-b, 533b.

64. *Rep.* 534c. Plato frequently describes this difference as one between "sleeping" and "waking" with respect to reality. The man of opinion, even "true opinion," is dreaming and dozing through life, 534c. Cf. *Rep.* 476b; *Polit.* 277d; *Phileb.* 20b. Dialectic is the instrument of "clear waking vision." *Rep.* 533c, 520c. The passage 534b-c, especially, suggests that the "raw material" as well as the condition of the mind prior to knowledge through dialectic is that of true opinion.

65. The word *katharmos* (purification) is used much more frequently in the dialogues than is *katharsis*, though the latter predominates in the *Phaedo*. Judging from *Soph.* 227d, Plato apparently makes no distinction between them as to meaning. Examination of his usage of *katharmos* indicates its close connection in his mind with both state and sectarian (Orphic) religious rites. *Phaedo* 69c; *Rep.*, 364e; *Phaedr.* 244e, 243a; *Laws* 868e *et al.* It is instructive, however, to note that *katharmos* is frequently defined as a process which removes the worst and retains the best. *Rep.* 567c; *Soph.* 226d, 227d; *Laws* 735b.

66. *Rep.* 510b, 511b.

67. *Rep.* 505a-b. Cf. *Charm.* 174b-c; *Laches* 198c; *Lysis* 220b f.

68. William Temple, *Nature, Man and God* (New York, 1949), 257.

69. *Phileb.* 31a.

70. *Phileb.* 22c, 28c, 29a f.; *Tim.* 41d, 90c; *Theaet.* 176b-c.

CHAPTER VIII

The Role of Love in Knowledge

.~.~.~.~.~.~.~.~.~.~.~.

For wisdom has to do with the fairest things and Love is a love directed to what is fair; so that Love must needs be a friend of wisdom, and, as such, must be between wise and ignorant.—*Symposium* 204b

.~.~.~.~.~.~.~.~.~.~.~.

1. CONTRARIETY AND THE PRIMAL AFFECTION OF THE SOUL

FOR Plato man is at once the agent and the victim of false opinion; if he misidentifies appearance with reality, he has none to blame but himself. He does this willingly, for his willing is not something different, but something identical with the prevailing bent of his affection.[1] This is so in spite of Plato's apparently conflicting assertion that no one voluntarily consents to falsehood and error.[2] The apparent contradiction is resolved, as we saw earlier, in Chapter III, by recognition of the fact that Plato is thinking of the essential volition, the real and true wish (*boulêsis*) of the soul.[3] This wish is described as the desire of the Good or the love of knowledge.[4] From the standpoint of this essential will or primal affection, no one voluntarily errs. Yet this contradiction in the human spirit constitutes both the tragic and the hopeful aspects of man's existence. Man is a tragic figure in that his imprisonment of mind is self-imposed. But that this condition is not the expression of his real and essential volition is his surviving hope of liberation.

The upside-down distortion of human existence, which, on the testimony of Callicles,[5] Plato readily accepts as the proper characterization of actual man, points, then, to a fundamental cleavage in human nature. It manifests itself in a contrariety between the apparent and the essential will, between affection for the apparent and for the real Good. It is for the purpose of exposing this conflict that Socrates engages in his exchange with Polus in the *Gorgias*.[6] There he tries to win acknowledgment of the fact that power to do wrong with impunity does not truly represent the real purpose of any man, but that his real wish and true "power" is to honor justice in word and action. But the cogency of this claim Plato could not fully establish until, in the *Republic*, he articulated the structure of the human soul and distinguished between the soul's inferior and superior appetition.[7] Then he was able to exhibit dramatically the contrariety implied in an exercise of reason which misidentifies reality in the first place and, thereafter, is exclusively occupied with manipulating appearances in the interest of securing the largest measure of private advantage.[8] For, to this exercise of intelligence, Plato opposes a reason, namely, the *logistikon*, which is commensurate with and conformable to the essential structure of Being. Thus Plato regards the task of *therapeia* as that of resolving the contradiction between the apparent and the essential will and, correspondingly, that between a merely technical and an essential reason.

To relieve men's blindness and to assist them to discover their essential will is the primary task of education. In the end, this self-discovery comes only by way of self-knowledge, assisted by the *elenchos*. The essential man, despite the vehement protest of the actual man, does "believe that doing wrong is worse than suffering it, and escaping punishment worse than incurring it."[9] The profound ambivalence of men toward the true Good is an underlying theme of the *Gorgias*. Until this self-disagreement is conceded,[10] as it is by Alcibiades,[11] there is no possibility of restoring to the powers and appetitions of the soul their proper "unison" and concord.[12] Meanwhile, Callicles is the brash but candid apostle of discord in the soul and contrariety (ἐναντιότης).[13] Against this contrariety Socrates sounds the warning that there is "disagreement" between Callicles and Callicles and that without assistance of the love of wisdom, Callicles is destined to live forever at odds with himself. The choice is now before him; it is his to make. It is the business of philosophy in the form of *elenchos* to disclose the antithesis and then, if possible, to solicit and enforce a decision.

The initial sign, then, of the essential desire of the soul is reigning contradiction in the human spirit made manifest in antinomic wills or wishes. It is this which prompts Plato to observe in the *Sophist* (228b), as well as in the *Phaedrus* (237d), that, in the case of most men, opinions, presumably true ones, are opposed to desires, anger to pleasure, reason to pain.[14] It is the same discord or deformity which was made so familiar in the *Republic*. In the *Timaeus* the antithesis is referred to in the proposition that "two desires naturally exist among men": the desire that serves the body and the desire of wisdom which serves the immortal part of the soul (88b). Here again are two wills. The one is rightly subordinate to the other in the harmonious life; but this is not man's normal condition; and, if *sumphônia* prevails at last, it is a painful achievement.[15] So in the *Laws*, as we find each actual man, he is "partly superior to himself and partly inferior."[16] The "self-inferior" is he in whom sensate desires, quite as in the *Republic*, tyrannize, contrary to nature, over the true "ruling principle."[17] The latter is not to be identified with an abstract theoretic reason but rather with *nous*, impelled and supported by eros, an affection which characterizes and inspires the philosophic nature.[18] It is the same eros which, in the *Laws* (688b), is said to attend and sustain wisdom, reason, and true opinion. So we have to inquire whether it is not with this eros that man's essential volition is to be identified. We have also to ask whether it is not upon the emancipation of this primal affection that the hope of education depends, above and beyond the contributions of the "sciences" and the indispensable assistance of dialectic.

Prior to the *Symposium* and the *Phaedrus*, Plato does not supply us with a direct examination of the theme of love. Nevertheless, it is widely alluded to in previous dialogues, especially in the *Lysis*, the *Phaedo*, and the *Republic*. From the *Lysis* we learn to suspect that the "neediness' of which desire is the manifestation is deficiency in respect of the ultimate Good.[19] In the *Phaedo* we perceive that the craving of "the lover of wisdom" exists in virtue of a recognized disparity between a present want and a sufficiency of which knowledge and reality are the abundant supply.[20] We learn that it is love of wisdom which distinguishes a few men from the many whose desire is riveted upon the corporeal.[21] We learn that truth is the ultimate desire, the prime love of the soul,[22] and that the essential man is one in whom *nous* is controlled by love of essential Being.[23] In the *Republic* the theme is continued. The lovers of wisdom are those "for whom truth is the spectacle of which they are enamoured" (475e). Hence it is the distinguishing mark of the philosophic nature to strive "emulously for true being." Such a one does not linger over particulars opined to be real, and his passion (*erôs*) is not blunted nor does his desire fail till he comes into touch with the essential nature of each thing. This he does by the exercise of that particular power, *nous*, to which belongs the capacity to apprehend essence (490a-b).

Plainly, that which distinguishes the philosopher, in the first instance, is not learning but love of it, not profession of truth, but aspiration for true reality. It is in his passion, not his possession, that Plato finds promise of "surcease from travail of soul" that stems from unresolved inner contrariety. The philosopher, appearing in the *Phaedo* and the *Republic,* is a man on the way to reconciliation with himself and, thereby, with essential reality. He is in process of overcoming the Calliclean split in the soul's life, the *anatropê* of human existence.

In the *Republic,* at one point pre-eminently, Plato provides a glimpse of the primordial volition of the real man. Plato is fully aware that, in its actual state, deformed by the warfare of antagonistic forces within, the true and really prior aspiration of the soul is scarcely discernible. So it is necessary to view the soul in a figure in order that its pristine nature may be seen relieved of the accretions and distortions attributable to its present existence. If we are to grasp its real nature, says Plato, ". . . we must note the things of which it has apprehensions, and the associations for which it yearns, as being itself akin to the divine and the immortal and to eternal being, and so consider what it might be if it followed the gleam unreservedly and were raised by this impulse out of the depths of this sea in which it is now sunk. . . ."[24] It is the soul's original and inherent proclivity or impulse (ὁρμή) that serves notice of its primary affection or volition.[25] Both here and in the *Phaedrus,*[26] Plato alludes to it as the soul's yearning—a yearning that he accounts for on the basis of kinship of *nous* with divine reality, but kinship imperfectly fulfilled.[27]

2. MISCONCEPTION OF EROS

For liveliness of interchange, humor, and exalted speech, the *Phaedrus* has hardly a peer among the dialogues. Virtuosity of metaphor and brilliance of imagery dazzle the reader, with the result that Plato's sheer artistry tends to obscure the two or three motifs skillfully woven into the fabric of the whole. These themes constitute the substance of the work; and, despite the stylistic exuberance, Plato is in keen earnest. Taken in the large, the dialogue may be considered a critique of prevailing notions of rhetoric with a view to a revised conception of its nature and purpose. Among other things, Plato gives notice that he intends to adapt rhetoric to serve his own purposes as an instrument of *therapeia.* In the course of the discussion, it becomes evident that rhetoric cannot be rightly conceived nor can the nature of its persuasive power be suitably interpreted apart from a correct understanding of the human being who is to be persuaded.[28] Consequently the symbolic account of the soul's constitution and travail forms the second principle element of the dialogue. Finally, neither the proper conception of rhetoric, redefined as dialectic, nor the nature of the soul itself can be understood without fully exploring the conception of eros. This third component provides a kind of tissue for the entire discourse.

If any of these three themes is ignored, the general bearing of the dialogue is likely to be missed. Nonetheless, a generalization is permissible about the entire work, which gradually forces itself upon the reader's attention. The dialogue may best be understood as an important part of Plato's effort to grasp and solve the problem of *therapeia,* in so far as this includes man's need for revolution of *êthos.* Therefore, in both the *Phaedrus* and the *Symposium,* Plato is intent upon disclosing the salutary dynamic of a certain noble love or madness which is inherent in human nature but is stifled and repressed.

With the assistance of dialectic, the superior affection of the soul may become liberated. Once freed, it may empower a transition from false opinion to a condition of knowledge and wisdom. Plato is, therefore, about to undertake a bold defense of the power and virtue of love. Stating his intention, he says: "We on our part, must prove that such madness is given by the gods for our greatest happiness; and our proof will not be believed by the merely clever but by the wise" (245c). In this Plato indicates not only his awareness of the novelty of the effort, but also his full comprehension that the proposed "proof" admits of no exception to the rule; namely that formal argument rarely convinces minds that are habitually ill-disposed toward truth.

Plato's treatment of eros was bound to encounter misunderstanding as well as incredulity. The civilization to which he spoke had come to flower and ripeness. Its state of mind had the formal clarity and precision of objects in space at high noon. It was as much occupied with things and immediate preferments as civilizations characteristically are. Its pedestrian vision was mostly circumscribed by the boundaries of sense. Its gods were as comfortable as other household familiars; otherwise they were adequately housed on the Acropolis. The chthonic deities of indigenous derivation had largely given way before the articulate, lofty, and formal splendor of the Olympians. Many Athenians had lost sensibility for the penumbra of mystery which, at the periphery, encircles and periodically threatens to encroach upon the neat clearing of experience within which the civilized mind seems content to domesticate its interests. The average Athenian, therefore, was predisposed to look with condescension upon the rhapsodies of the muses and older expressions of divine possession or prophetic frenzy. If Plato intended to speak soberly of eros and somehow make it serviceable to his *therapeia*, he could count upon initial prejudices, for eros was a little disreputable. Men of common sense looked with suspicion upon its raptures (231d). Moreover, it possessed a somewhat unsavory connection, in conservative minds, with various forms of effeminacy to which Plato himself alludes (239c-d).

For reasons prosaically represented in the speech of Lysias (231a f.), eros was suspect. This speech dispraising love introduces the main discussion of the *Phaedrus*. Without bothering to make distinctions and without specifying the kind of lover he depreciates, Lysias propounds the thesis that the non-lover is preferable to the lover on any score. The reasons are manifest: In his passion the lover is quite daft, devoid of sense and judgment. His actions are impulsive and wanting in consideration of his own best interest or that of his beloved. He is moved by blind passion unchecked by the real merits or defects in his beloved. His loyalty is unpredictable, and he is characteristically jealous.

Plato does not mean to challenge this exposé of the man of unbridled passion. He intends to register a demurrer, however, against lumping all lovers and all kinds of love in one heap. Secondly, he intends to uncover and refute the concealed assumption which, as in the speech of Lysias, identifies the non-lover with the man of calm sense, judgment, and perspicacity (232a). In the *Phaedrus*, Plato intends to contest the popular assumption that the life of reason is an unimpassioned life. He will show that the rational man is, in his own way, a lover, and he will contend that, uninspired by love, no man can partake of wisdom. Furthermore, Plato intends to prove that the so-called non-lover, in the absence of a higher love, is really a lover of himself, and that his applauded good sense is but a thin disguise for his calculated self-interest (256e).

Apparently much against his inclination, Socrates is prevailed upon to make a speech in dispraise of love. To the delight of Phaedrus, the exalted language of Socrates surpasses even the rhetoric of Lysias. Its almost total inconsequence, however, was Plato's ironical way of exhibiting the futility of pyramiding words, however euphonious and elegant. From the standpoint of dialectic, we should, however, not miss the point that the first speech of Socrates is a substantial improvement upon that of Lysias, for it begins with an honest clarification of terms and a generic definition of eros. As in the *Republic* (475b), so now in the *Phaedrus*, love is initially defined as any desire for something or other (237d), and, in human nature, two species of desire are distinguished. These are forthwith identi-fied with the "two ruling and guiding principles." The one is desire for pleasures and is identical with man's appetitive nature, the sensu-ous *epithumêtikon* of the *Republic* (439d). The other is said to be "acquired opinion" (ἐπίχτητος δόξα) which aspires after the best. This *doxa* we take to be a species of *doxa alêthês;* and although it is probably to be identified with the inculcated variety and is of con-ventional derivation, it nevertheless embodies undiscriminated truth.[29] When this opinion, controlled by intelligence, holds the balance of power in the soul, its force is called *sophrosunê*, good sense, or self-restraint (237e). But when sensuous desire irrationally con-trols, its rule is called *hubris* or excess (238a); and its overreaching takes sundry forms, depending upon the particular appetite which presently holds sway (238b).

With these preliminary distinctions in hand, Socrates ought to have been able to declaim in such fashion as to preserve the distinc-tions initially made and to avoid the self-contradiction against which he himself cautioned in the introduction to his discourse (237c). But Plato intends to show that oratory and set speeches are not reliable instruments of sincere inquiry. Inevitably they tendentialize the evi-dence because of polemical interest in the vindication of some avowed thesis. No set speech can lead inquiring minds to truth; it can only propound it on the assumption that the truth is already possessed by the advocate.

Covering his head, thereby to indicate that he is violating his own principles of dialectical procedure (237a), Socrates engaged in "shameless" discourse. He proceeded to deliver himself of dithy-rambic eloquence culminating on the same note which Lysias had enforced; namely, that a reasonable non-lover is much to be preferred to a distraught lover. The same presumption is also present: the supposition that the non-lover is one who manifests *nous* or intelli-gence (241c). No reference whatever is made to the two diverse kinds of love that were provisionally distinguished at 237d. Nor is there any acknowledgment of the implication that *epiktetos doxa* embraces a beneficent kind of eros. The speech, therefore, ends in the most patent *non sequitur*. Its conclusion, however, agreeably conforms with prevailing notions of "rationality" entertained by the advocates of sobriety. Ignoring the fact that he had already made one or the other kind of love pervasive of the soul's life, Socrates proceeded to substantiate the popular opinion that love *qua* love is tantamount to folly and ignorance (241a). He, too, spoke as though love and intelligence were mutually exclusive. Thus Socrates' first speech supported Lysias in the conception of an anaxiological or value-indifferent reason.

Having differentiated two sorts of love, the one laudable and rational, the other reprobate and irrational, Socrates proceeds to depreciate the inferior as though the latter embraced the entire class. Consequently, for reasons which Plato wished to disclose, the right beginning proved to be abortive. The reason is plain: In Socrates' first speech, dialectic is merely a tool of rhetoric. It is characteristic of rhetoric to favor some contention, espoused for partisan reasons, and to enforce its claims irrespective of its truth or falsity (261c). Illuminating and fruitful distinctions, made by dialectic, are brought to nothing when, with polemical intent, rhetoric summons supporting evidence to demonstrate a thesis which is championed out of some precommitment. This was only to say what had been insisted upon in the *Gorgias* (455a): that rhetoric, as practiced, is prompted only by the motive of winning the case. The speech of Lysias began by begging the question and then advanced it by special pleading.[30] Although it had a far more auspicious beginning, the discourse of Socrates illustrated the same fault.

Plato means to say that dialectic, as honest inquiry, and rhetoric, as commonly practiced, do not mix. The first speech of Socrates exhibits the incompatibility of the two methods. Subordination of dialectic to rhetoric entails the subordination of honest inquiry to prejudice and results in obscurantism. From this outcome, we are not to infer that Plato, on the other hand, regarded the pursuit of truth, through dialectic, to be a wholly disinterested quest. On the contrary, the only intelligence of which he has given us any glimpse is one that is solicited by the Good as manifested in "acquired opinion." As we proceed, we shall observe that much of Plato's irony is evidenced in the sly hint that a disinterested reason does not in fact exist. As regards the rhetorician's reason, it is interested and loaded with bias. Likewise, the alleged "calm good sense" of the so-called reasonable man is eventually found to be "inspired" also, but with a love of his own best interest.[31]

What is wanted, and this is what the *Phaedrus* undertakes to say, is not rational inquiry devoid of passion but, rather, inquiry controlled by a superior love of those realities that are, by right, the privileged interests and true "belongings" of the human mind.[32] Truth waits upon a proper love of it, but this love is repressed and requires emancipation. The first speech of Socrates has deprecated every form of eros by the banal exercise of disparaging the excesses of self-interested passion. His harangue was not only "shameless"; it was trivial. Nothing had been said which most men did not believe, for no one bothered to differentiate the kinds of love. Eros was assumed to be just one thing and that of small repute. Nevertheless Plato had other words to say in the *Phaedrus;* but first we shall consider the theme of love in the *Symposium.*

3. THE *Symposium:* LOVE AS MEDIATORIAL

The banquet of Agathon, celebrated in the *Symposium* with brilliant portraiture, scintillating repartee, and festive laughter, was devoted to the theme of love. Each of the speeches in honor of eros, far from being irrelevant to the tenor of Socrates' "key-note" discourse, contributes something, however obliquely, to the line Socrates is to follow.[33] Although the speeches of Agathon and his guests are suitable preludes, it is in the mantic speech of Socrates—offered in the name of Diotima as one honored of Zeus—that we are to find Plato's meaning most fully represented. There, among the important utterances of Socrates, is the statement that eros is a great spirit (202e), although it is but one among many *daimones.*[34] The whole of the spiritual (*to daimonion*) is "between" the mortal and the immortal, between the human and the divine.[35] "God with man does not mingle: but the spiritual is the means of all society and converse of men with gods and of gods with men . . ." (203a). The function of the spiritual, then, is mediatorial. Midway between the divine and the human, it makes each commensurate with the other in such a way that things complementary, but disjoined, are fashioned into a whole or All (202e).

Love, as one side or aspect of the spiritual, mediates between the human and the divine to establish community, which is already potential. Such a function of love as is here suggested was prepared for in a number of the preceding speeches. Agathon, for one, noted the power of love to expel alienation between persons and to admit intimacy in its stead (197c). Eryximachus called attention to the universal operation of amity, not merely among sentient beings, but also at physical and physiological levels of existence (186e f.). It is eros which everywhere introduces unity in diversity and is the author of "consonance" and "agreement" in place of variance (187b). Love, moreover, is said to be a "purveyor of friendship between gods and men" (188d).

If man is to have converse with divine reality and be turned around from Becoming to true reality, then Plato evidently is ready to entrust to eros the requisite power of communion. It is, indeed, quite permissible to suppose that the aspiring movement of the mind toward reality, so often noted in the *Republic*, is not distinguishable finally from eros. Eros seems to be a symbolic equivalent of the universal impulse toward the Good noted at *Republic* 505e. Or, again, it seems to be intimately allied with the tendency of "acquired opinion" to strive toward the best, as in the *Phaedrus*. It can scarcely be dissociated from the native upsurge or *nisus* toward Being to which Plato refers especially at *Republic* 611e. The mediatorial function of love had already been suggested by Plato in a memorable passage of the *Gorgias*, viz., wherever *philia* exists, there *koinônia* or community exists also. Then, adopting a mantic or prophetic manner reminiscent of the Diotimean words of the *Symposium*, Socrates says, "And wise men tell us, Callicles, that heaven and earth and gods and men are held together by *koinônia* and *philia*, by orderliness, temperance, and justice; and that is the reason, my friend, why they call the whole of this world by the name of order."[36]

Here, as in the speech of Eryximachus to which we have referred above, there is the clear suggestion that it is eros of a certain kind which secures organic consonance (*sumphônia*) in place of dissonance (*asumphônia*)—the sort of discord with which we found the soul of Callicles afflicted and rent asunder. Eros, it may be, has the power of banishing disunity and working in such a way as to unite the mind with its true objects. Subjectively considered, eros is, doubtless, the pristine desire of the soul; while, objectively considered, Plato probably understands it as the teleological lure of the Good.

Both in his exhortation to Callicles and in his rehearsal of the words of Diotima, we have examples of that half-rhapsodic and hortatory mode of speech which the Platonic Socrates used in alternation with acute dialectical probing. Together, they were the instruments of his maieutic art. As Alcibiades testified in the *Symposium*, Socrates' exhortations were as powerful in eliciting a tumult of inner compunction as they were mantic in nature (215e). They evoked, he confessed, profound "shame" for his depraved way of life and sharply confronted him with the question whether he could continue in his divided existence (216a-b). For Plato, shame (αἰσχύνη) is the tell-tale sign of contrariety in the human spirit—a contrariety becoming self-conscious and issuing in crisis.[37] In the case of Alcibiades, Socrates touches the nerve of philosophic love, hidden in the

bosom of one whose waking thoughts and prevailing incentives incline upon prosaic advantages and sensuous satisfactions. But, even
in its suppressed state, sensibility for a loftier good survives and the
mantic exhortation of Socrates can, now and again, awaken its dormant
vitality (218a). The words of the *muthos* are just suited to the
prophetic constitution of the soul;[38] for the soul is "prophetic" in the
sense that, where a measure of self-knowledge is induced, it is found
to be inspired and borne upward toward reality by an inherent and
irrepressible love of Being.[39]

But this love is not something distinct from intelligence as such.
It is the higher madness which characterizes the lover of wisdom and
impels him onward in the pursuit of truth. Love, as Eryximachus
observed, is "the attraction of all creatures to a great variety of things"
(186a). As love is the condition of community which obtains in the
physical order, so love, Plato believed, is the condition of such conformity of *nous* with reality as is essential for cognition at the level
of rationality. We might even say that knowledge is a species of the
more generalized friendship by benefit of which there is order and
community among all things. Manifestly, if this is so, there is no
status of cognition which is not also a status of affection. Where
affection is contrary, no cognition of reality is achievable. Hence,
Eryximachus got to the heart of Plato's conception of the role of love
in education when he said: "The master-physician is he who can distinguish between the nobler and baser loves, and can effect such
alteration that the one passion is replaced by the other; and he will
be deemed a good practitioner who is expert in producing love where
it ought to flourish but exists not, and removing it from where it
should not be."[40]

Love, then, belongs to the province of the Spiritual and it possesses, with the whole of the Spiritual, a mediating function. But
there is an ambiguity about love in its very nature. It is the offspring
of Resource, its father, and of Poverty or deficiency, its mother
(203b). Earlier, in the *Lysis*, it was said that the ground of *philia*
is desire, and desire is aspiration toward that of which, presently,
there is deficiency.[41] Analogously, in the *Symposium*, eros signifies
a want of which at the same time it is the desire of repletion. So
love symbolizes or, better, manifests the actual condition of man as
he exists, halfway between ignorance and wisdom (203e). This is to
be contrasted with the condition of gods; for since they are already
wise, they do not pursue wisdom (204a).

This midway condition of men Plato, forthwith, identifies with *orthê doxa* (202a). Furthermore, he denies that those who are basely ignorant desire wisdom. This is, of course, the condition of *amathia*, the ignorance of those who are satisfied in their ignorance, who feel no deficiency and, therefore, crave no enlightenment (204a). Accordingly, in them eros is stifled and suppressed. The love that aspires to that of which the soul has presentiment has no effectual working in them. And this constitutes the gravity of their plight, the near impossibility of their enlightenment.[42] But those who are midway, that is, are possessed of true opinion, are redeemable.

Like love, then, true opinion is "between"; and this is, indeed, what we learned earlier from the *Republic* (479d). And, as in the *Meno*, so here true opinion is said to be that which happily "hits on the truth."[43] Hence, while it cannot be called knowledge, neither can it be called ignorance or false opinion. But this state of mind, *orthê doxa*, is correlated with love; it is evidently inspired by it. It craves enlightenment; and, like the *epiktêtos doxa* of *Phaedrus* 237d, it strives after what is best. It pursues the good. In true opinion, the aboriginal love of truth and reality asserts itself; so, as was suggested in Chapter V, it is love of the "essence" in the complex of appearances which is the ground of hope that true opinion will advance to knowledge.[44] It is for this reason that, in the *Politicus*, Plato avers that men cannot advance to knowledge from false, but only from true, opinion.[45]

True opinion, then, is allied with eros or, better, we should say that true opinion is instinct with love or nerved by it. For this reason, in the *Meno* Plato can ally true opinion and moral aspiration in the lives of distinguished men (96e). They are, moreover, in Plato's view, divinely possessed. In some respects, their condition is daimonic; participating in the mantic life, they are in a way divinely enraptured (99d). Nevertheless, their condition falls short of knowledge, and to that end they must yet advance. However, despite the deficiency, in *Cratylus* 398c, Plato is prepared to say that "every good man, whether living or dead, is of spiritual nature and is rightly called a spirit." One wonders to what extent we may take Plato seriously when, in the succeeding etymology (398c), he derives *herôs*, hero, from *erôs*, love. Is the hero the daimonic man, the man of *doxa alêthês* who, yet unpossessed of the Good, still honors and pursues it through the tangled multiplicity of earthly appearances? In such a case, Plato's hero would be the philosopher, and Socrates would wear the crown.

4. The Higher Madness

Returning to the *Phaedrus*, we are to follow Plato as he distinguishes once more between the nobler and baser eros which, together, animate the *psuchê*. Can we locate more precisely that variety of love with which true opinion is allied and upon whose impulse depends the conversion of the soul? Nothing in this direction is achieved without "enthusiasm" (253a), for nothing less can counterbalance and prevail over the entrenched habituation of the mind manifested in false opinion and love of its deficient realities.

The first speech of Socrates had ended in contradiction and typical Socratic perplexity. Of course, it was all consummate irony and solemn make-believe. Nevertheless, it illustrated the power of self-refutation to disabuse presumption. When that occurs, as it is said in the *Theaetetus*, men "at length become strangely dissatisfied with themselves and their arguments; their brilliant rhetoric withers away, so that they seem no better than children" (177b). In his own case, Socrates shortly begins his recantation with the confession of acute inner dissatisfaction for his previous frenzied utterance. The inward monitor chides, and he is aware of discord and compunction within (242c). The latter is called "shame," which is a thinly disguised manifestation of the higher eros we seek to define.[46] By his own admission Socrates has sinned against eros. His characterization was really travesty; but this is against reason, for eros is a god or something divine, and can be nothing evil.[47]

Truth's reassertion of itself from time to time is no occasion for surprise from the Platonic viewpoint. Tradition, of course, associated love with divine things, even if the things were of Aphrodite. In Plato's thinking, tradition is neither to be ignored nor contemptuously discarded. It is to be examined and criticized. For knowledge proceeds from the tenuously and uncritically apprehended to what is articulately comprehended. If men generally took a dim view of love and despised it for its oblivious raptures, Plato nevertheless refused to leave the matter there or to abandon it altogether. He himself observed another kind of love, for Plato remembered Socrates. Surely, to the multitude, Socrates was a starry-eyed dreamer, an enraptured fool. How else, apart from the supposition of a kind of lunacy, could one account for Socrates' seemingly childish unconcern for the ominous drift of things at his trial? He had dared to remind his suspicious hearers of the Oracle's saying that none was wiser than Socrates. He tipped the scales woefully in the smarting immodesty with which he styled himself a "divine gift" to Athens. A stronger wind could hardly have been commanded for the flames of animosity already quickening. After his conviction, to mention public maintenance in the prytaneum violated all sanity in calculating ordinary human reactions. Plainly, Socrates was a fool, a widespread opinion for which men like Callicles and Thrasymachus were unreluctant witnesses.

Plato himself had no intention of denying the charge, only of clarifying it. To men fettered in the Cave, inured to the darkness, and convinced of the sole reality of passing shadows, a man accustomed to a brighter and larger vision could only provoke laughter as he stumblingly adjusted himself to the darkness of men's common day.[48] Nothing else could be anticipated save that denizens of the Cave should regard Socrates as mad. As a lover of wisdom, he revealed an infuriating disinterest in those things which ordinarily controlled men's affections. Of this Alcibiades, in the *Symposium*, was an eloquent, if somewhat tipsy, witness.[49] These things were sufficiently evident to all, but the Socratic madness was, to Plato, a divine daftness and a sublime lunacy. If Socrates was a fool, he was god's fool, because he was possessed of a divine inspiration ($\vartheta \varepsilon i \alpha$ $\dot{\varepsilon}\pi i\pi\nu o\iota\alpha$), a genuine passion for philosophy and the appropriate realities of its quest.[50] It was entirely understandable, as Plato observed in the *Phaedrus*, that the philosopher should be "rebuked by the vulgar, who consider him daffy and do not know that he is inspired" (249d). It was very much as Plato declared in the *Gorgias* (521e): Socrates was like a doctor tried by a jury of children on charges brought by a cook.

a. Calculating and Uncalculating Love

When, in the *Phaedrus*, Plato arrived at the place where it was possible to re-examine the nature of love, he prefaced the inquiry with a new hypothesis to be fully evaluated. The former supposition was already granted. Admittedly, the sensate lover is, by contrast with the sober non-lover, irrational to the point of derangement. The new supposition, however, is that the greatest of goods come to men through madness, provided it is of divine origin (244a).

A warning is now issued that we are not to be intimidated in our examination of eros by the many who aver that a "reasonable friend" is much to be preferred to one who is "divinely excited" (245b). To begin with, we should recall that in former times, *mania* was considered neither shameful nor contemptible. It was associated, we are told, with the "manic art" (244c). On the assumption that tradition does not wholly err in its esteem for *mania* but that, as usual, it requires revision, Plato sets forth, in brief review, four types of divine possession or madness which had flowered among the Greeks.[51] Although there is no clear warrant for dismissing the prophetic, mystic, and poetic kinds as inconsequential, it is true that Plato's preoccupation is with the fourth kind of *mania*, namely, the madness of love. But the madness of love has till now, in the *Phaedrus*, been placed in a most unfavorable light, either as inordinate sensual passion or as disguised self-love. Socrates' initial speech did, however accomplish something: It disclosed the fact that the lover's passion is commonly a distasteful, if masked, exhibition of self-seeking. His real interest is self-gratification. He is one for whom "everything is pleasant which does not oppose him, but everything that is better or equal is hateful" (238e). Such love stands self-condemned, for Plato is concerned to show that true love, the only ground of real friendship and community, reveals itself in ungrudging goodwill (*eunoia*). Far from being a love of self, it is, primarily, a love of ideal reality. Where it exists, it constitutes a bond of unity between men.[52] Without it, no such bond does or ever will exist.

One of the most fruitful contributions of the *Phaedrus* for ethical theory, one which is already anticipated in the *Gorgias*,[53] is the important distinction between uncalculating or "generous" love and the opposite, or ungenerous, variety. The seeming goodwill of ungenerous affection is really appetite, which the possessor wishes to satisfy.[54] Of great importance is Plato's recurrent indication in this dialogue that sensate love is reprobate, not so much because of its physical basis, as because of its inveterate selfishness (238e). It is "alloyed with mortal prudence and follows mortal and parsimonious rules of conduct" (256e). It does not and cannot manifest beneficence, since its possessor is unable to forget himself (240a). In contrast, the man inspired by love of ideal reality honors and imitates the object of his affection, holds it in awe and reverence (252d), and acquires therefrom new habits and an altered *êthos* (253a). By his love of eternal verities, he is liberated from jealousy, envy, and meanness (253b); and he is enabled therewith for the first time to exercise ingenuous goodwill toward his fellows.[55] He does not feign friendship; he is now truly a friend. Consequently Plato is able to say that it is the superior love or madness which gives "freedom to that which makes for virtue."[56]

Three loves are really implied throughout this discussion: the one is self-regarding sensate love. It may be either sensual or calculating. The second is true friendship, and the third, love of ideal Being (253a). Friendship is possible only on condition that the third form of love is vigorous and alive (253c). Plato is, obviously, contending that the *philosophos* is the only true lover and friend. He alone has been liberated from envy that springs from self-will and self-love (255b). Already in the *Republic* Plato had taught that the only "safe" guardian of the state is one whose love of truth extirpates concern for personal gain and private advantage, and whose primary love is centered in the eternal.[57] Finally, the distinction between "generous love" and "mortal prudence" is entirely apposite to the developing treatment of rhetoric in the *Phaedrus*. In contrast with rhetorical contentiousness and polemic (261e), dialectic may be pursued only by men of goodwill who undertake to discover truth rather than to enforce their own opinions and private causes.

b. *Theia Mania* or Divine Madness

In what is properly the third division of the *Phaedrus* (257d f.), which is principally occupied with a critique of existing rhetoric and a transformation of its current conception, Plato illustrates the efficacy of "division" in differentiating the kinds of erotic mania. Love belongs to the class of "doubtful things" (263b), but by cutting according to "natural joints," two classes of love are distinguished. One is the so-called "left-handed" sort. The other is a divine eros, "the cause of our greatest blessings" (266a). It is in the second part of the dialogue (242c-257c), however, that Plato provides a glimpse of these two species of love, together with their respective functions. It is here that the famous myth of the soul is unfolded with imaginative power. To determine the real nature of the soul is a task for long and superhuman discourse; but to describe it in a figure is an undertaking within human capacity. Therefore Plato resorts to a kind of celestial symbolics in an effort to vindicate his twofold thesis; *viz.*, that (1) madness is superior to "sanity" when it is a gift of the gods, and (2) it is the source of man's greatest happiness.

Accordingly Plato sketches the figure of the charioteer with his two steeds. The travail of the soul is analogous to Olympian contests, familiar to the Greeks. It suffices to recall that the driver guides two horses. One of noble breed, and pliant to command. He is a "friend of honor" joined with temperance and reverence.

The other horse is intractable and unruly. Viciously fractious, he is disobedient to the rule of the charioteer and outrageously bent upon sensuous satisfactions. According to the myth, there is an additional characteristic of soul in general, as of individual souls in particular; it is said that the soul is winged (246c): "Now when it is perfect and fully winged, it mounts upward and governs the whole world; but the soul which has lost its wings is borne along until it gets hold of something solid, when it settles down, taking upon itself an earthly body, which seems to be self-moving, because of the power of the soul within it."[58] In what follows, Plato indicates why the soul loses its wings; but we are interested especially in what the wings signify.

The interpretation of this symbolism is hazardous. Plato has warned us that "myth" as a whole is false, yet embodies truth. He has, likewise, voiced his distrust of "allegory" with its disguised meanings that must be ferreted out according to anyone's whimsy.[59] The function and truth-value of myth in Plato has, consequently, been the subject of speculation and controversy. Unquestionably, Plato employs myth whenever a subject exceeds the power of merely scientific understanding or, so to speak, stands upon the boundary between the ideal and the actual worlds.[60] Admittedly, he also employs myth in cosmology, as in the *Timaeus;* but this is a different sort of myth, required by his ontology, which decrees that no purely rational account of the world of Becoming is possible, since the Cosmos is a combination of Reason and Necessity. The problem of myth, however, can be over-refined, and, in the instance before us, it is plausible to take Plato at his word that dialectical treatment would be, in the present context, intolerably prolix. The subject-matter does indeed stand on the "boundary," and Plato understood the illuminating power of symbolism as employed in the hortatory method of Socrates. As J. A. Stewart has said, in myth Plato "appeals to that major part of man's nature which is not articulate and logical, but feels, wills and acts."[61] In Plato, as perhaps elsewhere, myth exists where the theoretical has not yet exhausted the whole exercise of reason and, therefore, where the practical or affective potencies of the soul are still integral with its total operation. Relevant to this, is the fact that the wing, which is the symbol of prime interest in the figure, is quickly sensed to denote the upward impulse of the soul toward abiding reality. We know what it stands for. It symbolizes the superior affection in the soul by which reason is inclined toward the Good and the acknowledgment of it.

The wing is the higher madness, the divine *mania*, which is the cause of man's greatest blessings. The wing is the "eagerness" of the mind to apprehend realities (248b). It is a manifestation of "kinship" between *nous* and the proper objects of intellection. The existence of this divine *hormê* has its ground in the original conformity between the mind of man and the intelligible order—an expression of their essential if unrealized mutuality. More than anything else, the wing, Plato says, partakes of the nature of the divine.[62] When some glimpse is gained of the good, true, and supreme realities, either in themselves or as beheld through "the darkling organs of sense" deficiently represented in particulars (250b), the wings of the soul grow and their lifting power (249d) is enhanced. Concomitantly, there ensues a renewal of awe or reverence which is perhaps as close as we come, in Plato, to the meaning of the English word "piety" with its denotation of worship.[63] *Aidôs*, or reverence, is reasonably understood as a quality attaching to *theia mania*, or divine madness. Plato intends to symbolize the superior eros by means of the wing: "Mortals call him winged Love, but the immortals call him the Winged One, because he must needs grow wings" (252c).

Inspired by *theia mania*, which both accompanies and promotes *anamnêsis* of intelligible reality, the mind becomes intent upon the objects appropriate to its peculiar range of cognition (249d). Therefore "of all inspirations" this is of the most sublime origin (249e). But a question is in order: How is the symbolism of the wing related to the figure of the charioteer with his two horses? As the myth unfolds, the two motifs become so intertwined that they are at times indistinguishable. Nevertheless, the best clue for interpreting the theme of the charioteer is its usefulness in accounting for the soul's loss of its wings and its gravitation earthwards.

Doubtless we overtax Plato's intention if we try to find in every detail of the myth some special import which it might feasibly bear. It is, therefore, precarious to account for mortal existence by the "fall" of the soul through defection to evil. It is possible that a certain disaffection of the soul is an occasion for its embodiment (248a), but this is not the principal cause, if we may judge from certain passages of the *Timaeus*, which have a better claim to be considered normative.[64]

In our fascination with the transcendent and ethereal surroundings of the charioteer's heavenly race, we may easily overlook the likelihood that the supercelestial course is only an analogue of the contest in which every human soul is presently engaged in the travail of its earthly way. Actually, this is indicated by the neat transposition of the whole theme to the context of mundane experience, which begins at *Phaedrus* 249d. Thereafter the same struggle, depicted in the loftier region amidst heavenly splendors, is enlarged upon and transposed to the scene of man's daily life. That this is the case—and we are not to be misled by the ethereal symbolics—is all but certain; and it indicates Plato's conviction that the soul of man is "winged" and aspires after truth and reality here and now. It catches glimpses of it, but is distracted and frustrated by the unruly appetitive power in its make-up and is turned toward "unrighteousness."[65] Hence, although every soul inclines toward superior reality and is possessed of an intuition of it (249b), its aspiration is inhibited and its vision is clouded (250b).

Considering more narrowly the figure of the charioteer, its significance is not over-obscure if we inquire, with Plato, why the soul loses its wings. It does so because the horse of ignoble breed is uncontrolled and, in its sensuous frenzy, overthrows the rule of the rightful guiding principle. That guiding principle is, in the figure, the charioteer in alliance with the horse of noble breed. But who are they? Many interpreters have found it plausible to identify the two with the *logistikon* and its ally, *thumos*, or the "spirited faculty" in the soul. Of this alliance we have plain and extensive evidence from the *Republic*.[66] Moreover, we have in the figure something very similar to the functional division of the soul into rational and irrational powers, which is also expounded in the *Republic* (440e).

Whether or not we wish to find in the charioteer and his steeds the familiar tripartite division of the soul, it is certain that Plato intends us to understand that the failure of the driver to gain vision of reality is attributable to the unruliness of a *dunamis* in the soul which waxes large with sensuous love and passion (248a). Manifestly this power is what is everywhere else identified with *epithumia* or sensuous appetition. Earlier in the dialogue, "two ruling and guiding principles" were distinguished. The one was sensuous desire. The other was acquired or true opinion. It was indicated that, when the appetitive power exercises mastery, it overcomes "rational opinion" and obstructs its proper function (238b). Likewise, in the myth, we are told that, through the agitation and ungoverned passion of the ill-bred horse, the charioteer may fail to apprehend or gain sight of realities (248a). There is a great rivalry and competition among the drivers so that their wings are broken and they are obliged to go away and feed upon opinion.[67]

All this, most probably, is only a parable of life. Even the periodic revolutions affording opportunity for the heavenly vision may be understood as recurring and ill-appropriated occasions for discernment of the Good.[68] These opportunities are lost to men through their preoccupation with the things of appetite. It is the familiar story of the Cave. Out of enlarging self-interest, men feverishly compete for sensuous goods and therewith, as Socrates made us to understand in the *Apology*, they become distracted and withdrawn from pursuit of superior realities (30a). Hence an inferior love obstructs knowledge and occasions ignorance. In so far as the appetitive eros enforces its rule and impedes the upsurge of the mind toward intelligible reality, it is responsible for the soul's loss of its wings. And this, indeed, is what we have already learned from the *Phaedo* as well as from the *Republic*.

Something more, however, remains to be said of the wing in relation to the charioteer and its ally.[69] We have identified the wing with the exalting divine madness. Here again, it is hazardous to press for precise equations, and the leading indication is that the superior madness characterizes the allies in their combined function. Love of reality, the *theia mania*, is an inherent uplifting force in the soul and pertains specifically to the whole mind. Once again, Plato is telling us in a figure that the mind of man is axiologically engaged, that is, it is solicited by the Good as the ultimate and privileged object of human volition. Plato also makes it apparent that failure in knowledge is attributable to a perennial struggle between a lower and a higher affection in which the inferior has, at least initially, gained the victory.

But in the *Phaedrus* Plato unveiled his discovery of something that might be called the "expulsive power of a new affection." It is none other than philosophic love or *theia mania*—the love of abiding and eternal Good. He asserted that it worked, as a by-product, to eliminate enmity among men (253b) and to introduce amity and friendship (255b). The divine eros did not eliminate self-interest, but it had the capacity to transform expressions of self-regard. More exactly, the higher madness pointed out the direction in which true "self-advantage" was to be found.[70] It transmuted the old reprobate eros, accepted with complacency by the many, into an uncalculating, free, and "generous love."[71]

Thus the *Symposium* and the *Phaedrus* disclose a daimonic principle for the liberation of man from the bondage of the Cave. It is the emancipating and effectual rule of the higher madness. Plato is assured that whenever the tyranny of sensate desire is overthrown and replaced by the rightful sovereignty of *theia mania*, there follows "a divine release from customary habits" (265a). There is the healing of man's greatest woe (252b), the cleft in his own nature. But in addition, and concomitantly, there is the beginning of renewal of knowledge out of the abundance of memory.[72] So there is "release" (244e), the release for which the philosopher longed already in the *Phaedo* (82d). It is release from the old *êthos* and *sunêtheia*. Conversion of *êthos*, then, relies also upon the impulse of love's upsurging power. Man is daimonic, spiritualized and inspired; and, as a consequence, he receives a new "character," fashioned in the likeness of the exalted object of his sovereign affection (253a). This, then, is Plato's "proof" that eros is the author of man's greatest blessings providing it is a gift of god.

NOTES

1. See *supra*, Ch. III, sec. 4. The will can scarcely be said to emerge in the dialogues as a separate power. *Boulesthai* regularly means to wish or desire; and *boulêsis* is, variously, wish, desire, purpose, or intention. The appetitive or affectional element is always present. It is no secret that Plato does not distinguish volition from appetition. It is clear from *Charmides* 167e and *Symposium* 205a that Plato has no hesitancy in equating *boulêsis* and *erôs*. This is reinforced by *Symposium* 192c and 193a. The latter place should be compared with *Lysis* 215e f., with its close association of *epithumein* with *philia*. Accordingly, *Cratylus* 420d may be trusted in the suggestion that voluntary (ἑκουσίως) choice or action (*cf. Rep.* 413a) is "yielding to the motion which is in accordance with the will (*boulêsis*)," that is, desire or what is aimed at (420c). It follows that action is free or voluntary when it follows upon the presently ruling appetition of the soul. *Cf. Rep.* 618b, 620a; *Laws* 904b. Thus there is always freedom of choice (αἵρεσις); but choice will follow the prevailing passion of the soul with the result that there is a true and false freedom. *Cf. Gorg.* 468e; *Rep.* 445b. True freedom will exist when (1) the true *boulêsis* or *erôs* of the soul prevails and (2) when it is regularly honored in decision and action. It follows, of course, that there is no such thing as liberty of indifference or absolute contingency of the will. This is for the reason that will is love, and the prevailing will is indistinguishable from prevailing appetition. Therefore it is not a separate power in the soul and is always involved in every exercise of the rational power, the *logistikon*. Every exercise of reason is inspired by some sort of love or desire. For the equation of love and desire, see *Phaedr.* 237d; *Laws* 837a.

2. *Cf. Protag.* 345d; *Rep.* 382b, 413a-b, 589c; *Soph.* 228b.

3. The following passages may be consulted for their indication of the essential wish of the soul: *Lysis* 220b; *Gorg.* 468c; *Rep.* 504e-505a, 611e; *Phileb.* 22b, 58d; *Tim.* 88b, 90d; *Laws* 803c. From *Phaedo* 98a and 99b, we are early put in possession of the answer. If it is of the very nature of intelligence, *nous*, to act from a choice of what is best, then, manifestly, the Good is the pole star of the soul. The

Lysis calls it the *prôton philon*. The teleology of the Good constitutes the true *boulêsis* or real *erôs* of man. Unless a man follows this leading, he does not do what he "really wishes" (*Rep.* 577d; *Gorg.* 467b).

4. Cf. *Rep.* 475e, 490a; *Gorg.* 468c; *Symp.* 206a.

5. *Gorg.* 481c.

6. *Gorg.* 466b-470b. The outcome is similar in the discussion with Callicles. Righteousness proves the best means of "self-protection." 522c-d. Cf. *Phaedo* 82b-c.

7. *Republic* 440a-b formally inaugurates discussion of the warring parties within the soul. Sensuous desires, contrary to rationality (*logismos*), constitute a faction (*stasis*) insubordinate to reason (440e). Of the "three principles" in the soul (443d), reason, anger, and sensuous desire, the second is allied with the first (440b), so that the struggle is really between the *logistikon* and the *alogistikon*, or two parties. (*Cf. Phaedr.* 238b-c; *Tim.* 88b.) The irrational appetitive power becomes the usurping "ruling passion" and "tyrant eros" of *Rep.* 573d-e. The two factions reappear, of course, at *Rep.* 589d ff.

8. Cf. *Alcib.* I, 113d; *Rep.* 485d, 419a, 495d, 586a; *Gorg.* 502e, 513a.

9. *Gorg.* 474b. Cf. 509e. The seemingly conflicting judgment of *Crito* 49c-d must be considered a statement suitable to the actual man or to the avowed amoralism of Callicles, as at *Gorg.* 503c. In any case the actual man will remain incredulous for such reasons as Plato supplies at *Republic* 527e and *Theaetetus* 176e ff. Cf. also *Protag.* 323b and *Phaedo* 69a.

10. *Gorg.* 482c. Cf. *Soph.* 228a, *Rep.* 572d.

11. Cf. *Symp.* 218a and *Alcib.* I, 118b, 126c.

12. *Rep.* 443e. Cf. *Gorg.* 507e ff.

13. *Gorg.* 482c. Cf. *Rep.* 442d, 591d; *Laws* 664e f.

14. Cf. *Phaedr.* 251a; *Rep.* 413c, 442c.

15. *Tim.* 42a-b, 44a-c. Cf. *Rep.* 443d.

16. *Laws* 626e, 645b. Cf. *Phaedo* 68c.

17. *Rep.* 442d, 443b. Contrast the illegitimate tyrannical ruling passion, *Rep.* 573a-e, 574e, 575d.

18. *Phaedo* 82c; *Rep.* 485c.

19. *Lysis* 217e-218b, 221e.

20. *Phaedo* 62e, 83a-b.

21. *Phaedo* 66c, 81a-e.

22. *Phaedo* 66b, 66e, 68a.

23. *Phaedo* 84a, 98a. This point is well stated and roundly affirmed by Gaston Milhaud, *Les Philosophes Géomètres de la Grèce* (Paris, 1934), 248, 251.

24. *Rep.* 611e.

25. In addition to *Rep.* 611e, instances of an elevating *hormê* are to be noted at *Phaedr.* 279a and *Phileb.* 35d, 57d. Suggestive but uncertain usage is found at *Rep.* 506e, 511b; *Parm.* 135d.

26. *Phaedr.* 251c, d. *Himeros*, yearning, is understandable in connection with the vehement love aroused by the recollection of essential beauty discerned through the particulars (250d). Cf. *Phaedo* 68a. It is awakened *erôs* and, almost surely, is akin to the hormic movement of the soul. Both *himeros* and *hormê* seem to be required to account for one of the two "leading principles" in the soul, namely, "acquired opinion which strives toward the best" (*Phaedr.* 237d). Cf. *Rep.* 517c-d.

27. Cf. *Phaedo* 66a; *Rep.* 490b; *Tim.* 90a; *Laws* 899d.

28. *Phaedr.* 269e-271c.

29. *Doxa alêthês* will take the form of either the inculcated variety (*Rep.* 430a-b, 538c, 574d, 601e; *Polit.* 309d), or the spontaneous variety (*Meno* 99b; *Rep.* 479e, 534c; *Polit.* 277d, e, 309c). The present interpretation of *epiktêtos doxa* does not have the support of prevailing commentary. R. Hackforth (*Plato's Phaedrus* [Cambridge, 1952], 41-42), who follows Taylor (*Plato*, 303) in translating *doxa*

as "judgment," takes it to represent "the condition of mind in which a man takes thought, reflects and weighs alternatives instead of thoughtlessly obeying the promptings of desire; . . ." This is not implausible especially when compared with *Phaedrus* 238b where it is indicated that desire sometimes overwhelms "rational opinion" that ordinarily strives toward the right. But this is precisely the hazard to which the inculcated variety of *doxa alêthês* is subject at *Republic* 413a. Men are said to have *dogmata* (412e, cf. 538c) and *doxa alêthês* stolen from them unwillingly by the "sorcery" of pleasure or fear (413c). Cf. *Gorg.* 493a. Thus there is here represented the same antithesis between a superior *doxa* and sensuous desire that we find expressly stated at *Phadrus* 237d. We seem to have the clear indication, then, that the soul is divided between contrary forces and that "acquired opinion" is inspired by desire for or loyalty to the Good. There is nothing strange in this. It is the nature of every form of true opinion, as we saw in Chapter V, to honor the true, the good, and the beautiful in their "appearances" but yet without discriminating the essence. Cf. *Rep.* 478e-479a, 490a-b, 534c.

30. *Phaedr.* 263c f.

31. Cf. *Phaedr.* 231a, 238e, 240a.

32. Cf. *Lysis* 221e; *Alcib.* I, 128d, 131a; *Rep.* 490b.

33. W. Jaeger, *Paideia*, II, 189.

34. *Symp.* 202e. The erotic *daimôn* of 202, as a species of the *daimonion*, has some relation, hard to define, with the familiar sign of Socrates, θεῖόν τι καὶ δαιμόνιον at *Apol.* 31d. Cf. *Phaedr.* 242b, *Rep.* 496c. The similarity lies in the mediatory character of both. Love, as a *daimon* among *daimones* in the *Symposium*, is perhaps to be correlated with the θεία ἐπίπνοια, the divine inspiration to which "true philosophic passion" is attributable, *Rep.* 499c. Certainly, this passion is not different from the "divine madness" which is the greatest blessing to mortals. *Phaedr.* 244a, d, 245c. We suggest that the connection between love as *daimôn* and the Socratic "divine sign" is that they both indicate the soul's sensibility of and responsibility to the lure of the Good. The "sign" is negative, it notifies of responsibility betrayed and is accompanied by shame (αἰσχύνη). *Phaedr.* 254c. Alternatively, when the higher eros or madness is vitalized, it is expressed in aspiration after reality and its psychological concomitant is awe or reverence (αἰδώς). *Rep.* 560d; *Epist.* VII, 337a.

35. *Symp.* 202e. The category of the Spiritual, as expressed in *Symp.* 202, is problematic in nature. From the psychological standpoint, the indications of its dynamic reality are given with the various forms of "manic" experience to which there is clear reference in the *Phaedrus* (244c). With it are also to be associated varieties of inspiration (ἐπίπνοια) and enthusiasm (ἐνθουσίασις) of divine origination. *Phaedr.* 249e; *Ion* 533e. Love, as *theia mania*, is another manifestation. *Phaedr.* 266a. In like manner, true opinion is called a divine inspiration (*Meno* 99d). Like prophetic frenzy, it is called *theia moira*, a divine dispensation. Cf. *Ion* 535a, 542a; *Meno* 100b; *Epist.* VII, 336e. But the Spiritual also has the basic connotation of life and vitality. Cf. *Rep.* 617e. See R. B. Onians, *The Origins of European Thought* (Cambridge, 1954), 403. Cosmologically considered the Spiritual becomes associated with motion, life, and *psûchê* through which all Being is animate. *Soph.* 248e. There is reason to believe that, eventually, all its functions, *viz.*, *daimones*, are embraced within the *anima mundi* of the *Timaeus*. Reality becomes ensouled, exhaustively dynamic, yet retaining structure. Cf. *Soph.* 249a, *Tim.* 41d.

36. *Gorg.* 507e. Cf. *Rep.* 500 c-d.

37. *Symp.* 216b. Contrariety in the spirit, evidenced in shame, is especially prominent in the following *Phaedrus* passages, 237a, 241a, 243b, 254c. The context is the warfare in the soul between two impulses symbolized by the noble and ignoble steeds. *Phaedrus* 254c suggests that shame is experienced on the part of the

nobler faculty of the soul following upon a victory of the inferior principle. *Rep.* 571c denotes the condition of the soul devoid of shame. *Rep.* 439e suggests the overcoming of shame through the momentary victory of desire. *Symp.* 178d extols the values of shame as an expression of noble love, *viz.*, the shame we feel for shameful things. Where the victory goes to the superior impulses of the soul, the ensuing condition is reverence or awe (*aidôs*) toward worthful things, see *Euth.* 12b; *Rep.* 465b, 560a, d; *Phaedr.* 251a, 253d, 254b; *Laws* 671d. For compliance with truth or the outcome of true argument out of compunction or shame, see *Gorg.* 508b; *Rep.* 502a.

38. See *supra; Ch.* I, sec. 3. *Cf. Phaedr.* 242c; *Symp.* 218b.

39. *Cf. Rep.* 501d, 517c; *Phaedr.* 253a; *Symp.* 206a.

40. *Symp.* 186d.

41. *Lysis* 221c-e. *Cf. Cratyl.* 428d.

42. For the thought, *cf. Rep.* 498a, 502a-b, 516d.

43. *Symp.* 202a. *Cf. Meno* 97c.

44. See *supra*, Ch. V, sec. 2. *Cf. Rep.* 490a-b. *Phaedr.* 250d-e.

45. *Polit.* 278d. The discussion of 277d-278e is concerned with the contrast between dreaming and waking knowledge, the passage from true opinion to knowledge. *Cf. Rep.* 534c.

46. *Phaedr.* 243b. *Cf. Soph.* 230d.

47. *Symposium* 202d denies that eros can be a *theos*, but the variance from *Phaedrus* 242c is not complete, for the statement remains indefinite whether eros is *theos* or only "something divine." In any case, the disparity is of little consequence.

48. *Rep.* 517a, 518a-b.

49. *Symp.* 219d. *Cf. Phaedo* 64b.

50. *Rep.* 499c.

51. *Phaedr.* 244b-245a. *Cf.* 265b-c.

52. *Phaedr.* 255e.

53. *Cf. Gorg.* 486a and 487a. The goodwill of Socrates is undissembling; that of Gorgias is, of course, not real, and Socrates is ironical. *Rep.* 499a indicates the kind of thing which characterizes discussions in the absence of goodwill. In contrast, see *Gorg.* 458a. It is instructive, in this connection, to compare the following passages: *Gorg.* 503c, *Rep.* 586a-b, *Laws* 731e, 875b-c and *Phaedr.* 247a, 478b. Anticipating the *Timaeus*, Plato, in the *Phaedrus*, teaches that the gods are devoid of jealousy and envy. *Cf. Rep.* 378c, *Euth.* 6b. It is their love for realities which causes them to be divine, *Phaedr.* 249c. The suggestion is offered that both the "fall" of the soul and its ignorance are attributable to rivalry, that is to egocentrism.

54. *Phaedr.* 241c. Plato quotes: "Just as the wolf loves the lamb, so the lover adores his beloved." The first Socratic speech was really an exposé of this kind of eros. It is prudential affection comparable to *Phaedo* 69a. The reference to "generous love," is at *Phaedr.* 243c. *Cf.* 253b and contrast *Rep.* 577e and 359c.

55. *Phaedr.* 255b. *Cf. Rep.* 580a. For Socratic goodwill, see *Phaedr.* 252e; *Alcib.* I, 131d; *Symp.* 218c; *Theaet.* 151c.

56. *Phaedr.* 256b. *Cf. Rep.* 576a, 577c. For liberation from the old *êthos*, see *Rep.* 541a and 561a.

57. *Rep.* 500b-c and 520c-d.

58. *Phaedr.* 246c.

59. *Rep.* 377a and 378d.

60. J. A. Stewart, *The Myths of Plato* (London, 1905), 57-59, 74.

61. *Ibid.*, 21.

62. *Phaedr.* 246d-e. The words are, "More than anything else which *pertains* to the body, it partakes of the nature of the divine." The phrase περὶ τὸ σῶμα strongly suggests that, however transcendent in its reference and impulse, the higher eros is, nevertheless, grounded in and is perhaps continuous with physical desire.

This is clearly suggested in the words of the *Symposium*. Love is an attraction of all creatures to a variety of things, and operates at the vegetative and physiological levels as well as in the craving of human souls for the beautiful. *Symp.* 186a. The famous ascent of the mind in *Symp.* 210a f. begins with physical desire which is sublimated in the rise to the intellectual love of absolute Beauty. Sublimation, of course, requires progressive transference of loyalty to successively more ideal objects. The higher eros is, therefore, the perfecting and fulfillment of the lower. *Cf. Laws* 837b-c.

63. The following *Phaedrus* passages may be examined for the use of σέβομαι, to revere or worship: 250e, 251a, 252a, 254b. The close connection with *aidôs*, reverence, is apparent and the common relation of the two to *erôs* is plain. Reference may be made to *Euth.* 12b f.; *Rep.* 465b; and *Laws* 729c, 798b, 837c, 917b. Reverence is the differentia of the religious posture, and it is impelled by both love and fear. Since the philosopher is a lover of true reality, he, quite evidently, defines the true religious man. If, furthermore, we can only speak of *erôs* according to *muthos*, it may follow that religion without the *muthos* is unthinkable. This, as a matter of fact, is the outcome in Plato if we may judge by *Laws* X.

64. *Tim.* 29e. The cause lies in the goodwill of the Demiurge, the cosmic architect, who is devoid of "envy" and desires that all creatures share his perfection to the limit of what is possible for them.

65. *Phaedr.* 248a, 250a, e, 253e.

66. *Rep.* 440b, 441a.

67. *Phaedr.* 248b. For a comparable rivalry, see *Rep.* 586a-b. For the meaning of *doxa* here, cf. *Phaedr.* 247e.

68. *Cf. Rep.* 508d, 498a, 518e f.

69. *Cf. Rep.* 439e. We might presume to identify the horse of noble breed with *thûmos*, for there is some obvious comparability between the latter, the "spirited faculty," and exalting love. But the equation is not secure. For example, if we compare *thûmos* with divine madness, it is strange that repeated references to the spirited faculty in the *Republic* do not uncover a closer affinity with eros than is, in fact, suggested. *Thûmos*, to be sure, typically manifests fidelity to all that is best, but it manifests itself especially in compunction on occasion of moral failure. It seems to be rather more the antagonist of evil than a proponent of good (440a-b). Thus it is sometimes expressed as "shame" and, in this respect, is something akin to the Socratic monitor (*Phaedr.* 242c, 243c-d). Even so, it is still true that the positive of "shame" is reverence, and the latter is also signified by the term *aidôs*, and this is intimately associated with love (*Phaedr.* 254e).

70. *Cf. Gorg.* 507e f., 522d.

71. *Phaedr.* 243c. Socrates alludes to this sort of goodwill and generosity in the case of Callicles, obviously in irony. *Gorg.* 487a, 521a. In the *Symposium*, Socrates himself is represented as the only worthy lover (218c). And the motivation is identified at *Phaedrus* 252e, *viz.*, the lover of Zeus desires the soul of his beloved to be like Zeus, like the Good. This is the basis for the aim of politics as stated in the *Gorgias*, *viz.*, "to make the citizens' souls as good as possible" (503a). It is precisely for this reason that, as Plato asserts of Socrates, the philosophic lover alone can be considered the true statesman. *Gorg.* 521e.

72. *Phaedr.* 250c, 254b. Both in the *Phaedrus* and the *Symposium* there is disclosed the way in which obstructed love of essential reality is gradually liberated in company with renewal of knowledge. The long-standing problem remains, however, for false opinion is enforced by inferior desire, and desire is, in turn, confirmed by ignorance. How then can the superior love get a start? Difficult as it is, through the "darkling organs of sense" there is for some a dim recollection of realities adumbrated in particulars (*Phaedr.* 250a-b). But among the ideal realities, Beauty shines forth most clearly to our senses (250d). And it is with the re-cognition of Beauty

in particularities, that Plato finds a likely starting-point for the ascent to ideal Being. The instrumentality or method will be, as in the *Republic* (511b), the dialectic of *elenchos*. Beauty, amidst the particulars, first awakens love of particular physical bodies (*Symp.* 210a-212b), then, of the beauty common to bodies in general. Next comes love of the soul as distinct from the body, then love of laws and institutions. In the fifth place, the mind is tutored to observe those *logoi* which become apprehensible to the mathematical sciences. Finally, there dawns upon the consciousness an immediate apprehension of "ever-existent Beauty"—that which, as a form of the Good, is devoid of supposition and self-authenticating.

CHAPTER IX

The True Rhetorical and Persuasive Art

~~~~~~~~~~~~~~~~~

Suppose, now, he who we say opines but does not know should be
angry and challenge our statement as not true—can we find any
way of soothing him and gently persuading him, without telling
him too plainly that he is not in his right mind?—*Republic* 476d

~~~~~~~~~~~~~~~~~

1. Pedagogy and Indemonstrable Knowledge

IT is not surprising that eventually the Athenian populace became
exasperated beyond endurance with the Socratic exposure of its
ignorance. After all, who was Socrates against so many? And Plato
encountered similar difficulties as a teacher. To the average man
Plato's claim was paradoxical, if not perverse. The Platonic Socrates,
as Callicles complained, was turning the facts upside-down. To minds
like his own, it was more likely that reliable knowledge was to be
drawn from sense data than from supersensible Forms. No one, not
even Plato, had ever "looked" at ideal essences; and the Idea of the
Good, alleged to be the one perfectly intelligible object, appeared
more nearly to be a forlorn surmise than a certainty. Plato could
share the ordinary man's bewilderment, and he could state it sym-
pathetically, as, for example, in the *Politicus*, where he observes that
"each of us knows everything that he knows as if in a dream and
then again, when he is as it were awake, knows nothing of it at all."[1]
None the less, Plato avowed in the face of widespread incredulity
that the majority confounded appearance with reality.

The conflict of claims forced upon Plato the need of an effectual
pedagogy. How was inveterate if not invincible ignorance to be
overcome? How is it possible, he asks in the *Republic*, to show
persuasively that men are not in their "right minds" when they claim
reality is that which they perceive? The severity of the problem
is not entirely attributable to Plato's sharp indictment of the common
mind, with its consequent resentment. Neither does the difficulty
stem alone from the fact that prevailing ignorance is "double" and
therefore obstinate and tenacious. Over and above these admitted

impediments, there is an additional factor which intensifies the problem. It is especially troublesome because it inheres in Plato's own conception of knowledge, the highest form of *epistêmê*. It is denoted by the second division of the second segment of the Divided Line. Plato calls its *noêsis* which is commonly translated "intellection." However, because Plato conceives it after the analogy of vision, it may suitably be termed intellectual intuition.[2] We are familiar with the fact that it is vitalized through the assistance of mathematical studies and dialectic, that its supreme object is the Good, and that its onset is culminative and sudden. The unique nature of this knowledge introduces difficulties for the teacher, and for three reasons.

First, in its highest form, knowledge is not at all a matter of demonstration, at least not in the usual meaning of the word *apodeixis*. The highest reach of knowledge is intellection to which, as at *Republic* 511b, reality authenticates itself. Secondly, *Symposium* 210e indicates that the knowledge in question possesses the character of immediate insight, direct acquaintance, and personal apprehension. Thirdly, attainment of this knowledge is conditioned by non-logical as well as logical factors. Habit of mind as we have noted, has a conditioning part to play in the success or failure of the event called knowledge. Important consequences follow from these facts. For example, how can any indictment alleging general human ignorance be vindicated, when the knowledge purported to be its antidote does not admit of rigorous demonstration? On what basis can Plato support his claim that things considered realities by ordinary men are not true realities so long as alleged knowledge of Being does not admit of some kind of public verification? It was precisely this difficulty which placed great burdens upon Plato's *paideusis*. He was still asserting in the *Sophist* that men confound appearance with reality (240d), but he was unable to gain assent to truth by way of necessary and incontestable inference. He possessed no coercive method for displaying reality in its true nature.

And there is every evidence that Aristotle perceived this difficulty. It is also likely that Aristotle was impatient over the apparent impasse and that, accordingly, he altered the conception of "scientific knowledge" in such a way that its findings could be regarded as cogent and necessary. He did not claim that all knowledge without exception is demonstrative. On the contrary, he held that "knowledge of immediate premises is independent of demonstration."[3] We must antecedently know the prior premises from which demonstration is drawn.

Infinite regress would destroy the possibility of knowledge altogether, and, therefore, must terminate in immediate truths which, as primary premises, are even better known than the conclusion.[4] The certainty of primary premises upon which necessary syllogism depends is a product of "rational intuition" or "induction."[5] Induction is the indispensable but indemonstrative ingredient in "scientific knowledge." Nevertheless, the ideal of scientific knowledge and the business of "first philosophy," as well as of mathematics and physics, are demonstration, *viz.*, the deduction of necessary consequences by means of rigorous connections from known "causes." Because the relation between premise and conclusion is, in the syllogism, equivalent to that between cause and effect, the truth of valid inference is incontestable and necessary.[6] Knowledge, properly considered, is made up of the truths of apodictic inference, and in this manner, whether wittingly or not, Aristotle contrived to make significant knowledge a matter of *apodeixis* or public verification by putting cognition under the tutelage of a defined method available to all.[7] By the same token he was able to relieve the knowledge process of the imponderables of private perspective.

Plato did not entrust so much to syllogistic method, for he had made it clear at *Republic* 533c that the certainty of conclusions from inference is not greater than the certainty of the premises. Furthermore, he was persuaded that the certainty of premises is conditioned by affective and non-logical factors in the human *psuchê*. The most stubborn obstacle in the way of knowledge is not the imperfection of inference or the cognitive instrument (*nous*) considered by itself, but the indisposition of the whole mind in respect to premises. Anything like conviction waits upon the concurrence of volition. Beset by this limitation, the highest knowledge possible to man cannot be, for Plato, the rigorous demonstration of reality to disinterested minds. Rather, as the *Phaedrus* shows, knowledge requires the proper reorientation of a *desiring* mind. It must incline toward reality in such fashion that discovery becomes possible. For Plato truth is not conveyed to the mind by deductive syllogism; rather the mind is conducted to a point from which reality discloses itself. This is the import of the parable of ascent to reality in the *Symposium* (210a-212a). The central theme of Platonism regarding knowledge is that truth is not brought to man, but man to the truth (*Rep.* 523a).

Since Plato perceived no way to evade the fact that wisdom is justified only of her children, he distinguished between wisdom and understanding, between dialectical and deductive proof. In the

Republic as elsewhere, dialectic conducts the mind to knowledge— *noêsis* or intellection (532b). Plato is ready to concede that logical inference does, indeed, derive the assured but hypothetical certainties of the sciences (533c). Dialectic, however, advances by finding in the *less* the *implications* for the *more*.[8] Deduction moves from the *more*, the hypothesis or premise, to the *less* or to the consequences for the less. The latter, Plato recognized in the *Republic*, is rigorously derived for all who concede the hypothesis from which inference originates (511d). With dialectical procedure, however, the implications of the *more* wait upon a disposition of the entire mind favorable to the acknowledgment of each succeeding *more* until, after many intervening steps, acknowledgment is secured and accorded to the highest intelligible object, the First Principle (511b).

This movement of the *elenchos* from the *less* to the *more* has been described by Leonard Nelson, in his essay on *The Socratic Method*, as the "art of *forcing* minds *to freedom*" and as the secret of the Socratic method.[9] Starting with any "experiential judgment," inquiry is made into the condition of its possibility. We "come upon more general propositions that constitute the basis of particular judgments passed"; and reflection proceeding in this way, there comes at length into view "the originally obscure assumption that lies at the bottom of the judgment on the concrete instance." Nelson describes this as the "regressive method of abstraction,"[10] a method which "employs reflection to lift the knowledge we already possess into consciousness."[11] What has been achieved is a banishment of dogmatism and resistance to the truth. What has been won is an acknowledgment of what was profoundly surmised but unhonored and unacknowledged.

But Plato knew that disposition to acknowledgment or "agreement" (ὁμολογία), even in the case of an initial judgment, unfortunately can be neither presumed nor constrained. Yet, as Socrates insisted in the *Crito*, it is requisite from the beginning to the end for successful completion of every inquiry (47a). In point of fact, however, dialectic encounters evasiveness and recalcitrance in the majority of men; and Socrates was always gratified, as in the case of Theaetetus, to find a nature inclining toward truth of its own accord without being unduly urged through all the intervening steps.[12] But because truth descried by dialectic counted upon a right disposition of the mind, the "leadings" of dialectic were not regarded by Plato as rigorously coercive. As each successive implication emerged and was, in turn, explored for its import, consent was not constrained but had to be accorded. Such knowledge, then, was in the keeping of volition. Acknowledgment could be withheld. Hence, the bearing of dialectical investigation could be deprived of its self-evidencing force; indeed, its "leadings" were not self-evident where a proper disposition of mind was lacking.

In one word, neither receptivity nor memory will ever produce knowledge in him who has no affinity with the object, since it does not germinate to start with in alien states of mind; consequently neither those who have no natural connexion or affinity with things just, and all else that is fair, although they are both receptive and retentive in various ways of other things, nor yet those who possess such affinity but are unreceptive and unretentive—none, I say, of these will ever learn to the utmost possible extent the truth of virtue nor yet of vice. For in learning these objects it is necessary to learn at the same time both what is false and what is true of the whole of Existence.[13]

Plato's conviction is clear: ultimate reality cannot be known by just any retentive and perspicacious intelligence; but it can be known by minds which in character possess affinity with the object of knowledge.[14]

Another, and second, barrier to cogent demonstration deserves mention. For Plato, the Good, as the intelligible First Principle, constitutes the ultimate premise of all thought and inquiry. It is the Principle through which everything else is known. Obviously, no subsequent deduction, employing the Good as premise, proves its validity. All deduction presupposes its validity. This circumstance is surely part of what Plato intends by the enigmatic assertion of the *Republic* that the Idea of the Good supplies "truth to the objects of knowledge and the power of knowing to the knower."[15] The Good, therefore, cannot be exhibited by deduction. Deduction requires some knowledge of it already, even if it is only the tacit assumption that truth is *better* than error, *i.e.*, more worthy of preference. The exhibition of the Good will not be by deduction but by a process we may best describe as *eduction*. The latter will be a drawing out from the *less* the implications for the *more*. As implicit awareness is transformed into explicit comprehension, knowledge comes into being. But, once again, this process cannot advance to fulfillment in the absence of "the habit of the Good." This "habit" can be nothing less than a condition and disposition of the entire soul favorable toward the acknowledgment of truth. It is manifestly identical with the new "habituation" of the soul which, in *Republic*

VII, Plato shows to be requisite for education.[16]   Through its em-
powerment the mind acquires some measure of conformity with its
object.

Plato did affirm that there is a kind of truth which admits of certain demonstration.   If we refer once more to the important *Republic* passages which differentiate the "sciences" from dialectic, it is
apparent what kind of truth is said to have apodictic certainty.   It is
the truth of mathematical science or the truths of the "understanding."   To be sure, as was indicated earlier, such truth is only hypothetical, even though it is demonstrative (511a).   By hypothetical, it
is meant that, unlike the knowledge of the Good, the truth of science
does not possess ultimate and unqualified self-evidence.   Its premises
are "arbitrary" and possess only limited self-authenticity.[17]

In preliminary fashion, we may now refer to a third aspect of
epistêmê which involved difficulties for Plato's pedagogy: It is that
the highest knowledge possible to man takes the form of immediate
and personal insight.   There are the well-known passages in both the
Symposium and the *Seventh Epistle* which indicate that dialectical
inquiry culminates suddenly in dawning vision of reality.[18]   Quite
apart from these signal passages, it scarcely needs laboring that, in
the *Phaedo*, the *Phaedrus*, and the *Republic*, the highest moment of
knowledge occurs when "the eye of the mind" attains "vision," however fleeting, of abiding reality.[19]   And the case is hardly altered at
all in the instance of the *Philebus* (59c) or in that of the *Timaeus*
(52a).   When the *organon* of knowledge is "kindled afresh," a vista
opens before the mind's gaze, and it beholds reality with "clear
waking vision" (527d).   Dialectic, in the *Republic*, is said to possess
the power of leading the best part of the soul up to a contemplation
of what is supreme among realities (532c); but not even dialectic can
display that object to every curious gaze.

Plato understood that there are limits beyond which even dialectical discourse cannot carry conviction.   Knowledge calls for a certain
commitment of the self.   In the absence of sincerity the most skillful
dialectician is unable to assist another to see.   There are some minds,
states the *Phaedrus*, so "fitted" for apprehension that words, sown
by dialectic, are able to "help themselves" and, of their own accord,
mature and come to fruition (276e).   However, there are others, as
Plato affirms in the *Seventh Epistle*, who are "morally" so indisposed toward truth that nothing would suffice to make them see
(344a).   It is not strange, therefore, that we find Socrates asserting
about the Good: "And, if I could, I would show you, no longer an

image and symbol of my meaning, but the very truth, as it appears to *me*—though whether rightly or not I may not properly affirm."[20]

The likeliest explanation for Socrates' inability to be affirmative in this matter is supplied by the *Republic*, namely, that the culminating moment of knowledge is immediate vision (517b). Its content Socrates can neither convey nor prove. He can only induce others to share it (540a). This is hardly "mysticism"! Its obvious analogue is to be found in the most elementary characteristic of direct sensible intuition. If, in some measure, we overcome the immediacy and, therefore, the privacy of our own sense perceptions, it is because others, with *common interests*, agree to share and acknowledge with us a common universe of denotation; and, doubtless, the requirements of day-to-day existence force us to do so. Plato is merely asserting that a comparable acknowledgment is indispensable for attainment of knowledge in a "higher" universe of discourse where, as the *Phaedrus* intimates, mutual interests are as indispensable to common knowledge as in the other sphere (256d).

Plato believed that deductive inference is absent in the case of immediate cognition of reality. If it were not so, the reality in question could be cogently deduced and the problems of pedagogy would be manageable. In the case of inference, something is ascertainably true if something else, upon which inference depends, is antecedently granted. Truths of the "understanding," therefore, are all of the hypothetical sort. The truth of *noêsis*—for there is only one, the Idea of the Good—is not hypothetical. Hence, neither can it be regarded as demonstrable. But, as we observed in Chapter VII, this fact does not detract from its truth-value. It possesses its own unparalleled kind of certainty.[21]

2. Two Modes of Certainty

Evidence is ample to indicate that there are two species of certainty embraced within the thought of Plato. The one is the self-evidentiality of the Idea of the Good, which alone satisfies the axiological character of thought. To be sure, the supremely intelligible is not uniquely self-authenticating, although it is unconditionally so. Justice, temperance, and beauty also authenticate themselves to the man who honestly consults the deliverances and intimations of his own soul. The other kind of certainty is the *apodeixis* or proof which belongs pre-eminently to the mathematical sciences.

Aristotle regarded this second mode of certainty as the criterion of truth in both metaphysics and physics. For him, science and philosophy were to become well-nigh indistinguishable because of his adoption of *apodeixis* as the standard of validity for every kind of organized and communicable knowledge. It was urgently necessary, therefore, that Aristotle should codify the rules of valid inference. This task he brilliantly executed in his *Analytics*, going altogether beyond anything Plato attempted.

Magnificent as was Aristotle's achievement in the science of logic, the motives prompting his efforts require to be recognized and assessed. If we may undertake to put together the pieces of a long-standing puzzle, let us note that Aristotle is found to be abandoning dialectic, as *elenchos*, together with knowledge of the supreme intelligible object and its accompanying and unique form of certainty, self-authentication. Aristotle chooses, instead, to put his confidence in the kind of knowledge which is hypothetical *and* demonstrable and which, accordingly, admits of public verification. Henceforth, proof (ἀπόδειξις) must be the condition *sine qua non* for all claims to scientific knowledge.

Aristotle is ready to concede that proof by way of inference presupposes axioms "which are not derived from more certain propositions but are immediately certain."[22] The most fundamental of these axioms are the "laws of thought," especially non-contradiction. The latter Aristotle regarded as the "starting point" of all other axioms.[23] In addition, there are the hypotheses and definitions of the special sciences which must be *taken* as first principles. For, Aristotle says, "it is impossible that everything should have a proof; the process would go on to infinity, so that there would be no proof."[24]

In order to arrive at the first principles or postulates of the sciences, Aristotle employed "induction," which ascends from the data of sense to universals and to conceptual definitions. By means of the latter, the facts of experience are eventually to be explained or rendered intelligible. The method proceeds by subalternation of particulars to universals. If we may take his own word for it, "induction" of universals is how Aristotle now proposes to reconceive the function of Platonic dialectic.[25] "Induction" serves to abstract and identify the τὸ τί ἐστί, the "what-it-is" of any sense datum; the resulting general concept is held to be the "starting-point" of all syllogistic or deductive reasoning.[26]

Evidently, then, Aristotle was prepared to transform the nature of dialectic quite beyond recognition. While, with him, it was a function of dialectic "to comprehend particulars under a general idea," this was, in Plato's conception, only an important portion of its total work, namely, that of division and composition.[27] But, furthermore, Aristotle did not hesitate to place Plato's dialectic in association with sophistry.[28] Dialectic treats as an exercise, he says, what philosophy tries to understand.[29] In this instance, Aristotle seemingly means the *elenchos*. From this standpoint dialectic is manifestly no longer an honored and legitimate part of philosophy; whereas, for Plato, it was almost the whole of *philosophia* proper, since the *elenchos* implemented the ultimate effort of *nous* toward reality. Apparently Aristotle regarded dialectic as a mere exercise, because it did not conform to the requirement of genuinely explanatory science. As Windelband states, this requirement is "the derivation of particular judgments from the universal."[30] In short, dialectic, understood as *elenchos*, does not consist of syllogistic deduction; therefore it does not attain to *apodeixis*. Defaulting in this respect, dialectic cannot secure knowledge which is scientific; for Aristotle expressed the judgment that "to be a matter of scientific knowledge a truth must be demonstrated by deduction from other truths."[31]

There is no escaping the conclusion that Aristotle largely abandoned the truth of self-authenticity for the truth of apodictic certainty, the truth of the syllogism. After all, only such truth was publicly verifiable. This judgment is not significantly altered by Aristotle's concession that the "laws of thought" are self-evidently true. If one is to have an intelligible world at all, something must be acknowledged as "given" in order that knowledge may get a start. At the moment it is enough to point out that Aristotle evaded Plato's problem of pedagogy by restricting knowledge to the sphere of cogent inference from acknowledged premises. Henceforth the character or disposition of a man seemed to be of no consequence in his attainment of *epistêmê*. Proof seemed to make both *êthos* and *erôs* irrelevant to the achievement of truth.

3. CRITIQUE OF RHETORIC AS A PERSUASIVE ART

For Plato, in contrast with Aristotle, the truth or the knowledge of ultimate reality (*i.e.*, "metaphysical" knowledge) is never necessary and never enforceable. Since assent cannot be required, because demonstration is not claimed, the right to dissent is always granted, and human freedom is respected. Likewise, although divine Reality is available for human cognition, it does not intrude itself upon human attention so as to constrain acknowledgment, but, rather, awaits it. Furthermore, Being, or the truth of Being, is in nowise so possessible that, by an exercise of syllogistic power, it may, in all cases, be displayed equally to the untutored, to the incredulous, or to the disinclined.

This is to say that for Plato divine Reality is not the attainment of a pure "theoretical reason." Neither does Reality admit of being exhibited by it. On the contrary, the reality in question is accessible only to a reason for which "practical" or axiological motivations are inherent. Accordingly, in the case of "metaphysical" knowledge, *assent* waits upon *consent*. Thus the knowledge in question is precisely knowledge through freedom, that is, through acknowledgment. So while Plato's *paideia* is designed to cope with pervasive human ignorance, his therapeutic pedagogy neither aims at nor pretends to supply any such logical *tour de force* as is, thereby, unable either to account for, to accredit, or to tolerate human error. For wherever apodictic knowledge is asserted, there denial of the liberty to dissent is implied. The Aristotelian reduction of metaphysical knowledge to the hypothetical and apodictic variety has always carried with it the implication of conformity; for where propositions are demonstrably cogent, conscientious objection is irrelevant and on occasion intolerable. But for Plato cogency is not anticipated in regard to the ultimate object of knowledge. What is required is not *apodeixis* but transformation of *êthos*. And furthermore it is precisely the case that in this domain there can be no knowledge unless it is conscientious.

For this complex of reasons, "metaphysical" conviction must necessarily be attained by some means other than *apodeixis*. In the interest of education, Plato was obliged to formulate a method neither polemical nor apodictic, but irenic. Consequently he found himself under necessity of reconsidering and redefining the existing art of persuasion, which hitherto had been almost exclusively the domain of the rhetoricians. Transformation of the persuasive art, its conception along new lines, comprises one of the two central objectives of the *Phaedrus* and has been so noted by Hackforth.[32] The other is clarification of the nature and efficacy of the higher madness.

The art of pedagogy which Plato is about to expound is not likely to have much in common with sophistry. Nor will it regard instruction as the transmission of information. Nevertheless there is reason to believe that, following the writing of the *Gorgias*, Plato's attitude toward rhetoric underwent some alteration. His earlier criticism of rhetorical practice, as we find it in the *Gorgias* and the *Euthydemus*, gives no quarter to its practitioners. But there are signs that Plato gradually came to concede a measure of similarity between the persuasiveness of rhetoric and the work of the dialectician. For the two methods had one characteristic in common. Neither could claim to secure incontrovertible proof. However different dialectic and rhetoric might be in other fundamental respects, both dealt with kinds of truth not logically enforceable—the one with matters of *doxa,* the other with those of *noêsis.*

Plato's critique of the prevailing conception of rhetoric is found in a number of dialogues but especially in the *Gorgias,* the *Euthydemus* and the *Phaedrus.* Generically considered, Plato defined rhetoric, according to function, as a producer of persuasion.[33] It was mainly employed in law courts and in the public assembly with the purpose of winning conviction on any subject dear to the orator's heart or prescribed by party interests. As Plato viewed the matter, however, the stigma attaching to rhetoric had little to do with its character as persuasion. There was nothing reprehensible about persuasive speech as such. Socrates himself had well understood the power of words. And, in the *Charmides* (157a), he had conceived words of the right sort as "charms" by which the soul might be cured of its ignorance and rightly nurtured in virtue. Already in the *Gorgias,* as in the *Crito,* Plato was prepared to assert that whoever teaches anything must, necessarily, in the course of teaching, also persuade.[34] The mathematician persuades as do the practitioners of the other sciences and arts. All of them secure conviction about verities relating to their peculiar subject-matter (454a).

Rhetoric, therefore, is not to be censured for the feature which it possesses in common with other arts and sciences. It is to be censured in so far as it makes persuasion its *exclusive* occupation. Plato's animus is directed, not against persuasion as a concomitant of instruction, but against the forensic temper which prizes success in verbal combat above responsibility to truth. Instruction ought to carry conviction in either the cobbler's art or in mathematics, for both kinds of "knowledge" distinguish truth from falsehood and are persuasive in regard to the truths of their respective subjects. If rhetoric is liable to criticism, according to the *Gorgias,* it is because it has no subject-matter except the "knack" of persuasion itself, *i.e.,* the inculcation of beliefs (453a). Because it possesses no distinctive material of inquiry in the province of which it is possible to say something is true and something else is false, Plato concluded that rhetoric is neither a science nor a true art (*technê*), but a "craft" or "skill" devoid of art.[35] The debased characteristics of rhetoric, as the Sophists had taught it, were to be looked for at three points in particular: the incentives prompting its practice, the means employed to win conviction, and the truth-value of the results it obtained.

a. Incentives Prompting Rhetoric

The incentives prompting the practice of rhetoric were readily apparent and openly acknowledged by its teachers. Rhetorical skill was the best means of winning the verdict in public debate and securing the kind of support necessary for the furtherance of private interest or party cause. Neither Protagoras nor Gorgias scrupled to commend his own brand of instruction upon this ground. Euthydemus exulted in his eristic tricks. Wielding words as his weapons, he was prepared to confute either true or false arguments of opponents with equal facility (272a). If matters of crucial importance for the well-being of the citizen and the community had not been at stake in the outcome of these contests, one might have dismissed the whole futile business as a sportive, if ludicrous, joust of words. Plato did in fact often describe it as "sport" and the combatants as hunters and sportsmen.[36] But he could not view with indifference the claim of Gorgias that the wily disputer, however ignorant of the truth, was quite able to subvert it and make a sorry spectacle of the truly informed specialist who happened to be inferior in forensic skill (452e). He could not regard as true art a sleight-of-hand which was able to make the same thing appear to the same persons as being at one time just and at another unjust.[37] Such practices were, plainly, traffic in untruth, and the practitioner was a merchandiser in appearances.[38] Truth was manifestly subordinated to the will and purposes of the disputant. This was the first and most damaging blight upon *eristikê* or disputation. It was always polemical and contentious in both spirit and intent.[39] Whether it was the speech of Lysias, as in the *Phaedrus*, or that of a Solon or a Pericles, the orator began with a presumed truth or an unexamined and antecedently adopted thesis (257e f.). He proceeded to support and enforce it, never to appraise its validity. His whole intent was in contriving by every persuasive trick at his command to get others to share, for some ulterior reason, the opinions he promoted. How, except by some incredible good fortune, could one expect truth to emerge concerning affairs either small or great?

b. Devices of Rhetorical Persuasion

If the incentives of rhetorical practice were reprobate, so also were the means it devised and employed to secure its ends. In the *Phaedrus* Plato went to the trouble, though with obvious satirical intent, of enumerating the various types of "proof" which the Sophists contrived for public debate. These were: narrative, testimony, confirmation from probabilities, and refutation; "covert allusion" and "indirect praises"; the proper uses of figure and metaphor; "tearful speeches" and techniques for arousing pity or fear. There were also forms of speech by which a Thrasymachus could arouse assemblies to wrath, then soothe again.[40] But in every case the device necessary above all others was to indicate adroitly in what respect the proposition to be enforced coincided with the opinions and prejudices of the assembled group.

Rhetoric was obviously a form of "flattery," and that is how Plato regularly described it.[41] In the effort to win his case, says Socrates in the *Gorgias*, the rhetorician always appealed to the predilections of his audience and dangled before it what was most pleasant to hear (464d). In this sense, Plato says the function of rhetoric is to persuade the multitude. And by the multitude he means the appetitive *dûnamis* in human nature which constitutes the "main mass of the soul," the part insatiably bent upon pleasure.[42] Thus rhetoric is discredited in so far as its method of producing persuasion is by accommodating argument to the ingrained prejudices, unexamined opinions, and unchallenged commitments of minds largely controlled by clamorous desires rather than by a love of truth.

c. Truth-value of Rhetoric

Finally, rhetoric, as practiced, stands condemned when measured by the results it obtains. It may successfully inculcate beliefs, but in so doing it accomplishes only a transfer of one man's opinions to another man's mind. Of the two forms of persuasion, according to the *Gorgias*, rhetoric is "a producer of persuasion for belief" (455a). It is the kind of persuasion, says Plato, from which we get belief without knowledge. There is another kind which eventuates in knowledge (454e). It is this which we propose to show that Plato subsequently identified with dialectic. From this judgment upon rhetoric, Plato evidently did not deviate; for in the *Theaetetus* he describes the role of the rhetorician as persuasion rather than as teaching (201a-c). Like jurors in courts of law, men are influenced to hold convictions about matters of which they have no first-hand knowledge but only hearsay. Correspondingly, in the *Phaedrus*, it is maintained that the maximum to be expected from rhetorical practice is "likelihood" (272e). It is a fabricated body of opinion imbued with tendentializing self-interest and effectually engrafted into other minds by surreptitious pleading. Among its average representatives, rhetoric was neither used nor recommended, so far as Plato could see, because of any genuine concern for truth.

4. The True Rhetorical and Persuasive Art

If it is true, as Plato affirmed in the *Gorgias*, that there is no teaching or learning in the absence of persuasion (453d), his *paideusis* must somehow include the art of persuasion. By now it should be apparent that Plato does not spurn persuasion as such. He does repudiate the craft which has no distinctive content and which makes inculcation of partisan belief its exclusive concern. We have already seen that in the *Gorgias* two forms of persuasion are alluded to. It is said that rhetoric produces persuasion for belief in the absence of knowledge, but there is passing reference to a different form of persuasion. From the second sort comes *epistêmê*, or knowledge in the privileged sense (454e). Plato, however, declines to enlarge upon the nature of the second kind of persuasion, although at 517a he alludes to an *alêthinê rhêtorikê*, a genuine art of rhetoric, which even the best of Athens' orators and statesmen failed to attain and of which, presumably, Socrates alone holds the secret. We must turn to the *Phaedrus*, evidently, for his supplementary treatment. There Plato definitively contrasts rhetoric, in its contemporary expression, with what he chooses to call "the truly rhetorical and persuasive art" (269d).

In the *Phaedrus* Plato intends to specify in what respect the art of dialectic is both like and unlike the theory and practice of rhetoric. A principal aim of the dialogue is to show that the persuasive art, which ought to inform rhetoric, is dialectic. It is a real art, not a craft, and it produces conviction in the soul (271a). It does not engraft other men's opinions. On the contrary, Plato indicates that by proper discourses its practitioners undertake to stimulate and induce men to seize hold of truth and reality for themselves.[48] A real, as distinguished from a pseudo, art of speech truly exists, but it needs definition. The *Phaedrus* shows that this art will take the form of "psychagogy," that is, a way of leading souls by persuasion (261a). According to the same standards by which rhetoric was found deficient, the true persuasive art will be seen to deserve approval and acceptance. It will be judged and found worthy by the test of its incentives, its manner of winning conviction, and the truth-value of its findings.

a. The Incentives of the True Persuasive Art

The *Phaedrus* is much occupied with the kind of incentive that must inspire any practice of rhetoric that can be considered a true persuasive art. Plato's prolonged effort to differentiate the inferior kind of eros from the divine sort is not at all irrelevant to the pervasive critique of rhetoric that controls the dialogue (266a). Preeminently, the true rhetorician (*i.e.* the dialectician) is a participant in the higher madness and, therefore, eagerly pursues knowledge of ideal realities. Unlike the common pleader before court or assembly, he does not marshal his argument in the service of private and factional concerns, for he has become liberated from ungenerous love.

Egotism specifically accounts for the phenomenon which Gorgias hardly blushed to admit; namely, that the skillful orator is able and willing to make men believe whatever he desires independently of considerations of truth. What other reason than self-interest could prompt men to contrive devices for swaying audiences to their will or to refute opponents with equal facility, whether the opponent's case was true or false? Plato's distinction between two sorts of love in the *Phaedrus* (266a) was essential for enforcing what he had already intimated elsewhere, namely, that rhetoric is but an instrument of self-advantage. The *Protagoras* makes plain Plato's conviction that it is the way of gaining affluence, prerogative, and dominion in politics (318e). All discussion, private or public, which is motivated by jealous self-regard and ulterior ends is not an instrument of truth, but, as the *Republic* suggests, only a tool for the acquisition of power or the successful merchandising of singular causes (365d).

The speech of Lysias in the *Phaedrus*, which Plato subjects to analysis (264a f.), illustrates the old device of begging the question. It begins with what ought to be the conclusion of inquiry; then, without suitable distinction between kinds of love, finds convenient reasons to buttress the prearranged and presumptuous contention that all lovers are to be shunned. As practiced, rhetoric was barefaced rationalization. It was truly *antilogikê*, the art of contending for one's own or party interests (261e). Prodicus, in the *Protagoras*, was speaking for Plato when he admonished Socrates and Protagoras that argumentation ought to proceed from "goodwill" (*eunoia*) between friends, not from emnity and dissension that ordinarily terminates in wrangling and strife (337b).

In the *Phaedrus* there is indication that Plato is trying to convey his conviction that there can be no escape from logomachy or from bias and partisan discussion so long as men are prompted by "mortal prudence" and the ungenerous or "left-handed" sort of love. Plato evidently intends to suggest a positive connection between the fruitless inconsequence of the speeches of Lysias and Socrates and the self-centered love they agree to censure.[44] He saw that the war of words, which described rhetoric, was only an expression of the jealousy, enmity, and partisanship that pervaded existing society. It was, as *Republic* 500b intimates, that same warfare at the verbal level. Therefore, before one can conceive of a truly persuasive art and of conditions essential for the fruitful pursuit of truth, he must become aware of the existence of a generous or liberal love (ἐλεύθερος ἔρως) (243c). The latter must embrace not only a love of essential reality but, as derivative, friendly feeling toward associates and "goodwill" toward them as partners, rather than as adversaries, in a common quest.[45] The incentives prompting discourse ought not to be, as with Euthydemus, pride of victory in oral combat, or, as deprecated in the *Phaedrus*, anxious quest for honors and fame for eloquence and wisdom (258a f.). The justifying motivation for any discussion or debate is endeavor after truth, and on the assumption that it yet remains to be found.[46]

Recurrently Plato refers to "goodwill" or a generous disposition as the prerequisite for sincere discussion.[47] He obviously intends to signalize the difference between the Socratic temper and that of Gorgias by the claim of Socrates that he is as glad to be refuted as to refute in the interest of finding truth and of avoiding error.[48] Despite Gorgias' ready protest that he, too, is ruled by identical sentiments, his words betray him. The rhetorician he describes prizes victory and, by profession, is an advocate of particular causes that require him to make the best of his case on every occasion (453a). Of necessity, therefore, he will proceed in a spirit of contentiousness rather than of inquiry (457d). No illuminating contribution or telling analysis made by an opponent is suffered to have its effect but must be countered and absorbed by diversionary rejoinders.[49] It was hopeless to anticipate that truth could emerge from the battle of words. As Plato stated in the *Theaetetus*, arguments become the masters of men rather than servants for the discovery of truth (173c).

A true art of persuasion, then, demands a "generous love"—something we might appropriately describe as a liberal mind. Along with other qualities, it seems to be required of the philosophic nature.[50] It is something altogether absent from the "tyrant soul" of the *Republic,* whose lower impulses have achieved complete mastery (576a). Hence it is the aim of education to liberate the "gentle part" of the soul from the brutish (591b). In the *Gorgias* Callicles praises philosophy as suitable for the young and conducive to liberality of mind (485c); but the same quality, bred by philosophy and fitting for youth, is childish and unmanly in maturity (485b). In mature years a man's personal advantage must be the rule—in business as in debate (484e).

Generosity of temper has its real source, according to the *Phaedrus,* in an emancipating love of wisdom which secures a "divine release from the customary habits" of the soul (265a). If there are liberal spirits, there are such because they are possessed of the higher eros. Plato means to say that the philosopher is the true rhetorician. Of him it may be said that, by persuasion and education, he guides his fellow seekers along the avenue of truth. He exhibits no jealousy or pettiness toward his companions, but strives earnestly to conduct them in the direction of a reality they mutually seek (253a). The true persuasive art is comprised of "fair and free discussions" whose single purpose is the discovery of truth. Plato believed that one large reason for the resolute ignorance of perverse humanity was its almost total unfamiliarity with unprejudiced discussion:

Neither, my dear fellow, have they ever seriously inclined to hearken to fair and free discussions whose sole endeavour was to search out the truth at any cost for knowledge's sake, and which dwell apart and salute from afar all the subtleties and cavils that lead to nought but opinion and strife in court-room and in private talk.[51]

In the *Seventh Epistle* Plato warmly declares that what is required in pedagogy is inquiry after truths, "proving them by kindly proofs and employing questionings and answerings which are devoid of envy" (344b). The objective of discussion, Plato continues to insist in the *Philebus* (14b), is not victory in debate but single-hearted devotion to truth.

b. The Means of Legitimate Persuasion

We may now consider the means of furthering valid persuasion. Indispensable preliminaries are definition of terms and a proper "division" of the subject-matter. Unless these steps are taken, discussion is bound to be fruitless.[52] As Plato commented in the *Republic*, the power of disputation (ἀντιλογική) is very great. Men fall into it, even against their will, and begin to wrangle whenever they have failed, initially, to make suitable distinctions. In that event, they engage in purely verbal contests and practice eristic rather than dialectic upon each other (454a). This observation is extensively illustrated in the *Phaedrus* and elsewhere. The principal fault with the speech of Lysias in dispraise of eros was not merely its haphazard structure (264b), but also its inexcusable failure to distinguish between the kinds of love before selecting the one to be depreciated. As a consequence, love, both good and bad, was rejected as reprobate (265c). The true persuasive art requires proper division and classification of the matter of inquiry and, in addition, the capacity to organize or synthesize the distinctive elements which become clarified by analysis (266b). In this way discussion may attain a cumulative conception of any problem under consideration (265d). Definition through division thus helps to forestall impulsive defense or refutation.

The methodology of the true persuasive art, however, has other aspects, and some of these are more germane to our immediate interest. It can hardly be overstressed that, in Plato's view, dialectic sets out upon a way of inquiry by no means fully charted. Its end results are to be determined only by the course of the discussion. In contrast, rhetoric predetermines its goal and then justifies it. Moreover, there is Plato's repeated insistence that the true persuasive art is a "joint-inquiry," shared by those who, disclaiming present certainty, cherish a common desire for discovery. Plato's notion of cooperative investigation deserves supplementary comment, because it not only unveils a distinctive feature of dialectic as *elenchos* but also discloses the way in which it is truly an irenic art.

During his conversation with Protagoras, Socrates gives utterance to his long-standing conviction that interchange with others in discriminating dialogue is wholly distinct from excursive harangue of public address.[53] In the *Meno*, with its brilliant illustration of the method of *elenchos*, Plato makes it clear that the crux of the process is joint-inquiry.[54] Discovery is made and knowledge comes to birth through cooperative investigation. The teacher interrogates. The learner makes replies without circumvention or defensiveness as answers commend themselves. Goodwill toward the advancement of the inquiry is required on the part of both the questioner and the one who answers. Meno's slave boy is pliable, unsophisticated, and largely without presumption; but joint-inquiry encounters obstacles when respondents are opinionated and "cagey" like Protagoras or Callicles. In such cases, answers will be evasive and qualified so as to protect antecedently espoused opinions which are presently being scrutinized.[55] Obviously, in this circumstance, the inquiry is not really shared or in common. It is not advanced in good faith by both parties, and genuine commitment to the enterprise is, as in the case of Callicles, evasively withheld (*Gorg.* 501c). The results of the effort are forfeited. Initial agreements or opinions that were up for examination are neither refuted nor confirmed because the series of steps has not been acknowledged by both participants.

If the true persuasive art is to have maximum effect, participants must be committed from the start; as, also, they must be in mutual agreement about the issues under consideration. At the beginning it is essential for all parties to understand and agree upon the subject of deliberation. For, says Plato, unless men come to an agreement at the beginning of their common deliberations, they will agree neither with themselves nor with each other, as they go on to reach the natural outcome.[56] Unless there is agreement at the beginning, there can be no mutual discovery or joint-acknowledgment of truth at the end. What is more, once *homologia* is secured and all parties have pledged themselves to the investigation, confidence may be placed in the outcome. Therefore the dialectician cannot accept condescending, tentative, or hypothetical agreement, as Socrates refuses to do in his conversation with Protagoras.[57] And, as Polus is warned, he must honestly consent to be put to the proof.[58] Socrates knows full well that condescension or feigned commitment to the inquiry at the start will inevitably rob the investigation of its fruits in sincere conviction at the end. But he also understands this other important fact: When a man's real and honest opinions are offered as the grist of joint-discussion, it is not his casual statements which are brought to the test, but the person himself. For Socrates confesses, "although my first object is to test the argument, the result will be that both I, the questioner, and my respondent are brought to the test."[59] This, of course, is what is required to lay bare the contradiction which Plato believes exists in the mind of a Polus or a Callicles—the contradiction between their professions and their profounder beliefs.[60]

With remarkable psychological insight, Plato (or perhaps Socrates) discerned that all argument is trifling and all demonstration is superficial which does not really involve the person of the investigator, his essential mind and genuine convictions, true or false. The accomplished rhetorician leaves men spectators of his virtuosity and legerdemain; and, even if he wins conviction by his dexterity, those who "believe" are usually hesitant to admit that his contentions are their own. With the *elenchos* the case is different: the interrogator and the respondent are jointly engaged in sifting the evidence and following, step by step, the unfolding import of the argument. *Elenchos* approximates more nearly to the true art of persuasion, because, where it secures real commitment and involvement of the mind of the participants, the results of discussion, in so far as they are negative, will not be refutations of opponents, but self-refutations of colleagues. As Socrates says to Alcibiades, "you are impeached of this by your own words out of your own mouth."[61] If men become angry when, little by little, they are finally tripped up and refuted by the Socratic *elenchos*,[62] neither Socrates nor dialectic is to be blamed, but the confuted ones who have been party to their own chastening and enlightenment.

When, however, men honestly submit to the examination of opinions and find, upon analysis and comparison, that they actually hold contradictory judgments about the same things, as Polus did about doing wrong and suffering it, then, as is said in the *Sophist*, they "grow angry with themselves and gentle toward others" (230b). Therewith, they are ripe for the apprehension of truth, and *elenchos* may have its fruition in deeper insights. The persuasive power of *elenchos* was to be seen in the way the eventual self-refutation, or, as it might be, confirmation was prepared for by a succession of antecedent agreements.[63] To these the respondent was himself a party, that is, if he was truly pledged to investigation. In this way dialectic contrives to make the results of inquiry, not alien and external, but one's own—not something imposed but something which, in the course of analysis, authenticates itself. True but obscured opinions are given a chance to surface and come to light. An account (*logos*) of them is rendered.

c. The Fruits of Joint-Inquiry

The aim of *elenchos* is not refutation or, more properly, self-refutation, though almost always this is involved; rather, the aim of *elenchos* is discovery and renewal of knowledge. Here also, dialectic does not achieve demonstrations and proofs before the eyes of reluctant and incredulous bystanders. Those who come to know anything through dialectic are persons who submit themselves to its discipline.[64]   They have become parties to an inquiry of which cross-examination, as the *Sophist* still contends, is the accepted instrument (230d).   The results of deliberation will be their own, not the words of another.   Thus Socrates (Plato) calls only the respondent himself as "witness."   The opinions of the many are irrelevant.[65]   So he declares: *"But if on my part I fail to produce yourself as my witness to confirm what I say, I consider I have achieved nothing of any account towards the matter of our discussion."*[66]   As enlightenment comes only through joint-inquiry, so the results will come in the form of personal convictions jointly shared.   Accordingly Plato does not hesitate to put in the mouth of Socrates these startling words to Callicles: "Hence any agreement (*homologia*) between you and me must really have attained the perfection of truth."[67]   *Homologia* is, as it were, the building-block of the Platonic *elenchos*, without which it would be powerless.   Obviously, it entails the consequence that, not words and ideas alone, but the man himself who holds them is profoundly involved and, as Socrates reiterates, himself is "put to the test."[68]

The genius of *elenchos*, the point Plato desires to stress, is that whatever eventuates in the course of cross-examination is not the examiner's importation, but the respondent's own contribution and finding.[69]   If there are summations and conclusions, they are the respondent's.[70]   He has not been shown; he has himself made a discovery.   In dialectical inquiry, a man is not spoken to; he speaks, and he himself supplies both the answer and the demonstration. Dialectic is the true rhetorical and persuasive art, because it permits a man to convict himself of error and, on the other hand, to confirm himself in the truth.   He is self-persuaded.   For this reason, Socrates admonished Alcibiades not to hesitate but to make answer if he wished to be persuaded: "and if you do not hear your own self say that the just is expedient, put no trust in the words of anyone again."[71]

In some respects, this counsel was Plato's own deepest wisdom. For him, the soul was "pregnant" with true opinions, but it became articulate only when plied and probed by the power of *elenchos*.[72] This interpretation at least makes sense of Socrates' remark to Callicles.   "I am certain," he said, "that whenever you agree with me in any view that my soul takes, this must be the very truth."[73]   But it is well to note the qualification: Truth is found by way of agreements which fellow seekers make in the course of dialectical conversation.   As if upon stepping-stones, discussion progresses from one secure admission to the next until the respondent discerns and declares the truth for himself. Like Alcibiades, he is confronted by the import of his own admissions.[74] Furthermore, Callicles, if he were an honest respondent, could trust the deliverances of his own mind, once they were sorted and sifted in joint-inquiry with one who loves the truth. In dialectic, Plato takes it to be a principle that it is not the questioner (ὁ ἐρωτῶν) but the one making answer who is the speaker (ὁ λέγων).[75] It was so in the case of Meno's slave boy. According to Socrates, the lad did not render a single statement that was not an answer out of the tumult of his own thought. To be sure the stirrings of reflection were precipitated by the maieutic art. In this art of Socrates, Plato believed he had found the incomparable instrument of *therapeia*.

In view of the fact that it is the unique power of dialectic actually to involve men in productive thought, induce them to speak for themselves, and deliver their minds of their own deepest presentiments of truth, Plato's continual strictures upon oratorical harangue are fully intelligible. Rhetoric did not provoke inquiry but inhibited it. In his role as solicitor and advocate, the rhetorician proposed to think for others through prevailing upon them to share his contentions. In contrast with dialectic, rhetoric succeeded in fostering belief rather than *educing* knowledge.

When we speak of the knowledge which dialectic evokes, however, we are now aware that it is not to be confounded with the demonstrable and hypothetical truths of the "understanding" in so far as these are deductive in character. It is the province of *elenchos* to treat primarily of man's axiological experience and with judgments issuing from it, with a view to ascertaining the implications for ultimate reality. It is permissible to say that dialectic is concerned with essential humane experience, with varying grades of *doxa*. Furthermore, the truths upon which men "stumble" in the process of dialectical inquiry remain inaccessible to those who, like Callicles, are disinclined to follow the arduous ascent. Accordingly it cannot be said that the findings of *elenchos* even approximate public verifiability or possess the kind of cogency that attends the truths of hypothetical *apodeixis*. This last statement may be qualified by the admission that the method of division, first fully formulated in the *Phaedrus*, undoubtedly was intended to afford to dialectic the advantage of greater precision. It assisted in definition of concepts and thus facilitated reflection by placing at the disposal of the reasoner an instrument for more accurate identification of "doubtful things." But if our analysis of division in Chapter V is essentially sound, the main *em-*

ployment of division—though not its content—is empirical. Its content is the *logos*-concept which, as we argued, looks two ways at once.[76] We now reaffirm the view that, in Plato's intention, the *elenchos* remains the prime method of strictly metaphysical inquiry. Hence, if we may trust the evidence of the *Sophist*,[77] the dialectic of *elenchos* retains priority as the privileged method of overcoming the "deformity," the worst ignorance of the soul, namely, *doxa pseudês* or the misidentification of true reality.[78]

The proper conduct of dialectical inquiry requires, as we have seen, undissembling commitment and self-involvement of persons to and in the process. Without this, the very data of research, the content of humane experience in the form of *doxai*, are lacking. In consequence, furthermore, discovery or enlightenment is in every way dependent upon the measure to which the respondent *allows* the inner depths of his experience to be "tapped" and its true import appraised. In the absence of decisive commitment, therefore, to the leadings of cross-examination, the effort will likely culminate only in refutation of one who insists on remaining an "opponent."

5. Insight and the Irenic Art

Plato found men in a condition of blindness. Appearance was confounded with reality, and, altogether, the truth of things was turned upside-down. But, as has been urged, knowledge of ultimate Being did not admit of impersonal apprehension through the agency of irrefragable deduction. Accordingly we find Plato recurring to the question how to deal with those who vehemently challenge his conception of Being. In the *Republic* he seeks a way of "gently persuading them" without resort to arguments *ad hominem* or personal rebuke. Undoubtedly, as we find Plato saying in the *Sophist*, it is necessary that adamant opponents improve in character before dialectic can have its salutary working (246d). For, as he affirms in the same place, those who are to be persuaded must be willing to answer or "discriminate" according to the rules of dialectic. In addition, they must be of a mind to agree on those points by means of which the discussion moves from step to step. Thus, although the philosophic pedagogue avoids "rebuke" and speaks in "gentle tones,"[79] Plato is somewhat at a loss how to proceed, for it is also true that he will "not grant the art of dialectic to any but the man who pursues philosophy in purity and righteousness."[80]

In the face of resolute perversity with which men confound the truth, Plato reaffirmed his view in the *Sophist* that the *elenchos* is "the greatest and most efficacious of all purifications" (230d). Plato knew that enlightenment encountered a resisting eros. Therefore, a kind of "charm" must be found. Resistance must not be intensified by frontal attack but must be circumvented. What better way than by encouraging men to participate in their own illumination? Can they resist truth, once they discover that it is of their own finding? In dialectic, as in nothing else, Plato believed he had found the irenic art.[81]

In the *Republic*, Socrates is made to ask: "Shall we, then, try to persuade him gently, for he does not willingly err, by questioning him thus . . . ?" (589c). Who does not understand that, in the heat of controversy, discriminating questions supply opportunity for deliberation and reconsideration? Precipitate claims are afforded a wider and richer context against which their partiality and half-truth may be seen and measured. Often motives for revision assert themselves, and the mind resumes a more fruitful course of reflection. At the very least, *elenchos* accomplished something like this. The truly persuasive art counts upon a certain right-mindedness which, under propitious circumstances, may reaffirm itself. Men do not willingly err; therefore, they may be persuaded. By this, perhaps, Plato means to suggest that in the course of dialectical examination man's native and irrepressible love of truth and reality, the divine eros, may slip its bonds, gather its strength, and reorient intelligence toward reality.

If we understand the maieutic method as it is described in the *Theaetetus*, we are prepared for the assertion that dialectic supplies the conditions, not of instruction, but of self-instruction.[82] There comes a cumulative vision to those who consent to examine and cross-examine, one after another, the import of their own admissions. Dialectic secures self-convincement, and in so doing it proves itself to be the irenic art.[83] It is never a way of enforcing conviction, but always a way of leading men to adopt the truth for themselves. Dialectic, as the best instrument of education, is a *psuchagogia*, an art of leading souls by persuasion (*Phaedr.* 271d.) It is, as was earlier suggested, the finally reliable pedagogy of conversion, and upon it, without doubt, Plato rests his hope of the moral and intellectual betterment of men and politics.

Innumerable instances of the unique power of dialectic meet us in the dialogues. Socrates finds himself confronted by a resourceful opponent, a Gorgias, a Protagoras, or a Callicles. First he obtains a pledge of initial agreement on some *doxa* apparently remote, but ultimately implicated with the fundamental issue of debate.   Then he explores successively the implications of each *homologia* for the next which is to follow.   He moves from the *less,* always in the direction of its implication for the *more.*   If his respondent is a man of goodwill, agreements will come readily.   If the respondent is wily and evasive, admissions will come in the form of reluctant and qualified concessions.   Eventually it will come to light that the initial *homologia* involved unforeseen consequences, and that the succession of implications accumulates in a conclusion at odds with the proposition previously affirmed.

The respondent now is confronted with an alternative and a choice.   Either he erred in making the initial and succeeding agreements leading to this evident, albeit discomfiting, consequence; or his previous opinions were without foundation.   If he decides that he erred in his initial *doxa* or somewhere along the way, he is obligated to indicate at what point and why.   If he concludes that he was ill-advised in making concessions to begin with, he is convicted of subordinating truth to prudential interests.   If he determines, willy-nilly, to reaffirm his original proposition, he must at least concede that he is on record for holding contrary or contradictory judgments.   Eventually he may be led to square himself with himself.   Meanwhile, like Alcibiades in the *Symposium,* the man will be self-convicted until he is self-convinced (216c).   This was the contrariety in the soul of Callicles which Socrates sought unsuccessfully to resolve through dialectic.   The final step *may* be the embracement of truth; but the decision remains with the individual man.

Quite apart from restrictions imposed by aptitude, the irenic method incurred a limitation which was to prove objectionable to minds unsatisfied with less than apodictic certainty.   The Aristotelian mind evidently was of such a temper.   The very fact that Plato, in the *Phaedrus,* was willing to call dialectic "the truly rhetorical and persuasive art" was enough, seemingly, to stigmatize it with Aristotle. It remains a mystery how Aristotle could possibly confound the persuasiveness of rhetoric with the kind of persuasion precipitated by *elenchos,* especially when the *Phaedrus* labored so diligently to differentiate the one from the other.   But the fact that Plato did not claim *apodeixis* for *elenchos* and dared to regard its function as only persuasive was evidently sufficient cause for Aristotle to link dialectic with sophistry.   His near-identification of sophistry and dialectic is, possibly, further explained by Aristotle's misunderstanding of the regulative function of decision in knowledge.   Quite plainly, if truth were dependent upon acknowledgment and acknowledgment, in turn, upon the right moral disposition, it could never be contended that matters of the highest moment, those of metaphysics, could ever meet the test as publicly verified knowledge. But this was what Aristotle required of everything that was to qualify as *epistêmê*.

For Plato, on the other hand, knowledge of ultimate reality took the form of self-authentication. It was the kind of knowledge that simply did not admit of demonstration. Divine reality, as it were, propounded itself to the disciplined and rightly disposed intelligence; and, although it could not be deduced, there were, as we have seen, conditions under which it might come to be acknowledged. Therefore Plato's pedagogy was so conceived as to encounter and cope with corruption of mind. It was an irenic method through which men might become both *self-convicted* of error and *self-convinced* of the truth. Now the alternative before them was either knowledge through acknowledgment or the Calliclean split self-consciousness, the intolerable condition of sustaining perpetual self-discord and self-disagreement (*Gorg.* 482b). The true rhetorical and persuasive art was the chief instrument of Plato's way of salvation, his *therapeia;* and upon it he placed his hope in the absence of some "stronger vessel," some "divine word" of revelation.[84] (See Appendix: Plato's Depreciation of the Written Word.)

NOTES

1. *Polit.* 277d. For the notion of knowing as in a dream, compare *Meno* 85c. In this connection, see *Rep.* 505e, 517c, 534c. It seems evident that presentiment of essential reality is what is meant by the dream state, and as 534c indicates the presentiment is in the form of *doxa alêthês.*

2. *Rep.* 511d, 527e, 534a.

3. *Post. Anal.* 72 b 18.

4. *Post. Anal.* 72 a 27, 71 a 28-30.

5. *Post. Anal.* 88 b 36.

6. *Post. Anal.* 71 b 20-33.

7. *Nic. Eth.* VI, iii, 4.

8. In the *Posterior Analytics* (71 a 4-10), Aristotle mentions two forms of "dialectical reasoning." They are induction and syllogism. It is characteristic of induction to exhibit "the universal as *implicit* in the clearly known particular." *Cf. Post. Anal.* 99 b 5-8. We have argued that the characteristic of dialectic in Plato's usage is discovery in the *less* of the "implications" for the *more.* It is a movement from the *derived* to the *implied.* If this be the case, there is close analogy between the movement of dialectical reasoning according to Plato and the induction of the "universal" by Aristotle. We might say that Aristotle has reduced Platonic dialectic from a transcendental to an exclusively empirical employment. It is induction based upon sense-experience instead of induction based upon the data of the moral consciousness, as in Plato. In the one case, we rise from the particular to the general

concept. According to Plato, we rise from "true opinions" regarding τὸ καλόν up to a First Principle in which they inhere.

9. L. Nelson, *Socratic Method and Critical Philosophy*, trans. T. K. Brown (New Haven, 1949), 15.

10. *Ibid.*, 10.

11. *Ibid.*, 16.

12. *Soph.* 265d-e. *Cf. Epist.* VII, 341e.

13. *Epist.* VII, 344a-b. *Cf. Rep.* 489c-d.

14. Pertinent here is the ingrained resistance of the prevailing *sunêtheia* of the Cave dwellers and the need of a new one. *Rep.*, 516a. In virtue of this, *nous* is "forcibly" disoriented from reality (519a). What is required is the *psuchê prosê-kousa*, the "fitting soul" of *Phaedrus* 276e. For the required affinity, see also *Rep.* 485c, 487a, 490b; *Soph.* 253e; *Laws* 663c.

15. *Republic* 511b does speak of a movement downward from the First Principle through successive dependencies, all of them Ideas, to a conclusion, also an Idea. This is the only reference in Plato, I think, to deduction from the Good. Actually, what is described is an ontological, not primarily a logical dependency, though the latter follows from the former. *Rep.* 517b-c.

16. See extensive discussion of this subject *supra*, Ch. VI, sec. 4.

17. *Rep.* 510b-511e and 533a-534e. Refer to treatment, Ch. VII, sec. 2. It has sometimes been supposed that mathematical truth comprised for Plato the norm or standard of philosophic verity. *Cf.* O. Toeplitz, *Das Verhältniss von Mathematik und Ideenlehre bie Plato*, Quellen und Studien, Bd. I (1931), 171, *passim.* This judgment cannot be sustained. Even A. E. Taylor's generalization, in reference to *Rep.* VI, xx-xxi, that we "cannot completely 'mathematize' human knowledge, but the more we can mathematize it, the better" is quite misleading (*Plato*, 295). To what extent this *is* true and to what province, namely to *empeira*, this applies can best be determined by examination of *Philebus* 56c-59b and *Protag.* 357a-b. If we consider arithmetic, among the propaedeutic studies of *Republic* VII, we see that it has as its first principles Unity and Indefinite Plurality (525a). Admittedly, these principles are *a priori* in a degree, exceeding the hypotheses of any other of the sciences. Their self-evidence and universality are proportionate to their logical ultimacy. In addition, in so far as arithmetic is pure and unapplied, its operations possess maximum clarity. Nevertheless, the *archai* of arithmetic, as of the other sciences, are not said to be devoid of assumption. On the contrary, they are suppositious (*Cf. Rep.* 511a, d; 533c). Only the Idea of the Good, which answers to the axiological bent of human intelligence, as we saw in Chapter VII, is declared to be a Principle without any supposition (*cf. Rep.* 510b, 511b). In Plato's thought, there is nothing transparently true for intelligence except the supreme intelligible, the Good itself, and, here, truth means self-authentication. Accordingly, it is unthinkable that Plato should have taken the norm and pattern of truth from the propaedeutic studies with their arbitrary *archai.*

18. *Symp.* 210e; *Epist.* VII, 341c, 344b. *Cf. Rep.* 519c-d; *Soph.* 265d.

19. *Rep.* 517b-c, 540a.

20. *Rep.* 533a. *Cf. Alcib.* I, 106d.

21. Verification through "authentication" is a theme which has received important modern statement by W. M. Urban, *Language and Reality* (New York, 1939), 215-226. Urban employs "authentication" as a means of verification where the empirical criterion of truth is inapplicable. Authentication involves "mutual acknowledgment" of values by communicating subjects. For Plato, it is certainly true that knowledge obtains when there is mutual acknowledgment, in dialectical converse, of a given universe of discourse. However, the authenticity of the Good is not dependent upon a *community* of acknowledgment. It is true that public knowledge of it would be so dependent. Plato dissents from those, including Aristotle perhaps, who insist

that there is no knowledge without public verification. Possibly, it is preferable to say that the function of *êthos* in knowledge causes Plato to *restrict* his public. With others, including Aristotle and most western philosophers of modern times, the public is not restricted. The philosopher aspires to make knowledge for every-body. With Plato, this would be the betrayal of philosophy and would also be regarded as futile.

22. W. Windelband, *History of Ancient Philosophy*, 252. *Cf. Met.* 996 b 26-30, 997 a 5 f.

23. *Met.* 1005 b 33.

24. *Met.* 1006 a 7-10. *Cf.* 997 a 11. For a detailed account of the *archai* of the sciences, *cf.* W. D. Ross, *Aristotle*, 42-49.

25. See *supra*, n. 8.

26. *Met.* 1078 b 24-26.

27. In Chapter V, *supra*, it was argued that Aristotle took over and utilized one part of Plato's total conception of dialectic. It was the joint-method of division and composition, by which the Form or "universal" is discriminated in the manifold of sense data. It was further argued that this method is suitable to the pursuit of empirical knowledge, and that its results are both hypothetical and apodictic. Now, we are asserting that it is to this sort of knowledge which Aristotle principally aspires. In Plato's language, it is *dianoia* or "understanding," the grade of knowl-edge inferior to *noêsis*. *Rep.* 533d f. Dialectic as elenchos is retained by Aristotle in the sense of "induction" of universals, but, as indicated in n. 8 above, it is denied all transcendental employment and, therefore, metaphysical significance.

28. *Met.* 1004 b 18, 1061 b 8.

29. *Met.* 1004 b 26.

30. W. Windelband, *op. cit.*, 250.

31. *Nic. Eth.* VI, vi, 1.

32. R. Hackforth (*Plato's Phaedrus*, 11) notes a difference between the *Gorgias* and the *Phaedrus*: ". . . whereas in the earlier [dialogue] Plato is content merely to contrast rhetoric and philosophy, in the later he seeks to harness rhetoric in the service of philosophy."

33. *Gorg.* 453a; *Phaedr.* 260c; *Soph.* 222c-d.

34. *Gorg.* 453d; *Crito* 51b, c. *Cf. Protag.* 352e; *Apol.* 35c.

35. *Phaedr.* 260e, and *Gorg.* 465a.

36. *Rep.* 539b; *Euthyd.* 271c-272a.

37. *Phaedr.* 261c-d.

38. *Soph.* 224d; *Gorg.* 459d.

39. *Euthyd*, 272c and *Soph.* 225c.

40. *Phaedr.* 266e-267e.

41. *Gorg.* 463a; *Rep.* 493b-c; *Soph.* 223a.

42. *Gorg.* 452e. *Cf. Rep.* 431a-b, 442a; *Laws* 689a-b.

43. *Phaedr.* 270b, 276e f. J. B. Skemp (*Plato's Statesman* [New Haven, 1952], 69) apparently can be cited in support of the view here asserted that the *Phaedrus* does proffer dialectic as the "real" art of rhetoric: "True Rhetoric can only be practiced by the man who is both a dialectical philosopher and a man possessed of real insight into human nature."

44. *Phaedrus* 243c suggests Socrates' own diagnosis of the problem: both speeches ignored the "generous" sort of love and held in view only the kind with which jealousy and enmity are concomitants. *Cf. Gorg.* 485a. This is the "left-handed" love of *Phaedrus* 266a. It is also the kind which is absent from the celestial com-pany of gods (247a). Its presence among other souls is the cause of the greatest rivalry and contention, and results in the eclipse of knowledge and the "fall" of the soul (248b). When, however, the divine madness reasserts itself, it banishes narrow-

ness and jealousy (253; *cf. Gorg.* 257d), and accounts for affection as well as disinterested concern for the enlightenment of the beloved (252e, 253c). This relationship is characterized by "goodwill" on the part of the lover (255b), and it is reciprocated (255a). So there comes about the possibility of truth-producing converse between man and man. *Cf. Symp.* 210c. This is the life of *philosophia* (256a) and *philia* (255e). In this way the *Phaedrus* spells out the suggestion of *Symposium* 203a, *viz.*, that the spiritual (*i.e., erôs*) is the means of society and real converse (*dialectos*) between gods and men. It is equally so of fruitful communication between men and men.

45. *Phaedr.* 253b. For partnership in search of truth, see *Gorg.* 487b, c, e; *Protag.* 336b; *Meno* 84c. Of course, in the instance of Callicles, Socrates is ironical. The opposite is the case; Callicles is neither conscientious nor well-disposed toward the discussion. Nevertheless, Socrates describes what is indispensable to fruitful communication and inquiry.

46. *Meno* 86b; *Hipp. Maj.* 288d; *Crito* 48a.

47. The goodwill (*eunoia*) of Socrates is referred to as inseparable from his use of the *elenchos* as part of the maieutic art. *Cf. Rep.* 474a, 533a; *Theaet.* 151c and, for the thought, see *Alcib.* I, 131c; *Symp.* 218c. However, this benevolence, implemented by *elenchos*, arouses anger as men are stripped of presumption, *Apol.* 23b; *Meno* 95a. But criticism is salutary if taken with goodwill, *Laws*, 635b. Attribution of "goodwill" to Callicles and Hippias is ironical. It is precisely what they do not have. *Gorg.* 485a, 486a, 487a; *Hipp. Maj.* 291e. In consequence, they do not sincerely *inquire* and are, therefore, eventually refuted but not self-confuted so that the result is not enlightenment.

48. *Gorg.* 458a, 461a; *Rep.* 499e.

49. *Rep.* 454a.

50. *Cf. Rep.* 486a, b. The exact denotation of "liberality" (ἐλευθεριότης), *Rep.* 402, is uncertain. It is here suggested that it is to be understood especially by reference to 591b, and in contrast to the tyrant soul of 576a. Compare the idea of *theia mania* as "divine release from customary habits" (*Phaedr.* 265a).

51. *Rep.* 499a.

52. *Cf. Gorg.* 457c; *Phaedr.* 237c, 265d; *Soph.* 218c.

53. *Protag.* 336b. *Cf.* the use of δημηγόρος at *Gorg.*, 482c; *Theaet.* 162d.

54. *Meno* 84c. Plato's words are "he will discover by searching with me." See also *Meno* 81d, 86c; *Protag.* 352e; *Gorg.* 472b; 487e; *Soph.* 218b.

55. See the following sequence, *Protag.* 331a, b, 332d, 333b, 334e, 335b, 338e, 360a-e. After *Gorg.* 497, the answers of Callicles are all condescending except occasionally when Socrates says something particularly provoking. The condescension is Callicles' way of evading the force of the argument or keeping it from touching him. He refuses to make genuine *homologiai* or commitments for which, subsequently, he can be held responsible. *Cf.* 497b, 499b.

56. *Phaedr.* 237c. *Cf. Crito* 49d, 47a; *Soph.* 218c; *Phileb.* 14b; *Theaet.* 170a.

57. *Protag.* 331c. *Cf. Gorg.* 497a.

58. *Gorg.* 474b.

59. *Protag.* 333c.

60. *Gorg.* 474b, 482b-c, 483a; *Theaet.* 177b.

61. *Alcib.* I, 118b. *Cf. Gorg.* 472c; *Meno* 85d; *Theaet.* 150d.

62. *Rep.* 487b; *Gorg.* 480e, 497b-c.

63. In the dialogues, illustrations of the cumulative outcome of a succession of *homologiai* are well-nigh innumerable, as an examination of Ast's *Lexicon* will quickly show. The following are adequately illustrative. It is to be noted that arguments based upon *homologiai* range throughout the dialogues and are especially prominent, among later ones, in the *Sophist* and *Philebus*. See *Alcib.* I, 116c;

Euthyd. 302e f.; *Gorg.*, 476d-e, 480e; *Meno*, 96e f.; *Rep.*, 478a; *Cratyl.*, 430a-b; *Soph.* 242c, 246d-247b; *Phileb.* 49e-50b, 60b f. *passim.*

64. *Gorg.* 475d. *Cf. Rep.* 494d. R. Robinson has suggested that in Socrates' usage the *elenchos* was "purely refutative" in function and that it was Plato who made the *elenchos* serve positive and constructive ends. *Plato's Earlier Dialectic* (Ithaca, N. Y., 1941), 188. This, as Robinson admits, involves a difficult historical question. Dialectic is bound to be refutative where Socrates encounters, as he so often does in the dialogues, hostile opponents. In this regard, however, perhaps too much credence can be given *Theaetetus* 210c.

65. *Gorg.* 474a. *Cf. Crito* 46d f.

66. *Gorg.* 472b. *Cf. Protag.* 331c.

67. *Gorg.* 487e. *Cf.* 486e.

68. *Protag.* 333c. *Cf. Symp.* 216b.

69. For the centrality of the concept of discovery (εὑρίσκειν) in attainment of knowledge, see Ch. IV, sec. 2. See also same chapter, n. 47. *Cf.* further, *Theaet.* 150c; *Cratyl.* 436a; *Phileb.* 16d, 34d; *Polit.* 287a.

70. *Meno* 85b-c; *Alcib.* I, 116d. *Gorgias* 474b-c shows Socrates preparing to convict Polus out of his own mouth, out of his own admissions.

71. *Alcib.* I, 114e.

72. *Theaet.* 148e.

73. *Gorg.* 486e. *Cf. Meno* 81d.

74. *Symp.* 216c.

75. *Alcib.* I, 113a-b.

76. See *supra*, Ch. V, sec. 3, a, for extensive discussion.

77. *Cf. Soph.* 230b-231b. Refer to earlier analysis *supra*, Ch. VII, sec. 2. On the basis of *Sophist* 226c f. we have argued that *diakritikê* stands for dialectic; henceforth to be conceived as embracing both the methods of *elenchos* and *division.* The fact that the latter does not eliminate the former has been fully argued in Chapter V. It is especially apparent from *Phaedrus* 276e and context. From the indications of the *Sophist*, however, it is to be anticipated that division will ordinarily be prominent in any use of dialectic. This seems to be the case in the *Sophist, Politicus* and *Philebus.* In the last, the *homologiai* and the language of *elenchos* are quite in evidence (28e). That a conjunction of the two methods is intended is suggested by 16a-b f. There is a possible, though doubtful, reference to *elenchos* at *Politicus* 285d-286a. The suggestion, however, is intensified in likelihood when the passage is compared with *Epistle* VII, 344b, and *Rep.* 533d.

78. *Soph.* 228c, 229c, 240d.

79. *Phaedr.* 268d-e; *Phileb.* 16a; *Laws* 885e, 888a; *Epist.* VII, 343e.

80. *Soph.* 253e. *Cf. Phaedo* 69b-c.

81. For the use of ἠρέμα and πρᾷον in connection with dialectic method, *cf. Protag.* 333e; *Cratyl.* 413a; *Rep.* 476d, 494d, 500a, 501c, 533d, 589c; *Phaedo* 83a; *Phaedr.* 268d; *Theaet.* 154e.

82. *Theaet.* 148e-151d. *Cf. Rep.* 537c.

83. At *Timaeus* 51d-e there is the statement that intelligence (*nous*) arises in us by teaching (*didachê*), with true reasoning, whereas true opinion arises by persuasion. The latter is moveable by persuasion, but *nous* is unalterable. This seems to contest the view that dialectic can be considered the truly persuasive art. We are familiar with the instability of true opinion (*Meno* 97c-98a; *Rep.* 508d), but what is to be said of intelligence which is immovable by the same? The apparent difficulty is obviated by noting that intelligence is immediately said to be stable because its objects, the "self-identical Forms" are stable (52a). It is one thing to hold that knowledge crystallizes through a process of self-convincement (persuasion) and another thing to say that knowledge, once attained, is undeviating. Both things are true without

contradiction. *Nous*, in the *Timaeus* passage, specifies the condition of metaphysical knowledge, such as *Republic* 534c. This, however, is not the kind of knowledge to which the cosmology of the *Timaeus* aspires, rather, to a subordinate rank that does not exceed probability (29c). Accordingly, the *elenchos* is not, properly speaking, employed in it at all.

84. *Cf. Phaedo* 85d.

CHAPTER X

The Sovereignty of the Good

Remember, the intellectual sight begins to be keen when the visual is entering on its wane.—*Symposium* 219a

1. Issues of Metaphysical Knowledge

IN the perspective of Plato, the sum of Being is not exhausted in Actuality; Becoming does not encompass all that is real.[1] The distinction between the Visible and the Intelligible, first plainly declared in the *Phaedo* (83b) and confirmed in the *Republic* (509d), is re-affirmed in the metaphysic of the *Philebus* (59) and in the cosmology of the Timaeus (28). These are commonplaces of Platonic interpretation today, although it is true that an older criticism (*e.g.*, Zeller) deprived Becoming of any "Being" and would, therefore, have regarded the statement that Being is not exhausted in Becoming as both gratuitous and misleading. Accepting, as more accurate, a dualistic or even a pluralistic interpretation of Plato's ontology, we have been inquiring into the grounds upon which Plato claims a privileged position for intelligible reality in the hierarchy of Being. In addition, our inquiry has examined the related problems of knowledge and ignorance, and more specifically, the enigma to which Plato recurs in the *Sophist*, viz., that "the eyes of the soul of the multitude are not strong enough to endure the sight of the divine."[2] But Plato despaired of introducing men to the total range of Being, apart from correcting the prevailing distortion of the soul's powers. Accordingly, Plato's conception of *philosophia* is basically soteriological, and his program of science and learning is not finally distinguishable from what he calls *therapeia*. This in turn must be explained by Plato's realization that impediments to ontological knowledge are attributable to anarchy in men's souls. And this is a fact available only to self-knowledge.

The consequence is that the proper starting-point for evaluating the Platonic ontology is the existing human situation. We do not get to reality save through man. This was central in the Socratic teaching. But we do not get to reality—certainly not the highest reality—save through a rightly oriented mind. Our purpose in this chapter is to explain how this principle operates in the actual processes of knowing: to show, that is, that the postulates of every inferential system, issuing in judgments of existence (ontological), are regarded by Plato as resting upon antecedent judgments of what is good. The ground of this interpretation must rest upon all that has gone before, especially upon the finding that, for Plato—conspicuously in *Republic* VI and VII[3]—the exercise of reflection is tendentialized by the prevailing *pathêma* of the whole soul, and that Plato does not look for attainment of knowledge of "most real Being" apart from revolution of *êthos*.

Now, however, it is essential to state that the question of suitable *êthos* is crucial primarily for the attainment of metaphysical knowledge. To be sure, *êthos* is presupposed and is operative in every exercise of cognition. It functions in sensible, opinable (*doxa*) and in technical (*technê*) cognition. But for these subordinate levels, Plato evidently believed that the prevailing *êthos* (*i.e.*, the sensate) requires no fundamental transformation for the attainment of knowledge. In point of fact, knowledge of Becoming (either critical or uncritical *doxa*)[4] requires little more than the eros of the lovers of spectacles, the same love, indeed, which inspires the "ignorance" of the Cave and is sufficient to account for the probable truths of empirical generalization, or what, in the Cave, passes for wisdom.[5] To be sure, the so-called "ignorance" of the Cave is, taken by itself, not really ignorance but *doxa*, and only becomes ignorance, that is, *doxa pseudês*, when, in addition, its empirical objects are asserted to be ultimate reality. Such a judgment confounds Becoming with Being. In opposition thereto, Plato makes his metaphysical claim: It is the object of *noêsis*, not *doxa*, that denotes the transparently intelligible and superior reaches of Being. And it is primarily in the attainment of this prospect that Plato understands the condition of the *entire* soul to be decisively influential. Here a suitable *êthos* is requisite; and, in default of right character, knowledge cannot be completed. In short, according to this view, *êthos* is determinative of the possibility or impossibility of metaphysics.

With Kant, the Aristotelian word, "metaphysics," passed under a cloud. For Kant, metaphysics was impossible, and phenomenalists since Kant's day, but for different reasons, have labored ingeniously to make the impossibility permanent. By way of his carefully wrought definition of theoretical knowledge in his first *Critique*, Kant presumed to banish metaphysics. However, what Kant perhaps did not fully recognize was that the metaphysics he rejected in the first *Critique* he reinstated, somewhat transformed, in the second. The reinstatement was partially effected by his "moral argument" grounded in the "moral consciousness." With it, though perhaps not quite intentionally and in his own peculiar way, Kant made his peace with Plato. For when we refer to Plato's theory of Forms, especially to his teaching on the awareness of the Good, we are in the domain of his metaphysics—the province of the Intelligible, the Divine. We have crossed the line between existence and essence, between the spatio-temporal frame of Becoming and the ever-abiding invisible and Eternal.[6] Plato felt obliged to acknowledge essence on pain of forfeiting every possibility of supplying an intelligible account of the world—both the cosmic order *without* and the moral order *within*. As this writer reads Plato, the moral order within, as in Kant's case, always provided for Plato the primary data for the interpretation of reality. Although, in the later dialogues especially, Plato undertook to relate the Cosmos *without* to the causality of the Good,[7] initially, the Good was apprehended *within*. This extension of the causality of the Good to embrace Becoming, so prominent in the *Timaeus* and the *Laws*, explains in part the elaboration of ontology in the later dialogues, with its articulation of the scale of Being.[8] But Plato seems always to have understood what Kant obliquely affirmed, that the true starting-point of metaphysics is man's axiological consciousness, and, furthermore, that it does not afford the kind of knowledge which can be apodictic.

It has not been the intention of this study to enlarge the bulk of an already extensive literature relating to Plato's theory of Forms. Nevertheless, the Forms have been presupposed as any discussion of Plato must presuppose them; and this is perhaps the best way to begin a consideration of them, *i.e.*, to view the Forms as necessary presuppositions of the structure of experience *within* as well as the structure of the world *without*, when both these spheres of experience are earnestly interrogated. Throughout this investigation our concern has been to exhibit those factors that, on the one hand, impede and those that, on the other, encourage recognition of these Ideal presuppositions. Accordingly, questions centering upon mutual relations among the Forms, their possible subsumption under the Idea of the Good, the relation of Forms to divine Intelligence, the place of "mathematicals" among them or in an intermediate position, their relation to particulars—none of these questions, all quite important in themselves, has come to the fore.

Only this has been assumed, that, for Plato, Being is possessed of an Ideal Structure which is represented, but is not exhaustively represented, in the order of the existent Cosmos. That Structure is "given." It has deficient representation in the Cosmos. It also constitutes the *metron* of intelligibility and reality for the knowing mind. Moreover, the Ideal Structure is, at it were, recapitulated as the structure of human intelligence itself. Thus, for Plato, man is microcosm, and *nous* is the indication that man is participant in something Paul Tillich has lately described as "ontological reason."[9] For Plato the Ideal Structure serves notice of itself more or less forcefully in human consciousness and the tokens of that notification are recognizable in the presentiments of *doxa alêthês*, true opinion, that, in most men, resist entire suppression.

It is now commonly acknowledged that Plato's ontology embraces a scale of Being. Intimations of such a scale appear quite early in the dialogues. It is already clearly hinted in the *Phaedo*, where the difference between sensible and intelligible reality is indicated by the "deficiency" and imperfection that characterize the realm of particularity or Becoming (74d f.). In the *Republic* (477a), Plato locates Becoming between Being in the privileged sense—most real and most intelligible—and Not-Being, which is devoid of formal structure. The last category reappears in such dialogues as the *Sophist*, the *Philebus*, and the *Timaeus*, but under diverse and often enigmatic forms, as the material principle.[10] All three categories, in ascending worth and therefore in ascending reality, are comprehended in Plato's completed ontology. But pre-eminence belongs to Ideal Structure, conceived both as transcendent and as pervasive of the Cosmos.[11] The question whether the Ideal Structure is to be considered as essence alone or as *Nous*, embracing essence, is a special problem within Plato's metaphysics and theology. The problem, unfortunately, can scarcely be considered here. Notice has already been taken of the difficulty that Plato encountered in the course of his reflection, in trying to maintain distinction between a supreme *Nous* and the Good, considered as the supreme intelligible object.[12] But this problem, too, calls for special treatment and cannot detain us. The point here to be stressed is the absolute antecedence and objectivity of the Ideal Structure which is still quite plainly alluded to in the *Timaeus*.[13] In a sense, our whole study has focused upon the questions: Why are men ignorant of its reality, and how is that ignorance to be overcome?

In order to find answers to these questions, we have sought to follow Plato in his diagnosis of the plight of man and in his suggestion of an appropriate therapy.

In what follows, nothing is said which is to be understood as calling into question the absolute objectivity of the Ideal Structure of reality, either as transcendent or as deficiently represented in the sphere of Becoming. The sole purpose is to show on what grounds, within the knowing subject himself, the Intelligible World becomes, or else does not become, discriminated in knowledge. In short, the intention is that of indicating under what conditions metaphysical knowledge is possible, or else impossible. The bearing of our whole study should have made it plain that the Ideal Structure is available or accessible to human intelligence by reason of man's essential kinship (*suggeneia*) with intelligible reality, and that failure of cognition or, better, re-*cognition*,[14] must be attributed to the unsuitability of the "whole soul" which, in the absence of proper therapy, declines to probe its own depths or exercise its full reach.

2. The Nature of Judgment

It has been argued in the previous chapter that *epistêmê*, issuing from dialectic, is not regarded by Plato as demonstrable. Now it may be added that, if such knowledge were rigorous, a decision, *krisis*, would have no legitimate part in judgments. For example, the judgments (γνῶμαι) of "scientific knowledge," as Aristotle understood them, are necessary, and Plato had previously so regarded them.[15] For this reason they are apodictic. Their truth is not optional. Where there is demonstration, there is no room for decision, no place for a deliberative yes or no. Assent is constrained on the part of those who are sufficiently acute to understand the syllogism. According to Aristotle, if there is "scientific knowledge," there will be demonstration. If there is demonstration, inference will have proceeded *from* "necessary premises" *by way of* "necessary connections" *to* necessary conclusions.[16] Given the validity of primary premises, inferential reasoning may arrive at results to which no exception may be taken. Hence there will be no place for either voluntary agreement or dissent, or for exercise of conscientious preference or choice.[17]

Apparently, then, whenever knowledge has become apodictic, *i.e.*, "scientific," the judgment is no longer a decision; rather, it has been deprived of "decisiveness." Aristotle distinctly observes this consequence, noting that it is not possible to "deliberate" about necessary and demonstrable truths.[18]   He is therefore inclined to assign all preferential and deliberative functions of reason to the sphere of "prudence" (φρόνησις) rather than knowledge.[19]   Such decision as is allowed to operate in the formation of judgments is assigned to the "practical" function of reason as distinct from the "theoretical."   Thus the scientific faculty (τὸ ἐπιστημονικόν) is distinguished from the deliberative or calculative faculty (τὸ λογιστικόν).[20]   The judgments of the latter alone rightly permit the intrusion of preference.   Thus it is not surprising to find Aristotle referring to a "theoretical reason" which is purely so, since it is said to be devoid of all practical considerations.[21]   And Aristotle must be credited with a full comprehension of what he was about.   With clear intent, he subordinated Plato's highest cognitive faculty, the *logistikon*, to a yet more exalted faculty, called the *epistêmonikon*.   He conceived the latter as a faculty of pure scientific cognition (*i.e.*, logical) from which all notices of valuation, all preferences of the will, are eliminated and whose syllogistic findings are, in consequence, regarded as apodictic.   Herewith Aristotle engendered not only the illusion of pure objectivity in knowledge but, applying it to the subject-matter above and beyond physics, fathered the fundamental error of Western philosophy, to be corrected by Kant, that metaphysics could and ought to take the form of necessary or apodictic knowledge.

By contrast, Plato conceives no operation of the *logistikon* as devoid of preferential or valuational motives.   For Plato, as A. E. Taylor rightly contended, a distinction between a superior speculative or theoretical reason and a subordinate practical reason is not contemplated, since "the two spheres are inseparable."[22]   Apparently it never occurred to Plato to conceive of the operations of intelligence except as prompted and inspired by better or worse practical or axiological incentives.   As we have seen, man is the subject of a higher as well as of a lower eros, and it is the higher which urges and impels the mind in the direction of ultimate reality, impeded though it may be by the promptings of the inferior love.   For Plato, then, it was fatuous to suppose that metaphysical knowledge, or the issues of ontology, could be settled without reference to the total disposition of the knowing subject—without, more exactly, the conscientious concurrence of the whole man.

On one occasion Aristotle himself recognized that, according to Plato's tripartite division of the soul, appetite or desire (ὄρεξις) is found in each "power" of the *psúchê*.[23]   Although, from the passage, it is not clear whether Aristotle means to adopt the view himself, it does rightly indicate Plato's opinion that there is no "faculty" of the soul, including *nous*, from which incentives of affection are absent. Aristotle, however, believed he could locate an operation of reason in which deliberation, *i.e.*, volition or βούλησις, had no valid part to play. This seemed likely to Aristotle because syllogistic reasoning had the appearance of necessity. With respect to it, preferential notices of the mind seemed quite impertinent.

Nevertheless, the question remains, and it is a question of prime importance with Plato, whether the first premises of all thought are not, in great measure, deposited by predisposing interest or valuation. In such a case, it will result that the *prius* of every sort of knowledge is a recognized and acknowledged or unrecognized and unacknowledged *purpose*.

If our study of Plato has shown that volition is profoundly implicated in the knowledge process, it is now in order to say more precisely what this entails for competing world-views. Whenever *ultimate reality* is in question, it is fully evident to Plato that the first premises, or *archai*, of thought steer the course of reflection. It is for this reason that, at *Republic* 485d, Plato takes note of the indispensability of the proper eros in the philosophic nature. If a man's desires are strongly directed toward sensuous fulfillments, his aptitude for superior cognition is weakened. It is the sort of thing of which Socrates complains at *Phaedo* 83d: Overwhelming sensuous interests dictate that nothing is real or true which is not first descried and then confirmed by those same interests. It is this, again, to which Plato alludes at *Republic* 519a. The vision of so-called clever men, the cave-dwellers, is quick to discern such data of reflection as interest them, as suit their *sunêtheia*. Thus, if essential reality is ever to be apprehended, the whole soul must suffer a "conversion," thus transforming from uselessness to usefulness the cognitive power (*nous*) whose "potency" has not been in question, but only its employment. Since, it was the unconverted soul which was responsible for the first principles of the world-view of the Cave, Plato was convinced that such hypotheses as these are not beyond question and are, in truth, resultants of foundational valuation. First principles are decisive for knowledge; but "decisiveness," in this connection, carries its literal meaning. That is to say, first principles, in great part, derive from, or have their justification in, antecedent notices of volition—it being remembered, to be sure, that for Plato there is no real distinction between volition and affection. The will is not distinguishable from the prevailing affection of the whole mind.[24]

In this context, whenever we speak of interest or volition, *eo ipso* we refer to some objective of interest or some end of volition. As axiologically engaged, the mind contemplates or prefigures a good, even if it is only some sensuous good, some apparent good. In terms of that good, together with its co-ordinate purpose, some first principles commend themselves to thought *as implementations* of the mind's present objective. A judgment about the Good, or some species of it,[25] is, therefore, in Plato's view, always the usually unconscious source of hypotheses which, eventually, lead to knowledge of some sort or other. With this in mind, we are able to see, in the famous *Republic* passage (509d), not only why the Idea of the Good is pre-eminent in the intelligible world but also why it is said to transcend essence, *ousia*, with surpassing power. *Ousia* means here, as elsewhere, being in general. If our interpretation is valid—and it relies upon the more extensive analysis of Chapter VI—Plato is saying that initial working principles devolve from a prior decision about some species of the Good; and from these principles, in turn, are derived the various conceptions of Being, depending upon what species is most honored.

Plato accepted the fact that there is a variety of available first principles. Among the many, some are more fertile for valid interpretation of reality than others. Nevertheless, first principles are, invariably, expressions of value-interest. Consequently they will be more or less adequate for knowledge of reality in proportion as the interest engendering them conforms to the supreme measure of worth, the Good-in-itself. First principles, for example, which are engendered by an interest in manipulating the physical environment, will be too partial or restricted to implement investigation of the full range of Being. In contrast, such a first principle (*archê*) as Socrates insisted in getting "agreement" upon from Crito,[26] as preliminary to dialectical inquiry, may lead up, as in the manner indicated at *Republic* 511b, to a Principle devoid of all supposition, to the metaphysical ultimate, the Good itself.

As there can be no systematic knowledge without employment of working hypotheses, whether in the deduction of the sciences or in induction of dialectic (*Rep.* 511), so there are no hypotheses which are not grounded in a choice or a decision about the Good, generically considered. It was, therefore, evident to Plato that the absolutely foundational consideration governing "metaphysics" is the antecedent, and usually unexamined, choice which men make about the Good. In the final analysis, every query about first principles, and the conception of reality deriving therefrom, resolves itself into the question: What, in actuality, has been taken to be ultimately preferable? The validity of first principles, governing resultant conceptions of reality, can be finally estimated, therefore, only by an axiological criterion.

This insight forced upon Plato the realization that the question about the nature of reality is both initially and ultimately settled by a decision regarding the Good. What is it that is absolutely preferable, or what is it that comprises the object of ultimate concern? Furthermore, Plato perceived that unless there is a native, inexpugnable, and essential preference of the soul, reality must remain unknowable; for, unless this is so, the first principles governing inquiry will be determined by an *existing* multiplicity of incompatible judgments of what is good. The universe, unavoidably, will dissolve in a diversity of "rationalized" perspectives. In the light of our previous study, it should not be necessary to argue extensively that Plato avowed a native, original, and sovereign preference of the human mind. It may be associated with the *theia mania*, the superior eros of the *Phaedrus*, or with the "hormic" movement toward intelligible reality as in the *Republic*, the *Philebus*, and the *Timaeus*.[27] If we would know the direction in which we are to look for ultimate reality, we must, according to Plato, attend to the vector, as it were, of the soul's ultimate preference together with its object.

In probing the soul to discover its axiological center of gravity, Plato was seeking not only a solution to the moral problem but at the same time a solution to the problem of knowledge. Instead of ignoring the fact that apprehension of Being is conditioned upon valuation, thereby fostering the notion of value-indifferent cognition, Plato accepted the fact. He made *epistêmê* precarious by conceding its axiological foundation. But he secured its possibility and made it a courageous, if hazardous, enterprise by showing that veridical knowledge depends upon the emancipation of a "divine affection" which, at one time, gives "wings" to thought and assists the mind in realizing its potential conformity with ultimate Being. He made the condition of knowledge of reality a love of it. Knowledge becomes dependent, not upon disinterest, but upon such interest as "inspires" the mind, allured by the Good and drawn to it. *In ordine cognoscendi*, then, *axia*, or value, takes precedence over "being" and, hence, transcends *ousia* with surpassing power.[28] But what is true *in ordine cognoscendi* is also true *in ordine essendi*. The Good is not only determinative in the order of knowing; it is also primary in the order of Being.

The latter means that, for ultimate reality, it is not other for it to Be and to be Good.

3. KNOWLEDGE AS PERSONAL DECISION

In the *Republic* the aim of Plato's *paideusis* is to precipitate decision in favor of the unconditional superiority of justice to injustice (360e). To achieve this end it was necessary fully to develop a theory of human nature. When the soul was explored, it became apparent, to those who had committed themselves to the inquiry, that justice was as necessary to the life of the soul as health was to the life of the body. Throughout the dialogue Plato was engaged in vindicating Socrates' contention in the *Crito*: The soul is benefited by the right and ruined by the wrong.[29] Nevertheless the truth of Socrates' claim could become convincing only when the transcendent relations of the soul with the divine order were exposed to view. It is impossible to understand Plato's method in ethics unless it is realized that he saw no possibility of defining human good apart from the ultimately serious context in which mankind stands.[30]

Now knowledge of the metaphysical environment does not take the form of irrefragable conclusion from inference. The very form and rationale of the dialogues suggest that knowledge derives from a succession of joint-agreements, usually provisional and subject to subsequent rejection or confirmation by further analysis. Confirmation (βεβαίωσις) involves at least two conditions: first, that a succeeding *homologia* is fully implied by a previously conceded hypothesis; secondly, that by subsequent analysis a proposition proves fruitful for advancement of the inquiry. Admittedly, the fruitfulness of successive hypotheses is, in large measure, governed by the declared aim of discussion. This, however, would prove no qualification at all except on the supposition that the problem investigated is genuinely meaningful. But, if the inquiry is meaningful, something else is implied; and that is a mutually acknowledged universe of discourse, such as, for example, is required by Socrates in the *Crito* 46b-48d.

There is obviously little possibility of fruitful inquiry into the merits of justice as compared with injustice if the respondents acknowledge no real distinction between the two, or if, as in the case of Thrasymachus, injustice is redefined as justice. As a matter of fact, however, Plato did not believe that, in such cases, dialectic was really at an impasse; for there are virtually no human beings totally obtuse to the solicitations of higher goodness. Entire "shamelessness" or

irreverence toward the Good—Plato's equivalent for "total depravity"
—is feasible but an extremely rare phenomenon.[31] Those who pretend
indifference or express contempt are covertly at odds with their own
essential nature and deepest sentiments.   In such cases, as we have
seen, the function of dialectic is to assist the morally "shameless" man
eventually to square himself with himself or make a "true concord
of his own life."[32]

Nevertheless productive inquiry is most fully assured when men
come to an agreement at the beginning of discussion.[33]   This is to
say that initially they must acknowledge the meaningfulness of the
investigation.   But to acknowledge meaningfulness is to acknowledge,
at the same time, an intelligible context, a universe of discourse, in
the framework of which the express aims of investigation have significance.   Manifestly in weighing the merits and nature of the modes
of virtue, there is tacitly presupposed a minimum principle—the
antithesis between good and evil.   Those who fail to concede or are
oblivious of so fundamental a distinction can hardly begin to inquire
into the nature of moral excellence.   If men have no basis for common deliberation or no common will (*koinê boulê*) in regard to the
starting-point (*archê*) of discussion, they cannot engage significantly
in joint-investigation.[34]   In the absence of such a common will, discussion would be, at best, only contention between parties whose
standpoints remain hopelessly at odds.

In reference to a passage in the *Republic*, Paul Shorey has dis-
cerningly pointed out that "Despite his faith in dialectic Plato recognizes that the primary assumptions on which argument necessarily proceeds are irreducible choices of personality."[35]   The passage in question finds Plato asserting that his entire claim for the "potency" of
the organ of knowledge, once it is purified, to apprehend non-sensible
reality will not be credited by those whose "vision" is blinded by their
"habituation" to sensuous interests and experience (527e).   He had
been saying that sensate affection misdirects the cognitive faculty so
that it perceives only the "shadows" of the Cave.

In the judgment of the cave-dwellers, the claim that the organ
of knowledge may descry "intelligible" as distinct from "visible"
reality will appear stuff and nonsense.[36]   Those, however, who have
willingly engaged in the stages of inquiry and have, from the start,
consented to make initial and then successive agreements as the argument progresses, will now, at length, share in a common acknowledgment of the outcome.[37]   But at the terminus, as at the beginning, a
decision is required.   The conclusion, like the initial premise, is not

forced (ἀκούσιος). It remains optional, and voluntary (ἐκούσιος). In dialectic a judgment is not a necessary conclusion, but more nearly a decision. It is quite truly a *krisis*, that is, a decision of the entire mind involving volition.

As we noted in the previous chapter, the power of dialectic is manifested in *educing* consent, so that conclusions of inquiry are the investigator's own results, which he can disclaim only by disregarding his already avowed commitments. Because, throughout the discussion, consent has been repeatedly accorded, the concluding judgments are literally choices and self-determinations. Therefore it is rather evident that where volition does not *concur* knowledge will not *occur*.

According to Plato, *nous*, the organ of knowledge, is in fact an "organ of judgment."[38] If, however, truth and reality are to be rightly "decided,"[39] decision will be by means of experience, intelligence, and discussion; and, above all, it will be a decision of character.[40] As we might anticipate, the "organ of judgment" is not a pure noëtic faculty. In its integrity of function, volitional incentives operate in conjunction with the intuitional power. Although it is true that the affective power influences the intuitive, it is in their cooperation that knowledge exists. However, true *epistêmê* obtains only when the mind is governed by affection directed to the supreme Good. It is for this reason that Plato commonly expressed the view that the best criteria of truth are to be located in the decisions, not of the sensate man, but of the lover of wisdom.[41]

At this point we may conveniently refer to the statement of Shorey, quoted above. It is not only true that the prime assumptions of argument are "irreducible choices of personality"; in point of fact, all the intervening stages and the culminating judgment, as well, are in like manner such "irreducible choices." But when we mention the word "personality," we really denote what Plato called the "entire soul."[42]

Lest we assume that Plato was quite exceptional in holding that virtue is the condition of knowledge, it is well to keep in mind that Aristotle was neither unaware of nor entirely unfavorable to the idea. In the *Nicomachian Ethics* he says: "But the Supreme Good only appears good to the good man: vice perverts the mind and causes it to hold false views about the first principles of conduct. Hence it is clear that we cannot be prudent without being good."[43] This is a wise saying. Actually, however, it represents a restricted use of the Platonic principle as the context shows. Since full evaluation is out of the question here, it is only possible to observe that

Aristotle concedes the influence of volition only in reference to the "first premises" of moral or "prudential" reasoning. In this domain valid premises are not likely to be attained by men of vicious character.

With Plato, on the other hand, the premises of all reflection whatsoever involve and reflect the valuational preferences and purposes of the inquiring subject. Plato recognizes no function of reason which is axiologically neutral. Consequently, the incentive of all inquiry is some tacit or acknowledged "good" which interest proposes and then promotes. This, as we are about to argue, is as applicable to the concern of the sciences as to that of dialectic.

4. DECISION AND FIRST PRINCIPLES

If it is true, as A. E. Taylor has claimed, that Plato sought to derive the hypotheses of the special sciences from the Idea of the Good,[44] the likeliest way to understand such derivation is to see that the hypotheses of the sciences are actually specialized expressions of the inherent axiological bent of intelligence. The postulates or hypotheses of the sciences are rational formulations of the *purposes* to which the sciences are devoted. These purposes, however partial or particularized, are, generically considered, modes of the Good. In such a case the *archai* of the sciences would constitute no exceptions to the rule that, in its essence, all reasoning is axiologically inspired. The first principles of the sciences, no less than the hypotheses of dialectic, are manifestations of the insuppressible and ultimate concern of *nous* for the Good. In this manner, as the sufficient reason or final cause of all first principles, including those of the sciences, the Idea of the Good supplies, as Plato asserted in the *Republic*, "the power of knowing to the knower" (508e).

To illustrate the decisive character of all first principles, including those of the sciences, is admittedly not easy, mainly because the data of the dialogues is mostly limited to *Republic* VII. The Platonic sciences, represented in Book VII of the *Republic*, are abstract and theoretical rather than concrete and applied.[45] The incentive prompting these sciences is hardly distinguishable from interest in truth as such, although they are concerned with specialized provinces of truth. There are indications that Plato regards the sciences as partly inspired by aesthetic concern for perfection of form.[46] Moreover, the sciences, although they afford truth of a certain rank, are instrumental to a yet higher knowledge; for the knowledge which science affords assists the mind to apprehend intelligible Being and, at length, to achieve intellectual intuition of the Good. With Francis Bacon, on the contrary, the motivation of "natural philosophy" is application. His interest is one of control and exploitation of physical nature for man's comfort and convenience.[47]   Science had no such limited purpose for Plato.   Applied sciences he described in the *Republic* as rather vulgar and "mechanical" (522b).   In the *Philebus* (55e-57d), he takes a more favorable view; however, he still rates the applied sciences below the theoretical and these, in turn, are subordinate to dialectic, which aims at intelligible and immutable Being (57d f.).   The justification of the pure sciences is not the measurement of land, exact accounting in business, the prediction of eclipses, or calculation necessary for navigation and construction. These purposes the sciences may indeed serve.[48]   But the true aim of the sciences is, principally, to habituate the mind to the use of pure thought and to "convert" the soul from the world of generation to that of essence.[49]   Anomalous as it may appear to our modern viewpoint, the justification of the sciences is, for Plato, their serviceability for moral and spiritual ends.   Pursuit of them facilitates apprehension of ultimate reality.   By that "measure" men and cities might conceivably govern themselves in righteousness.[50]   In the case of both Bacon and Plato the sciences possess utility; but their conceptions of utility are quite different.   Nevertheless, in both instances, the scientific enterprise is controlled by a judgment of value and of purpose.   It is a decision about the "good" which engenders the sciences and justifies their existence.

In what sense, now, may it be said that the hypotheses of the sciences depend upon a value-judgment?   First of all, they presuppose a particular and delimited frame of meaning.   In the case of geometry and stereometry, that frame of meaning is supplied by extension, respectively, in two and three dimensions.[51]   In the case of astronomy, we are warranted in saying that there is added a dimension of time and the phenomenon of motion.[52]   Extension, time, and motion, together constitute what we may call the *material component* of the frame of meaning.[53]   The meaning-situation, however, is incomplete apart from the interests and purposes which the inquiring mind entertains with respect to the given spatio-temporal continuum.   Its interest is evidently one of exact quantitative description of the given continuum by means of numeration and unit measurement.[54]   The purposive character of the arts and sciences is recognized by Plato in the *Philebus* as well as in the *Republic*.[55]   In the *Philebus*, as in the

Republic (528e), Plato is still subordinating the utilitarian purposes of applied mathematics (*technê*) to the superior purpose and superior accuracy of "philosophic" mathematics (57a-d). And this, in turn, is subordinated to dialectic (57e). And although dialectic has the least utilitarian value, nevertheless, it has the "greatest regard for clearness, exactness, and truth."[56]

It is to the purpose which informs the sciences that we are to look for the *formal component* of the frame of meaning. However, it must be admitted that in the case of the pure or "philosophic" sciences Plato's interest is so concentrated upon their instrumental value for "highest knowledge" that he tends to neglect their more immediate end, namely, that of delineating by means of mensuration and geometrical operation the given continuum or *material component* of the frame of meaning. But it is plain that, in the case of the pure sciences as also in the applied, the pervasive principle of Plato's ontology is relevant: In them also the Unlimited is presupposed,[57] and intelligence is at work undertaking, not so much to apply as to discover, the Limit or Form which contributes structure and thereby intelligibility to the *material component*. As Plato explicitly recognizes in the *Republic*, the operations of geometry or stereometry and the calculations of pure astronomy cannot proceed without presupposing the second and third dimension (528b). We may indeed abstract all sensuous qualities (525c), but we must *think* depth-dimensional extension; and we must do so too in calculating ideal motions of ideal astronomical objects (529d). This *thought* is a necessary presupposition of the three branches of Platonic "mathematics" in question, and there is good reason for supposing that Plato later symbolizes the object of this thought in the *Timaeus* in the form of "ever-existing Place" (52b). It is, moreover, quite as ultimate ontologically as ever-abiding self-identical Form (52a). It is, as has been indicated, a species of the Unlimited of the *Philebus*.

There is analogy between the actual world viewed as a "combination" of Limit and Unlimited, as in the *Philebus*, and the situation in the sciences. Each science presupposes a *material component* of the frame of meaning as well as a form-conferring purpose supplied by intelligence. The purpose, considered as human, is a species of the Good. It denotes an interest in the intelligible arrangement of the continuum. This does not mean that the human inquirer actually confers the formal structure. It only means that his value-charged interest answers to the measure of goodness which already is represented in the structure *there*. Knowledge in the sciences, quite as much as the *epistêmê* deriving from dialectic, is possible because of the *analogia* obtaining between reality and the knowing mind.[58] Here too, furthermore, knowledge requires conversancy with the Good, for its content equally derives from the Good its power of being known.

We are in a position now to raise again the question why Plato regarded the hypotheses of the sciences as possessed of a measure of self-evidence and yet, at the same time, as arbitrary. Further, we are interested in the question why, although the findings of the sciences are "conclusive," Plato regards the resulting knowledge as being inferior to that attained by dialectic—and this not merely in the *Republic* (533d) but also in the *Philebus* (57e f.).

In the interest of rendering an intelligible account of plane surfaces (528a) and the depth-dimensional continuum, or in the interest of arithmetic calculation, certain hypotheses immediately commend themselves. Plato alludes to a few of them:

For I think you are aware that students of geometry and reckoning and such subjects first postulate the odd and the even and the various figures and three kinds of angles and other things akin to these in each branch of science, regard them as known, and, treating them as absolute assumptions, do not deign to render any further account of them to themselves or to others, taking it for granted that they are obvious to everybody.[59]

Apparently, Plato believes that the postulates evince themselves, as it were, and possess some measure of self-evidence. Nevertheless they are "arbitrary" and, hence, deficient in truth-value. The immediate explanation for their arbitrariness is that they are left unexamined and unverified. But there is a further and less obtrusive reason. They are arbitrary also, and more fundamentally, because their truth is conditional. It is conditioned upon the conjunction of a specialized frame of reference together with certain interests or purposes which prompt reflecting intelligence in dealing with the context. Given the *material component* of the frame of meaning (the rudimentary spatio-temporal continuum), and given also the purpose and incentive of rendering it intelligible by ordering it through measurement, thereupon certain hypotheses propound themselves as minimal requirements of articulate arrangement. Thus, if there is a point, it has *relata*. If it has *relata*, there will be lines. If there are lines emanating from a single point, there will be angles. If there are angles, there will be the "three kinds" to which Plato refers, and so on.

The postulates are arbitrary, moreover, for a cognate reason: They have applicability, and hence validity, only within a specialized frame of reference and as presupposing commensurate and, therefore, delimited purposes. Accordingly they will possess little if any self-evidence outside that context. Thus, that a straight line is the shortest distance bet.~een two points is self-evident only if the context is restricted to plane surfaces. Much less has it relevance in the domain of personal or political relations where the truth of the proverb would more likely prevail, that the longest way round is often the shortest way home. In like manner, in the sphere of ethics it is not very meaningful, as Plato knew, to affirm with Protagoras in the dialogue of that name (349c), that virtue is equal to the sum of its parts. And absurdity is complete when, in the *Parmenides*, there is an effort to understand the causality of Ideas by the geometric symbolism of the relation of parts to a whole (131c).

The consequence is that the validity of the postulates of the special sciences is narrow and conditional. *Validity is conditioned upon the frame of reference to which the postulates are relevant; and validity is also conditioned upon purposes, suited to and commensurate with the context, for which alone the postulates commend themselves.* Since, then, the postulates are only conditionally valid, they are also arbitrary. It follows, nevertheless, that a special science is sufficiently established, first, if its postulates are genuine resultants of the conjunction of *context* and *interest*, and secondly, if the inferences by which the interest is advanced represent real connections of the subject-matter. However, Plato realized that the express aims of the sciences are prescribed by the possibilities inherent in the context-of-interest. Therefore, he concluded that the postulates or hypotheses of the sciences are severely restricted in denotation. They are expressions of fragmentary and partial human concerns, occasioned by a particularized context-of-interest.

To summarize: Because the purposes of any science are dictated by interest, which purposes, in turn, are occasioned by the particular framework of spatio-temporal arrangements, the hypotheses of the sciences are expressions of *interest-in-context*. They are formulations of preference and purpose in terms of a given meaning-situation. But because the hypotheses are expressions of interest-in-context, they are arbitrary in so far as they pertain only to that context and because the interest-in-context itself does not exhaust the sum of genuine human concern. Accordingly, the first principles or postulates of the sciences unavoidably express only a fragment of the total Good that is relevant to the wholeness of human experience.

It was therefore manifest that scientific knowledge (*dianoia*), operating from postulates or hypotheses of limited denotation—although admitting of *apodeixis* within its province—is nevertheless deficient in truth.[60] The reason for this, Plato evidently concluded, is that no hypotheses of a science or a group of sciences are capable of expressing the ultimate interest of the "whole soul" or of satisfying its aspiration after the all-embracing Good. However rigorously derived, the merely scientific account of reality falls short of the amplitude of meaningfulness required by the human spirit considered as answerable to the highest intelligible Object.

As we undertook to show in Chapter VII, there is, in Plato's thought, only one unqualified First Principle. It is the Idea of the Good. It is the Beautiful-in-itself, but preëminently the Good-in-itself, which answers to the inherent axiological impulse of the mind. As has been continually urged, Plato is quite ready to concede that the truth of this proposition is available only to one who is possessed of proper self-knowledge.[61] For the hypotheses from which dialectic moves up to the Principle "without supposition" are, as in the case of Polus or Callicles, unavailable for want of it. For want of self-knowledge neither Polus nor Callicles is disposed to heed the suppressed but surviving "true opinion" regarding the just and the unjust. Thus, each represents a man divided against himself (*Gorg.* 482b), a man holding contrary opinions at the same time about the same things (*Rep.* 603d). Only in resolving the conflict in favor of true opinions is thought supplied with the hypotheses that, with the assistance of dialectic, may lead on to the apprehension of metaphysical reality.

If these observations are valid, the consequences are plain: Although the hypotheses of the sciences are genuinely decisional, *i.e.*, are expressions of interest-in-context, the truths deriving from them are of subordinate ontological significance as compared with truths secured by way of the judgments and agreements of dialectic. To make this clearer it is necessary to mention two factors. First, the hypotheses explored by dialectic evince themselves from a different and more inclusive meaning-situation than those of the sciences. They derive from man's responsible consciousness of the True, Beautiful, and Good—from the axiological as distinct from the "positive" universe of discourse. It is in the axiological province that Plato believed the distinctively humane and supremely meaningful are to be found;

for the humane is the best index to the divine.[62]   Secondly, by exploring successively the implications of the initial hypotheses of
dialectic, the mind is conducted, by way of its own admissions, to
eventual apprehension of the supreme intelligible object, the unconditional *Archê* of all thought.

The hypotheses of dialectic, then, represent valuations of a different order from those of the sciences, because they are occasioned by a
different interest-in-context.   Nevertheless, the hypotheses of the
sciences are no less decisional in nature, since they too reflect and
express preference regarding a delimited "class" of the Good.   We
can say, therefore, that because all hypotheses of whatever sort are
rational constructs, formulations suitable to some interest-in-context,
they are *ipso facto* the outcome of valuational judgment.   Consequently, since what comes to be known of the sum of reality is known
by exploration of initial principles, it is plain that axiological concern
—controlling the perspectival field and evincing the principles—
governs the outcome of ontological knowledge.   To put it plainly,
metaphysical knowledge is impossible unless the knower passes beyond both the interest-in-context pertaining to *doxa* and that pertaining to science (*dianoia*) to the richer interest-in-context of distinctively humane (*i.e.*, axiological) experience.   The "hypotheses" of
humane experience are identical with the surviving true opinions
about the just, the right, the excellent, the beautiful, and the holy.
It is these that Socrates characteristically explored with the aid of
elenchos.

Thus it seems to have been Plato's conviction that what comes
to be known (not what *is*) of the scale of available Being rests back
upon "irreducible choices of personality"; for these are in large
degree responsible for the postulates from which every kind of formal
reflection proceeds.   If the interest-in-context is the one suitable to
the sciences, inference will ordinarily proceed deductively to apodictic
conclusions, which, however, remain only hypothetical.   If, on the
other hand, the axiological consciousness in conjunction with human
life and action constitutes the interest-in-context, reflection, with the
assistance of dialectic, may advance from vestigial "true opinion" to
a state of cognition called *noêsis*.   In it the event of metaphysical
apprehension takes place.   Therefore, when ontology or judgment of
existence is in question, the literally decisive factor in the outcome of
knowledge is, rather plainly, the fundamental concern, or the sovereign valuation of the mind.   If, for example, the prevailing concern
is the sensuous *boulêsis* of the cave-dwellers, it will be largely re-

sponsible for propounding the kind of realities with which phenom-enalistic knowledge is, as Plato affirms both in the *Republic* and the *Philebus*, content to deal.[63] Again, if the interest-in-context is re-stricted by irreducible choice of personality to that pertaining to the sciences, then reality in its total reach will surely escape detection until an alteration of *êthos* supplies other materials and incentives for reflection. The metaphysical question, then, falls back upon the nature of *êthos*; and Plato has no solution, no *therapeia*, except the conversion or revolution of the entire soul.

5. Preference for Certainty: Aristotle and Bacon

The decisional character of working hypotheses means that, for Plato, the sum of available truth has a direct correlation with the totality of *bona fide* human preference. Truth comes to exist in judgments which are the products of inquiry prompted by legitimate interpretations of the Good. Among these truths, those of the sci-ences will be surely included. But the truths which are derived by way of dialectic have, for Plato, a privileged position and significance as well as greater certainty. They possess greater certainty despite the fact that the truths of dialectic are decisional from first to last.

The nature of dialectical knowledge will be, to use a word too much in currency to be unambiguous, "existential." By "existential" it is here specifically meant only that the truths of dialectic are not available except through personal decision. However, this is only to say, although the word is important, that the truths of dialectic are *acknowledgments* of the inquiring mind. To attain them, as Socrates said in the *Crito*, some good or goods must frankly be con-ceded in order to implement the process of investigation and to pre-pare the way for the ultimate agreement or conclusion (49d).

In contrast with those of dialectic, the truths of the sciences are products of necessary inference. To be sure, Plato regarded the truths of the sciences as possessing only hypothetical validity because their postulates are "arbitrary." Nevertheless, if we ignore the arbitrary character of the hypotheses, truths deduced from them have necessity. Because they are resultants of rigorous inference, they seem to be independent of personal preference and the vagaries of human valuation. Hence the "objectivity" of scientific truth is just exactly its *apparent* want of "decisiveness." If we disregard the premises of demonstrable knowledge, it is its nature to be entirely non-decisive. Accordingly it comes about that non-decisive knowledge acquires, superficially, the title to certainty.

There is no doubt that the disposition to ignore the decisional character of first premises has gained for demonstrative knowledge a certain prestige. From the time of Aristotle this has been the case. Because he was enamored of the certainty of the syllogism, Aristotle was inclined to accept the truth of necessary inference as the standard of truth in general and as the criterion of knowledge in the privileged sense. He expressly rejected the view, however, that everything qualifying as knowledge is of the demonstrative variety.[64] At one point he came so near to Plato's conception of dialectic as to suggest that it is "a process of criticism wherein lies the path to the principles of all inquiries."[65] And in both the *Metaphysics* and the *Nicomachean Ethics* he elevates wisdom above scientific knowledge, declaring that the former is the most sovereign and authoritative kind of knowledge.[66] However, on closer inspection, his words are found to be more honorific than substantial; for we find that wisdom is defined as "scientific knowledge" conjoined with "intelligence." The latter is a kind of immediate apprehension by which, at least occasionally, Aristotle declares that first principles of demonstration may be intuited.[67] In short, whatever the most perfect mode of knowledge may be, whether wisdom or something else, its essential ingredient for Aristotle is demonstration. By demonstration he means, in his own words, "a syllogism productive of scientific knowledge, a syllogism, that is, the grasp of which is *eo ipso* such knowledge."[68] Correspondingly, we observe a tendency to relegate decisional truth to the limited sphere of practical considerations, where, because of valuational choice, necessity is not obtainable in judgments. In this sphere Aristotle conceded that judgments are really decisions, and truth is really decisive.[69] It is desirable to understand why Plato preferred decisive truth and Aristotle necessary truth.

If people desire certainty in knowledge, they will do so for definable purposes; and it is also probable that they will have to settle for a somewhat more restricted body of "knowledge" than those who are more latitudinarian in their conception of verity. They may, nevertheless, acquiesce to the limitation if they can be fully assured about the cogency of their restricted domain. Also, they are not likely to be perturbed by narrowing horizons if they agree to ignore the preferential nature of the *postulates* of necessary reasoning. It is not unfair to say that Aristotle contented himself in this respect with the constant reminder that first principles of the sciences are intuitively self-evident and that, in any case, it is not possible to get demonstration in everything without regress to infinity.[70] To a considerable extent, he was willing to accept the arbitrariness of first principles without much attention to the fact that their arbitrary nature was a consequence of specialized interest-in-context.

In some instances, as we have noted, Aristotle inclined to regard first premises and definitions as apprehended by a kind of intuitive act of *nous*.[71] On the whole, however, we are probably justified in regarding his method of "induction" as the way in which the mind attains to first principles or the premises of syllogism. Induction starts from sensation. From recurrence and persistence of sense impressions comes memory; from memory comes experience; and from experience, the universal is conceived and stabilized.[72] Judging from the important passage here referred to in the *Posterior Analytics*, it seems evident that induction is itself what Aristotle elsewhere calls an intuitive act of *nous*. He indicates that induction, which stabilizes "true universals," is the way we get to know the premises of scientific or discursive knowledge.[73]

At this point, however, we must enter a demurrer; for it is a real question whether universals, in themselves, rightly constitute the premises of science. No doubt their "definitions" are among first principles; but there is a considerable chasm between a universal and a judgment in which it is incorporated. Hypotheses are, for the most part, judgments constituted by what it is desirable to say about the universal. This consideration itself is one aspect of the larger question whether an unsolved problem of Aristotle is not an insufficient account of the origination of first principles. Plato recognized that what is said about universals, either in definitions or postulates, amounts to a registering of preference engendered by interest-in-context. Even in regard to Aristotle's foundational axiom, "non-contradiction,"[74] he nowhere observes that its validity is guaranteed by other than the mind's preference for meaningfulness as opposed to absurdity. This is undoubtedly an ultimate preference of the human mind and, however original, is an implicit judgment about the Good. However we approach the matter, analysis seems to vindicate the claim of Plato that first premises are decisional in nature, and, therefore, that the aspiration for necessity in knowledge has fulfillment only by ignoring the preferential nature of postulates.

There remains, however, a possibility that, as a principle of thought, "identity" is even more fundamental than is "non-contradiction" and that it is non-decisive in character. Plato was aware that knowledge is possible only in virtue of a certain fixity or stability of concepts.[75] The basis of all knowledge whatsoever is the recognition of identity. In the *Sophist* Plato makes it clear that the known must be identical with itself; but, as self-identical, it is also "different" from other knowables. Hence identity presupposes difference; and difference, identity. Now, however, Plato also conceded no genuine identity to particulars, because they are in continual alteration.[76] Therefore identity belongs only to the Form or Idea which is "ever-the-same"; or, as Aristotle would say, identity properly belongs to the universal. Disregarding the self-identical Forms and confining attention to sensible experience, it is immediately apparent that identity, upon which identification relies, is valid only for "practical purposes." In point of fact, Plato claimed that there is no real identity or "equality" between things in the natural world;[77] but, for the requirements of ordinary perception, identity is postulated or, better, presupposed. The conclusion must be either that identity is a principle derived *a priori* as Plato believed, or it is an "hypothesis," an implicit decision of the mind, made in the interest of such identification as is indispensable for empirical knowledge.

Francis Bacon is a thinker who in more recent times shared with Aristotle a preference for certainty in a delimited sphere of knowledge. In some respects, however, Bacon possessed a better explanation of his preference for *apodeixis* than did Aristotle. Aristotle had certainly agreed with Plato in esteeming wisdom, the knowledge of primary causes, above the truths of applied sciences and arts, especially in so far as the latter aimed merely at "utility."[78] Bacon, however, was not abashed to alter this position and to make utility the prime incentive of inquiry. He was responsible for the dictum that "the true lawful goal of the sciences is none other than this: that human life be endowed with new discoveries and powers."[79]

Bacon was frank to say that all knowledge is justified by use and action, for he saw more clearly than most others before him the connection between knowledge and man's power over nature.[80] In Bacon's opinion, Aristotle "made science a bond-servant of logic" by interpreting the particular through the universal.[81] In contrast, Bacon proposed to ignore first principles as indemonstrable and to confine his efforts to the discovery of "middle axioms," or what he elsewhere designated as laws of nature. These are to be known through observation and experimentation; for "middle axioms" are the fruit of experimentation with sensible particulars.[82]

Bacon's *novum organum* is the method of experimentation. By means of it, real connections between natural events may be ascertained and such certainties achieved as enable men to invent "commodities" and control their environment. Very shortly, Bacon was able to announce that the measure of certainty in knowledge is proportionate to the degree of utility it possesses. Prediction, manipulation, and control are suitable and adequate indices of truth. Experiment provided those certainties mainly worth considering. If *this* appeared certain, it was because Bacon had antecedently decided that all certainties of any consequence advance the "kingdom of man" or his power over nature.[83]

Placing "revealed" or supernatural knowledge in a separate province in which reason has no competence, Bacon was content to identify truth with utility. By this procedure he accomplished the virtual reduction of all *philosophia* to "natural philosophy" or science. On Bacon's showing, therefore, philosophy for generations has had nothing to do; indeed, it has had no proper existence. Furthermore, because others, often unwittingly, have shared Bacon's identification of truth with utility, it has come to pass that experimental knowledge is popularly regarded as the standard of validity in every sphere of inquiry. Questionable as this notion may be, no small part of the prestige of modern science rests upon the avowed Baconian determination to ignore first principles, to attend only to fertile connections between observable events, and to codify the "laws" of their sequence.[84]

It is pertinent to remark, therefore, that the cogency of experimental truths is proportionate to the measure of common consent to estimate validity in terms of utility. Manifestly, then, the first principle of experimental knowledge is a judgment of value and a registering of purpose. It is an estimate of "good" by reference to which knowledge is adjudged useful or not useful and, therefore, validated or invalidated, true or indeterminable. The possibility of prediction and the power to control events by a knowledge of efficient antecedents is taken by Bacon to be the most likely indication of possession of truth. It is not Aristotelian deductive certainty secured by the subalternation of particulars to universals.[85] The certainties of the *novum organum* depend upon the valid determination of "middle axioms" or "laws of occurrence," inducted by discriminating observation, manipulation, and generalization from particulars.[86] Baconian science rests content with laws of nature, not because, in themselves, they afford a sufficiently intelligible account of reality, but because they provide a sufficient account *for practical purposes,* *i.e.,* to enhance the power of man over nature. This, in fact, is all that Bacon ever claimed for them.

Examination of both Aristotle and Bacon, then, leads to the plausible conclusion that both the certainty of syllogism and that of experimental science are more apparent than real and are strictly *hypothetical.* The certainty of syllogism, Aristotle's term for scientific knowledge, is conditioned upon the reliability of first principles, according to his insistence. But, with greatest of goodwill, it cannot be admitted that Aristotle's premises are certain or apodictic. Their certainty, as Plato always contended, is conditional. They presuppose what we have termed interest-in-context and are products of decision within a given and artificially delimited frame of meaning.

The acute Bacon knew what he was about when he abandoned all effort either to explore or to validate first principles and confined attention to the induction of "middle axioms" or proximate causes. He did so, as he declares, because Aristotelian principles are sterile and profitless for a knowledge of nature.[87] In addition, he recognized that they did not admit of certification. That Bacon succeeded in dispensing with Aristotle's first principles, such as substance, form, matter, and the laws of thought, cannot be credited for a moment. He employed them, but without formal notice.

When it came, therefore, to recognizing his own presuppositions, Bacon's acuteness was blunted. He did not, for example, take note at all of the foundational preference upon which he formulated his *novum organum.* Nevertheless, it was his first principle. It was the value-judgment that material utility is the privileged and well-nigh solitary criterion of significance. Consequently he defined truth and utility as one and the same thing.[88] The revolutionary character of Bacon's decision is visible in his unhesitating intention to identify wisdom with the knowledge that supplies power to man for the manipulation of his environment.[89] With Bacon, wisdom and science were incautiously equated, and that equation was to become a prime assumption of modern man. "Sapience" consists in knowing what is serviceable to material interests—"whosoever knoweth any form [law] knoweth the utmost possibility of super-inducing that nature upon any variety of matter. . . ."[90] And many have shared with Bacon the assumption that there is no greater desideratum.

From this state of mind, a momentous consequence follows. Just as Aristotle had defined knowledge and truth as "conviction arrived at in a certain way," namely, the way of syllogism,[91] Bacon, likewise, identified truth with those inductions arrived at in a "certain way." This time, however, it is the way of experiment, the method of "natural philosophy." Under such conditions, nothing is supplied credentials of truth unless it is brought forth by the one useful and sovereign method.

To such a conclusion Plato would raise a dissenting voice. The way to truth is not one, but many. There are different avenues suitable to different spheres of reality. Dialectic is fitted to explore first principles and the highest reaches of Being. Deduction is an appropriate method for the mathematical sciences, especially since they were considered mainly abstract rather than concrete. In such sciences, knowledge advances, as Aristotle so clearly perceived, by exhibiting real relations between a first principle and its particular instances. If the connections are real and not specious, the conclusion will be rigorous, even if only hypothetical.

Finally, when knowledge is sought about matters of fact—which Aristotle himself distinguished from those of "reasoned fact"[92]—Plato will have no quarrel with Bacon or anyone else who insists that the proper method of knowledge is not deduction from universals, but generalization from identifiable, efficient antecedents and connections. It is true that Plato had little or nothing to say on the subject, but it is also true that he consistently refused to regard pure abstract truths of science as applicable, without qualification, to particular concrete events. In this way, he was prevented from the error of applying the deductive method of theoretical science to the investigation of physical phenomena. By contrast, perhaps the cardinal error of Aristotelian science was the assumption that the syllogistic method was equally suitable for the advancement of theoretical science and "natural philosophy," even though Aristotle was aware of a difference between the two.

The full explanation of Aristotle's mistake cannot be given here, but a prime factor can be mentioned. First, it is axiomatic with Aristotle that we have knowledge of anything when we are able to specify the cause. But, further, Aristotle conceived connections between the terms of syllogism after the analogy of efficient causality. Thus, in any demonstration, the premises are regarded as the "cause of the conclusion."[93] On the strength of this analogy, therefore, the inferential system is conceived adequate to supply explanation of matters of fact quite as readily as it may supply the theorems of geometry. In this way, as Bacon complained, Aristotle reduced natural philosophy to logic.

We are able to say, then, that Bacon was not in opposition to Plato, as he supposed, when he revolted against the science of Aristotle. Doubtless he was on solid ground in claiming that to know the particular only through the universal, and not in its efficient connection with the fabric of actual events, destined the mind never to know the particulars according to the "mode of their production." As Bacon understood the case, the power for altering the physical world according to human purposes did not derive from knowledge of universal concepts. Therefore he set about formulating a new order of universals, the "laws of nature." He did so by faithful observation of natural sequences to the end of identifying truly efficient antecedents. When generalized, these new universals were the "middle axioms." Upon knowledge of them "the fortune and affairs of men" manifestly depended, in Bacon's opinion.[94]

Against Bacon's *novum organum* Plato would probably have nothing to say in so far as it claimed to be a method for investigating physical nature. But there is a feature of Bacon's thought against which he would have strenuously cautioned. Plato would have refused assent to the hidden premise upon which Bacon made sweeping claims for the sufficiency of the experimental method. The premise is comprised of a value-judgment which Plato would have regarded as entirely defective. *He would have contended that there is no warrant for claiming for the novum organum the sole prerogative of defining the criterion of truth, unless one antecedently agrees with Bacon that the only truth worth having is that which affords man power over nature. Only on the ground of such a partialized conception of the Good can the sufficiency of truth derived from the experimental method be conceded at all.* Bacon's identification of truth with utility would have been for Plato the sign of fundamental distortion in axiological preference that called for a revolution of *êthos*.

Although Bacon was well acquainted with Plato's analogy of the Cave, he identified the shadows and darkness of human error with the received traditions of men.[95] He did not notice the kind of "knowledge" which Plato attributed to the prisoners of the Cave. Plato had referred to "experts" among the cave-dwellers. They receive highest honors among their fellows, because they are "quickest to make out the shadows as they pass and best able to remember their customary precedences, sequences and co-existences, and so are most successful at guessing at what was to come. . . ." (516d). Here, as Paul Shorey noted, the modern positivist conception of causation is shrewdly anticipated. But the more interesting point is: Plato links what we may properly call empirical knowledge with certain estimates and decisions about the "good" to be sought. The cave-dwellers are committed to empirical knowledge because of their particular kind of *êthos*. Already in the *Phaedo* Plato had prepared the way for affirming that their judgment of what is *true* is largely determined by their estimate of what is *good* (81b). They are engrossed with sensible realities because they are controlled by sensuous interests. Such intelligence partakes of the *anatropism* which turns reality "upside-down." It is preoccupied with "precedences, sequences and co-existences" because of the predictive value of such observation. Knowledge of this sort is justified by its mundane utility; but, for Plato, that sort of utility is a distinctly subordinate aspect of the real Good. Consequently a *method* conceived in order to implement the preference for utility cannot, for Plato, possibly represent the norm of verity. *Truth is no higher in honor than the value-judgment by which its discernment is implemented.*

6. THE FINAL PREFERENCE OF THE HUMAN MIND

We return now to final consideration of Plato's conviction that the sort of truth which is decisional is of greater moment than the kind which is apparently necessary. We have examined "scientific knowledge," to which Aristotle accords high, if not the highest, honors. It is comprised of the apodictic conclusions of necessary inference. We have considered the mode of certainty which Bacon devised by way of his *novum organum*. Evidently, the cogency of both sorts of knowledge is conditional, because, in both cases, the procedures which seem to afford certainty do so only in virtue of a delimited frame of meaning. This is equivalent to saying that inference (whether of syllogism or experiment) rests upon hypotheses dictated by the interest-in-context presently dominant. Plato regards such hypotheses as inadequate for the most fruitful interpretation of reality, because he questions the sufficiency of the value-judgments from which the hypotheses receive their self-evidence. It is now our business to define the basis of Plato's misgivings.

We may begin by reiterating our previous finding; namely, that there is no starting-point of knowledge which is not decisional when analyzed to its roots. Bacon's experimental knowledge is no exception. Aristotle cannot evade the indication that his most fundamental principles are self-evident only *for* specifiable interests-in-context and that even the "laws of thought" actually depend upon expressions of value-preference, however apparently universal these may be.

Plato's analysis of the knowledge-process seems to suggest, then, that there is no achievement of knowledge which is not conditioned by a prior decision about the Good or, more specifically, about what is worth knowing. If this circumstance entails the consequence that there is an element of so-called "subjectivity" in knowledge, Plato accepts the inevitable with equanimity. Because of his anthropology, this subjectivity is not vicious. Man is not cut off from ultimate reality; and, in his essential nature, he mirrors the Real. Therefore Plato was disposed to believe that reality is not known except as we consult, not a part, but the entire experience of the subject who knows.

In Plato's view, the quest for certainty by way of *apodeixis* is both inadequate and futile. The quest for certainty by this route evidently sustains itself just so long as the investigator refrains from critical examination of the foundational valuations which, while they remain unmolested, supply his postulates with self-evidence. Untroubled by dialectical probing, initial principles or postulates seem adequately secure. They appear so in proportion as the knower is wholly engrossed in some particular interest-in-context. But when, by some shift of interest and perspective, a man is alerted to the partiality of his valuations, his hypotheses are likely to be seen for what they are: self-authenticating only *for the purposes* or "good" which, hitherto, controlled his interest. However, this circumstance —and the point is to be carefully noted—does not imply that the hypotheses are not valid at all. They may be thoroughly fruitful for advancing inquiry in the particular area which they serve; but there may be other and wider purposes for which the postulates have no relevance, and there may be loftier spheres of reality which they do not help to illuminate. Just this, it may be affirmed, is what Plato believed about the hypotheses of the propaedeutic studies described in *Republic* VII. He regarded them as arbitrary because they rest upon valuations and implement purposes which, in his judgment, cannot possibly be identified with the ultimate concern of the human soul. The hypotheses of the sciences are rightly accredited for the advancement of the interest-in-context they represent. But it is erroneous to regard them as unconditionally certain or as wholly adequate instruments for the exploration of essential Being. There are, however, hypotheses, those of dialectic, which have superior self-evidence and are of greater fertility for the perfection of knowledge.

Plato's preference for decisional as distinguished from apodictic knowledge is intimately connected with his general teaching concerning the correlation of knowledge with *êthos*. The bearing of the foregoing study shows how central is Plato's conviction that knowledge of reality is conditioned upon virtue and that true Being is inaccessible to ill-disposed minds. Consequently, since Plato finds mankind predominantly in a state of contrary affection, *paideia* requires a revolution of *êthos*. Truth, he holds, does not even begin to germinate in alien states of mind.[96] Plato's education requires, in company with intellectual discipline, emancipation from bondage to the inferior eros. This appetition, as we have noticed, enslaves and represses the aboriginal aspiration of the mind for "most real Being." But there is no possibility of attaining to the highest truth available to *nous* apart from decision for it, or, initially, for its indications in the form of *doxa alêthês*. It was on this basis that it was argued in the previous chapter that metaphysical knowledge must be, in Plato's view, conscientious in nature. The decision in favor of superior truth is really a manifestation of *theia mania*. Therefore, Plato declared in the *Phaedrus* that the higher eros is the "author of our greatest blessings" (266b). When the divine affection becomes lively, as a new "habituation" replacing the old *sunêtheia*, it is, most probably, what Plato calls "the habit of the Good."

With Plato, that which men know or which they take to be reality rests upon judgments they make respecting the Good or its species. If, therefore, we are to adjudicate among the various judgments about the Real, we must revert finally to the question about the real Good. Is there some Good-in-itself to which all others are referred for their justification? Is there some Good in the light of which other claimants to the title may be ranked? Plato's answer to this question is discovered by attention to what he regarded as the final and irreducible preference of the human soul. If we are seeking the ultimate preference from whence derive the most significant initial postulates of rational thought, then, in our deliberations, we must not confine attention to the object and fail to consult the subject of knowledge. The pre-Socratic "physicists" will, therefore, not be proper guides in this matter. On the other hand, neither will Protagoras or those of his temper supply the clue. The Sophists, to be sure, accentuate man the subject; but, although they make man the "measure of all things," the man who measures, on Plato's showing, is the sense-bound denizen of unexamined life in the city-state. Neither the a-humanism of the Ionians nor the uncritical humanism of

Protagoras provides the data from which an index to the truly preferable may be taken. The Ionians are absorbed with the objects of the "outlook." The Sophists are distressingly deferential toward the "unregenerate" subject of experience. They are so indiscriminately accommodating toward every whim and unexamined preference of all individuals that the universe dissolves into a multiplicity of incompatible interest-bred assertions that are made about it.[97]

Plato was reduced to the conviction that the only reliable course for the discovery of the truly preferable, the norm of goodness, is the path Socrates chose. It is the way of self-knowledge. In the first chapter of this study, the claim was defended that the teleological world-view of Plato takes its rise from the Socratic reading of the *psuchê*. By earnest attention to his own innermost experience, by self-consultation, and by probing the deeper levels of his own inwardness, Socrates discerned in the pronouncements of his *psuchê* more than could be credited to the deliverances of sense and more than could be accounted for by deferring to the social context. In large measure, the ontology of Plato, especially the metaphysics of the Forms, is an effort to provide and define a status for that "more."

From the inward apprehension of what is best, Socrates discovered the likeliest clue to what is most real. Therefore, when Socrates abandoned "physical investigations" of the Ionian sort—observing that they achieved no more than "probable" knowledge—and followed the ancient directive of the Delphic oracle, he was establishing the foundational principle of Platonism. In the injunction γνῶθι σεαυτόν (Know thyself) Socrates, and Plato after him, discovered what he took to be the right approach and the finally reliable method for the interpretation of reality. It was trustworthy because it ignored neither the subject of knowledge, as the Ionians did, nor the object of knowledge as the uncritical subjectivism of Protagoras did. The Socratic principle of self-knowledge gave recognition to the obvious but easily ignored fact that reality is not known, save as it is apprehended by knowing subjects. At the same time it preserved from the Ionians such a proper humility toward the object as does not succumb to sophistic vanity; namely, the arrogance toward Being which, from the circumstance that experience is subjective in fact, infers that it is also subjective in reference. Plato is willing to accept the view that "man is measure" only with limitation. *Man indeed reflects or mirrors reality, but he mirrors an objective Ideal Structure which measures man.*

It is to be expected, therefore, that the prime data for metaphysical reflection, in the Socratic-Platonic method, will be taken from the sphere of human inwardness, that is, from the qualitative distinctions which are native to humane experience as such. There may be other methods which attempt to interpret reality by means of categories or principles less congenial to the human spirit. Reality may, for example, be interpreted in mathematical, geometrical, or mechanical symbolism. For Plato these projects are permissible and admirable. Only it must be recognized that such symbolism has limited application and supplies no more than a truncated view of the scale of Being. Furthermore, however useful such systems of notation may be for certain purposes, they provide an account of reality which is deficiently intelligible. There is an explanation for this fact. It is that such systems do not answer to the primary and, therefore, privileged category of meaning by which *nous* is determined. Measured by the chief axiological concern of the human mind, the symbolism of mathematics and mechanics construe reality in a fashion that is meaningful only for a restricted field of interest. Taken alone, symbolic systems of this kind actually produce an account of Being from which all but a species of logical and aesthetic value has been evacuated.[98] Inspired by the quest for certainty in the sphere of physical explanation, the notation of mathematics and mechanics construes reality in terms which are partly alien to the human spirit. It divorces the subject of knowledge from the object by constructing a world-view in which there is no real place for the human knower with his ineradicable axiological concern.

For Plato the index to truth about reality is the whole man, faithfully interrogated with reference to the entirety of his experience. With this principle in hand, Plato believed he could go a long way toward illuminating and, perhaps, resolving the strife of systems. Plato is not content to leave the question of reality to the mercy of rival human interests and initial principles which consequent decisions produce and enshrine. Reality would be devoid of coherence. A universe would not, in the strict sense, be possible. There would be only a variety of symbolisms, each claiming to supply the adequate notation for the final rendering of truth. If prevailing interests govern primary hypotheses, then the truly prior and privileged valuation of the human *psuchê* must be discoverable if the scale of Being is to be knowable. By reference to the privileged norm, other concerns must receive their subordinate rank and place. The matter may be summarized thus: The values which are implemented by the hypotheses of the sciences are, as contrasted with those of dialectic, only instrumental. Alternatively, those valuations which supply the "starting-points" of dialectical ascent to the First Principle are more nearly intrinsic, although they too must at last have their justification in the *ne plus ultra*, the Idea of the Good in which they are grounded as their supreme co-implicate.

What, then, is the ultimate and, therefore, privileged category of meaning in Plato's universe, and how may it be discovered? In answer, it may be said with some assurance that Socrates, through self-attentiveness and examination, was conscious of a magisterial moral claim upon him. The obligation was binding and unconditional, and it suggested to Socrates, as to Plato, that the soul was solicited by a higher loyalty beyond the self. Plato informs us that Socrates was alerted and answerable to a norm of excellence, taking the form of a divine summons. Precisely for this reason, as we saw in Chapter I, Socrates whimsically described the soul as *mantikon*, or oracular. And, on the strength of this conviction, Socrates urged that a man's first business was the proper tendance of his soul.[99]

In Socrates' experience there was the intimation of a standard of goodness, of order, of proportion which Plato believed the chaotic society of his day urgently required. In the individual's life the acknowledgment of such a *metron* might reconcile the warring factions in the soul and secure harmony and integrity in place of self-discord. But the imperative of the Good is not merely a ground of action which issues in *eudaimonia*. Its acknowledgment is also the pre-condition of highest knowledge. It has been argued that the norm of the Good is given universally in human experience as it was given to the awareness of Socrates; but only on condition of candid self-knowledge may it become known. It is known only in so far as it is honored by the whole mind. Its solicitations or notices may register in human awareness in the form of true opinion, but they may easily go unheeded. Reality, with which the soul is "akin," to which it is ultimately conformed, and which constitutes its maximum context, is not known unless it is *decided for*. Nothing, seemingly, finally conduces to knowledge of the First Principle except honest self-consultation with the aid of dialectic.

If this interpretation of the source and spring of Plato's metaphysics seems to give undue prominence to the Socratic standpoint and consequently to the data of the moral consciousness, then at least it may be rejoined that, in the specifically metaphysical province of Plato's ontological inquiry, Socrates is regularly the principal speaker. This is true not only of the *Republic* and the *Phaedrus* but also of the *Philebus*. Among the later dialogues of Plato, it is especially the *Philebus* that has the right to be considered meta-physical in intent. Its ethic cannot be established without its meta-physic. Nevertheless, it has not been our insistence that the Good is exhausted in the moral. The moral is a mode of the Good, prob-ably the privileged mode. All the same, the Good embraces all excellence whatsoever. It is the Intelligible as such or the Ideal Structure of Being considered as the harmonious proportion of all excellencies in coherent unity.[100]

The sovereignty of the Good had consequence for Plato's view of the world. To the Socrates of the *Phaedo*, mechanical explanation of the Cosmos by way of *stoicheia* seemed unprofitable (98c). Such an account failed to satisfy the requirement of the mind for intelli-gibility. Following the suggestion of Anaxagoras, but consulting his own *psuchê*, Socrates discovered that intelligence is so constituted that nothing is transparently intelligible, nothing satisfies its criterion of meaningfulness, except power or action governed by a choice of what is best (99b). It was, as was argued in Chapter I, upon this insight that Plato found support for the teleological interpretation of the world—a view which characterizes Plato's cosmological think-ing from the "autobiographical passage" of the *Phaedo* to his final statement on the subject in the *Laws*. The privileged symbol for the interpretation of the existing world is there said to be "the mental energy of the will aiming at the fullfillment of good."[101]

The inexpugnable axiological determination of intelligence re-quires, for satisfactory explanation of the Cosmos, causality, not in terms of mere positive antecedents or even mathematical ratios, but determination in terms of intelligent purpose controlled by a Good. If there still remains such dissent as Bacon's protest that "final causes" have no utility for the investigation of nature, Plato's answer will always be: Such investigation is not enough! Neither man's significance nor his end is exhausted in his mastery of nature. Plato was fully aware that there is no "proof" of the teleological world-view, because there is no "proof" of the reality and supremacy of the ideal Good. Both may remain "moonshine" for those who refuse to consult with candor and honesty their own inwardness. If self-examination is withheld, ignorance remains well-nigh invincible. In that case, the only remaining refutation of intransigent minds will be the one Socrates explicitly noted in the *Gorgias* (482b). If men refuse to acknowledge the sovereign imperative of the Good, then they are destined to live at odds and in perpetual discord and faction with themselves. The penalty for man's non-recognition of the true

First Principle is the demoralization, even annihilation, of his own essential nature—the ultimate absurdity, one would suppose, into which the human spirit can fall. But this, precisely, is Plato's version of the present "fallen" condition of man.

NOTES

1. In the *Phaedo*, the "actual" is the particular thing which strives toward "essence" but falls short (74d f.). At *Republic* 477a, as at *Timaeus* 49e, particular things partake of inherent ambiguity since they can be said neither "to be" nor "not to be." At length, this suggested to Plato "actuality" or "existence" as the peculiar status of Becoming, but he could articulate this status only with the help of his material principle. This, in its cosmological expression, as in the *Timaeus*, is the Receptacle (51a). It is that "wherein" particulars come to be and cease to be (49e), since "it is somehow necessary that all that exists should exist *in* some spot and occupying some *place*" (52b). Hence, place (*chôra*), and probably also time (*chronos*), as at *Timaeus* 37-39, are differentia of actual as distinct from Ideal being.

2. *Soph.* 254a-b. This is reminiscent of the like disability to which any of the cave-dwellers is subject when turning from the objects of *doxa* to the intelligible sphere without the Cave. *Rep.* 515c, 516a-b, 518a.

3. *Rep.* 518c, e, 519a-b.

4. See earlier treatment of the concepts above, Ch. V, sec. 3, a. The cosmology of the *Timaeus* is a form of probable knowledge (29c-d) because its object, Becoming, is a combination of Reason and Necessity (48a). Knowledge, here, most likely, may be said to have the status of critical *doxa*. It employs an analogy, or *paradeigma*, as we have seen was customary in the case of division. The pervasive analogy is the "Living Creature" (ζῷον) (*Tim.* 30b) patterned after the quite enigmatic intelligible and all-perfect Living Creature (31b), or the ὃ ἔστι ζῷον (39e). (Cf. *Soph.* 248e where Plato, possibly for the first time, seems to attribute life, soul, and mind to τὸ παντελῶς ὄν, most real Being.) However, in the stereometrical account of the so-called "Platonic bodies" (53c f.), there is a further and quite different refinement of *doxa* by the application of mathematics to elementary bodies. Here, Plato means to show how applied mathematics secures real *technê* in the sense of *Republic* 522c and *Philebus* 57; and mathematical physics gets under way. But this, as *Philebus* 47e-58a shows, will not be considered the proper subject of dialectic nor the highest object of human knowledge. *Cf. Rep.* 511b. Quite otherwise, it deals not with "eternal verities," but only with transient "becomings" (γιγνόμενα) of past, present, and future—physical realities in time and space. *Phileb.* 59a. *Cf.* 27a; *Tim.* 28a, 49e; *Theaet.* 157b.

5. *Rep.* 516c. *Cf. Laws* 886b for a "grievous unwisdom which is reputed to be the height of wisdom." The instances are not wholly comparable, but are so, nevertheless, in their common disregard of the teleology of the Good.

6. *Cf. Phaedo* 79a f.; *Rep.* 585c; *Phaedr.* 247c; *Phileb.* 61d-e; *Tim.* 51d.

7. For the causality of the Good, see *Phaedo* 99c; *Rep.* 509b, 608e; *Laws* 967a. The concept is admittedly ambiguous because of Plato's indecision about the relation of "God" and the Good. *Cf. Rep.* 380c; *Tim.* 29e. It is, perhaps, when Plato undertakes to exhibit the causality of the Good *in cosmology* that he is found to introduce the efficient causality (ποίησις) of a supreme Intelligence as the only acceptable symbol. *Cf. Phileb.* 26e, 27a; *Soph.* 265c; *Tim.* 30a; *Laws* 892a-b. It is in this mode that the causality of the Good is extended to the outward world. As apprehended *within*, in man's moral consciousness, the causality of the Good takes the form of the Idea of the Good, the ultimate object of man's axiological concern. As such it tends to be the Final Cause. In cosmology, however, where causality must

take the form of *poiêsis* (making), *Soph.* 265e, the causality of the Good is inadequate, and Plato requires the agency of soul activity. At this point, first clearly suggested at *Sophist* 247e-248e, Plato returns to a full-fledged consideration of the causality of God, which had been dropped from the time of writing of the "autobiographical passage" of the *Phaedo* (96-100). Phillip H. DeLacy ("The Problem of Causation in Plato's Philosophy," *Classical Philology*, XXXIV [April, 1939], 2) is, I think correct in the view "that from the first God was an important element in Plato's thought, but Plato did not suggest in the early dialogues any means of harmonizing God and the Ideas in a single system" (p. 104). He is, furthermore, mainly right in suggesting that in the later dialogues Plato sought a solution to the problem of causality, not by way of Ideas, but in "the purposive activity of souls" (p. 106). And DeLacy makes a signally important contribution in urging that Plato's reassertion of the causality of soul is "a natural outcome of the principle that true causality is ethical responsibility" (p. 115). It is against this background that we would have to give serious attention to the Demiurge of *Tim.* 29e f. if the theological question were to receive the attention it regrettably cannot receive in this present study.

8. The logical derivation of the scale of Being, already adumbrated in *Republic* 477-478, is worked out in the *Sophist* (254-259). It has its "metaphysical" formulation in the *Philebus* (23c-27b) and its cosmological illustration throughout the *Timaeus*, where the three principal components, disregarding the Demiurge, are: ever-existent Being, becomings (γιγνόμενα), and Necessity or the material principle (52d). Dialectic as the art of discrimination (*diakrisis*) has large usage throughout the delineation, but dialectic as *elenchos* has limited relevance because its proper employment is mainly metaphysical as suggested by *Philebus* 57e and *Sophist* 246d. Accordingly, *elenchos* has no use because no relevance in the *Timaeus* until it is perhaps alluded to at 90c as the proper *therapeia* for the attainment of immortal as distinguished from mortal knowledge. Cf. *Tim.* 52c.

9. Paul Tillich, *Systematic Theology* (Chicago, 1951), I, 72f.

10. See *supra*, ns. 1 and 8. See also *supra* Ch. VII, n. 13.

11. Plato's developed doctrine of Becoming as a mixture of the Limit (Form) and the Unlimited (Indefinite Multiplicity) (*Phileb.* 24, 25) and the view of the Cosmos as a conjunction of Reason and Necessity, characteristic of the *Timaeus* (48a), suggests an immanence of Ideal structures. Cf. *Tim.* 50c, 52d. But these are said to be "copies" of those always existent (50c). Possibly they are to be identified with mathematical proportions or "numbers," and so intermediate between particulars and Forms. In any case, even in the *Timaeus* the antecedence and transcendence of Forms is retained with modification. Cf. *Tim.* 52d, 27d. It has been stated that pre-eminent reality still belongs in the later dialogues to Ideal Being. This has been strongly challenged by Phillip H. DeLacy in his important essay "The Problem of Causation in Plato's Philosophy" (see *supra* n. 7). DeLacy has urged that in the later dialogues "the causality of the Ideas" is replaced by the causality of soul "as a self-subsistent transcendent force" (p. 108). He assumes that in the earlier period soul, including that of God, must be regarded as an "instance of particularity" and belong to a lower order of reality than the Ideas. Therefore he seems to infer that, with the emergence of soul-causality into unambiguous reality in the later dialogues, "the ontological hierarchy of the early theory of Ideas is destroyed" (p. 109). We must, however, admit this later clarification respecting soul-causality without agreeing that the hierarchy or scale of Being is much altered thereby. In the first place, it is not true that soul ever was regarded by Plato as an "instance of particularity." Already in the *Phaedo* (97c), as in the *Phaedrus* (245c-d), soul is an eldest principle. Secondly, it is, rather, that not until Plato positively takes up the distinctively cosmological task that he is led, as in the later dialogues, decisively to correct the ambiguities relating to soul-causality, which had prevailed since the writing of *Phaedo* 99c-d. Thirdly, in the *Sophist* and *Philebus*, Plato en-

larged the concept of Being to include Ideas, Soul, Becoming and Not-Being (*Phileb.* 23c-d), although the relationship between the causality of the first two was left finally incompletely determined by Plato. If the question was indeed left unresolved, then there is, to be sure, no clear indication as to the primacy of either. The issues raised here calls for full length treatment, but a certain sort of primacy of the Ideal Structure is at least rather plainly indicated in the fact that the Demiurge of *Timaeus* 29a is beholden to the eternal ideal Paradigm in his ordering and creative activity.

    12. See *supra,* Ch. VI, n. 60, for fuller discussion.

    13. *Cf. Tim.* 28c-29c, 31a, 48e, 52a.

    14. For significance of "re-cognition," see *supra* Ch. IV, sec. 2.

    15. *Post. Anal.* 72 a 25, 88 b 30. This judgment is based upon the analysis of Chapter VII above and has its basis, especially, in interpretation of *Republic* 510b, d, 511d, 533c. These passages in their context exhibit beyond much doubt the distinction in Plato's mind between the *deductive* method of the "arts and sciences" and the *inductive* or eductive method of dialectic. Aristotle retained and elucidated the deductive method in his logic of syllogism; and, because of his empirical conception of the origin of concepts, transformed the induction of dialectic into the theory of "abstraction" of universals. Plato does not question the *necessity* in deductive syllogism, but insists upon its purely hypothetical value (533c). For the superior truth-value of dialectic, *Republic* 510c and 511b-c should be compared with *Philebus* 57e-59d. In the late dialogues, the latter passage must be considered a *locus classicus* for indication of Plato's continuing dependency upon dialectic, as distinct from *dianoia,* as the privileged procedure where metaphysical knowledge is the desideratum.

    16. *Ibid.,* 73 a 23, 88 b 33; *Top.* 100 a 25; *Nic. Eth.* VI, iii, 4; vi, 3.

    17. *Nic. Eth.* VI, v, 3; vii, 6.

    18. *Ibid.,* VI, v, 3.

    19. *Ibid.,* VI, vii, 6.

    20. *Ibid.,* VI, i, 6.

    21. *De An.* 432 b 28; 433 a 14; *Nic. Eth.* VI, ii, 3.

    22. A. E. Taylor, *Plato, the Man and His Work* (New York, 1932), 295.

    23. *De An.* 432 b 7.

    24. See *supra,* Ch. VIII, n. 1.

    25. See *Lysis* 219c for subordinate goods dependent upon the ultimate Good. Also see *Philebus* 54c for instrumental good considered as in the class (*moira*) of the Good.

    26. *Crito* 49d. This is taken to be a definitive passage indicating the nature of the initial "hypotheses," or subordinate first principles, with which the dialectic of *elenchos* works up to the ἀνυπόθετος ἀρχή of *Republic* 510b and 533c. It is the kind of *archê* which figures prominently in all the pre-*Republic* dialogues. It is obviously a datum of the moral consciousness. It is illustrated at *Gorgias* 474b; but here Plato encounters the typical resistance to its acknowledgment, which it is part of the role of dialectic to overcome. The upward ascent of dialectic awaits upon joint-consent or joint-decision with regard to the premise of discussion (*Crito* 49d).

    27. *Rep.* 517c, 611e; *Tim.* 90a; *Phileb.* 35d, 57d; *Phaedr.* 279b.

    28. See *supra,* Chs. VI, sec. 4, and VII, sec. 2.

    29. *Crito* 47d-e. *Cf. Laws* 727b, and *Rep.* 619c.

    30. *Epist.* VII, 344b. *Cf. Rep.* 506a.

    31. *Rep.* 560a, 571c, 573b, 577e; *Phaedr.* 251a.

    32. *Laches* 188d. *Cf. Gorg.* 474b, 482b-c; *Rep.* 443e, 560a; *Soph.* 230b-c.

    33. *Phaedr.* 237c; *Gorg.* 457d; *Rep.* 612e; *Protag.* 352c.

    34. *Crito* 49d. Such a starting-point as this is to be identified with the hypotheses and *hormai* of *Republic* 511b from which the metaphysical employment

of dialectic takes its rise. If it is contested that this is only a moral datum, then it has been our contention that, in Plato, access to ultimate reality is pre-eminently by way of axiological experience; and this is why its final object is the Good.

35. *Plato: The Republic* (London, 1942), II, 174, fn. *c.* on 527e.

36. *Cf. Rep.* 527e and 517a.

37. *Rep.* 527e. For additional uses of συνδοκέω to indicate provisional agreement, *cf. Rep.* 460e; *Protag.* 331b, 340b; *Hipp. Maj.* 283b.

38. *Rep.* 582d. *Cf.* 518c, 527d.

39. *Rep.* 582a-e. *Cf. Laches* 186e; *Phileb.* 41d.

40. *Laches* 188c-d; *Soph.* 246d, 253e; *Laws* 663c. There is possibly an oblique reference to this viewpoint in the hypothetical reply of Protagoras to Socratic criticism (*Theaet.*, 167a-b). A bad condition of soul (πονηρὰ ψυχῆς ἕξις) engenders corresponding thoughts, while a better condition engenders better thoughts, but not, according to Protagoras, truer ones. It is here that Plato goes beyond Protagoras and asserts, if better, then, also truer. The "habit of the Good" (*Rep.* 509a, *cf.* 592a), as argued *supra*, in Ch. VI, sec. 4, is the precondition of knowing the Good, or supreme intelligible reality.

41. *Rep.* 582d-e; *Phaedo* 66a-c, 67b; *Phileb.* 40b.

42. *Rep.* 518c, 586e.

43. *Nic. Eth.* VI, xii, 10.

44. *Op. cit.*, 294-295.

45. *Rep.* 525d, 526d, 527a-d, 528c.

46. *Rep.* 529b-d.

47. *Cf. Novum Organum*, VIII, 113, 147, 162, and *Of the Interpretation of Nature, Works*, VI, 50, 73.

48. *Rep.* 525c-d, 527d, 528e.

49. *Rep.* 525c, 526a-b, 530c.

50. *Rep.* 526e, 531c, 540a.

51. *Rep.* 528b, d. Stereometry or solid geometry, usually considered as having been given rigorous scientific form by Theaetetus within the Academy, required the third dimension (αὔξη) or augmentation. The meaning of αὔξη is perhaps best indicated by *Laws* 894a. Sensible bodies are recognized as having depth (βάθος) in the stereometrical account of the elements at *Timaeus* 53c.

52. *Rep.* 528b, e, 529d. For Plato, time is the number or measure of motion. *Tim.* 38b-c, 47a. Length of time is a coordinate of the uniform movement of bodies through measured space. See the author's article, "Christian and Greek Views of Time," *Journal of Religion*, XXXIII, 4, 1953. In the *Timaeus*, as in the *Republic* (530c), astronomy is propaedeutic to philosophic wisdom in that the revolutions of reason in the heaven may prompt the revolution of reason within and lead to ascertainment of "the absolutely unvarying revolutions" that are divine (47b-c).

53. This so-called material component of the frame of meaning is admittedly a construction drawing in part upon the developed ontology of the later dialogues. We are attempting to infer the reasons for Plato's explicit awareness in *Republic* VII that the hypotheses or postulates of the sciences are, at once, both self-evident and yet arbitrary (510c). In the *Republic* (524c), and even earlier in *Protagoras* (357a-b), Plato has isolated the principle of indefinite or intrinsic duality, which was to become the root concept of materiality. See author's unpublished dissertation, "Not-Being and the Problem of Evil in Plato," Ch. III. It is this principle which becomes the Unlimited of the *Philebus* and is "fixed" by the Limit to produce *Becoming*, or the class of the Mixed (26a f.). The cosmological expression of the material principle is extension in three dimensions, or depth-dimensional place and, in the *Timaeus*, is symbolized in the Receptacle. This place, however, does not by any means exhaust the meaning of the Receptacle. It is now suggested that, despite the apparent indication in *Republic* VII, Plato cannot account for the postulates of geometry, stereometry,

and astronomy without positing as "given" the ideal material continuum embracing depth dimensionality, motion, and probably time. How otherwise, for example, can he speak at *Republic* 529d of ideal movements, "of real speed and real slowness in true number [Time] and all true figures?" Motion and figure, however ideal, require for their bare conception a continuum of space, and also of time, if motion is uniform (*Tim.* 47a). *Timaeus* 52b makes it pretty clear that depth-dimensional place is the "non-sensuous" continuum, the "rational" presupposition of bodies and bodies in motion. Whether we need to distinguish with L. Robin (*Études sur la signification et la place de la physique dans la philosophie de Platon* [Paris, 1919], 43) "intelligible" from "sensible" space remains problematic, for it is a question whether Plato regards space as sensible at all. Bodies are sensible (*Phaedo* 81b; *Laws* 894a). Rather, the spatial continuum, as one form of materiality, is the necessary presupposition of physical magnitudes and, in this way, is intelligible. It is an aspect of Necessity. It is also the presupposition of pure sciences dealing with points, lines, surfaces, angles and so on.

54. *Rep.* 522c; *Phileb.* 55e.

55. *Rep.* 526e, 527a-b, 531c; *Phileb.* 57b.

56. *Phileb.* 58c. *Cf. Tim.* 52c.

57. It is customary with Plato to insist that pure *arithmetic* discourses only of pure numbers, never "numbers attached to visible and tangible bodies." *Rep.* 525d; *Phileb.* 56d-e. But it does not follow that there is no material component of the arithmetic frame of meaning. On the contrary, this is just exactly required and specified. It is the concept of "indefinite" or "unlimited plurality" (525a). The latter, in conjunction with "unity," the Limit of *Philebus* 25e, engenders every actual number between one and infinity. *Cf. Phileb.* 17e and *Parm.* 144a. In the case of geometry and stereometry, depth-dimensional space is tacitly recognized as the material component (528b, d), but the concept is not developed until much later in the *Timaeus.* See also Ch. VII n. 33.

58. *Tim.* 47b-c.

59. *Rep.* 510c. *Protagoras* 349c and *Parmenides* 131c suggest that another postulate of geometry, not mentioned but perhaps alluded to, is that the whole is greater than a part and equal to the sum of its parts. *Meno* 86e f. represents a derivative hypothesis, not a primary postulate; however, it is taken as true and so is hypothetical and arbitrary. *Sophist* 244c and *Meno* 87c represent the dialectical use of hypothesis: If something is allowed to be so, what follows for the nature of Being or the teachability of virtue? *Parmenides* Pt. II, illustrates this method extensively. *Phaedo* 100a represents, perhaps, Plato's earliest reference to hypothesis of this sort.

60. *Cf. Rep.* 531d, 533d; *Euthyd.* 290c; *Phileb.* 57d-e.

61. Intimation of this conviction, so apparent in the earlier dialogues, seems to be reaffirmed at *Philebus* 63b-c in a context, which, as contrasted with most of the later dialogues, possesses a distinctly metaphysical import.

62. *Rep.* 589d. *Cf.* 501b; *Phaedo* 95c, also *Tim.* 41c, 47c; *Laws* 899d-e.

63. *Rep.* 516c. *Cf. Phileb.* 59a.

64. *Post. Anal.* 72 b 18.

65. *Top.* 101 b 3.

66. *Met.* 996 b 10; *Nic. Eth.* VI, vii, 2.

67. *Nic. Eth.* VI, vii, 3, 5; viii, 9. *Cf. Met.* 981 b 30, 982 a 1.

68. *Post. Anal.* 71 b 17-18.

69. *Nic. Eth.* VI, ii, 2-3; vii, 6; x, 1.

70. *Met.* 997 a 5-15, 1005 b 10 f. *Cf. Post. Anal.* I, 19-21.

71. *Nic. Eth.* VI, vi, 2; viii, 9; xi, 4; *Post. Anal.* 100 b 5-15.

72. *Post. Anal.* 99 b 35-100 a 10. *Cf. Nic. Eth.* VI, iii, 3.

73. *Ibid.*, 100 a 3-10. Aristotle's "induction" is really not so very different

from Plato's account of the formation of general conceptions. *Cf. Phaedr.* 249b, 265d; *Rep.* 596a. The principal difference is that Plato regards the process as *anamnêsis*, which presupposes a transcendental reference of *nous*. Correspondingly, a different anthropology is presupposed.

74. *Met.* 1005 b 12-35.

75. *Parm.* 135b-c. This claim rests particularly upon Plato's theory of the co-implication of Identity and Difference as worked out in the acute analysis of the *Sophist* 254b-260c.

76. *Tim.* 49a-e, 50c. *Cf. Cratyl.* 389b-390e, 440a-e.

77. *Cf. Phaedo* 74c-75e.

78. *Met.* 981b 20; 982 b 22.

79. *Nov. Org., Works,* VIII, 113. *Cf.* 147, 160, 162, 206.

80. *Of the Proficience and Advancement of Learning, Works,* VI, 223; also *Nov. Org., Works,* VIII, 67-68 and *Interpr. of Nat., Works,* VI, 28, 36, 48-49, 73.

81. *Nov. Org., Works,* VIII, 70-71, 84.

82. *Interpr. of Nat., Works,* VI, 84; also *Nov. Org., Works,* VIII, 104, 138, 148.

83. *Nov. Org., Works,* VIII, 99, 147.

84. *Interpr. of Nat., Works,* VI, 64. *Cf.* J. S. Mill, *Auguste Comte and Positivism* (London, 1907), 6, 14-15.

85. *Post. Anal.* 71 b 29-33.

86. *Nov. Org., Works,* VIII, 167, 206.

87. *Interpr. of Nat., Works,* VI, 64.

88. *Nov. Org., Works,* VIII, 156.

89. *Advancement of Learning, Works,* VI, 223.

90. *Ibid.*

91. *Nic. Eth.* VI, iii, 3-4.

92. *Post. Anal.* 78 b 30-79 a 15.

93. *Post. Anal.* 71 b 20-35.

94. *Nov. Org., Works,* VIII, 138.

95. *Advancement of Learning, Works,* VI, 278.

96. *Epist.* VII, 344a. *Cf. Rep.* 409b.

97. *Theaet.* 171b-c; *Cratyl.* 386a-c.

98. *Cf.* Aristotle, *Met.* 1078 a 30-35. H. Weyl points out that, in the world of mathematical physics, we are introduced to the "essence of things." Leaving our "human nature" behind, we are transported into a world of "flawless perfection" and pass beyond the distinction between good and evil. *The Open World* (New Haven, 1932), 28-29. Evidently Dr. Weyl thinks he is offering us a boon. It does not cross his mind that he is supplying only the mathematician's paradise evacuated of all but mathematical meaning. Plato would say that such a paradise has truth only for the limited purposes of the mathematician; and Aristotle long ago recognized that mathematical perfection is only a fragment of the Good. *Met.* 996 a 25-30.

99. *Apol.* 29e, 30a, 36c; *Gorg.* 503a, 504d.

100. See *supra*, Ch. VI, n. 60.

101. *Laws* 967a. *Cf. Phaedo* 99c; *Cratyl.* 413c; *Soph.* 265c; *Phileb.* 26e, 28c; *Tim.* 29e. Each of these passages supports the general view that Plato found no way to solve the cosmological problem without recourse to an intelligent Cause actuated by loyalty to the Good. Indeed, as we have urged from the beginning, to be intelligent and motivated by goodness is, for Plato, one and the same thing. Teleology and the Good, therefore, are conjointly represented by a cosmic intelligence which comes closer than anything else to being Plato's God.

CHAPTER XI

Wisdom: The Fruit of Therapeia

How fine it would be if wisdom were a sort of thing that could flow out of the one of us who is fuller into him who is emptier, by our mere contact with each other, as water will flow through wool from the fuller cup into the emptier.—Symposium 175d

1. GREEK WISDOM IN ITS SUCCESSION

IT has been said by St. Paul "that Jews ask for signs, and Greeks seek after wisdom."[1] No doubt these words point to a profound distinction between the Hebrew and the Greek mentality; but if it was characteristic of the Greeks to pursue wisdom, it is worth recalling that, in his own day, Plato was not greatly impressed by the fact. To be sure, Plato was always committed to the view that, among the goals of human existence, wisdom had priority. In the *Laws* he is still echoing the thought of the *Apology* in affirming that "what destroys us is iniquity and insolence combined with folly (*aphrosunê*)," while "what saves us is justice and temperance combined with wisdom (*phronêsis*)."[2] Wisdom is always, in Plato's thought, closely associated with a knowledge that saves.[3] Moreover, with him as with Socrates, it is hardly permissible to speak of wisdom save in combination with righteousness or, conversely, of righteousness save in combination with wisdom.[4]

In the *Phaedo* wisdom is described as that condition in which the soul is liberated from the distractions of sense and has unhindered communion with ever-abiding realities. Wisdom, indeed, is the realization of the native conformity of the soul with essential reality (79d). In the *Republic* "the knowledge which alone of all forms of knowledge deserves the name of wisdom" is that attained by the philosophic guardians (429a). And from the subsequent course of the dialogue, we know that this form of knowledge is *noêsis*, or discernment of the Good. And we learn that the Good is that paradigm of measure and proportion according to which the philosophic guardian first orders his own life in harmony and justice and, thereafter, that of the auxiliaries and the citizenry in so far as that is possible.[5] In this way the saving wisdom of the few, to whom rule properly belongs, is to some extent participated in by the many. Thus the city-state itself, in some degree, partakes of a reflected wisdom (428d). And in such a way as this the hope, which still survives in the thought of Plato's *Laws*, is to be realized, *viz.*, that in so far as possible the state shall come to resemble a wise man's head (964d).

But Plato's notions of wisdom were eccentric to those of his age, and he knew it. Many and various were the conceptions that laid claim to the title of wisdom. The earlier dialogues are often devoted to examining the credentials of these pretenders. In the *Philebus* Plato recurs to his long-standing conviction that, of all the virtues, the one to which almost everybody lays bold, if pretentious, claim is wisdom. Contentious about their special candidates, men are full of strife and the false conceit of wisdom (49a).

For his own conception of wisdom Plato was, initially, in heavy debt to Socrates. Somehow, Socrates fell heir to the strange and perennially unpopular notion that "human wisdom" is of trifling worth.[6] He interrogated the representatives of the various "knowledges." He discovered that artisans, poets, politicians, and Sophists were all, in their line, adept enough in pursuing their espoused objectives. Physical investigators might analyse and combine the constituent "elements" of all things,[7] but there was a general ignorance of ends worth pursuing and no unanimity or stable comprehension of what constituted human excellence, or more properly defined human destiny.[8] Socrates testified with the help of Plato in the *Phaedo* that the "kind of *sophia*" which investigates *phusis* he early explored with eagerness but finally abandoned. He did so, not because, as he ironically stated, he was unfitted for it, but because it supplied an account of the world that was, for him, deficiently intelligible (96a). The conception of wisdom had to be capacious enough to embrace the unique data of man's axiological awareness, which alone supplied a *telos* and a destiny for human striving. So Socrates could not properly conceive of wisdom save, first, by taking a longer and deeper look at man himself. And he at least hints in what direction wisdom is to be sought. It is indicated in his characteristic admonition to his contemporaries: Your first concern is to know yourself and the means for the perfection of the soul in righteousness.[9] Wisdom is a life devoted to the attainment of such truth as perfects the soul; and perfection of the soul is, if we may judge from the *Phaedo,* to become assimilated to the Divine in excellence.[10]

Disagreement and uncertainty about the nature of wisdom survived the best efforts of Socrates and Plato, as one might expect, so that the writer of the *Epinomis* could assert that what mortal man should learn in order to be wise had neither been stated nor discovered (973b). This deficiency he essays to make good. He is so far faithful to his master, Plato, as to deny that wisdom can be identified with knowledge pertaining to the arts or the ordinary sciences. However "necessary" to human life these may be, they do not constitute wisdom (974c-d). It is not possible, either, for him to disbelieve "that we must deem the good man to be wise" (989a), a conjunction which Plato had in truth alluded to in the closing words of the *Phaedo.* In point of fact, there is every indication that the prevailing conception of wisdom was revolutionized by Socrates, elaborated and enriched by Plato, and somewhat denatured by Aristotle—all within the bounds of a century. Although Stoicism preserved, with eccentric emphasis, an aspect of Socratic wisdom in the form of the self-sufficient sage, the Platonic concept of wisdom, after Aristotle's recension, was destined for perpetual ambiguity. From this ambiguity, Thomism of the high Middle Ages did not assist it to escape;[11] and neither the Renaissance nor the Reformation had much interest in doing so. With the ascendancy of "natural philosophy" in the seventeenth century, a temper of mind ill-equipped for comprehension of Platonic *sophia* was fostered and still survives.

Throughout the Christian era, and now and then since the Renaissance, there has been occasional recognition that Greek wisdom was not simply identifiable with scientific learning. But for the most part, the contrary supposition prevailed and very nearly to the extent that Aristotle prevailed. In Plato's thought, wisdom appears to be both something less and something more than "science" of the metaphysical object. But, for Aristotle, wisdom is identical with rigorous knowledge of primary causes, principles, and Being *qua* Being.[12] Over the nature of wisdom, therefore, there is division between Plato and Aristotle; and this divergence of viewpoint constitutes a significant parting of the ways between the two major traditions in European philosophy.

Differences about the nature of Greek wisdom continue to find expression in modern times. No less a scholar than Maritain declares that Greek wisdom

. . . is human wisdom, rational wisdom. It is not the wisdom of philosopy aspiring to be wisdom of salvation. It is a wisdom of philosophy with an order of its own, following its own line of *perfectum opus rationis*, a perfect work of reason. But here is no longer any question of a wisdom of salvation and hôliness, a wisdom of eternal life. It is a wisdom of here below, a wisdom of earth.[13]

Such characterization of Greek wisdom may find partial support in the views of Aristotle; but Plato is also a Greek, and it is precisely the character of Platonic wisdom to declare for the insufficiency of theoretical reason. The wisdom of Plato embraces aspiration for salvation. The soteriological concern of Plato for both the individual's destiny and that of society is a distinguishing presupposition of Platonic *sophia*. But, even of Aristotle, it is over-simplificaton to suggest that wisdom exhausts itself in knowledge of "the existence of that which is not God."[14] To be sure, Aristotle's concern is for an "aesthetically" complete Cosmos in which "God" is the keystone of the universal arch. Aristotle's interest in God doubtless implements his desire for complete scientific explanation of the world. But the notion that Greek wisdom is purely "human wisdom and rational wisdom" is an exaggeration that will hardly bear scrutiny unless we assume in advance, with Thomas Aquinas, that the sharp alternative to human reason is supernaturally revealed truth.

Admittedly, Greek wisdom does not presuppose, as does Christian thought, discontinuity between the creature and the Creator; nevertheless, even Aristotelian wisdom "looks up." It relies upon a measure of continuity between the human and the divine. In Plato, of course, the two are not finally divorced. And even with Aristotle, the intellect is the divine in man.[15] In knowledge man the knower becomes identical with the object, not with respect to "matter," but with respect to "form."[16] The same holds true for knowledge of "God," the supreme knowable. Here also the knower is identical *in knowledge* with the object known. Hence, in this respect Windelband rightly inferred that "a difference between it and the divine spirit cannot be made out."[17] It is for this reason that Aristotle was willing to say in the much disputed passage of the *De Anima* that the mind, when fully acting, is identical with its object and is imperishable and immortal.[18] It is one in knowledge, apparently, with the imperishable and eternal *ousia* of God. In *theôria*, it is one with the Eternal.

Thus it appears dubious to assert, even of Aristotle, that "Greek wisdom experienced at a decisive moment a sense of the real which is offered to our human mind and experience, and of the existence of that which is not God."[19] In view of the fact that Aristotle equated wisdom with knowledge of the metaphysical object, such an assertion seems unaccountably out of balance.

Yet it is true that Aristotle's conception of wisdom, conceived as *knowledge* of "primary causes and first principles," has largely prevailed in European philosophy. Francis Bacon, as we have seen, made a radical departure from both the Platonic and the Aristotelian traditions when he identified "sapience" with knowledge of the "laws of nature" derived by experiment, and thus reduced philosophy to natural science.[20] But when we turn to Descartes we find him adopting the Aristotelian position with little variation. The sovereign good for man, he tells us, considered by the light of natural reason apart from revelation, "is none other than the knowledge of truth through its first causes, *i.e.*, the wisdom whose study is philosophy."[21] To this extent, therefore, the "father of modern philosophy" remained faithful to the Aristotelian conception of *philosophia*. Wisdom is knowledge of the truth, especially of the highest intelligible object, the First Cause, and the Being whose existence is necessary.

With Plato, wisdom is not simply knowledge of the supreme intelligible object. Wisdom, moreover, is not a resultant of the exercise of theoretical understanding. The term *sophia* signifies an involvement of entire human nature and the dependency of the ultimate cognitive moment upon the affective life of the knower. Wisdom, therefore, is in no sense identifiable with "science," the knowledge-content of which would, in Aristotle's view, be available to competent knowers irrespective of *êthos* or character. Therefore wisdom is, in Plato, a term which connotes an inescapable contingency in knowledge. Descartes vaguely perceived this and noted a difference between Plato and Aristotle. The former, he said, did not claim ability "to discover anything for certain"; whereas Aristotle, altering Plato's method, took first principles to be certain, and derived demonstrable consequences therefrom. But Descartes observes that there is no evidence that Aristotle succeeded in vindicating the certainty of first principles.[22]

Descartes is not to be credited when he attributes Plato's tentativity in truth-matters primarily to the influence of Socrates. To be sure, Socrates' avoidance of dogmatic assertion was proverbial; but Descartes exhibits no grasp of the profound reasons for Plato's own distrust of dogmatic affirmation in metaphysics. This defective interpretation was not exceptional and reflects no particular discredit upon

Descartes. The scholastic tradition, in which despite his innovations he was firmly rooted, had for the most part, through dependence upon Thomas, forfeited understanding of the influence of *êthos* upon knowledge.

2. PLATO'S CONCEPTION OF WISDOM

Wisdom is a paramount desideratum of all Plato's reflection and writings; yet no single dialogue is expressly devoted to the theme. The *Phaedo*, doubtless, comes nearest to doing so, and, after it, the *Republic* and the *Philebus*. The composition which might have made *sophia* its special subject, the *Philosophos*, was evidently never written, although Plato has left us notice he had proposed to write it. The dialogue was to have been a parallel and contrasting piece with the *Sophist*.[23] We are warned that the delineation of the philosopher would be as difficult as that of the Sophist, but for opposite reasons. Whereas the Sophist is hard to discover because he hides in a kind of "darkness," the darkness of false opinion, the philosopher is equally difficult to make out because he dwells midst dazzling light.[24]

Central as is the concept of wisdom, then, in Plato's thought, its precise denotation is not easy to come by. Whether in the *Protagoras* (333a) or in the *Laws* (964b), wisdom is, of course, intimately associated with the so-called cardinal virtues, courage, temperance, and justice. And yet, in a sense, it embraces all the virtues, since the knowledge which is essential to wisdom is the condition of the other virtues also. The *Protagoras*, for example, labors to make it clear that the knowledge of wisdom is the precondition of all virtue, whereas, by contrast, ignorance (*amathia*) is the cause of vice (358c). Wisdom seems possessed of an ambiguous nature, for it involves at once a cognitive and a moral condition of the soul. This ambiguity clearly attaches to it in the *Phaedo* (79d), where the *pathêma* of the soul called wisdom presupposes, at one and the same time, a cognitive state and also assimilation in goodness to the nature of divine reality that is known.

To understand Platonic wisdom is to begin by observing that its conception is governed by Socrates' reversion from "the investigation of nature," as noted in the *Phaedo* (96a), to a concern for and an investigation of the *psuchê*. For Plato, quite as much as for Socrates, self-knowledge is the beginning of wisdom; for, to the *psuchê*, Reality makes itself available not only in a distinctive but in a definitive way. Socrates understood his vocation as a divine directive to urge men to " tend" their souls; but to "tend" the soul is, in the first place, to "attend" it and faithfully to consult it. If men would do so, then Socrates was prepared to believe that none could finally disagree with him that right is better than wrong and that doing evil is worse than suffering it.[25] Moreover, if men would attend their souls, they might stumble upon the same realization that came to Socrates, to which also he testifies in the *Phaedo*, that intelligence is inherently prompted by a preference and concern for order, beauty, and goodness (98a, 99b). It was in terms of these categories, as "hypotheses," that Socrates undertook apparently a new and distinctive method of causal explanation—to discover in these *logoi* the truth of realities (99e f.).

The approach to reality by way of the deliverances of the critically scrutinized soul has a significant result. The Real, hitherto called *phusis* and conceived as more or less concrete by the exteriorized mentality of the nature philosophers, is moralized and spiritualized. *Phusis* is no longer apprehended solely by way of external perspective and analysis; hence *phusis* is no longer known primarily in its extended and quantitatively determinable arrangements. It is now known as it impinges upon man's inwardness, the sanctuary of meaning and value. Reality becomes enriched in denotation as the avenues of its apprehension are enlarged to include the avenue of distinctively humane experience. Reality comes to embrace those features of which the axiological moments of human experience are signs and tokens. It is this reality with which both Socrates and Plato believed the soul to have essential *koinônia* and to which they regarded the soul as essentially akin. Wisdom would most likely consist in actualizing or perfecting that "kinship"—a position which is as fundamental to the *Timaeus* as it is to the *Phaedo*.[26] It is not strange, therefore, but entirely suitable to the changed perspective, that the conception of wisdom should be altered. The "investigation of nature" gives way to what was for the first time properly called *philosophia*. Reality which is loved is transformed in content. It is now love of that range of being which is "recollected," however dimly, and is clarified only by the assistance of the sciences and dialectic. But, in all, it is the kind of being that is available, initially and primarily, to the honest and perceptive glance of self-examination. Wisdom, considered on its cognitive side, will mainly consist in discovery and acknowledgment of what turns up in the process of dialectical inquiry.

Obviously wisdom will not consist in the findings of physical investigation; if otherwise, why would Socrates abandon them? Neither will wisdom consist in the certainties of necessary deduction or syllogism; if otherwise, why would Plato in both the *Republic* and the *Philebus* leave these behind for the superior discoveries of dialectic?[27] When Plato returns in the *Timaeus* to physical investigation, the findings are never called wisdom, but only something between knowledge and opinion, admitting of probability or "likelihood" (29b-c). We may, however, suppose that, while such knowledge deals, as the *Philebus* indicates, not with eternal verities but with transient productions of temporality (59a), it is nevertheless that portion of scientific understanding (*dianoia*) which has a respected and integral place in a comprehensive account of the world.

Finally, it is obvious that wisdom is remote from the mental state of one who is surfeited with knowledge of many things. Plato is fond of contrasting the moral earnestness of Socrates with trifling polyhistors among Sophists like Hippias and Prodicus. The "knowledges" which encumber their minds are incredibly numerous, but the content is "fifty-seven varieties" of odds and ends.[28] In an effort to distinguish the wisdom of the philosopher from a mélange of information, Plato reminds us that neither the wisdom of the *polis* nor that of the individual consists in "manifold knowledges." Granted that the mass of folk are "lovers of spectacles" and always take delight in learning some new thing,[29] there is nothing here to assure accruing wisdom. And no matter how encyclopaedic a man's mind or how learned he may be in the sciences, he is not therefore equipped to give "good counsel" either to himself or to the state.[30]

Of all forms of knowledge, therefore, the kind which alone approximates to and deserves the name of wisdom is, as the *Republic* states (429a), the kind which is attained only by the highest rank of guardians. They are, to begin with, naturally of a philosophic nature (490e), possessed of a spirit of truthfulness (485c), apt to learn and of good memory (486c), and with a mind endowed with measure and grace (486d). Moreover, the guardian of highest attainment must be a lover of truth striving after true being, not lingering over the particulars of sense and *doxa* (490a). Instead, he will cherish true opinions and, with the aid of the sciences and dialectic, at length discriminate the essential reality of each thing, laying hold of it with that part of his soul, doubtless the *logistikon*, with which it is "akin" (490b). So there will be begotten in him intelligence and truth. But, this is not all; the wisdom of the guardian must include knowledge of existence as well as essence. He must have learned to know the ideal reality of things and yet not fall short of others in experience (*empeiria*).[31] The wisdom of the guardian-philosopher does not consist merely in apprehension of abiding reality, but in his disposition and capacity to make his "vision" relevant to life and in his desire to do so. Judging from the *Republic* and the *Philebus*, therefore, it is apparent that wisdom cannot properly be equated simply with knowledge or with the contemplation of Being. The wise man or philosopher-statesman does not fulfill his calling in attaining intellectual intuition of reality; on the other hand, he cannot fulfill his role without it. No one can be an acceptable guardian of the historical *polis* until he has at least begun "naturalization" procedures in "the city whose home is in the ideal."[32]

The picture of the wise man of the *Republic*—his qualifications, discipline, and attainment—strikes us as excessively idealized and calculated to engender despair. It is not strange that the writer of the *Epinomis* should justify his own sober misgivings in asserting that "it is impossible for men to be blessed and happy, except a few" (973c). Plato, however, did not intend to propagate a forlorn hope. The philosophic guardian, like the state he rules, is only a paradigm pointing in the right direction, and Plato anticipates no more than approximate attainment (*Rep.* 472c f.). We are closer to Plato's intention when we observe that, in the larger sense, wisdom begins its life in the human spirit coincident with the mind's passage from the "dream state" of the multitude to the waking condition of the philosophic searcher. The dream state, as we have seen, is "the mistaking of resemblance for identity," confounding sensible realities with real Being, as at *Republic* 476c. It is contrasted with the case of the more perspicacious mind that is able to discriminate the "self-beautiful" from the particular things that participate in it (476d). The error of the dreamer is that of the cave-dwellers and the Sophist,[33] who doze through this present life, confusing imperfect realities with essential Being. Wisdom, on the contrary, stirs to life in the soul of man when, with "clear waking vision," and with the aid of the sciences and dialectic, some few have learned to distinguish reality from the shadows of the Cave.[34] But advancement in wisdom is an arduous process calling for the concerted effort of the entire soul, its intellectual in concert with its affective powers.

But now it must be reaffirmed that the lover of wisdom is also one whose perspective is altered and who no longer shares the inverted standpoint of the sensate mind. Such a man is not the unwitting victim of false opinion or double ignorance, which, according to Callicles' admission, turns value and reality upside-down. For the correction of this distortion both the propaedeutic studies and dialectic are necessary means. They assist in the banishment of false opinion, and, concurrently, in the transformation of *êthos*. Indeed, since knowledge (*epistêmê*) and virtue (*aretê*) are mutually dependent, we have the clear indication that wisdom requires the combination of knowledge and virtue in a single life. It is even likely that wisdom presides over or, indeed, consists in the combination. In this event, a merely intellectualistic conception of wisdom would quite miss Plato's meaning. Furthermore, if wisdom is *epistêmê* conjoined with *aretê* in the soul, then wisdom should turn out to be the exact opposite of *amathia*, double ignorance, the soul's prime "deformity." Wisdom, however, may be viewed from two related standpoints. It may be conceived according to the internal economy of the soul's powers. Also it may be understood in relation with the destiny or the final end of man. In both cases, wisdom will embrace a cognitive and an ethical component.

3. Wisdom as Concord in the Soul

There is a passage in the *Laws* dealing with ignorance which deserves close attention in tracking down the meaning of Platonic wisdom. Plato asserts that ignorance (*amathia*) in its greatest form is that which is always in process of dissolving the order of states. Consequently the lawgiver will endeavor to implant wisdom (*phronêsis*) in so far as possible and root out ignorance, for ignorance is also folly (688e). The "greatest" and worst form of ignorance is then described:

That which we see in the man who hates, instead of loving, what he judges to be noble and good, while he loves and cherishes what he judges to be evil and unjust. That want of accord (*diaphônia*), on the part of the feelings of pain and pleasure, with the rational judgment is, I maintain, the extreme form of ignorance, and also the "greatest" because it belongs to the main mass of the soul. . . .[35]

Socrates in his apology had described a kind of ignorance which would be regarded as most reprehensible (29b). It is that ignorance which typifies those who "take no thought for wisdom," who scorn things of the most importance and care for those of lesser worth (30a). A similar perversity is mentioned in Socrates' exhortation to Polus in the *Gorgias*, that the latter is, for all his seeming candor, misconstruing to himself his real and true convictions (474b). The distortion involved in the greatest ignorance is, likewise, suggested in the ambivalence of Alcibiades in the *Symposium*. Alcibiades, who is normally all too capable of suppressing purer incentives, cannot under the protreptic speech of Socrates, wholly disown a higher loyalty enjoined upon him (216b). But when untroubled by Socratic exhortation, he is quite able to promote what he judges evil and unjust, and with no great remorse of mind.

This extremity of ignorance, as defined in the *Laws*, is closely allied to the two kinds of evil in the soul described in the *Sophist* (227e). The one is called a "disease," the other a "deformity." Each reinforces the other. The disease is internal disagreement. Opinions, presumably true, are opposed to desires, righteous anger to pleasure, reason to pain (228b). The deformity is attendant and consequential. It consists in false opinion; and false opinion misses the mark, confounding appearance with reality. This state of mind is one of "disproportion" (228c), and it issues frequently in the false conceit of knowledge (229c). Against common opinion, as we saw, Plato insists that this ignorance is morally censurable, for it is "vice" when it arises in the soul (228d). Altogether, as in the *Laws* (689a), ignorance, according to the *Sophist*, exists in conjunction with unhealthy discord in the soul, consisting of affection at odds with "rational judgment." Ignorance, says Plato in the passage quoted from the *Laws*, exists when men love what is opposed to their real judgment of the noble and good. Ignorance is, indeed, understandable as something very like the suppression of "true opinion" through the ascendency of a contrary affection. In our passage, Plato describes it as opposition to rational judgment or to "the *doxa* according to reason" (689a).

This circumstance, of course, presupposes Plato's pervasive conception of a fundamental contrariety in the psychic life between the inferior and superior eros. In the *Republic*, as we have noted, it is symbolized as antagonism between the "rational" and "irrational" principles (439d). Similarly, in the *Phaedrus*, the human soul embraces "two ruling and leading principles." The one is innate desire for pleasure. The other is said to be "acquired opinion"—a species of *doxa alêthês* as we have argued—which strives for what is best (237d). In the passage of the Laws, Plato now, once more, alludes to this duality (689b). The inferior principle is represented by the appetitive multitude, the "main mass of the soul," with which we are fully familiar from *Republic* 442a and 588d. The other power, which at *Republic* 590d, Plato calls "the divine governing principle," is, in the *Laws*, represented under the collective form of "knowledge, opinion, or reason" (689b). Hence, Plato seems to reiterate in the *Laws* what he made unmistakable in the *Phaedrus, viz.,* that the inferior affection may overmaster "rational opinion" (238b), and the result is the greatest form of ignorance.

To summarize, it is manifest that for Plato ignorance or false opinion signifies, not alone intellectual error, but an unethical condition of the whole soul whereby a man is self-deceived, beguiled through the over-persuasiveness of unrestrained appetitive urges. He is at cross-purposes with himself. As Plato recurrently states in the *Republic,* he is an "enemy to himself," choked with "inner faction" and a dreadful want of "self-agreement" (352a). Accordingly, at the cognitive level, he entertains contrary opinions about the same things at the same time and teems "with countless such self-contradictions" (603d). So he harbors the "involuntary lie" in the soul, wallowing in ignorance (535e). The "involuntary lie" is defined as "deception in the soul about realities."[36]

The outcome is plain enough: In Plato's view the greatest form of ignorance is false opinion, and, while it manifests itself, on the one hand, as intellectual error, it is at the same time a condition of folly (*aphrosunê*) and moral obliquity. Hence it is not surprising that we are reminded in the *Timaeus* that folly is of two sorts; the one is madness, and the other is ignorance (86b). The correlation of *amathia* and *aphrosunê* in the dialogues is fairly commonplace.[37] And in the *Protagoras* it is early suggested that folly is the direct opposite of wisdom (332a).

We have looked thus closely into the nature of the greatest form of ignorance on the supposition that it may help, by contrast, to disclose the nature of wisdom, the greatest form of human excellence. It is interesting that at *Republic* 354b, although the reference is casual, Plato links vice with ignorance and virtue with wisdom. But the direction taken there had previously been explored in the *Protagoras,* where the tenor of discussion led to the agreement that folly is the opposite of wisdom (332e) and that wisdom entailed knowledge (360d). If, as has been established, intellectual error presupposes disharmony and strife among the soul's powers, correspondingly it is quite possible that Plato regards wisdom as presupposing an opposite condition, one of harmony and concord. In that case, wisdom evidently would characterize the man in whom there is "accord" between affection and "right reason." He would be one in whom the higher eros is emancipated, as in the *Phaedrus,* and such a love would prompt the organ of cognition toward truth and reality rather than impede and divert it, as when the inferior eros exercises dominance. This would entail "release," as the *Phaedrus* asserts (265a), from old established habits. Wisdom would be advancing, then, in the measure that men begin to honor true opinions or, more exactly in the words of the *Republic,* do not linger over particulars (490a) but search and peer through the manifold of sense for the "self-beautiful" in the complex of the many (507b). No doubt it is in this connection that Plato speaks of Eros as "desirous and competent of wisdom," and, in the same place, as halfway between ignorance and *sophia,* quite in the same way that "true opinion" is also said to be.[38]   Thus, true opinion, together with the eros that actuates it, would be the beginning stage in the advance to wisdom.

In these circumstances, wisdom would presuppose that discord and contrariety in the soul are resolved, so that a man, in the opposite way from ignorance, is coming to approve what he judges good and excellent, while he disapproves and rejects what he judges to be depraved. This, in point of fact, is how Plato describes the man of wisdom in the *Laws.* He is "the man who has his feelings of pleasure and pain in accord with the dictates of right reason and obedient thereto."[39]   The implication becomes fully clear if we advert to the earlier teaching of the *Republic,* for there also wisdom is attributed to him who has tamed the brutish part and liberated the gentle. The entire soul reverts to a better order (591b) and the appetitive nature is harmonized and attuned for the sake of "concord" in the soul (591d).

Plato's meaning is unmistakable: As ignorance is the fruit of discord, and hence of vice in the soul, so wisdom is, on the contrary, the fruit of concord or of virtue. Judging from Plato's maturer reflection in the *Phaedrus,* the predicate "wise" is too great for man and belongs to God alone. Much more suitable is the phrase "lover of wisdom" (278d). So perhaps we do not rightly speak of wisdom as a fully attainable condition, but we can suppose that wisdom is coming to birth whenever men eagerly pursue such knowledge and excellence as is prescribed by the aboriginal aspiration of the mind. In this condition, a man is acquiring integrity of being in place of contrariety. He is becoming wise, as the *Republic* puts it, in that he is becoming "one man instead of many, self-controlled and in unison" (443e). Such a one is variously described by Plato as possessed of *harmonia, philia,* and *metriotês,* that is, harmony, inner friendliness, and proportion.[40] He is contrasted with that worst condition of the soul, devoid of freedom and true friendship (576a), enslaved, and never able to honor what it truly wishes (577e). It is for these reasons also that, in the *Philebus*, wisdom is described as assimilation to "measure, moderation and fitness" (65d). This assimilation is, if we understand Plato aright, the establishment in the soul of that order, beauty, and symmetry which, in eternal Being, is the ever-existing Good.[41] Thus, the Eternal comes to be truly mirrored in the human soul by being recapitulated there. The man of wisdom is the true microcosm of essential reality.

We are led to the conviction, then, that for Plato wisdom is indistinguishable from what, in the *Republic*, he describes as "the possession and habit of the Good" (509a, 592a). It will be recalled that this concept was earlier examined in Chapter VI. We found it to be descriptive of the inward disposition of the entire soul, indispensable to knowledge of most real Being. The *Philebus* also is in search of that *hexis* and *diathesis*, disposition, of the whole life which may be called *sophia* (11d). Now, at this point, we are able to conclude that wisdom is, indeed, a condition of cooperation between the cognitive and volitional powers of the soul. At one time, it embraces the highest knowledge possible to man (*epistêmê*) and also that healthful integrity of the soul's powers which is virtue. Each makes the other possible in actual attainment. Hence wisdom is in fact the conjunction of intellectual understanding and virtue in the same life. The enigma of Platonic wisdom, both its attainment and definition, is that there is no possibility of the one (knowledge) without the other (virtue).

4. PLATO's *Therapeia*: AN EVALUATION

The marriage of knowledge and virtue, either in the individual life or in the body politic, is the principal goal of Plato's *therapeia*. This conjunction is *sophia*, and it is the true wisdom that promises salvation to men and to society. What is needful for the individual is, by analogy, needful for the *polis*, for it is Plato's opinion that the state ought to "resemble a wise man's head and senses, on the ground that it possesses within itself a similar kind of wardenship."[42] Plato turned from a political career to the pursuit of philosophy in order to discover a cure, a *therapeia*, for immoralism and societal disintegration. The course he chose he defended; for in the *Gorgias* his ultimate approbation for Socrates was that the latter, contrary to the common notion, was the only Athenian of his time who attempted the "true art of statesmanship" (521d).

Plato was always inspired by the figure of Socrates, who was at the same time "the wisest and most righteous man" he had encountered among the Greeks. Socrates was the wisest of his contemporaries but, also, if we may take the words of the *Republic* as fashioned upon his person, he was "the figure of a man 'equilibrated' and 'assimilated' to virtue's self perfectly" so far as that is possible to humankind (498e). In one historical personality, Plato discovered the principle which was to govern largely his concept of philosophy. Plato found exalted knowledge and virtue combined indissolubly in a single human being, and the combination was wisdom. Moreover, the wise man was the happy man, blessed in the integrity and self-agreement of his own *psuchê*. Plato also discerned in Socrates one who was sufficient to himself. Socrates was the true *autocratês*, not because he ruled over many, but because he ruled over himself.[43] Contrary to the opinion of Polus, he was a man who really exercised "power" and possessed it.[44] From the person of Socrates, Plato made a discovery which was to shape his reflection upon human destiny. He caught sight of the principle that virtue and knowledge are mutually dependent absolutely. He learned what was soon to be forgotten, even by his academical succession, that truth about the nature of the Real is unattainable by intelligence, however acute, which "ethically" has no *rapport* with its object.

The knowledge of ultimate reality is not the product of necessary inference but is discovered through *acknowledgment* as the mind is assisted by dialectic. Hence, the decisive epistemological principle of Platonic metaphysics is, as Augustine had the acuteness to perceive, the dictum of Socrates: "It cannot be that the impure attain the pure."[45] This is Plato's warning to every metaphysical effort which, without "clean hands and a pure heart," aspires to knowledge of the Absolute. It is also the prophecy, which seems to have been borne out by the history of European philosophic effort, that the attempt to make metaphysics into scientific knowledge eventuates in the atrophy of metaphysics itself.

Wisdom exists wherever the native appetition of the soul for the trans-empirical Good prompts, supports, and confirms the *organon* of knowledge in locating and discriminating most real Being. Then, mind and heart agree and the man becomes not "wise" but a lover of wisdom. Without this *harmonia* "not even the smallest fraction of wisdom can exist"; and this harmony is the saviour of men and cities.[46]   Therefore, strange though it be, Plato prefers this self-accord above expert calculation and all training and accomplishments which foster agility of soul in the arts and sciences.   Simple ignorance, he asserts, is never alarming; much more perilous is a wide variety of "knowledges" and learning without wisdom.[47]   For Plato there is no necessary connection between sheer intellectual acumen and wisdom, because wisdom is "the habit of the Good."   It is hard-won vision of reality conjoined with the love of it.   It is the antithesis of *amathia*, which turns reality "upside-down."   The philosopher is one who has emerged from the self-imposed darkness of shadow-knowledge and sees reality right-side-up.   He ascertains the orders of Being according to their proper scale and rank, and in contrast with the multitude, he subordinates what is less to what is of greater worth.   In so doing, he reverses the practice for which Socrates, at his trial, censured the Athenians.

Plato has been allowed to speak; what now may be said regarding the sufficiency of Plato's *paideusis*.   Explicit criticism has been deferred, but the reasons are obvious.   Our principal effort has been to place the thought of Plato in a perspective from which it can be understood, but which, in the history of interpretation, was early obscured by the Aristotelian reaction.   With Plato, all knowledge whatsoever and metaphysical insight in particular involve the concerted functioning of the powers of the entire *psuchê*.   Knowledge is not an achievement of disinterested theoretic reason.   For Plato, there was none.   In all knowledge whatsoever, first principles are engendered by interest-in-context and are, therefore, "decisive" in the manner already described.   Consequently the issue of knowledge lies with the orientation of volition.   If this is true, then, the momentous and definitive question is: What is the Good, or what is the privileged preference of the human mind?   The answer to this question will inevitably shape the nature of every ontology, that is, man's answer to the question: What is real?   But that only forces us back to the query: What is, *in fact*, man's pristine preference, his essential proclivity, his ultimate concern, his supreme *conatus?*

This issue immediately involves a problem regarding the sufficiency of Plato's *therapeia*.   It is true that when Socrates consulted his *psuchê* he found it to be unconditionally solicited by a Good which laid him under binding responsibility to the right as opposed to the wrong.   This encounter with Reality conferred upon him, and as he believed, upon man generally, the status of moral being.   Henceforth the ultimate preference of the human *psuchê* was, for him, plainly defined as the Good. But it was so defined *for* Socrates only because he acknowledged it. Now, then, what shall be done for the man who fails to acknowledge because he presently prefers something other than the Good? This is the heart of Plato's problem and the formidable obstacle to his *paideusis*. The true comprehension of reality hangs in the balance upon a decision or valuation which, by antecedent inclination, a man either is or is not disposed to make. The eventuality of knowledge or ignorance depends upon the focus and balance of volitional forces of the soul. But how shall wrongly disposed volition be altered so as to be rightly disposed?

Plato's problem is intensified by his own diagnosis of the human plight. False opinion is an "affection" in the soul;[48] that is to say, ignorance of true Being results from the domination of the sensuous eros as the inferior *dunamis* among the soul's powers. Our analysis, furthermore, has shown that the condition of double ignorance is one of self-deceit. The native impulse of *nous*, tending in the direction of intelligible reality, is repressed and obstructed, not by an external power, but by the force of the inferior eros. This inferior conation expresses the soul's own preference and "decision" for something less than the true Good. Hence, men are in a Cave of ignorance and, by their own decision and choice, wedded to *doxa* and its objects. Therefore men are willfully ignorant, although it is decision in opposition to the *conatus* of their essential nature, and their false opinion is the "involuntary lie."

In the extremity of man's plight, Plato offers a defined *therapeia*. It includes, as we undertook to show, *metastrophê* or "conversion" of the entire soul, involving the affections, by which *nous*, the organ of cognition, is reoriented rightly with respect to prime reality. This is revolution of *êthos*. But now the question becomes insistent: Granted the need of alteration of *êthos* or the habitude of the soul, has Plato's *therapeia* adequate resources to achieve this end? If ignorance of essential reality is basically the resultant of censurable preferences, how may these preferences be transmuted and transformed?

Plato has no simple answer. He depends upon the emancipating power of the propaedeutic sciences and upon the power of dialectic. The efficacy of dialectic is, first, to encourage self-knowledge; second, to induce *aporia* and void presumption; and third, to solicit agreement to evident truths which, by implication, involve ulterior consequences. Minor acknowledgments lead to hidden, but certainly implicated, major ones. But in the last analysis, *homologia* may be withheld and decision may be insincere. Consequently the culminating insight or discovery which should eventuate at the end of dialectical inquiry may be inhibited and the discussion terminate only in acknowledged or unacknowledged refutation of the intransigent respondent. There is no assurance, then, that dialectic will be efficacious. Knowledge, which waits upon the concurrence of volition, cannot confidently be predicted in any individual case; it is always contingent.

Not even dialectic, then, may with certainty be relied upon to effect the soul's conversion of *êthos* and its "release from bonds" of ignorance. Yet there is no evidence that Plato ever altered his conviction that dialectic was the supreme instrument for the deliverance of the soul and the truly persuasive art. Dialectic supplies the "living and breathing word" which "plants and sows in a fitting soul intelligent words which are able to help themselves, . . . which are not fruitless, but yield seed from which there spring up in other minds other words capable of continuing the process forever."[49] But does this mean that even dialectic waits upon a certain *fitness of soul* and that, wanting suitability, its power is blunted? A simple affirmative would be untrue to Plato's mind. Dialectic does, in many cases, actually achieve alteration of *êthos*. Yet, it can fail. But where it fails, Plato has a final word to say, namely: At least dialectic may lead a man to the point where he recognizes that the place at which he has arrived in dialectical interchange is contradictory to his starting-point. That is the crossroads to which Socrates conducted the minds of Polus, Callicles, and Alcibiades. But he left it to them to decide which way they would go and whether, henceforth, they would live in self-accord or in perpetual disagreement with themselves.

According to the genius of dialectic, men, when they are really convicted of error, are self-convicted, and when they are committed to truth, they are self-committed.[50] Plato was never able to improve very much upon Socrates' reply to Callicles' disparagement of philosophy, as that reply is found in the *Gorgias*. The words, to be sure, are Plato's, but, through them, we catch a glimpse of Socrates:

Philosophy always holds the same, and it is her speech that now surprises you, and she spoke it in your presence. So you must either refute her, as I said just now, by proving that wrong doing and impunity for wrong done is not the uttermost evil; or, if you leave that unproved, by the Dog, god of the Egyptians, there will be no agreement between you, Callicles and Callicles; but you will be in discord with him all your life. And yet I, my very good sir, should rather choose to have my lyre, or some chorus that I might provide for the public, out of tune and discordant, or to have any number of people disagreeing with me and contradicting me, than that I should have internal discord and contradiction *in my own self*.[51]

Here is Plato's answer as Socrates gives it. The test of truth is not in being in agreement with others, however great the throng, but in being in agreement with one's self—by being in accord with the soul that has native kinship with divine reality. And herein is indicated, also, the therapeutic power of dialectic. It has the capacity to conduct the mind of inquirers from erroneous opinions to the threshold of valid insight and knowledge. It can bring a man to assent to propositions contrary to the ones with which he started; but dialectic cannot secure the crowning decision for the truth that has come to light in the process of investigation. It is as Socrates confessed to Polus: "If on my part I fail to produce yourself as my *one witness* to confirm what I say, I consider I have achieved nothing of any account towards the matter of our discussion" (472b). In the final analysis, truth of this order is an attainment of personal insight through decision, and there is no substitute. In the final analysis, this kind of truth is not demonstrable but, plainly, confessional in nature; for *homologia* is not only agreement and admission, it is confession of truth and consent to reality.[52] The real question is how long a man can endure unresolved contrariety in his own spirit. The insoluble problem of Plato's *therapeia* is identical with the unanswerable question: How long can a man live at odds with himself and with his deepest presentiments of truth?

In Plato, this question has no answer. It is always possible that, under the impelling power of dialectic, men may be led to resolve the inner tumult of their souls in favor of the supreme Good which everlastingly solicits their acknowledgment. On the other hand, like Alcibiades, men may successfully subvert the intimations of truth and goodness which haunt the dim recesses of consciousness as ghosts that staunchly resist exorcism. If, on the other hand, the tension within the soul terminates in explicit acknowledgment of ideal reality and goodness, discriminated by dialectic, a man may be counted blessed. In that event, the inner discord and contradiction will be resolved. In its place will come a condition of self-agreement, measure, and harmony. Then a man will have attained to both knowledge and virtue in a single movement of the whole soul—to that symmetrical and harmonious state which is called wisdom.

To be sure, in the hands of a skillful pedagogue like Socrates, dialectic may contrive to revolutionize the *êthos* of many; but is its range wide enough and powerful enough to be an instrument of social salvation?[53] Even in the case of individuals, there is no assurance that dialectic will secure the fruits of its intent. It remains altogether possible that Alcibiades, a type of the man forever hung over the void of indecision, and others can contrive a moderate compromise within themselves. Alcibiades no doubt did find a tolerable adjustment of the strife of purposes within him. If the more sensitive spirit of a Socrates found contradiction insufferable and resolved it by a decision in favor of the Good, his resoluteness was exceptional. Of this fact Plato was always impressed, and he also knew that society exacted of Socrates the ultimate price of integrity. The world, as Plato well knew, supplies suitable incentives for those who prefer comfort to courage, and it is not impossible that men will always find a way to moderate and contain their strife of spirit and inner compunction about the Good, while they indefinitely postpone decision and pretend ignorance of its claims. For this eventuality Plato's *therapeia* has no ready antidote; nor is an infallible one likely to be found.

It is at this point, perhaps, that the philosophy of Plato, great as it is both in its diagnosis of the human plight and in its scheme of *therapeia*, looks beyond itself to a larger conception of divine grace. There can be little doubt that, subsequently, Christian thought, on the one hand, found an ally in Plato: specifically, in his conception of the contingent, decisive, and non-demonstrative nature of knowledge of things Divine and of the inescapable necessity of transformation of *êthos*. On the other hand, in the view of St. Augustine, the resources that Plato did not possess for the completion of his task, Augustine believed to be discoverable in "the Mediator twixt God and men," who moved the reluctant affections and induced acknowledgment of Divine reality where it had been halting or withheld. This, for Augustine, was the impulse and the ground of his own *Confessions*.[54] So the theme of *homologia* found its further implementation in the later Christian *therapeia*. Thereafter, although often obscured and ignored, it became a basic principle in the Christian conception of theological knowledge.

NOTES

1. I *Corinthians* 1:22.
2. *Laws* 906a. Cf. *Apol.* 30a, 36c; *Rep.* 443e f.
3. *Protag.* 356e, 357a; *Rep.* 433c, e; *Laws* 965a.

4. *Cf. Apol.* 29e, 36c; *Protag.* 360d; *Phaedo* 68a-c, 79d; *Rep.* 433e, 621b; *Symp.* 184c-d; *Theaet.* 176b-c; *Laws* 689d.

5. *Rep.* 540a, 484c-d, 428d, 442c.

6. *Apol.* 23c.

7. *Phaedo* 96a-97b.

8. *Apol.* 20b.

9. *Apol.* 29e, 30a-b, 36c; *Crito* 47d-e; *Symp.* 216a; *Alcib.* I, 129a.

10. *Phaedo* 67b, c, 79d, 82b-c. *Cf. Theaet.* 176b-c; *Tim.* 90d.

11. T. Aquinas, *Summa Theologica*, Dominican Trans. (London, 1920), Pt. I. QQ. I. 6. Thomas deviates but little from the Aristotelian conception of wisdom as knowledge of the first Cause. Wisdom is knowledge of divine things. However, Thomas distinguishes between such knowledge as has its first principles furnished by natural reason, and knowledge which has its first principles from revelation. The latter will entail superior wisdom.

12. *Met.* 982 a 2.

13. J. Maritain, *Science and Wisdom* (New York, 1940), 10.

14. *Ibid.*, 11.

15. *Nic. Eth.* X, vii, 8; viii, 13.

16. *De An.* 430 a 18, 431 a 1-5, b 21. *Cf. Tim.* 69c-e, 90e.

17. *History of Ancient Philosophy* (New York, 1906), 281.

18. *De An.* 430 a 23-24.

19. Maritain, *op. cit.*, 11.

20. See *supra*, Ch. X, Sec. 5.

21. *Prefatory Letter to Principles of Philosophy*, *Works* (ed. Haldane and Ross, Cambridge University Press, 1931), I, 205.

22. *Ibid.*, 206.

23. *Soph.* 254b.

24. *Soph.* 254a.

25. *Gorg.* 474b; *Crito*, 49b; *Apol.* 30d, 32d.

26. *Cf. Phaedo* 79e, 80b, d, 86b; *Tim.* 47d, 90a, d.

27. *Cf. Rep.* 532d; *Phileb.* 57d f.

28. *Euthyd.* 292e; *Gr. Hipp.* 281d, 285e; *L. Hipp.* 368a-d.

29. *Rep.* 475d.

30. *Rep.* 428b; *Laws* 689c, 819a.

31. *Cf. Rep.* 484d, 539e; *Phileb.* 62b.

32. *Rep.* 592a.

33. *Rep.* 476c, 520c, 534c, and *Soph.* 233c, 235a f.

34. *Rep.* 533c.

35. *Laws* 689a.

36. *Rep.* 382b. *Cf.* 577d; *Laws* 730c.

37. *Gorg.* 514e, *Phaedo* 81a; *Rep.* 382c; *Theaet.* 176d.

38. *Symp.* 203d, 202a.

39. *Laws* 696c. *Cf. Phaedo* 73d for the notion of "right reason," which is there associated with *anamnêsis* and which, in Chapter V *supra*, we have linked closely to *doxa alêthês.*

40. *Cf. Rep.* 443d, 490d; *Phileb.* 64e-65d; *Laws* 628c, 693c.

41. *Phileb.* 64a. *Cf.* 64e-65a.

42. *Laws* 964d. *Cf. Rep.* 369e.

43. *Cf. Rep.* 387d.

44. *Cf. Gorg.* 470a.

45. *Phaedo* 67b. *Cf.* 79d, 80d, 82d; *Phaedr.* 250c; *Soph.* 246d, 253e; *Laws* 689c-d.

46. *Laws* 689d.

47. *Laws* 689c and 819a. *Cf. Rep.* 491d-e, 519a.

WISDOM: THE FRUIT OF THERAPEIA

48. *Rep.* 382b.

49. *Phaedr.* 276e.

50. *Alcib.* I, 114e; *Gorg.* 472b, 474a; *Symp.* 216b-c.

51. *Gorg.* 482b-c.

52. It is remarkable that F. Schleiermacher, Plato scholar that he was, should have used the fundamental word of Platonic dialectic, *homologia*, to signify "confession" of faith. *The Christian Faith* (Edinburgh: T. & T. Clark, 1948), 79. To be sure, this has ample precedence in the New Testament, *e.g.*, II Cor., 9:13; Heb., 3:1, *et al.* The New Testament usage is itself of great importance, for it suggests that Christian knowledge is the kind in which there is mutual sharing or agreement respecting a common insight or conviction that, nevertheless, does not pretend to *apodeixis*.

53. If it is contended that in the *Laws* Plato broadened the basis of his educational scheme to embrace the whole people, it must nevertheless be conceded that, according to his own words, it was a "second-best" society under law. *Laws* 875d. And to this law men were to be conformed from childhood by a carefully devised process of conditioning and association. The fact that Plato permitted no questioning of the laws and required universal assent "with one mouth and one voice" to their unimpeachable validity is sometimes considered an indication of Plato's "failure of nerve." *Laws* 634d-e. The discovery of truth was the prize of philosophic *paideusis*, but it was a hard and strenuous way and few were suited to undertake the rigors of the discipline. *Epist.* VII, 450b f. Yet, this "second-best" was not a conclusion to which Plato came reluctantly in old age; he was already alive to the problem in the writing of the *Republic* (466d, 471c f.). What the *Laws* indicates, perhaps, is Plato's admission that the higher *paideusis* is not a sufficient instrument of *social* control; it must be reinforced and supplemented by law as the most readily available restraint to lawlessness.

54. For a more ample treatment of these themes and appropriate references to the works of Augustine, see the author's article "Faith and Reason" in *A Companion to the Study of St. Augustine,* ed. R. W. Battenhouse (New York: Oxford University Press, 1955), 304-310.

Plato's Depreciation of the Written Word

IT has been argued that in the face of false opinion and resistance to truth Plato found in dialectic a method of self-confirmation in knowledge.[1] Only by making a man party to both his own confutation and enlightenment was it possible to circumvent and eventually transform the intransigence of the ill-disposed soul. The end was achieved by soliciting a succession of inconspicuous, but momentous, agreements. The termination of discussion brought with it the inescapable obligation to comprehensive acknowledgment or irresponsible denial. Men were brought face to face with an option. Brought into the open by dialectic, it was forced and could no longer be eluded.

Given this background, we are better prepared to understand why Plato puzzled his interpreters by his strictures upon the written speech and the carefully composed treatise. The derogatory utterances are confined to the *Phaedrus,* to the *Seventh,* and to the *Second Epistle.*[2] A critique of written discourse is the dominating theme of the famous "philosophical digression" in the *Seventh Epistle.* C. Ritter and Paul Shorey, among modern scholars of stature, have declared against its authenticity. The majority of experts, however, who credit the genuineness of the *Seventh Epistle,* also accept the digression as integral and not as interpolative.[3] The digression contains Plato's striking assertion that there does not, nor ever will, exist a written speech dealing with his most important doctrines (341c). The philosophic digression follows this assertion and constitutes an explanation. At the end of this discussion, Plato's depreciation of the written treatise is reiterated with the statement that reasons have now been given why no man of "moral earnestness," who treats subjects of moment, commits them to writing. Rather, he allows them to abide "in the fairest region he possesses." This region, we may believe, cannot be other than mind or *nous* (344c).

The bulk of commentary upon this enigmatic contention has been both great and lively. In the nineteenth century, it gave rise to the hypothesis that the dialogues do not represent Plato's real thought and that he retained secret doctrines which were elucidated to a coterie of disciples in the Academy. These teachings constituted what Aristotle referred to as Plato's "unwritten discourses." The gratuity of such a theory was fittingly and effectively challenged by Grote long ago and is no longer reputable.[4] Nevertheless it is still important to press Plato for an explanation of this depreciation of written exposition as an avenue of either teaching or learning.

If our conception of the truly persuasive art is defensible, it should follow that Plato would abjure dogmatic or didactic instruction, either public or secret, as wholly incompetent to effect education and induce *epistêmê*. On this account, the written treatise would receive no more consideration than the same prompt dismissal accorded by Plato to the "set-speech" of the rhetorician. As a matter of fact, such a dismissal of the written word is not confined to the *Epistles* but is precisely what we find at the conclusion of the critique of rhetoric in the *Phaedrus*. Indeed, the entire third section of the *Phaedrus*, beginning at 257e, undertakes to discuss and appraise speech-making as prose composition, both oral and written. Plato begins with the observation that "the proudest of statesmen are most fond of writing and of leaving documents behind them" in order to perpetuate their names for wisdom. Rounding out the discussion, Plato states that no man earnest for the increase of knowledge will write in ink or sow his thoughts with written words (276c). He would be an utterly simple person who supposed that anything in writing would be clear or certain. Words, once written, preserve a solemn silence when questioned, or they keep on saying one and the same thing (275c). The written word contains, necessarily, much that is playful and never deserves to be treated very seriously. This applies to the recitations of modern "rhapsodes" delivered orally to sway men's minds (277e). Lysias, Homer, and Solon are to be gently but firmly informed that all prose compositions are, pedagogically, of trifling worth unless each writer can support his compositions by discussion, that is, by *elenchos* (278c).

For Plato truth is no dead word of the past, and no authority, however venerable, is a substitute for the "living and breathing word" which is sown by intelligent discourse (276a). In the first place, those who write treatises are controlled by the wrong incentives. Like the rhetoricians, they presume to possess the truth and seek only for likely ways of transmitting it to others. But, in addition, even if they possess wisdom their instruction is fruitless, for truth in high matters is not transmissible in such a way. Its content does not admit of transference and its proofs are of a different order.

Plato's second objection is that the didactic method either in written or in oral speech miscalculates the difficulties in the path of enlightenment and, therefore, entirely misconstrues the true method of persuasion. If the writer of treatises, like the orator, desires only to instill beliefs, the varied repertoire of "proofs," such as the rhetorician uses, will be good enough. If, on the other hand, knowledge requires learning what is true and false about "the whole of Being," as in the case of virtue and vice, then positive or didactic utterance falls beside the mark. Teaching and learning respecting Being encounter obstacles impervious to preceptual methods (*cf. Soph.* 230a f.). In the *Phaedrus*, the obstacle is the "inferior love" in the soul. In the *Republic*, it is a *sunêtheia* or "habituation" by which the soul is disinclined toward truth and reality. In the *Seventh Epistle*, it is an "alien state of mind," a corruption of *êthos*, and a want of "affinity" for the desired object of knowledge (*Epist.* VII, 343e-344a). In the *Sophist*, it is a morally reprobate mind which obstructs the influences of free and fair discussion (246d). Men of evil nurture do not so much as seek after knowledge of true Being (*Epist.* VII, 343c and *Soph.* 246b). Therefore there is little to be gained by haranguing them unless, in the process of interchange, they can be encouraged to alter their basic attitude toward the realities in question.

In consideration of these factors, *didachê*, teaching, whether by verbal harangue or by formal treatise, is impotent to secure knowledge of reality to refractory minds. This, incidentally, is part of the explanation Plato offers for his inability to make headway with instruction of Dionysius II and also for the latter's complete incapacity to give reliable account of the "knowledge" which formed the content of Plato's own doctrine. It was not that Dionysius lacked intellectual acuteness. Rather, by Plato's testimony, he was indisposed to undertake the rigors of preliminary and dialectical disciplines, and, in addition, he was unable to cleave to *philosophia* as that "daily mode of life" requisite to final enlightenment (*Epist.* VII, 340b-341a).

Consequently, in all such cases, the written word could scarcely be counted upon for real persuasiveness. It could easily be "reviled" by those who had no mind to its import or were devoid of the sort of goodwill indispensable for its appropriation. Moreover, the written word did not know to whom to speak and before whom to be silent when speech was useless (*Phaedr.* 275d-276a; *cf. Laws* 891a). In short, the dead word of the page was unfitted to cope with the obliquity of man's affective disinclinations toward truth—truth which the written word, nevertheless, might embody in some measure. But in whatever degree truth relating to ultimate reality proved susceptible to positive verbal expression, Plato affirmed that his own statement would be the best exposition of his particular doctrine (*Epist.* VII, 341d). There seems little reason to doubt that the famous passage on the Good in the *Republic* is one instance of such an attempt. Even here, language points only in the direction of a reality which intrudes itself upon the mind's sight as the reward of arduous discipline in sciences and dialectic.

A third ground for distrust of the written word may be reasonably attributed to Plato. It has to do with the nature of effective persuasion. The *Republic* has made us familiar with the need for a "conversion" of the entire soul in order to enable it to "endure the contemplation of essence and the brightest region of being." Those, however, who have suffered no such alteration of *êthos* are wont to ridicule the philosopher, whose larger purview they do not and cannot share (*Rep.* 517a, 518a). Hence, claims for a wider environment of the mind meet with easy refutation among those sharing only the perspective of the Cave. Plato refers to this situation in the *Seventh Epistle*. Men are content with the images of things, τὰ εἴδωλα; therefore, when the philosopher gives positive expression to his insight in speech or writing, he is easily confounded by those who, not participating in the stages of dialectical agreement, are not possessed of the series of steps by which the philosopher arrives at the summit of apprehension (343c-d).

Now Plato regularly asserts that dialectic aims at knowledge of the essence. But in regard to anything whatever, the knowledge-process embraces five factors, three of which are: the name, the definition, and the particular thing. In the fourth place, there is true opinion, knowledge, and intelligence. The object of each of these is essence, which is the "Fifth," or the reality-in-itself. Intelligence approaches most nearly in kinship to the "Fifth." Intellection is, of course, knowledge in the highest degree (*Epist.* VII, 342c-d). Although dialectic does not concern itself with the "particular," it may take note of the name and the definition. Its main occupation, however, is with the sphere of the "Fourth," and we cannot be far wrong in assuming that its function is to transform "true opinion" into knowledge or intellection. At this point, we may begin to see that didactic exposition, oral or written, encounters insurmountable obstacles.

In the first place, Plato says that knowledge of Being is brought to birth with greatest difficulty only on condition of long application to the subject and continual "living with it" (341c). Secondly, when knowledge comes, it dawns "suddenly" as a discovery; and, in default of this insight, nothing less can be a substitute (344b). Thirdly, related to the need for a right disposition of the mind toward truth, there is the fact that nothing but joint-inquiry—implemented by questions and admissions "devoid of envy"—can elicit, one after another, the acknowledgments that may issue in final "conviction" about the "Fifth," *i.e.*, reality-in-itself. But, if all of this is prerequisite to knowledge of Being, it is entirely understandable why Plato should look with misgivings upon the written treatise. In comparison with living dialectical intercourse, its resources were negligible, if not completely incompetent.

We are now prepared for a final observation about the nature of *elenchos*. Dialectic is the truly persuasive art, because it employs a form of verbal interchange which procures conviction in the minds of the participants. It builds upon agreements, but its instrument is the *elenchos*, by which error is divined and eliminated. The primary meaning of the verb ἐλέγχω seems to have been "put to shame." In Plato's usage the original meaning is retained, but discourse, or cross-questioning, becomes the instrument for inducing shame. If the *elenchos* "confutes," it does so by convicting of error through putting respondents to shame—shame over contradiction among their own confessed opinions. We have endeavored to show that the genius of dialectic lies in its power, first, to win acknowledgment of self-contradiction, then to procure consent to the "leading," not merely of the argument, but to deep-lying and obscured convictions. Thus, in the case of Polus and Gorgias, Socrates' fundamental aim was to arouse from slumber true opinions which each feigned to disavow but really believed (*Gorg.* 474b, 482b-c). His purpose was to exhume truth buried under rationalization so that men would acknowledge it, if for no other reason than "for very shame" (*Rep.* 501e; *Gorg.* 508b). Because the *elenchos* has the power of revealing a man's disagreement with himself, the method of dialectic alone is capable of inducing inner conditions favorable to the discrimination and acknowledgment of repressed but true opinions.

Because of the nature of double ignorance and in view of the power of the *elenchos*, nothing but dialectic is able to "constrain" a man to "decide for" or acknowledge the "Fifth," *i.e.*, true reality (*Epist.* VII, 343d). Quite apparently, this compulsion is, at the same time, both logical and moral. Because the highest knowledge, like the worst ignorance, involves the entire moral and intellectual nature, Plato was justified in declaring that such knowledge does not even get started if a man's morals (τὰ ἤθεα) are bad.

NOTES

1. See *Rep.* 533c for the use of βεβαίωσις, confirmation in knowledge through dialectic. *Cf. Phileb.* 14b-c.

2. *Phaedr.* 273d-278d; *Epist.* VII, 341b-345a; *Epist.* II, 314a-c.

3. G. C. Field's judicious and perceptive review of the problem of genuineness of the letters is surely among the most instructive and balanced of treatments. *Plato and His Contemporaries* (London, 1930), 197-201. J. Harward, *The Platonic Epistles* (Cambridge, 1932), 59-79, provides an excellent account and appraisal of the debate over the genuineness of the letters. Along with Field, Taylor, and Burnet, he credits the "digression" to Plato. Both Harward and R. S. Bluck (*Plato's Seventh and Eighth Epistles* [Cambridge, 1947], 181) provide convenient tabulation of prevailing scholarly opinion regarding the several letters. Under the weighty authority of E. Zeller and H. T. Karsten, German scholarship during the nineteenth century was negative toward all the letters. B. Jowett concurred, but at mid-century G. Grote strongly supported their authenticity against the German tendency. *Plato* (London, 1865), I, 220. Ritter's formidable opinion was favorable to the narrative portion of *Epist.* VII, but did not accredit the "philosophic digression." *Neue Untersuchungen Über Platon* (München, 1910), 329 f. Shorey, with customary incisiveness, was negative to the letters in general, with only moderate confidence accorded to VII. *What Plato Said* (Chicago, 1933), 40-50. For a useful review of French scholarly opinion, *cf.* A. Dies, *Autour de Platon* (Paris, 1927), 266-71. Glenn R. Morrow (*Studies in the Platonic Epistles* [Illinois Studies in Language and Literature, XVIII, 3-4, 1935], 47-60) is a recent and among the very best witnesses to the authenticity of *Epistle* VII. His fair and full attention to the most pertinent and long-standing objections to Platonic authorship, balanced by his masterful exhibition of the positive evidence, is impressive and convincing.

4. G. Grote, *Plato* (London, 1865), I, 226-231.

Index

Abstractionism, the method of, 118, 119, 218, 265

Academy, the, 100, 305

Acquired Opinion, 191, 192, 194, 196, 206, 207, 292

Actuality, the meaning of, 120, 276

Adam, James, 157, 181, 182

Affection, in relation to ignorance, xix, 60, 111, 112; its function in knowledge, 59, 147; transformation of, 144. See also *Pathêma*

Aidôs. See Reverence

Aisthêsis. See Sense perception

Aitias logismos. See Casual reasoning

Alcibiades, ambivalence of, 8, 20, 186, 194, 300; view of Socrates, 198; self-refutation of, 230; as self-convicted man, 235, 292; as man of indecision, 301

Allegory, 201

Amathia. See Ignorance

Analogia entis, 44, 257

Anamnêsis. See Recollection

Anatropê (anatropism), as inversion of reality, xxi, 12, 45, 269, 291; as distortion of human nature, 42, 47; definition of, 45-47, 63; as ontological inversion, 139, 146; as divided self-consciousness, 188

Anaxagoras of Clazomenae, 20, 22, 23, 153, 275

Anoia, as folly, 67

Anthropology. *See* Man

Antilogikê, as disputation, 225, 228

Antisthenes of Athens, 5

Aphrosunê, as folly, 46, 140, 146, 293

Apodeixis, as ideal of knowledge, 139, 142, 213; method of, 169, 218; of the sciences, 216; of mathematics, 216, 217; modes of, 217-19; the nature of, 246; as scientific knowledge, 262; its

impossibility in metaphysics, 275. *See also* Certainty; Truth

Aporia, as perplexity, 21, 50, 79, 82, 83, 85; its function in dialectic, 176

Appetite. See *Epithumia*

Appetitive faculty, nature of, 47, 61, 190; influence in relation to knowledge, 61, 63, 144, 148, 149, 159, 203, 298

Apuleius of Madaura, 73

Aquinas, Thomas, 284, 285, 302

Archê. See First Principles

Archer-Hind, R. D., 29

Aretê, nature of, 14, 36, 44, 293-95; Callaliclean view of, 47; according to Protagoras, 77, 78. *See also* Virtue

Aristeides of Athens, 35, 37, 79

Artistotle, on the nature of certainty, xvii, 212, 217-19; on philosophy, xviii, 286; on Socrates, 17, 53; on the will, 75; on classification, 117, 121; on abstractionism, 118; empiricism of, 121, 138; on the priority of the universal, 124, 138, 156; conceptualism of, 132, 157; on the active intellect, 138; on restriction of the *a priori*, 138, 139; on disinterested reason, 139; on induction, 139, 218, 263, 280; ideal of knowledge, 139, 142, 213; *êthos* irrelevant to truth, 139, 219; definition of scientific knowledge, 143, 212, 218, 219; on mathematics, 155, 183; on syllogism, 171, 213, 278; his qualitative view of bodies, 181; on Plato's derivation of number, 182; attitude toward *elenchos*, 218, 219, 235; logic of, 218; metaphysics as scientific knowledge, 220; on verification, 238; on demonstrative knowledge, 246, 262; the *epistêmonikon*, 247; on theoretical reason, 247; on decisional knowledge, 253; his preference for certainty, 262; the reduction of empirical science to logic, 267; error of Aristotelian science, 267; on deduction, 278; on wisdom, 284, 286; on immortality, 285

Arithmetikê, 164, 166

Aspiration, of the mind, 43, 67, 109, 149, 184, 195, 271, 291, 294. See also *Hormê; Himeros*

Association, the principle of, 55, 108

Astronomikê, 163, 168, 183, 256, 279

Atheism, 72

Augustine of Hippo, 52-55, 62, 73, 296, 301

Auxiliaries, 7, 283

Aviary, the parable of, 84, 125, 126, 127

Axiology: the axiological determination of the mind, 16, 23, 24, 25, 43, 64, 139, 275, 288; precedence of the axiological problem, 55; the primacy of axiological awareness, 55, 68, 86, 273, 279; in respect to the Good, 153, 159, 160, 179, 204. See also *Theia mania; Nous*

Bacon, Francis, idols of, 56; the place of mathematics in science, 181; the aim of natural philosophy, 255; conception of utility, 255; rejection of Aristotelian logic, 264; preference for certainty, 265; nature of certainty, 265; experimental method of, 265; utility the criterion of truth, 265; reduction of philosophy to science, 265; his first principle as decisional, 266; first principle of, 266; identification of wisdom and science, 266; Plato's probable refutation, 268, 275; his conception of wisdom, 286

Barker, Ernest, 6, 29

Beare, John I., 158

Beauty, its function in knowledge, 209, 210

Becoming, the nature of, 15, 25, 32, 46, 90, 106; as possessed of real being, 49, 116, 117; knowledge suitable to, 106, 110; as intermediate being, 114, 116, 137, 245, 276; as the class of the mixed, 120, 155, 201, 277. *See also* Intermediate being

Being, as ever-abiding, 46, 106; as embracing Becoming, 49, 116, 278; as most real being, 56, 58, 106, 114;

296; the knowledge of most real being, 71; accessibility of, 81; Parmenidean view of, 114. *See also* Ideas; Forms

Being, the scale of, 106, 242, 244, 245, 277

Belongings of the mind, 13, 81, 192

Blindness of the mind, 143, 145, 146, 150, 159, 186, 233

Body, as tomb of the soul, 19, 60; as obstruction to knowledge, 55, 58, 60, 146, 147, 157; nature of bodies in general, 279-80

Boulêsis, primary meaning of, 66-67. *See also* Volition; Freedom

Burnet, John, 14, 17, 23, 88, 157, 160, 170, 309

Callicles, 12, 33, 34, 35, 45, 47, 48, 84; defines goodness as power, 33; anatropism of, 47, 185, 291; his resistence to enlightenment, 150, 232; split self-consciousness of, 183, 194, 229, 236; as apostle of discord in the soul, 186; as actual man, 206; dispraise of philosophy, 227; evasiveness of, 229, 239

Causality, mechanical, 22, 275; teleological, 22-23, 275, 281; of the Good, 23, 244, 276; real, 146; of the Ideas, 152, 277; of the soul, 277. *See also* Good

Causal reasoning, 94, 95, 102-3, 110

Cave, the, 44; knowledge characteristic of, 45, 61, 65, 111, 140, 144, 145, 146, 290, 307; as the predicament of man, 47; symbol of *anatropê*, 47, 140, 148; the way of egress from, 140, 143, 150, 167

Certainty, of self-evidence, 179; modes of, 217-19, 269; superior certainty of dialectic, 261; the preference for, 261, 264. See also *Methodos*

Chalcidius, 54, 73

Character, 53. See also *Êthos*

Choice, relation to intelligibility, 23; the most fundamental, 186, 261; definition of, 205; as ground of hypotheses, 249; involved in knowledge, 253

Christian thought, 52, 285, 301, 302

Cicero, 54, 73

Civilization, xvi, 34, 189

Classification. *See* Sciences

Color, theory of, 151, 159

Composition, method of, 115, 173, 174. See also *Sunagogê*

Conceptualism, 115, 116, 119, 132

Conformity, primordial the: of mind with reality, xix, 42, 43, 44, 50, 57, 58, 81, 83, 87, 147, 202; as virtue, 44, 57; as wisdom, 282. *See also* Epistemology

Conscience. See *Suneidêsis*

Contradictory conception, 39, 182

Contrariety, in the soul, 185-88, 207, 208, 229, 275; crisis in, 194, 235, 292, 300; resolution of, 294. *See also* Soul; Shame

Conversion, as therapy of soul, xxi, 147; discussion of, 147-50, 157, 158; the method of, 150; the means of, 161-80; as basic to education, 161, 298, 307. See also *Metastrophê*

Cornford, F. M., 49, 100, 115, 119, 121

Correlation, of knowing and being, 106, 114, 115, 116

Cosmology, discussion of, 22; causality of the good in, 25, 72, 276; knowledge suitable to, 276; of the *Timaeus*, 276, 279

Cosmos, nature of, 72, 145, 153, 201, 244, 275, 277

Criticism, place of, 15, 19, 129; rationalistic, 40; of tradition, 197, 199

Cynicism, 23, 35

Daedalus, images of, 94, 102

Daimones, 193

Daimonion, 24, 97, 193, 207

Damphier-Whetham, W.C.D., 181

Dante, 4

Death, 3, 13, 55, 56, 58

Deduction, subordination to dialectic, 167; nature of, 170, 171, 174, 219, 237; irrelevance of, 215; relation to induction, 218, 277. *See also* Dialectic

Deficiency, conception of, 55, 74, 108, 112, 164; of self-evidence, 178

Deiformity, of man, 43, 96

DeLacy, Phillip H., 277

Delphic Oracle, 197, 198, 272

Democracy, import of, 34, 35, 48

Descartes, René, 163, 286, 287

Dewey, John, 50

Diagrammata, 88

Diairêsis, 115. *See also* Division

Diakrisis, 118. *See also* Division

Diakritikê, 119, 121, 172-73, 240. *See also* Dialectic

Dialectic, its relation to dialogue, xvii; as inquiry, xviii, 226; nature of, xviii, 8, 82, 103, 116, 214, 236; the function of, xix, 8, 83, 84, 96, 109, 112, 231, 232; the distinctive data of, xx, 168, 214; as joint-inquiry, 82, 88, 91, 228, 231, 308; as self-instruction, 88, 230-32, 299, 300; the misuse of, 96; as *diakritikê*, 117; as instrument of conversion, 148, 149, 167, 298; the limitations of, 150, 299, 300, 301; the preamble to, 162; the power of, 166-77, 214; value for philosophy, 167; relation to sense experience, 167, 168, 308; the aim of, 169, 177, 216, 288; as ascent to a first principle, 170, 171, 175, 278; as subordinated to rhetoric, 192; Aristotle's transformation of, 218, 236, 238; Aristotle's objections to, 219. *See also* Division; *Elenchos*

Dialogues, purpose of, xvii, 6, 8, 100, 251; depreciation of, 305

Dianoia. *See* Understanding

Dichotomy, method of, 172, 174, 183

Didachê, conception of, 78, 80, 306

Didactic instruction, Plato's avoidance of, 6, 79, 286; the weakness of, 143, 305, 306

Diogenes of Sinope, 12

Dionysius of Syracuse, 181, 306

Dissos Logos, doctrine of, 39, 49

Divided Line, 106, 157, 175, 212

Divine summons, 23, 24, 275

Division, method of, 115, 117, 118, 172-75; first employment of, 116, 172; Plato's use of, 116, 277; as instrument of classificatory science, 118; as empirical discrimination, 118, 119, 183; of doubtful things, 173, 184, 232; its employment of paradigms, 174, 184

Dogmata, value of, 101

Doxa. *See* Opinion

Doxa alêthês. *See* True Opinion

Doxa, critical, 116, 119, 120, 127, 276

Doxa pseudês, definition of, 111, 243. *See also* False Opinion

Dreaming, condition of soul, 22, 44, 45, 84, 95, 98, 102, 113, 184, 211, 290. *See also* Waking life

Dualism, in anthropology, 19, 61; epistemological, 39, 117, 122
Dunamis, as faculty, 17, 42, 46, 146, 203

Earp, F. R., 13
Education, the problem of, xxi, 32, 47, 135, 144, 211-17, 220; the nature of, xxi, 140, 161; not conveyance, 136; as conversion, 147, 157, 161; conception of in the *Laws*, 157, 158, 162; need of self-knowledge, 186; dependence upon eros, 187, 298; requisite habituation for, 215, 150-55; sufficiency of, 297. See also *Paideia*
Education, nature of, 215, 232, 253. See also *Elenchos*
Effluences, 159
Eidôla, as image, 110, 131, 140, 162, 307
Eidos. See Forms; Ideas; Being
Elenchos, genius of, xviii, 231; as instrument of metaphysics, xviii, 121, 214, 219, 233, 236; the nature of, 8, 82, 83, 88, 171, 214, 308; the Socratic, 82, 171; as clarification, 171, 230; the data of, 171-77, 179, 232, 278; as distinguished from division, 172-75, 277; as purification, 173; as not demonstrative, 214, 219, 300; as eduction, 215, 232; as self-convincement, 216, 229, 233, 236, 299, 330; its likeness to rhetoric, 221; as the irenic art, 228, 230, 308; as self-instruction, 231-35, 299. See also Dialectic
Empedocles, epistemological principle of, 50, 158, 159
Empeiria, nature of, 135, 136, 138, 155; need in statecraft, 136, 155, 290; defined, 182
Empiricism, of the *Theaetetus*, 114; method of, 118, 121; Plato's attitude toward, 126, 128
Epiktêtos doxa. See Acquired Opinion
Epistêmê, as true knowledge, 35, 78, 86, 87, 114, 117, 181, 295; the criterion of, 93; difficulties of attainment, 212-17; as non-demonstrable, 212, 213, 246; the influence of volition upon, 213, 248, 298; as acknowledgment, 214, 298; as personal insight, 216, 300, 308. See also Knowledge

Epistemology, of Protagoras, 38-41; monistic types, 40, 60; epistemic conformity, 42, 81, 87; of Plato, 49, 106; basic principles of, 58, 83, 86, 87, 139, 154, 296; critical monism in, 156; love necessary to epistemological conformity, 195. See also Conformity; Knowledge
Epithumêtikon. See Appetitive faculty
Epithumia, role in knowledge, xxi, 59, 60, 61, 64; as desire, 55, 60, 61, 65, 66, 191, 203; contribution to ignorance, 55, 59-62, 67, 146
Eristikê, as disputation, 222
Eros, the inferior kind, xxi, 64, 226, 292, 294, 298; the superior kind, 15, 64, 66, 113, 197-205, 226, 271; function in cognition, 59-68, 112-13, 195, 292, 293; kinds of, 66, 186, 191, 200, 292; emancipation of superior kind, 149, 294; the pristine eros, 187, 195; popular disrepute of, 189-91; generic definition of, 190; as spirit, 193; as mediatorial, 193-96; power of, 194; as offspring, 195; a sign of deficiency, 195; as mediate between ignorance and wisdom, 195; as lure of the Good, 206; continuity with physical attraction, 208; as requisite for wisdom, 294. See also Love
Error, as misidentification of reality, 43, 71, 111-14, 122, 124; as voluntary-involuntary, 63-68, 96, 185; ontological, 140-41. See also False opinion
Eryximachus, doctrine of, 193, 195
Essence, as cognitive object, 86, 115 143, 151, 167, 172, 176, 244; knowledge of, 307-8
Essential being, 55, 84, 109, 114, 137, 186, 289
Ethics: the moral consciousness, 22-25, 274, 280; basis of moral obligation, 24, 274-75; and metaphysics, 251, 275; moral being, 297; knowledge and morality, 309
Êthos, as disposition of soul, xix, 149, 150, 158; the prevailing kind, 36, 37, 162; as decisive for knowledge, 53, 55, 243, 298, 299; its role in ignorance, 53, 59-62, 149; a definition of, 149, 158; as habit of the Good, 154; the revolution of, 177, 189, 199, 243, 271, 291. See also Character
Euclid, 169

Euclides of Megara, 5
Eudiamonia, as well-being: the Socratic view, 10, 11, 20, 274; nature of, 31; false notion of, 37. *See also* Happiness
Eunoia. See Goodwill
Evenus, 13
Evil, in the soul, 62, 202, 292. *See also* Contrariety
Eye, of the soul, 146, 147, 157, 170, 177, 216

Faculty, of the soul. See *Dunamis*
False Opinion, as morally censurable, 62-68, 293; nature of, 111, 114, 143; discussion of, 113-15, 122-29; as interchanged opinion, 123; as misidentification, 125, 156; as not the starting-point of knowledge, 176, 196; difference from *doxa,* 243; as deformity, 292; as greatest ignorance, 293. See also *Doxa pseudês*
Field, G. C., 27, 309
First premises, conditional truth of, 257; as decisional in nature, 259, 260, 261, 262. *See also* Hypothesis
First principles, without supposition, xix, 170, 176, 259; the true first principle, 24, 177-80, 259; of thought, 24; as ultimate reality, 33, 117; as aim of dialectic, 117, 120, 167; of the sciences, 212, 218; decisive in cognition, 248; purposive basis of, 249, 273; ignored by Bacon, 265
Flux theory, 25, 39, 41, 49, 56
Forgetfulness, 43, 61, 66, 81, 91
Forms, Socratic view of, 14, 23; rationale of, 32; as prepossessions, 43, 81, 86, 90, 91, 128; as recollected, 55, 81; participation in, 109, 110, 111, 151; as ingredient in particulars, 113, 137, 181; relation to particulars, 116, 158; function in cognition, 127, 137, 156; relation to the Good, 152-54; the theory of, 244, 277. *See also* Being; Ideas
Frame of meaning, the material component of, 255, 256, 257, 279, 280; the formal component of, 256
Frank, Erich, 66, 75
Freedom, nature of, 47, 51, 205; of free will, 66, 75; as emancipation, 69, 149, 166; for virtue, 199; of choice, 205; in knowledge, 219, 220. See also *Boulêsis;* Volition
Freeman, Kathleen, 28, 49
Friendship, the basis of, 193, 194, 199, 200, 204, 295; true friend, 200

Genus, 120, 152, 173, 174
Geometry, 169, 178, 280
Gnôsis, 91, 106, 137. See also *Epistêmê*
God (*theos*), the Socratic view of, 11, 15, 16, 53, 54, 56; Plato on, 23, 58, 73; and the Good, 160, 276, 277, 281; Aristotle's, 285
Good, the Idea of: relation to *nous,* 17, 22, 23, 33, 43; Socratic view of, 23, 275; metaphysic of 29, 32, 177, 178; defined as power, 33; dislocation of, 43; nature of, 43, 44, 154, 275, 282, 295; as norm, 69, 70, 84, 152, 272, 274; notices of, 97, 274; true opinion of, 103; discussion of, 150-55, 159; as final cause, 152, 153, 194, 283; primacy of, 160, 179, 249, 297; self-evidence of, 178-80, 216, 217, 237, 259; as ultimate premise, 215; function in knowledge, 249, 254; as ultimate preference, 250; relation to self-knowledge, 274. *See also* Causality
Good, the habit of, 154. See *Hexis*
Good, the moral, 24, 275
Goodwill (*eunoia*), nature of, xx, 74, 199, 208; function of, 94, 239; in truth seeking, 226-28; need of, 235, 307
Gorgias of Leontini, 35, 36, 222, 226, 308
Grote, George, 305, 309
Grube, G. M. A., 59, 150, 158
Guardians, 7, 48, 88; true rulership of, 33, 200; knowledge of, 104, 282, 289; need of experience, 136, 155, 290; qualifications of, 289; wisdom of, 289-90

Habituation, need of alteration, 67; wrong kind, 140, 144, 149, 306; its role in ignorance, 149; nature of, 149; new kind, 153, 199, 204, 215, 271; breakup of wrong kind, 204-5, 227, 294; its role in knowledge, 212, 215
Hackforth, R., 206, 220, 238
Happiness, in relation to virtue, 10, 196; greatest, 189. See also *Eudaimonia*

Harmonia, of soul, 10, 44, 186, 293, 294, 300

Harward, J., 309

Hegel, G. W., xv, 30

Heidel, William A., 28

Heracleitus, 17, 25, 39, 60

Hexis, inferior kind, 146, 150; relation to ignorance, 146; habit of the good, 150-55, 271, 279, 295; general nature of, 157, 160; new kind, 199. *See also* Habituation

Hiedel, F., 29

Himeros, 184, 188, 206. *See also* Aspiration

Hippias of Elis, 37, 60, 289

Hobbes, Thomas, xvi

Homer, 7, 17, 305

Homologia (acknowledgment), role in dialectic, xviii, 214; as confession of, 25, 300, 301; as not enforceable, 215, 219, 298, 300; role in metaphysics, 220, 231; role in joint-inquiry, 229; cumulative result of, 230, 239; progressive movement of, 231-35, 308; nature of, 234-35, 251. *See also* Irenic art; Knowledge

Hormê, pristine impulse, 64, 188, 194, 196, 201, 294; as aspiration of the mind, 149, 247, 271; as impulse of dialectic, 180, 279; ground of, 202; the basis of, 202. *See also* Aspiration

Hubris, 48, 75, 191, 272

Human bondage, nature of, 47, 60, 61, 74, 140-47, 156; of the mind, 147

Humanism, Socratic-Platonic, xx, 42; Protogorean, 42, 271

Hypothesis, as starting-point of knowledge, 169, 171, 176, 178, 274; as arbitrary, 169, 170, 174, 178, 218, 280; the destruction of, 170, 177, 179; those of *elenchos*, 171, 177, 179; the self-evidence of, 175-80, 257; as of limited denotation, 178, 258, 259, 260; the purposive nature of, 178, 249, 256-61, 273; the adequacy of, 249, 258; fruitfulness of in dialectic, 251; the validity of, 258; the decisional nature of, 259, 260, 263. *See also* Knowledge

Ideas, as ideal structure, xvi, xix, 111, 117, 159, 245, 272, 278; transcendence-immanence of, xvi, 246; the function of, 23, 25; as self-identical,

107, 115, 119, 120, 132, 136, 137, 264; as mingling with particulars, 109, 110, 116. *See also* Forms; Being

Identity, role in cognition, 90, 285; principle of, 164, 264

Ignorance, cause of, xxi, 59-62, 68-69, 113, 128, 162; double ignorance, 46, 51, 59, 63, 67, 71, 111, 129, 149; as involuntary, 46, 62, 63, 72; as morally censurable, 46, 53, 67, 68, 144, 148, 279, 292; as folly, 46, 62-68, 140; as *pathêma* of the soul, 60, 65; as voluntary, 63-68; the kinds of, 63, 68, 70; simple ignorance, 63, 297; as vice in the soul, 67, 73; as unrighteousness, 68; greatest form of, 161, 291; as opposite of wisdom, 291; the definition of, 297

Immoralism, 36, 295

Immortality, 28, 56, 59, 91, 98, 99, 285

Impiety, 15, 18, 72, 76

Indefinite plurality, the principle of, 164, 280

Individualism, 34, 35, 41, 48

Induction, the method of, 215, 218, 236, 278

Intellectual intuition, the nature of, 14, 81, 97, 119, 212; as outcome of dialectic, 214; object of, 217, 243, 282, 290

Intelligence. See *Nous*

Intelligibility, norm of, 179, 180, 259, 272-76

Intelligible world, structure of, 136-37, 159; condition of, 156, 219, 275; ultimate intelligibility of, 179-80, 275; deficiently, 283

Intermediate being, 114, 137. *See also* Becoming

Involuntary lie, 46, 72, 161, 293, 298

Ionian physicists, 16, 28, 271, 272

Irenic art, 220, 227, 228, 230, 231, 233-36

Irrationality, of soul, 47, 157, 191, 292; faculty of, 149

Jaeger, Werner, 14, 15, 26, 144, 157

James, William, 4

Joint-inquiry. See Dialectic

Judgment, divine, 19, 28; cognitive, 45, 70; nature of, 107, 112, 157; ontological, 243; practical, 247

Justice, character of, 9, 11, 12, 13, 32,

34, 282; defined as power, 33, 185; as contrary to nature, 35; abstract, 109

Kant, Immanuel, xv, xvi, 90, 99, 243, 244, 247
Katharmos, 173, 184. See also *Katharsis*
Katharsis, function of, 18, 20, 55-59; as condition of knowledge, 54, 56; as related to conversion, 161. *See also* Purification
Kinship, of the soul, 4, 18, 43, 64, 96. See also *Suggeneia*
Koinônia, 14, 58, 60, 81, 120, 194, 288
Knowledge, as apodictic, xviii, 216, 218, 242, 246, 247; as event, xix. 40, 147, 148, 150, 151, 154, 180, 212, 260; as related to character, xix, 59, 154, 216, 299; as regulated by interest, xxi, 59, 112, 146, 149, 258; as personal discovery, 7, 45, 87, 88, 93, 98, 212, 213, 308; as incomplete, 56, 60; obstructions to, 60-62, 68, 69, 83, 143, 166, 279; subjectivity in, 72, 270; that makes for virtue, 78, 81, 87, 90; as non-transmissible, 80; as conformity, 81; as recognition, 87, 90, 124, 148; as direct acquaintance, 93, 212; as vision, 93, 142, 217; as empirical, 115, 116, 119, 120, 136, 174, 182, 183, 268; through dialectic, 117, 308; through conversion, 135, 298; as progressive, 157, 231, 252; as self-agreement, 160, 300; as friendship, 195; as non-demonstrable, 212-17; 219, 220, 300; as hypothetical, 216, 218; as self-convincement, 236; objectivity in, 247; specious, 261; as acknowledgment, 261, 274, 275, 288, 296. See also *Epistêmê*
Knowledge, as *a priori*: in Plato's thought, 64, 84, 86, 90, 95, 97, 98, 103, 116, 128, 142; Aristotle's rejection of, 138, 139; as mathematical, 164
Knowledge, as decision: in Plato's thought, 235, 236, 248, 252, 254, 271, 300; Aristotle's denial of, 246; in reference to the Good, 250; regarding first principles, 254, 259, 297; as personal dicision, 261, 274, 299, 309; Plato's preference for, 271

Law. See *Nomos*

Laws, of thought, 139, 156, 164, 218, 263; of nature, 268
Light, analogy of, 151, 158
Limit, the, 120, 132, 155, 159, 256, 277
Livingstone, R. W., 6, 8, 15, 26
Logistikon, 47, 186, 203, 247, 289.
Logos, as form, 23, 25, 40, 119, 120, 167; as proposition, 107, 119; as account, 109, 110, 230; as universal concept, 115, 116, 118; the concept of, 118, 119, 120, 127, 133, 233; as *mia idea*, 118, 119, 120, 130; as mathematical, 164, 166
Love, as volition, 66, 75, 186, 187, 260; as liberal or generous, 199, 204, 226, 238, 239. *See also* Eros
Lysias, speech of, 190, 226, 228

Maier, Heinrich, 5, 26
Maieutic art, 20, 194, 232
Man, kinship with reality, xvi, 4, 18, 42, 136, 180; actual and essential, xxi, 37, 41, 42, 180, 185, 186, 187, 276; the plight and misery of, xxii, 47; deiformity of, 4, 43, 44, 96, 136; integral, 10, 293-95; responsibility of, 16, 17, 24, 26, 42, 97; affords access to reality, 23, 42, 44, 84, 242; axiological consciousness of, 23-25, 142; end of, 24, 57, 58, 291; as measure, 43; first habitation of, 145; darkness of, 146; as microcosm, 157, 180, 245, 270, 272, 295; ambivalence of, 186; as self-inferior, 187. *See also* Axiology; Contrariety
Mania, as madness of love, 199; two kinds, 66, 67, 200. See also *Theia mania*
Maritain, J., 284
Materialism, 39, 71, 72
Mathematikê, principles of, 120, 125, 126, 164, 182; as applied, 120, 133, 182; as *a priori*, 133, 163; Aristotle's view of, 155, 183; function of, 163; in physical theory, 181, 276; certainty of, 216, 217; as portion of the Good, 281
Matter, so-called Pythagorean, 39, 40, 49; as material principle, 116, 151, 159, 163, 181, 276, 279, 280; as continuum, 183, 280
Meaning, privileged category of, 273-75
Mechanism, of vision, 151, 154, 159

Memory, 115, 119, 124, 128, 131, 133

Metaphysical knowledge, nature of, 219-20; reduction to science, 220; conscientious nature of, 220, 271; false conception of, 247; foundations of, 249, 272-73; as not theoretical, 297

Metaphysics, the data of, xx, 129, 232, 244, 272, 274; the starting point of, 4, 129, 272, 273; of the Good, 32, 34; Plato's alleged abandonment of, 115, 116, 117, 119; the place of, 117; dependence upon *êthos*, 243; the province of, 244; atrophy of, 296

Metastrophê, 147-50, 158. *See also* Conversion

Methodos, empirical, 118; classificatory, 118, 120; diacritical, 119, 173; dialectical, 167; demonstrative, 169, 213; experimental, 181; Socratic, 214; eductive, 215; inductive, 215, 218; Aristotelian, 218-19; irenic, 228

Metron anthropos, doctrine of, 38, 41, 43, 49. *See also* Sophists

Mia idea. See *Logos*

Milhaud, G., 206

Mixed Class, 120, 132. *See also* Becoming

Mnêmê. See Memory

Monism, 40, 50, 117, 120, 130, 156

Monotheism, 54

Mores, prevailing, 13, 34, 37, 48; truth-value of, 101, 112, 129

Morrow, Glen R., 309

Multitude, of citizenry, 19, 33, 37; ignorance of, 42, 43, 60, 88, 130; resistance to enlightenment, 42, 162; in the soul, 47, 68, 146, 223, 292

Murphy, N. R., 107, 108

Mystery religions, 19, 57, 74

Mythology, of Dionysos Zagreus, 18; nature of, 20, 73, 201; Promethean, 41, 95, 97, 136; *Phaedrus* myth, 58, 84, 200-5; Orphic, 60, 74

Natorp, Paul, 117

Nelson, Leonard, 7, 214

Nescience, as correlated with Not-Being, 106

Nilsson, M. P., 28

Noësis. See Intellectual intuition

Noëtic union, 137; as species of *philia*, 195

Nomos, 34, 44, 49, 129, 162, 181

Not-Being, conception of, 116, 132, 245; as material principle, 151, 245, 279

Noumenon, 91, 99, 100

Nous, as divine intelligence, 15, 22, 23, 28, 33, 145, 153, 281; nature of, 17, 20, 23-26, 148; as seat of rational life, 17, 20, 41, 147; as axiologically determined, 22-23, 53, 54, 64, 139, 153, 159, 273; kinship with reality, 42-43, 105, 307; reality accessible to, 42, 86, 100, 143, 147; conformity to Being, 43, 130, 145, 148; as corrupted, 58, 67, 70, 72; as purified, 58; objective referents of, 107, 148, 149, 153, 180; disorientation of, 144, 146-49, 237; as redirected, 148-50; as not impotent, 149; as instinct with eros, 187, 213. *See also* Axiology

Nous and the Good, mutual correlation of, 23, 179, 205, 275; separation of, 33; symmetrical relation of, 153, 159, 160; tendency to unite, 160, 245

Number, whole, 120; theory of, 120, 164; ontological status of, 164, 277; pure, 164, 166, 182, 280; derivation of, 182; as measures of motion, 279

One-and-Many, 110, 120, 130, 176, 294

Ontology, mechanistic, 25, 26, 275; Plato's, 25, 114, 137, 155, 272; dependency of, 55, 71, 250; Sophistic, 114, 122; Plato's later, 116, 244, 245; main objective of Plato's later ontology, 116, 137; basis of ontological knowledge, 242, 260, 272, 279. *See also* Being; Forms; Ideas

Opinion, influenced by desire, 61, 65; objects of, 90, 114, 149, 157; nature of, 103, 109-11, 129; ideal content of, 110, 112; definition of, 111, 117; as minimum cognition, 114, 127, 129; instability of, 118, 153. *See also* Acquired Opinion; False Opinion; True Opinion

Organon of knowledge, 43, 44, 61, 135, 143, 147, 150, 253, 296

Orphism, 18, 19, 57, 60, 161, 177

Orthê doxa, 89, 92, 101, 196

Orthodoxy, 15, 19

Orthos logos, 88, 89, 99

Paideia, Plato's, 4, 31, 42, 54, 62, 69, 86; as true politics, 31, 81; popular,

104; impediments to, 212, 298; according to the *Laws*, 303. *See also* Education

Paideusis, as scheme of education, 4, 32, 212, 224

Paradeigmata, as forms, 33, 43, 44, 278, 282; as general conceptions, 174, 184, 276, 290

Parmenides, refutation of, 114, 122, 130; error of, 120

Particulars, as objects of *doxa*, 55, 109, 117, 151, 158; deficiency of, 55, 108, 112, 137; equivocation of, 94, 165, 166, 182; ontal status of, 117, 276

Pathêma, in relation to cognition, xix, 60, 65, 112, 243. *See also* Affection

Pathêmata, 60

Pedagogue, true, 24, 82, 83, 85, 87, 227

Perception. *See* Sense perception

Periagogê, 147-50, 158. *See also* Conversion

Pericles, 31, 35, 48, 80

Persuasion, subordination of inquiry to, 36, 37; true art of, 72, 305. *See also* Rhetoric

Phantasia, 111. See also *Sensum*

Phantasma, 40

Phenomenalism, xxi, 38, 39, 45, 49, 111, 112, 141; Plato's final answer to, 275

Philia. *See* Friendship

Philodoxia, 46, 111, 112

Philosopher, the nature of, xx, 55-59, 112, 187, 227, 239, 290, 291; as statesman, 31, 290; rarity of, 43, 162; need of experience, 135, 136, 290; self-agreement of, 188; as true friend, 200, 209, 227; as true rhetorician, 227

Philosophia, nature of, xv, xxi, 11, 53-54, 219, 239; beginning point of, xvi, xx, 242, 259; the denaturing of, xvi, 167, 265, 286; function of, xix, 30; as salvation, xxi, 45; as purification, 56; as conversion, 144; impossibility for multitude, 162; chief instrument of, 167, 219; as daily mode of life, 306

Phronêsis, 67. *See also* Wisdom

Phusis, investgation of, 16, 17, 21, 22, 40, 53; ultimate, 54, 72, 288

Piety, 34, 35, 202, 209

Plato, the interpretation of, xv, xvii, 30, 53, 242, 243; influence of Socrates upon, 3, 5, 6, 274; tentative pessimism

of, 3, 4, 7; his estimate of Socrates, 6, 7-9, 162, 196, 197, 198, 296; his deviation from Socrates, 25; his main purpose, 30; basic principles of, 159, 213, 272, 296; the ultimate faith of, 180

Pleasure, 9, 31, 57, 61-65, 104, 146, 292

Pleonexia, 34, 48, 85, 181

Politicians, 31, 33, 37, 48

Politics, state of, 3, 4, 30-32; true aim of, 31, 81, 295

Politikê technê, 78

Polus, 29, 34, 296, 300

Polymathy, 69, 70, 289, 297

Positivism, xvi, 49, 141, 268

Power, in the state, xxii, 33, 48, 51; corruption of, 181, 225; true power, 185, 296

Preference, sovereign kind of, xxi, 215, 250, 269, 271, 274, 288, 297; relation to ontology, 65, 72; as volition, 67

Pre-Socratic thought, 16, 17, 271, 272, 288

Propaedeutic studies, 69, 162-66, 306

Protagoras of Abdera, as teacher, 36, 78; anthropology of, 38; similarity with Plato, 38; phenomenalism of, 38, 40, 114, 115; modern parallels to, 40; methodological agnosticism of, 40; error of, 120; uncritical subjectivism of, 272

Prôton philon, 175, 176

Protreptic, of Socrates, 20, 194, 195, 201, 292

Psuchagogy, 20, 224, 234. *See also* Irenic art

Psuchê, Socratic views of, 12-16, 17, 20, 24, 274, 275; Orphic view of, 18, 19. *See also* Soul

Psychology, tripartite, 46, 47, 51, 61; functional dualism in, 47, 64, 75; alteration of Socratic, 146

Purification, as means of knowledge, 18, 54, 56, 58, 71, 148, 154; relation to conversion, 148; instrument of, 173-74. See also *Katharsis*

Pythagoreanism, so-called, 18, 161

Rationalization, 9, 13, 309

Reade, W. H. V., 73

Reason, as discursive, 15, 119, 178; impediments to, 60, 248; object of, 131; value-indifferent, 139, 248

Reason, practical, xvi, 70, 220, 247; theoretical, xix, 70, 139, 187, 220, 247, 297; inseparability of from theoretical, 247
Receptacle, 116, 181, 256, 279
Recollection, its nature as learning, 55, 57, 81, 91, 95, 108, 118, 281; as reclamation, 81; relation to true opinion, 108; alleged abandonment of, 121; failure of, 128; excursus on, 133; literal meaning, 137, 148
Religion, 34, 40, 48
Reverence, 20, 95, 96, 100, 202, 208
Rhetoric, characterization of, 221-24; as flattery, 31, 223; as persuasion, 221, 223; Plato's attack upon, 36; defects of, 36-37, 232; as disputation, 192, 222, 305; revised view of, 220. See also Persuasion
Rhetoric, true: incentives of, 225; means of persuasion, 227; kindly proofs of, 227, 308; its use of division, 228; nature of, 234-36, 305, 308. See also Irenic art
Rhetorician, 226, 230
Ring of Gyges, the, 32
Ritter, Constantine, 152, 160, 309
Robin, Léon, 280
Robinson, R., 240
Rogers, A. K., 14, 26
Ross, W. D., 157, 159

Schiller, F. C. S., 40, 49
Schleiermacher, F., 303
Sciences, use of classification in, 117, 121, 127, 132; classificatory, 118, 121; applied, 168, 256, 264; utility of, 264; as power, 264
Sciences, the pure: the uses of, 69, 168, 255; the value of, 70, 163, 254; nature of, 121, 163, 168, 255; the defect of, 170, 289; deduction in, 174; the hypotheses of, 178, 218, 257, 258; Plato's subordination of, 179, 275; the hypothetical and demonstrative truth of, 216, 218; as scientific knowledge, 219; the archai of, 238
Scientific faculty, of Aristotle, 242
Self-advantage, true, 12, 36, 85, 204
Self-agreement, 10, 160, 188, 300
Self-deception, 46, 62, 63, 65, 67, 140, 148, 185
Self-disagreement, in the soul, 161, 186, 197, 293; as the Calliclean split self-consciousness, 188, 194-299

Self-ignorance, 47
Self-imprisonment, 148
Self-inferiority, 186
Self-injury, 12
Self-instruction. See Elenchos
Self-interest, 9, 34, 47, 82, 190, 199, 204
Self-knowledge, the requirement of, xx, 21, 160, 274; the content of, 22-24, 272, 273; value of, 186, 272, 275; as wisdom, 283, 287
Self-mastery, 10, 294, 295, 296
Self-transcendence, 24
Sense-bound, man as, 42, 46, 57, 62
Sense perception, as source of knowledge, 39, 111, 114, 136, 143; function of, 46, 106; instrumental value of, 55, 114, 168, 183; relation to doxa, 109, 119; possibility of, 136, 137
Sensum, 112, 116, 127, 165. See also Phantasia
Sextus Empiricus, 50
Shame (aischunê), role in education, 8, 96, 194, 207, 209, 308; as sign of contrariety, 194
Shamelessness, 251
Shorey, Paul, 103, 153, 160, 252, 253, 268, 309
Singer, Charles, 181
Skemp, J. B., 238
Society, prevailing character of, 33, 34, 36, 295
Socrates, distinctive standpoint, xx, 242; revolution of, xx, 12, 16, 17, 53, 54, 272; his influence upon Plato, 3, 4, 70, 180; true portrait of, 5, 10, 11, 226; principal concerns, 6, 10, 21, 32, 274; as provocateur, 8; as servant of truth, 8; integrity of, 9-11, 287; vocation of, 11, 12, 15, 74, 287; religious tendency, 14; impiety of, 15, 18; as teleologist, 22, 180; first principle of, 24; divine sign, 24-25; as true autocratês, 296
Socratic problem, the, 7, 14, 54
Solipsism, 41, 49, 93, 272
Solmsen, F., 28, 48
Solon, 7, 305
Sôma. See Body
Sophia. See Wisdom; Phronêsis
Sophists, as conventionalists, 13, 36, 37; connive at prevailing ethôs, 32, 36; as teachers, 35, 36, 37, 272; ontology of, 71, 113, 114, 129; Plato's agreement with, 79; anthropology of, 272;

error of, 290. See also *Metron anthropos*

Sophrosunê, as temperance, 37, 57, 90, 191, 294

Soteriology, Plato's, xi, 4, 20, 59, 236, 242, 285

Soul, aberrations of: pathological condition of, xxi, 68, 146; depravity of, 24, 96, 148; dual appetition of, 64, 197; tyranny in, 64, 66, 149, 187, 206, 295; bondage of, 139-47; deformity of, 173; disease in, 173, 292; contrariety in 185-88, 206, 229. *See also* Contrariety; Evil

Soul, the: perfection of, 10, 11, 18, 57, 284; the Socratic view of, 12, 15, 41, 64, 272, 297; as man's dearest possession, 12, 14, 26; its access to reality, 14, 23, 38, 44, 56, 84, 91, 273; as seat of knowledge, 14, 86; as prophetic, 17, 97, 274; its kinship with Being, 18, 24, 42, 83, 96, 100, 202, 274, 288; the faculties of, 47; conversion of, 143, 147-50; concord in, 186, 295; the true ruling principle of, 187; the pristine *eros* of, 187, 188, 195, 288. See also *Psuchê*

State, ideal, 32, 34, 290; the rationale of, 33-34; the second-best, 181; as reflected wisdom, 283; the norm of, 295

Statesmanship, true, 31, 32, 48, 209, 290; need of experience for, 155, 290

Stenzel, Julius, 115, 116, 117, 118, 119, 121, 132, 172, 183

Stereometry, 276, 279, 280

Stewart, J. A., 201

Stoicism, 284

Suggeneia, 50, 87, 96. *See also* Kinship; Soul

Sumphonia, 187, 194

Sunagogê, 15, 115. See also *Diakritikê*

Suneidêsis, 24

Sunêtheia. *See* Habituation

Syllogism, the premises of, 139, 141, 169, 213; its premises arbitrary, 170; the rules of, 171; Plato's evaluation of, 213; as the truth of certainty, 219, 262; its analogy with efficient causality, 267; defect for empirical science, 267

Symbolism, 43, 47, 84, 136, 144, 146, 151, 159, 188, 194, 201, 203; the privileged symbol, 168, 273, 275

Tabula rasa, 124, 127, 128, 135

Taylor, A. E., 14, 18, 99, 157, 159, 237, 247, 254, 309

Technê, value of, 60, 69; as art, 72, 136, 155; nature of, 136, 141, 182, 276

Teleology, 22, 25, 272, 275; no proof of, 275; in relation to the Good, 23, 281

Telos, 22, 25, 283; the Good as, 153-54

Temple, William, 180

Theia mania, 202, 204, 205, 250, 271

Theia moira, 35, 49, 97, 129, 181

Themis, 34

Themistocles of Athens, 31, 35, 79

Theomorphism, 44

Therapeia, nature of, xi, xxi, 47; the function of, 25, 58; as requisite to knowledge, 71, 144; as conversion, 147, 189, 298; evaluation of, 150, 295-301; dialectic as the instrument of, 232, 233, 234, 236, 299; the goal of, 295

Thompson, E. S., 103

Thrasymachus of Chalcedon, xxii, 33, 34, 35

Thumos, the: as a *dunamis* of the soul, 47, 203

Tillich, Paul, xvi, 245

To Apeiron. *See* Unlimited

Toeplitz, O., 237

To Meson, as the mean, 182

To Metaxu, 114. *See also* Intermediate being

To Metron, as measure, 33, 38, 48; as the essential man, 42, 272; as the Good, 84, 153, 274

To Peras. *See* Limit

Transcendence, experience of, 14; transcendent reach of the soul, 15, 143; denial of, 40; of the Good, 152, 177, 249; of forms, 245

True Opinion, nature of, 35, 65, 84, 88, 91, 93, 94; subversion of, 64, 292; influences upon, 67, 111, 112; inferiority to *epistêmê*, 93, 94, 102, 109, 122; inconstancy of, 94, 96, 110; stabilization of, 94-96, 102, 171, 176, 260; as presentiment of ideal being, 97, 101, 308; content of, 103, 114; relation to *nous*, 103, 130; condition of, 113, 125, 128, 137; as data of *elenchos*, 172, 176, 289; as beginning-point of knowledge, 196, 260, 271, 289

Truth, as personal discovery, xvii, 6-8,

212, 231; as not transmissible, xviii, 7, 77-80; as hypothetical, xviii, 170, 216, 218; as demonstrable, xviii, 212, 213, 216; as self-authenticating, xix, 45, 86, 170, 178, 216, 219, 237, 273-76; general accessibility of, 7, 139; the Protagorean destruction of, 41; as decisional, 72, 235, 236, 260; prior awareness of, 82-88; presentiments of, 83, 84, 86; criterion of, 87, 141, 237, 269; as reality, 151; dependence on the Good, 152, 153; as prime love of soul, 187; basic theory of, 212; scientific, 261, 262. *See also* Knowledge; Sciences

Ultimate reality, knowledge of, xvi, 236, 296; access to, 14, 272; accessibility of, 139, 219, 287; initial premises of, 248; clue to nature of, 272, 288; the nature of, 288
Unconditional obligation, 23-24, 26, 274
Understanding, the nature of, 81, 118, 178; developed view of, 119, 120, 289; as distinguished from *epistêmê*, 169, 170; as subordinate, 175, 178; as classificatory knowledge, 175, 238. See also *Dianoia*
Unity and plurality, principle of, 164, 166, 178, 237, 280
Universal, the (*To Katholou*): as concept, 115, 124; Aristotle's view of, 138, 156; Plato's view of, 156; the induction of, 218, 236, 238, 263; relation to *hypothesis*, 263
Unlimited, the, 120, 132, 155, 159; as potentiality, 164; principle of, 256, 277
Untersteiner, Mario, 39, 40, 49
Urban, W. M., 237

Valuation, distortion of, 12, 42, 46; influence upon cognition, 67, 248, 260; determination of hypotheses, 249, 270; as decisive in metaphysical knowledge, 260, 298; the primary valuation, 273. *See also* Axiology
Value-awareness, 17, 25, 275, 283. *See also* Axiology
Value-judgment, 260, 269, 273
Values, transvaluation of, 12, 13, 16
Varro, Marcus, 54, 73
Verification, the method of, 105, 237; limits of public, 212, 213

Vice, of the soul, 67; as productive of ignorance, 294
Virtue, the teachability of, 3, 36, 78, 80, 81, 87; the appearance of, 9; its relation to happiness, 10; as the aim of life, 14, 31, 291; the criterion of, 34; inadequate sources of, 34-38; the Sophists as teachers of, 35; as not transmissible, 35, 79, 80; civic, 36, 78; as conformation to Being, 44, 57, 58; as linked with knowledge, 53, 77, 79, 80, 81, 86, 87, 291, 296; of the philosopher, 56; the summit of, 57; as knowledge of the Good, 70; as not natural, 80, 92; as wisdom, 293. *See also* Knowledge
Vision, of the soul, 146, 149, 152, 156; physiology of, 147; mechanism of, 151-54, 158, 159; as intellection, 212; as knowledge, 217, 297
Volition, causality in ignorance, 62, 65, 260; as two-fold in nature, 64, 66; as real wish of the soul, 65, 185, 187; as man's essential will, 65, 67, 185; as appetency, 66; meaning of voluntary, 66; function in cognition, 248. See also *Boulêsis*; Freedom

Waking life, of the mind, 44, 104, 184; by the assistance of dialectic, 88, 92, 111; through mathematical studies, 166; wisdom as, 290. *See also* Dreaming
Weyl, H., 281
Wild, John, 45, 47, 61, 159
Windelband, W., 157, 219, 285
Wisdom, as highest knowledge, 57, 169, 285; the definition of, 58, 291, 295, 297; desire of, 186; as saving knowledge, 282; nature of, 282, 283, 287, 294; denaturing of, 284, 286; Aristotle's view of, 286; as self-agreement, 294, 295; as habit of the Good, 295; as harmony, 300. See also *Phronêsis*
World view, the mechanical, 16; the axiological-humane, 16, 25; the teleological, 22, 25, 272, 275; the criterion of truth of, 142, 269; the sensate, 143
Written treatise, the: Plato's attitude toward, xvii, 304, 306, 308; Aristotle's view, xvii; depreciation of, 304-9

Xenophon, 4, 5, 15, 17

Zeller, Eduard, 24, 117, 242, 309